AMBOINA, 1623

Amboina, 1623

FEAR AND CONSPIRACY
ON THE EDGE OF EMPIRE

Adam Clulow

Columbia University Press
New York

Columbia University Press
Publishers Since 1893
New York   Chichester, West Sussex
cup.columbia.edu
Copyright © 2019 Columbia University Press
All rights reserved

Library of Congress Cataloging-in-Publication Data

Names: Clulow, Adam, author.
Title: Amboina, 1623 : fear and conspiracy on the edge
of empire / Adam Clulow.
Description: New York : Columbia University Press, [2019] |
Includes bibliographical references and index.
Identifiers: LCCN 2018058385 | ISBN 9780231175128 (cloth : alk. paper) |
ISBN 9780231550376 (e-book)
Subjects: LCSH: Ambon Island (Indonesia)—History—17th century. |
Trials (Conspiracy)—Indonesia—Ambon Island. | Nederlandsche Oost-Indische Compagnie—
History—17th century. | East India Company—History—17th century. | Netherlands—
Foreign relations—Great Britain. | Great Britain—Foreign relations—Netherlands.
Classification: LCC DS646.69.A43 C55 2019 | DDC 959.8/52—dc23
LC record available at https://lccn.loc.gov/2018058385

Columbia University Press books are printed on permanent and durable acid-free paper.
Printed in the United States of America

Cover design: Elliott S. Cairns
Cover art: *The Most Savage and Horrible Cruelties Lately Practised by the Hollanders
upon the English in the East Indies* (Presborow, 1624). Nationaal Archief,
The Hague, States General, 1.01.02, inv. no. 12551.62-3.

Contents

Illustrations

Note to the Reader

Dutch East India Company sources make use of the Gregorian calendar, which was ten days ahead of the Julian calendar used by the English. To provide some uniformity in dates, I have wherever possible converted all dates found in English documents into the Gregorian calendar. There are significant inconsistencies in the names of Dutch East India Company ships and employees as they appear in the sources. In general, I have either maintained the original spelling or chosen the most common variant. As is standard in studies of this period, I have employed the shorthand Dutch and English to describe the two sides involved in the Amboina conflict, even while acknowledging that both companies drew from a far more expansive labor pool. Most studies in English of this case refer to it as the Amboyna trial. As this book draws more heavily on Dutch archives and scholarship, I have used the variant Amboina, which appears most commonly there. Across the early chapters of this book, I have made extensive use of an important compilation of Jan Pieterszoon Coen's letters: H. T. Colenbrander and W. P. Coolhaas, eds., *Jan Pietersz. Coen: Bescheiden Omtrent Zijn Bedrijf in Indië*, 9 vols. (The Hague: Martinus Nijhoff, 1919–1954). To enable easier reference within this vast source, I have provided a brief description of the primary sender and recipient in the notes. These descriptions are intended to guide the reader but they are not comprehensive and do not include all of the individual senders or recipients.

Acknowledgments

I have worked on this book on and off for close to a decade and a half since 2004, when I first encountered the Amboina case during a research trip to the British Library. In that time, I have received invaluable help, support, and guidance from a wide range of people and institutions. Without them this book would never have been completed. My first debt is to Adam McKeown, a brilliant historian and remarkable teacher who died at a tragically young age while this book was being written. Adam was a mentor to me while I completed my doctoral dissertation at Columbia and he served from the day I met him as my model for what a teacher and scholar could be. He encouraged me to pursue this project and weighed in as I wrestled with endless early drafts. In his scholarship, his generosity, and his humanity, Adam was an inspiration to me and so many others, and he is sorely missed.

Over the past decade, I have presented different aspects of this project numerous times and have always emerged with fresh insights and ideas. David Lurie, my wonderful PhD supervisor, encouraged me to present this work at the Donald Keene Center at Columbia and pushed me to sharpen my views on the trial. If there is a single origin point for this project and so much of my research since, it is the first course I took with David, Japan Before 1600, which forever changed my trajectory as a scholar. I owe a special thanks to Lauren Benton, who invited me to present my work at Vanderbilt; Siyen Fei, who arranged for me to give a paper at the

[xi]

Annenberg Seminar series at the University of Pennsylvania; and Rusty Kelty, for a wonderful public event at the Art Gallery of South Australia. Many scholars gave generously of their time to read a series of ramshackle and imperfect drafts. Martine van Ittersum, the groundbreaking scholar of Grotius and the Dutch East India Company, read an entire draft of the manuscript and greatly improved it with her comments. I was privileged to host Dani Botsman, Lauren Benton, and Jan Lauwereyns in Melbourne on separate visits while I was finishing the manuscript, and all three shaped it in crucial ways.

I started work on this project as a PhD student at the Historiographical Institute at the University of Tokyo. There I am grateful to Matsui Yōko and Matsukata Fuyuko for welcoming me into their remarkable research center. In Tokyo, I was privileged to work with the library left by Iwao Seiichi, the great chronicler of the Japanese in Southeast Asia, whose formidable work has continued to inspire me in the decades since I first read it. At Columbia, I am indebted to Carol Gluck, Henry Smith, and Greg Pflugfelder for all they did to support my research. Once I finished my PhD, I was fortunate enough to spend a year at Princeton University as part of the Fung Global Fellows Program while I worked on part of this project. There, Michael Laffan and Saarah Jappie generously aided me with the translation of a series of Malay documents, while Michael Gordin, Helder De Schutter, David Kiwuwa, Priti Mishra, Brigitte Rath, and Ying Ying Tan provided the company of an extraordinary group of scholars.

My first publication related to this project was in *Itinerario* in 2007, and I remain very grateful to the editors and anonymous readers for their help in guiding that article through to final publication. Jack Wills, another remarkable historian and towering figure in the field who also passed away recently, read drafts of the article and gave freely of his encyclopedic knowledge. Across the years since I started my PhD, Leonard Blussé, the great pioneer of studies of the Dutch East India Company in Asia, inspired me to always go back to the archives with fresh vigor while pushing me to sharpen the chapter on Japanese mercenaries.

The bulk of work on this project was completed at Monash University, where I have taught since 2008. When I arrived at Monash with the ink of my dissertation barely dry, I was fortunate enough to be placed in the office next to Ernest Koh, the most generous of all colleagues, who has provided a constant source of support and encouragement. I am grateful as well to numerous colleagues, including Clare Corbould (who read a crucial early draft), Seamus O'Hanlon, Noah Shenker, Daniella Doron, Carolyn James, Michael Hau, and Susie Protschky, as well as to three successive heads of schools, Al Thomson, Megan Cassidy-Welch, and Christina Twomey, for giving me the time and space to pursue this research. Three much esteemed and vastly generous senior colleagues, Bain Attwood, David Garrioch, and David Chandler, all read drafts of the full manuscript and contributed hundreds of suggestions and comments. I am also very grateful for the support provided by an Australian Research Council Discovery Early Career Research Award, which gave me time off teaching to complete this project.

At Columbia University Press, I owe special thanks to two wonderful editors: Anne Routon, who first encouraged me to pursue this project, and Caelyn Cobb, who shepherded the manuscript through to final publication with great patience and skill. I am especially grateful to the anonymous reviewers, who provided pages and pages of insightful commentary. I think it is fair to say that my initial draft of the manuscript did not fully persuade all of them, and I would like to thank each of the readers for their exceptionally detailed and helpful comments, which picked up far too many assumptions while pushing me to sharpen my argument. I cannot be sure that what follows will convince them all, but I am certain that the manuscript was vastly improved as a result of their time and effort, and I offer my profound thanks.

As part of the wider project, I created an interactive website to introduce students to the 1623 conspiracy trial at the center of the book. The website was generously supported by Monash University, which provided both funding and resources. I found the best of all possible institutional partners in the Roy Rosenzweig Center for History and New Media at George Mason University and I owe a special thanks to Kelly Schrum, the wonderful director of Educational Projects, Chris Preperato, James McCartney, and Joo Ah Lee. Without their work, the website would never have come into being. At Monash, Sam Horewood, now a PhD candidate at Duke, provided indispensable help in designing, improving, and managing the website, while Justine Vincin helped me with the seemingly endless transcriptions of primary sources. In London, Andrew Deakin, a distinguished barrister, gave freely of his time to review a vast stack of materials and record videos for students, in addition to talking me through the intricacies of weighing up compromised testimonies.

As part of the preparation for the website, I was privileged to host a conference on the two companies at the Internationales Wissenschaftsforum

Heidelberg at the University of Heidelberg. The conference was generously sponsored by the International Research Award in Global History, which was offered jointly by the Department of History and the Cluster of Excellence "Asia and Europe in a Global Context" at Heidelberg University, the Institute for European Global Studies at the University of Basel, and the Laureate Research Program in International History at the University of Sydney. I would like to thank Roland Wenzlhuemer, Glenda Sluga, and Madeleine Herren-Oesch for their support. Over three days, we gathered many of the leading scholars of the companies. I am especially grateful to Alison Games, Rupali Mishra, Philip Stern, Tonio Andrade, and Leonard Blussé, all scholars I have admired for years, for agreeing to sit for interviews and for giving so freely of their insights. In particular, I would like to thank Alison Games, who is completing her own much-anticipated book, *The Invention of the Amboyna Massacre*, for her generosity in discussing the intricacies of the trial.

Taking the Amboina trial into the classroom has been a high point of my career as a teacher and I am very thankful to the hundreds of students at Monash who participated in different versions of the trial exercise. While I cannot name them all, their encouragement and energy sustained me in finishing this book, even as their perceptive comments helped me rethink the mass of evidence. Special thanks are due to Bernard Keo, who so expertly guided discussion in tutorials along with Sam Horewood. At Brandeis University, Xing Hang trialed the website and supported the project in countless ways. At Leiden University, Tristan Mostert, a PhD candidate who represents the model of a new generation of superb VOC scholars, generously agreed to use the website in one of his classes and put me in contact with his impressive cohort of students while improving a number of chapters with his comments during an immensely productive shared visit to London in 2018, while I was working on the final edits.

While the scale of the Amboina archive is daunting, it is also stored at three of the most accessible archives in the world, where it has been my pleasure to spend hundreds of hours working through stacks of material. I am grateful to all the staff at the British Library in London, the National Archief in The Hague, and the National Archives in Kew for everything they do to make projects like this possible. Once my daughter was born at the halfway point through this project, it became far more difficult for me to make the long trip from Australia to archives in Europe. I am grateful first to Nadia Kreeft and then to Mariska Heijman, who both made many visits on my behalf to The Hague and scanned seemingly endless series of documents. Both provided invaluable help as well when I stumbled in my transcriptions or translations, gently pointing out when my strange route into seventeenth-century Dutch via Afrikaans had steered me in the wrong direction.

My parents, my two brothers, and my extended family have been a constant source of support. My father dived into the depths of Roman-Dutch law on my behalf, sending me copy after copy of obscure South African law journals and reading numerous drafts. My wife Anna and my daughter Esther tolerated a project that seemed to sprawl forever outward, while filling the spaces between with joy. This book is dedicated to my oldest and dearest friend, Andrew, who has been by my side for approaching forty years, since we were five. Although we have not lived in the same country for decades now, he has been a constant source of encouragement and inspiration. I could not have asked for a better or more generous friend and I offer this book in thanks for a debt of friendship that can never be repaid.

Maps of Southeast Asia, Amboina, and the Banda Islands

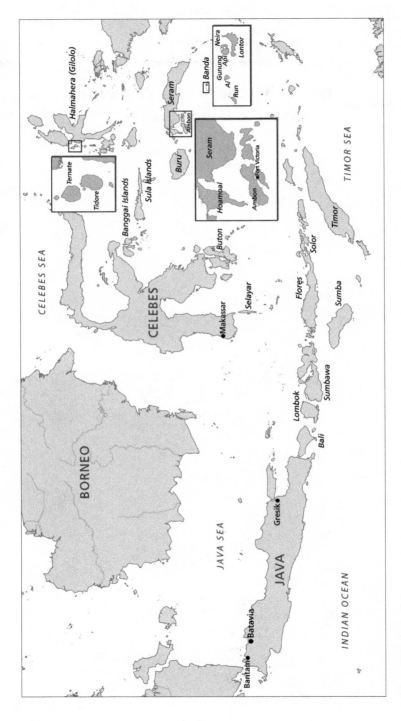

Map of Southeast Asia

(*Top*) Map of Amboina. (*Bottom*) Map of the Banda Islands.

AMBOINA, 1623

Introduction

The Company and the Colony

O n February 23, 1623, a young Japanese soldier called Shichizō
was arrested by his Dutch employers. The night before he had
been overheard asking suspicious questions about the defenses
of a key Dutch East India Company (Vereenigde Oost-Indische Compagnie
or VOC) fortification located on Amboina, a remote set of islands in what
is now eastern Indonesia.[1] Called before the governor, Herman van Speult,
Shichizō denied everything.[2] He had done no such thing; he had been in
his bunk sleeping, in the barracks eating, anything but on the walls of the
fort. When members of the guard were summoned to confirm the charges,
Shichizō admitted that he had been asking such questions but insisted that
his inquiries had been prompted simply by curiosity. The answer served
only to inflame Van Speult's suspicions. These could not have been idle
questions. They must have been leading somewhere, to some hidden and
terrible purpose. And Shichizō could not be acting alone. Someone must
have instructed him to investigate the defenses of the fort, and that party
must be close at hand with the ambition and means to seize control of
Amboina, which was prized for its rich crop of cloves and other precious
spices. When Shichizō continued to be "stubborn," the governor decided
that he must be tortured to reveal the truth.[3]

There was no apparatus for torture in the fort. Instead, the most commonplace of objects would serve to extract answers: some rope, a doorframe, and large pots of water. Shichizō's arms and legs were wrenched

apart and bound roughly to the doorposts. As he struggled, a cloth was placed over his mouth and tied tightly behind his head. One of the Company's soldiers began to pour water over his head while another stood behind him, pulling the cloth around his mouth. The water gushed in, filling Shichizō's mouth, then his sinus cavities, the sodden cloth pulling tighter and tighter as he desperately sucked in air. This "torture of water," or waterboarding as it is more commonly known to us today, produced a confession: that Shichizō had joined a plot orchestrated by a group of English merchants based nearby to seize control of the fortification and ultimately rip the spice-rich island from the Company's grasp.[4]

Authority for the subsequent investigation was handed over to Van Speult's subordinate, Isaaq de Bruyn, the advocate-fiscal (*advocaet-fiscael*) or chief legal officer on the island.[5] Armed with Shichizō's confession, De Bruyn proceeded to arrest, interrogate, and torture the remaining ten Japanese soldiers in the garrison, all of whom confessed to signing on to the plot in return for a promise of 1,000 reals, a huge sum far in excess of their yearly earnings.[6] On February 26, De Bruyn turned his attention to the merchants attached to the small English East India Company (EIC) trading outpost in Amboina. He started with Abel Price, who had been named by Shichizō as the primary intermediary between the Japanese and their coconspirators. Waterboarded, Price promptly confessed to a role in a conspiracy aimed at the "taking of the castle, and the murdering of the Netherlanders."[7] The ringleader of the plot was identified as Gabriel Towerson, the forty-nine-year-old chief agent of the English company's trading post on Amboina.

As De Bruyn worked his way through the English contingent at Amboina, further torture sessions appeared to uncover an array of additional plotters, including a mestizo slave overseer and warriors from the hostile polity of Luhu on the nearby Hoamoal Peninsula, who had all joined together in a sprawling conspiracy with Towerson and his Japanese accomplices. On March 8, the Amboina judges—an improvised tribunal made up of VOC officials, merchants, and captains—convened to render judgment on the conspirators for "treason against the state" (*crimen leasae maiestatis*).[8] They returned a predictable verdict: guilty, although a last-minute decision was made by the governor to spare a number of English merchants.[9] Early in the morning of March 9, the convicted were led out to the empty ground in front of the fort. There, a total of twenty-one men were beheaded, one by one, with a single stroke of a sword. Although this brought the trial to an end, the aftershocks of what had happened on Amboina would continue to reverberate out for decades.

When news of the case reached London at the end of May 1624, it sparked immediate outrage from English East India Company officials. The first polemical shots were fired not by the English, however, but by VOC supporters, who published a short pamphlet, *Waerachtich Verhael vande Tidinghen ghecomen wt de Oost-Indien*, or *A True Declaration of the News That Came Out of the East Indies*, designed to defend what had happened.[10] Widely believed to be the work of a senior Dutch official, the pamphlet denounced the "terrible conspiracy" (*groweliicke conspiratie*) while offering a measured defense of the legal proceedings.[11] The EIC was quick to respond, commissioning its own account later titled *A True Relation of the Unjust, Cruell, and Barbarous Proceedings Against the English at Amboyna in the East-Indies, by the Neatherlandish Governour and Councel There*, which was compiled on the basis of the testimony provided by a number of survivors who had made their way from Amboina to London in the intervening year. Packed with rancorous attacks on Dutch tyranny, it argued that the charges were nothing more than the "forged pretence of a Conspiracie."[12] Such accusations were magnified by King James I, who thundered sporadically against what he viewed as the judicial murder of his subjects, and by the publication of graphic although largely invented depictions of savage torture, such as the one that adorns the cover of this book.[13] Propelled by a trickle and then a torrent of anti-Dutch rhetoric, the episode morphed from a trial into the "Amboyna massacre," a label that has remained connected to the case ever since.[14]

These clashing arguments and pamphlets meant that a legal case that had taken place thousands of miles away from Europe in a distant part of Asia swiftly emerged as a focus of bitter dispute between traditional allies in Europe. Beginning in 1624, it became a consistent feature of Anglo-Dutch relations as angry letters, pamphlets, and delegations were exchanged across the North Sea. By 1627, and facing a threat from a new king, Charles I, to embargo Dutch shipping passing through English ports, the States General in the United Provinces agreed to convene a special tribunal to investigate the conduct of the original Amboina judges. Hampered by clashes over jurisdiction, the subsequent investigation limped on until 1632, when the surviving officials were predictably exonerated. The verdict did nothing to dampen the controversy, and the case roared back to life whenever anti-Dutch sentiment was on the rise. After decades of failed attempts, the

English government, now under the direction of Oliver Cromwell, succeeded in extracting an acknowledgment of wrongdoing in the aftermath of the first Anglo-Dutch War (1652–1654). It came with a substantial payout for the surviving relatives of the merchants executed on Amboina, although there was no possibility of punishing the original judges, who were long dead.[15]

Even though the settlement ended the formal legal dispute, the case flickered back into sharp focus whenever English relations with the Netherlands came under stress. In 1673, a full fifty years after the execution of Towerson and his compatriots, John Dryden penned a new play, *Amboyna, or the Cruelties of the Dutch to the English Merchants: A Tragedy*, denouncing VOC brutality. In it, he excoriated Van Speult, and the Dutch nation more generally, condemning the "base new upstart commonwealth" for daring to "doom the subjects of an English king."[16] The trial resurfaced again during the Anglo-Boer War (1899–1902), when it was used by English writers to illustrate the essential villainy of not only the seventeenth-century Dutch but also, more tenuously, their Afrikaner descendants in South Africa.[17] Even today, the trial continues to court controversy, featuring prominently in Giles Milton's hugely successful popular history *Nathaniel's Nutmeg*, which condemned the Dutch in virtually identical terms to those first deployed nearly four centuries earlier.[18]

Over the years, scholarly writing on Amboina has been dominated by two questions. First, and most urgently, scholars have debated whether or not there was actually a plot to seize control of the fort and hence if the charges leveled against the English and the Japanese were justified. Not surprisingly, historians have tended to split along national lines, with British writers generally insisting that no plot existed.[19] One argues that "a terrible mistake was made at Amboyna in that the executed Englishmen were innocent of the plans ascribed to them," while a second dismisses the charges as nothing more than a "pretext" lacking any substance.[20] In contrast, many Dutch historians who have taken up the topic, including in a series of foundational articles written in the early twentieth century, agree that there was some sort of conspiracy and thus a basis for VOC action, even as they have been highly critical of the ramshackle nature of the legal proceedings themselves.[21]

Running parallel but generating less heat has been a second question concerning the impact of the Amboina conspiracy trial on relations between England and the United Provinces, whose longstanding alliance was shaken by the controversies unleashed by the case. For scholars like Anton Poot, the 1623 trial played a key role in shaping the nature of relations in the uneasy period that preceded the three Anglo-Dutch wars.[22] Other historians have focused on the English company's sustained attempts to use the apparatus of state to secure action from the United Provinces. Anthony Milton has shown how the EIC attempted to mobilize public opinion through a potent combination of petitions, pamphlets, and paintings, while in an important new study Rupali Mishra has used the trial's controversial aftermath to illuminate the awkward and constantly shifting alliance that existed between the English company and the state in this period.[23] Adopting a global frame, Alison Games has examined how two events, in Virginia in March 1622 and in Amboina a year later, became embedded within the charged category of "massacre."[24]

My first encounter with the case came in 2004. Stepping gingerly at first, I quickly found myself sucked into the nearly four-centuries-old debate over whether or not there had been a plot. One reason the question seems both answerable and yet out of reach is because of the surprising scale of the archive. In contrast to the vast bulk of seventeenth-century colonial cases, which left a very limited set of records, the Amboina trial produced a massive archive that sprawls across multiple repositories. This includes the original trial record prepared by Isaaq de Bruyn, which contains the individual confessions of the accused, the charges, and the final verdict, as well as a huge trove of additional materials produced by the two companies as they fought bitterly over the legality of the original case.

On the English side, the most important new testimony came from six survivors of the trial, who were called before the Admiralty Court in 1624 after they arrived back in London.[25] These depositions were matched on the Dutch end by an even more expansive set of materials. As tensions mounted, the VOC summoned the surviving Amboina judges first to Batavia and then to the United Provinces. They were deposed in both places, providing detailed answers to 139 questions in 1625–1626 and then to 189 questions in 1628.[26] Both companies, moreover, scoured isolated outposts across Asia to dredge up additional witnesses who, though they had not participated in the original case, were present on Ambon at the time.[27] These materials were then fed into a series of detailed pamphlets that laid out each side's arguments while laboring to demolish, point by point, any opposing claims.[28]

The product of this extended clash between dueling claims and witnesses is an archive that runs to thousands of pages of original documents scattered across the British Library in London, the National Archives in Kew, and the Nationaal Archief in The Hague. Unlike most legal documents from this period, including the terse and largely formulaic judicial materials conventionally produced by the VOC, the Amboina records are remarkably detailed. The witness depositions, which span hundreds of manuscript pages, lavish attention on the smallest of points while providing elaborate accounts of the individual stages of the trial. But for all its size and specificity, the archive is also elusive. Virtually every witness was on someone's payroll, whether the VOC, the EIC, or one of the rival governments, and each sought to craft a version of the case designed to guarantee ongoing support from their sponsors. Putting together the different versions of the case and trial itself creates a dizzying *Rashomon*-like kaleidoscope of plausible interpretations. Depending on how you weigh individual pieces of evidence, it is possible to present a wide spectrum of positions ranging from clear guilt to absolute innocence, as well as every shade of gray in-between, with each interpretation backed up by its own well of materials.

By 2014, after almost a decade of research, I was still mired within the same debate over guilt or innocence with no end in sight. Frustrated, I decided that I had to try something different. With the help of the Center for History and New Media at George Mason University, I built a website (www.amboyna.org) designed to lead undergraduates through the intricacies of the trial. At its center we placed an interactive trial engine called "What's Your Verdict," which presented the most compelling evidence offered by the VOC (dubbed the prosecution) and their English opponents (the defense). Breaking down a complex case into constituent parts, we arrived at six key questions that have to be answered one way or the other in order to come to a verdict. For each, the site presents the arguments mobilized by both sides, in conjunction with the most important pieces of evidence. To tap into a different kind of expertise with trials and testimony, we asked a distinguished London-based barrister, Andrew Deakin, to work through all the materials. Generously agreeing to waive his fees, he ploughed his way through a huge stack of Amboina files and then sat through hour after hour of filmed interviews designed to guide students through the materials and the challenges of weighing up divergent testimony.

After hundreds of hours of consultation, design, and construction, the website went live in 2016. It was trialed first with multiple classes at Monash University in Australia, then at Brandeis University in the United States, and finally at Leiden University in the Netherlands.[29] Students worked through the materials, completed the trial engine, and then arrived at class ready to debate and defend their conclusions. When these tests were complete, we made the website publicly available, and since then thousands of visitors from across the world have worked through it, with their verdicts all recorded in our database.[30]

On the most basic level, the results of this experiment were enormously gratifying for someone who had spent years in largely solitary engagement with the Amboina archive. Although some students tossed off a verdict after racing through the materials, many others confided to me that they had become engrossed by the details of the trial, trawling through the sources and coming back again and again to key points. Equally important, having hundreds of pairs of new eyes examining familiar material proved a revelation for me. By homing in on points that I had dismissed too quickly and forcing me to defend lazy assumptions in class, these students helped me think through the mass of Amboina evidence.

Trying and retrying the case in seminar after seminar convinced me as well of three basic points. First, it is very difficult to mount a convincing defense of the big plot pictured by the advocate-fiscal. This involved a diverse set of groups—English traders, Japanese soldiers, warriors from Luhu, and a slave overseer—all of whom were required to work together with precise timing to seize the castle and subdue its defenders. And yet even after an exhaustive search conducted by the advocate-fiscal of English papers and possessions, there was no sign of any actual links between the different participants or of the kind of communication that would have been necessary to facilitate such a conspiracy.[31] The point was freely admitted by the Amboina judges themselves, who acknowledged that they discovered no "Bookes or Writings [that] . . . did any wise touche this enterprize."[32] Even more telling, the confessions themselves, which form the only evidence put forward by the advocate-fiscal, do little to buttress the notion of the grand conspiracy. No single confession, including that by the supposed ringleader, names all of the alleged plotters, and the accused often seemed to be confessing to entirely different schemes centered on themselves rather than involving a coordinated union of anti-Dutch parties. Some of the Japanese soldiers interrogated by the advocate-fiscal, for example, confessed under torture that they—rather than the English—were the key conspirators, while the other plotters only feature in a single confession or not at all. In fact, even as they admitted their own involvement in the plot, a number of the accused specifically refuted, even under torture, the notion of a sprawling conspiracy involving local allies. When these facts are put together, it is difficult to support the view that an organized conspiracy involving all of these different groups existed.

Second, the slimmed-down version of the Amboina conspiracy, that some English merchants based in Kota Ambon had plotted something, seems unlikely but also impossible to definitively disprove. The spotlight falls squarely on Gabriel Towerson, the ringleader, who had supposedly orchestrated the whole plot, gathering the conspirators, pledging them to loyalty, and guiding their actions from behind the scenes. But as D. K. Bassett first pointed out, an examination of Towerson's private correspondence dispatched when he was supposedly preparing the plot shows not a man scheming against the Dutch but rather someone who was reprimanded by his superiors for being too close to the VOC governor.[33] In September 1622, that is, just a few months before he had supposedly gathered his followers to plan their assault on the fort, Towerson lavished praise on Van Speult for his "upright harte," which made a him a reliable and trustworthy ally for the English in Amboina. Rather than assembling weapons and additional resources for the plot, Towerson asked for special gifts to be prepared for Van Speult, including a "chaine of gold" and some beer. It was such a warm request directed toward a key competitor that it quickly earned him a sharp rebuke from his superiors.[34]

It is also true that such an enterprise would have been an enormous gamble for Towerson and his fellow plotters, who had never shown themselves as anything more than the most mediocre of EIC servants. While English pamphleteers writing after the trial significantly inflated the size and strength of the garrison, the fact remained that even if an attack was clearly feasible in theory it would have been very difficult for the core group of conspirators to seize a well-defended fort in the middle of a Dutch-controlled colony. And, it would have been virtually impossible for them to hold on to their prize once the dust had settled. The VOC had a formidable military presence in the region and would certainly have committed all available resources to retake the fortification. Equally, it was far from certain that Towerson's superiors, who were in the process of withdrawing from their outpost in Amboina, would have leapt to his defense.

And yet, even with these reservations, we cannot rule out the possibility that there might have been some kernel of a plot, that a handful of English merchants, perhaps in an angry exchange or an alcohol-fueled discussion, might have fantasized about striking back against the Dutch, whom they resented bitterly for a host of perceived offenses. While such whispered conversations did not approximate the sprawling conspiracy pictured in the legal proceedings, the interrogations conducted by the advocate-fiscal may in fact have stumbled upon the traces of some sort of speculative discussion directed toward the castle. For all their detail, the sources do not allow us to penetrate the clandestine conversations of the dozen or so English merchants based in Kota Ambon in the months leading up to the trial, which may have contained their own inchoate schemes.

But third, and most important, my experience in the classroom convinced me that I had been asking the wrong question. The debate over guilt or innocence has a momentum all of its own, a well-worn groove rendered smooth by generations of dueling writers, but it is also in essence a political contest, extending from the controversy that first erupted in 1624, that seeks to apportion blame either to the Dutch or the English. It serves, moreover, to close off more avenues of investigation than it opens, pushing us to a question that—in the absence of an elusive "smoking gun" that I have seen no trace of in the archives—cannot finally be answered while shutting down other areas of investigation that can yield results. Accepting its basic parameters acts to narrow the frame, cutting a sprawling case down to the motivations and means of a handful of English merchants, while blinding us to what was happening around them.

Once we push beyond this familiar question, however, a different and more productive avenue of inquiry opens up, focused not on the familiar cast of English merchants but on the Dutch officials gathered in Amboina, whose actions drove the case forward. If we are to believe the traditional thrust of English-language scholarship, there is no mystery here, for we know exactly what Van Speult and De Bruyn were thinking when they first accused the English of plotting against them. According to this view, Amboina was a site of "very great strength," where the long-term project to dominate the spice trade was coming to final fruition in 1623.[35] Here the Dutch were firmly entrenched, their defenses secure, and their garrison possessed of overwhelming strength that made them, in the words of one scholar, absolute "masters of the Clove and Nutmeg Archipelago."[36] And this strength and confidence allowed Van Speult to cook up a plan to eject the English from Amboina.

For centuries now, beginning with the very first publications in 1624, scholars writing in English have emphasized that the trial was a deliberate, methodical, and carefully calculated act. In this view, Dutch authorities on Amboina fabricated an overarching conspiracy in order to eject the English from the Spice Islands and thereby secure control over the lucrative trade in cloves. Such an explanation, which posits a conspiracy not on the English but on the Dutch side, was first suggested by the so-called Amboyna men, the survivors of the case, who declared that the "bloody and murderous massacre [at Amboina] . . . was premeditated by the Dutch."[37] It was immediately seized upon by EIC officials and pamphleteers, who made it a central charge in their long campaign to depict the Dutch in Amboina as bloody tyrants.

In the early twentieth century, the notion of an underlying VOC conspiracy was enthusiastically embraced by a string of patriotic chroniclers of British Empire, who accused Van Speult of toying with the English "as a cat might play with a mouse" before springing "upon his victim [to] crush him out of existence."[38] Even now, it remains a strikingly consistent and durable feature of many English-language descriptions of the case.[39] One recent history of the British Empire asserts that Towerson and his fellow merchants "were tortured to death . . . in an exercise of brutality designed to frighten off others," while an influential study of Anglo-Dutch rivalry treats the trial as an "atrocious judicial murder" that was engineered by a Dutch East India Company in the process of obtaining a "predominant position in the Indian Ocean and East Asia [though] a combination of commercial expertise and the ruthless use of force."[40]

Once we start to look more closely at the Amboina trial, however, any notion that it was part of a carefully orchestrated masterplan to eject the English quickly falls apart.[41] Rather than a ruthless feat of judicial maneuvering, the case formulated by the advocate-fiscal, Isaaq de Bruyn, was a legal mess that succeeded in violating many of the rules of Dutch justice. The most stinging criticism came not from the English but from De Bruyn's own superiors, who derided the trial documents prepared by the advocate-fiscal as essentially worthless. The problem was that he had not followed the "appropriate style of justice" by, among numerous other errors, failing to make sure that confessions obtained through coercion had been properly confirmed by the accused outside the torture chamber.[42]

It was also politically disastrous. In addition to censuring the legal proceedings, senior Company administrators in Batavia were appalled by the decision to stage a mass execution of English subjects at the conclusion of the trial when the prisoners could have been held until instructions had been received from Batavia, or simply shipped to the Company's headquarters for the hierarchy to render judgment there. VOC officials were no strangers to large-scale trials. In the nearby Banda Islands, Van Speult's fellow governor, Martinus Sonck, had presided over a mass conspiracy trial the previous year that had resulted in the execution of dozens of Bandanese elders. But, viewed in cold political terms, it was one thing to execute a group that the Company believed fell completely under its authority and quite another to behead the subjects of the Dutch Republic's oldest and most important European ally. The fact that the trial came at a moment in which the two companies were in a state of formal alliance that committed them to profit sharing and joint military operations, with constant exhortations from The Hague and London to do nothing to jeopardize this relationship, made the news even more difficult to digest. When they heard about the execution of ten English merchants, Van Speult's superiors were furious that "clemency" had not been shown "with respect to a nation that is so close a neighbor."[43]

In the final assessment, Amboina was the most disorderly of cases that stunned and disoriented even the VOC hierarchy. How then to understand it? How to explain an interrogation that escalated so quickly from suspicion to torture to execution, brushing past standard restraints in the process, and a trial that was so poorly executed, with such a flawed judicial record that it seemed perfectly engineered only to incite massive controversy? Together these questions form a different Amboina riddle that sits alongside the timeworn debate about guilt and innocence. This book represents my attempt to answer these questions and thereby to present a different view of the 1623 trial. Rather than starting with the legal proceeding themselves, it focuses instead on the territory where they took place and what was happening there in the weeks and months before Shichizō first appeared on the walls of the fort.

Despite its importance, Amboina has been largely sidelined in discussions of the case, which have concentrated on Towerson and the English merchants under his command. This tendency has served to effectively detach the conspiracy trial from the place out of which it emerged and which shaped its course and outcome. In fact, looking at Amboina in February 1623 reveals a very different picture from that conventionally presented in English-language scholarship. Rather than a stable node of

Dutch power, it was a site of intense volatility that was about to descend into a three-decade cycle of war and pacification known as the Amboinese Wars.[44] And instead of a bastion of strength and confidence, the VOC settlement at the center of the supposed plot was convulsed by waves of fear that broke one after another upon its residents.

Amboina in 1623

Today, the island of Ambon and its surrounding territories have largely receded from public attention. In the seventeenth century, however, they were a vital hub on global networks of trade that was aggressively fought over by competing Asian and European powers. Part of the Malukus (Moluccas), a remote archipelago in modern-day Indonesia famously known as the Spice Islands, Amboina stood at the center of the lucrative trade in precious spices. While Banda was associated with nutmeg and mace, Amboina was famous for cloves, which formed, in the words of one Dutch official, "the riches of the Ambonese . . . their gold and silver."[45] In 1605, the VOC had taken possession of one corner of Amboina when Steven van der Haghen accepted the surrender of the Portuguese fortification of Nossa Senhora da Anunciad.[46] Later renamed Castle Victoria by Dutch authorities, the fort was located on the southern part of the small island of Ambon, in a settlement, Kota Ambon, which became the Company's key headquarters in the territory.[47]

Kota Ambon was the Company's first possession in Asia.[48] From the walls of Castle Victoria, the governor administered a wider administrative area labelled as Amboina in VOC sources. Expanding over time, it came to encompass the island of Ambon, itself comprised of two parts, Hitu in the north and Leitmor in the south, connected by a narrow neck, the Hoamoal Peninsula in western Seram, as well as a number of scattered islands including Boano, Kelang, and Manipa.

While scholarship on the trial has continued to resolve around a familiar set of issues, Amboina is a very different story. There, knowledge of the Dutch colonial presence has advanced in leaps and bounds thanks especially to the pioneering work of Gerrit Knaap, by far the most prolific and influential historian of Amboina, who has contributed a series of foundational books, articles, and source compilations. These include his groundbreaking monograph *Kruidnagelen en Christenen: De VOC en de bevolking*

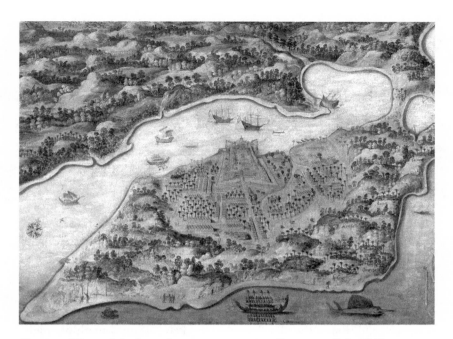

Figure 0.1 View of Ambon. Anonymous, c. 1617. Courtesy of the Rijksmuseum, Amsterdam. SK-A-4482.

van Ambon 1656–1696, and multiple articles in Dutch and English examining the nature of warfare in Amboina, the changing demography in Kota Ambon and the wider province, the relationship between the Company and local powers like Ternate, the nature of the colonial apparatus, and a host of other topics.[49] This work has been expanded and augmented by contributions, some focusing specifically on Amboina, others looking more generally at the early history of the VOC, by a number of innovative scholars, including Jur van Goor, Martine van Ittersum, Leonard Andaya, Jennifer Gaynor, J. Keuning, Muridan Satrio Widjojo, Peter Borschberg, and others.[50]

What follows draws heavily on such scholarship, while focusing much more narrowly on what was happening in the weeks and months leading up to the trial. Here, the sources are more limited. In contrast to the vast archive associated with the Amboina case itself or the ballooning records of the later colonial period, there is a more restricted pool of documents from this period. While Van Speult exchanged regular correspondence with the VOC hierarchy, especially the governor-general in Batavia, and his fellow administrators in neighboring territories, these letters, many of which are collected in a vast compilation edited by H. T. Colenbrander and W. P. Coolhaas, provide a relatively narrow window, and there is no *Dagregister*, the detailed record of daily events that is such a vital source for other parts of the Dutch Empire.[51]

One way to peer into Amboina in 1623 is by using the supposed plot itself in a different way. In her groundbreaking study of rumors and conspiracy theories in colonial Africa, Luise White argues that the fictive vampire stories that she describes offer a way for historians "to see the world the way the storytellers did, as a world of vulnerability and unreasonable relationships."[52] It is the very "inaccuracies in these stories" that make them, White argues, "exceptionally reliable historical sources." Building off White's insights, this book treats the conspiracy articulated by Van Speult and De Bruyn as a source in its own right. When the advocate-fiscal conjured up a sprawling plot involving multiple parties, he did so by tapping into an existing grid of imperial concerns, fears, and vulnerabilities. In this way, each addition to the plot, however unlikely, means something, highlighting a pulsing point of anxiety in the minds of VOC officials on Amboina.

With this framework in place, we can revisit the 1623 conspiracy. At its center were of course the English, but they were joined by three Asian groups that have been largely dismissed in past analysis, which has focused almost exclusively on Towerson and his countrymen. According to the advocate-fiscal, who we know used a mixture of torture and prompts to extract the confessions that he wanted, Towerson had colluded with the polity of Luhu on the nearby Hoamoal Peninsula, which had thrown off the confines of a restrictive treaty designed to control the clove trade. Eager to eject the Dutch from Amboina, Luhu had, the advocate-fiscal insisted, agreed to dispatch hundreds of warriors to join the plot. Also implicated was Augustine Peres, the overseer of the castle's population of slaves, who, despite the fact that he had not been identified by any of the other plotters, was dragged into the torture chamber. He would, De Bruyn argued, have brought his charges over to the English side, thereby swelling the ranks of the plotters with more than a hundred slaves drawn from across Asia. Finally, there was a small contingent of about a dozen Japanese soldiers, who would betray their masters by launching an attack from within the walls of Castle Victoria.

It is difficult to imagine a more diverse array of conspirators: warriors attached to a key Malukan hub in the clove trade, slaves pulled from across Asia, and mercenaries from Japan. The involvement of such different groups raises obvious questions about the likelihood of such an expansive conspiracy, but it also reveals something about the nature of the Dutch East India Company and how it was changing in this period. Although there is an ongoing tendency to treat the VOC as an essentially commercial organization focused primarily on trade, it was always a composite body that pursued a route to profit that ran through the expansion of Dutch power in Asia.[53] This feature can be traced back to the company's foundational document, the 1602 charter, which gave the new organization a suite of effectively sovereign powers, including the right to conduct direct diplomacy, the right to maintain military forces, and the right to seize control of territory by building fortresses and strongholds.[54] Because it combined the attributes of both corporation and state, the Dutch East India Company operated from the beginning as much as a political and military actor as a purely economic one.[55]

Arriving in the region determined to push its way into rich trading circuits, the VOC used the powers granted in its charter to morph over time from a maritime enterprise with only the most limited presence on land into what Jur van Goor calls a "mixed Asian–European state" that occupied a place alongside other Asian states in regional networks of war and diplomacy.[56] It did so by seizing territories like Ambon or Jayakarta (later Batavia), which turned the organization into a territorial power overnight, and by constructing a sprawling network of treaties that bound it tight to a range of rulers and polities.[57] When these treaties were violated, the VOC responded with force, gradually pushing out the limits of its influence and seizing new territory and subjects in an effort to ensure final compliance. As it dove deeper and deeper into the region's politics, the organization turned increasingly to Asian settlers to populate its colonies, Asian slaves to provide labor, and Asian fighters to wage war alongside its troops.[58]

The result of these converging developments was a process of what one scholar calls "Asiafication," in which the organization found itself transformed by its encounter with the region even as it transformed those territories under its direct control.[59] This change took decades to complete, but it was given vital impetus by Jan Pieterszoon Coen, the most influential of the early governors-general (in office 1618–1623, 1627–1629) and Van

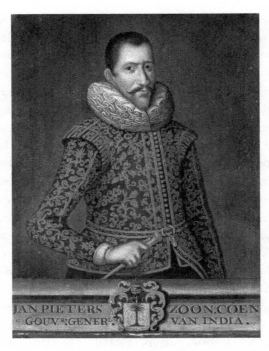

Figure 0.2 Portrait of Jan Pieterszoon Coen. Anonymous, 1750–1800. Courtesy of the Rijksmuseum, Amsterdam. SK-A-4528.

Speult's direct superior, who pushed the organization aggressively into Asian politics.[60]

The eventual outcome of this process was a hybrid, a European empire with Asian roots headed by a governor-general who was converted from a chief merchant into a kinglike figure widely recognized as such by surrounding rulers.[61] This transformation was not, however, an easy one, a smooth melding of European and Asian structures into something new. Instead, the Company's attempts to enforce its treaty rights thrust it into bloody campaigns of pacification or long and unpredictable wars, while its reliance on Asian soldiers, settlers, and slaves exploded into sporadic episodes of mass violence as suspicions were turned in toward groups both alien and familiar.[62]

This returns us to the three sets of Asian conspirators supposedly implicated in the Amboina conspiracy. For officials on the ground, the Company's Asian strategy came to unleash new terrors that by 1623 appeared to crowd menacingly around Castle Victoria. Just two years earlier, Coen had launched a massive invasion of the nearby Banda Islands designed to finally subdue that troublesome archipelago. Intended to secure the Company's political mastery, the campaign instead sent shock waves running through the wider Spice Islands. In the weeks before the trial, a series of attacks apparently planned by Luhu and its allies across the Hoamoal Peninsula seemed to have opened up an ominous tear in the colonial fabric. In their wake, VOC merchants, including two men who would later sit in judgment at the Amboina trial, arrived in Castle Victoria carrying terrifying reports of attacks in the night and mutilated bodies. As officials gazed outward to enemies beyond the walls of Castle Victoria, they speculated nervously about the possibility of a slave revolt bursting out from within or whether their Japanese soldiers, unfamiliar troops transported from thousands of miles away into the heart of a vulnerable VOC outpost, might switch allegiances without warning.

These fears were magnified by the presence of the English, the last group of alleged conspirators, who occupied a sinister place in the Dutch colonial imagination. Arriving late in the region with few resources and limited military strength, the English East India Company was a perennial thorn in the side of the VOC as it constantly probed for weaknesses and opportunities to exploit. But even though they did act as a stumbling block to Dutch plans, EIC agents also came to assume an oversized stature in the minds of officials like Coen and Van Speult, who constructed a potent feedback loop of fear and distrust that ran through their correspondence. This intensified after the signing of the Treaty of Defense in 1619, which pushed English merchants, now recast as commercial partners, into the center of VOC establishments across Asia. The result was that dire warnings about inevitable English treachery reverberated through the letters sent to Amboina in the months leading up to the trial.

Put together, the picture that emerges of Castle Victoria in 1623 is one of a center in crisis as the governor and the garrison confronted a host of threats—some authentic, others the product of dark colonial fantasies—that seemed to challenge the very survival of the VOC presence there. Rather than feeling strong, therefore, the Dutch in Amboina felt acutely, overwhelmingly weak. In this way, the conspiracy case itself was driven by a potent combination of genuine crisis, imagined threat, and overpowering fear that propelled the rapid escalation from suspicion to torture, gave shape and form to the sprawling plot, and pushed it forward to a final bloody climax.

In making this argument, I build off an important 1942 article by Willem Philippus Coolhaas, the prolific historian of the Dutch East India Company, who first called attention to what he described as the "psychosis of fear" (*angstpsychose*) in Amboina.[63] The date of the article, written either directly before or during the early years of the Nazi occupation of the Netherlands, was not coincidental. In Coolhaas's own words, "The last years, and particularly months, have caused us to learn how great an influence rumors can have, and how they can eat away at our feelings of safety and security." In identifying the "psychosis of fear," Coolhaas's work brilliantly anticipated a new wave of scholarship focused on the role of anxiety and panic in European expansion that would start to appear decades later.

As they pushed outward in the early modern period, Europeans were, to borrow Jean Delumeau's evocative phrasing, engaged in a "permanent dialogue with fear."[64] In recent years, scholars have shown that colonial anxieties were a structural part of European expansion, creating a feeling of "helplessness" that shaped the imperial experience.[65] In an important new collection focused on the Americas, Louis Roper and Lauric Henneton have argued persuasively that fear was "a fundamental component in the lives of early modern settlers," while Mark Meuwese, Remco Raben, Markus Vink, and others have highlighted the potent "combination of fear, uncertainty, and excessive violence" that dominated daily existence in Dutch settlements in the Americas and Asia.[66] Such works have shown that fear was baked into the nature of European expansion, forming the omnipresent companion for merchants, soldiers, and settlers in the Americas, Asia, and elsewhere.[67]

Although Coolhaas acknowledged the corrosive nature of anxiety in Amboina, he returned toward the end of his 1942 article to a far more conventional position by arguing that VOC officials in Amboina had in fact discovered a genuine plot that linked together multiple conspirators.[68] This book builds on Coolhaas's insight but aims to trace the longer genealogy of the trial by showing how a period of change and crisis prompted VOC officials to summon up a sprawling plot that stitched together an array of colonial nightmares into an overarching conspiracy. My goal here is not to defend the Dutch in Kota Ambon or to cast them somehow as the anxious victims of their own empire but rather to understand how a sense of emergency could drive a ramshackle prosecution that ended in a mass execution in front of Castle Victoria.[69] As such, I draw inspiration from studies like Mary Beth Norton's *In the Devil's Snare: The Salem Witchcraft Crisis of 1692*, which seeks to tie a sprawling witchcraft prosecution that, like its counterpart in Amboina, broke free from conventional restraints to a wider political crisis along a colonial frontier.[70]

The first part of what follows examines mounting tensions in Kota Ambon. Chapter 1 explores the volatile political environment across the Malukus as VOC's attempts to enforce a series of restrictive treaties generated increasing resistance. Chapter 2 moves inside the walls of Castle Victoria to examine the slave population in Amboina and its overseer captain, Augustine Peres. Here, the governor-general's plans to populate the Spice Islands with compliant workers, coupled with the opening up of new slaving hubs in South Asia, triggered an increase in the number of slaves in Kota Ambon just as the wider security situation appeared to be deteriorating. Chapter 3 looks at the contingent of Japanese soldiers based in Castle Victoria. Although there were only around a dozen Japanese recruits in Kota Ambon, these soldiers represented the tip of an ambitious plan pushed by a small group of Dutch officials to harness Asian military manpower to fight the Company's wars. Chapter 4 focuses on English East India Company merchants in Asia and their place in the wider VOC world. Finally, chapter 5 shifts to the trial itself by attempting to trace the potent combination of fear, ambition, and incompetence that underpinned the legal proceedings.

While part I seeks to explain the nature of the trial, part II takes aim at yet another Amboina mystery: how a chaotic and panic-inflected response to the questions of a young Japanese soldier came to be presented and widely understood, including by modern scholars, as a methodical legal process carefully and deliberately engineered to achieve a clear purpose. This change stemmed, I suggest in chapter 6, from an unexpected convergence between the strategies pursued by the two companies after news of what had happened in Kota Ambon reached Europe in May 1624. Drawing on two competing groups of witnesses, both the VOC and the EIC sought to obscure the disordered nature of the trial at Amboina in order to strengthen their respective positions. For EIC officials selling a story of Dutch treachery, De Bruyn could not be an inept bungler if he was a malicious agent of a wider plot to expel the English. And for Dutch East India Company representatives eager to avoid damaging political consequences, there was every reason to quash their own doubts about the advocate-fiscal's competence in favor of a new version of the trial that emphasized its orderly nature. The result of this convergence was to erase whole parts of the original proceedings and open the way to a new interpretation of Amboina as a methodical legal process designed, depending on perspective, either to brutally cheat or to rigorously enforce justice.

Finally, chapter 7 seeks to trace the long aftermath of the case in both Europe and Asia. It shows how EIC efforts to extract compensation foundered for decades before being unexpectedly revived by Cromwell during the first Anglo-Dutch War. In addition to tracking this long controversy, the chapter returns to Amboina to examine what happened to this colony in crisis in the years after 1623. Here the timelines converge unexpectedly. Just as negotiations over the original conspiracy trial were wrapping up in Europe around 1654, Amboina was in a process of violent transformation as a new administrator, Arnold de Vlaming van Oudtshoorn, made use of a brief spasm of bloody rebellion against Dutch rule to remake a contested landscape.

Conspiracies and Empire

By any measure, the English East India Company waged an extraordinarily successful propaganda campaign against its Dutch counterpart that has shaped accounts of the trial ever since. But another reason the vision of the Amboina trial as a strategic maneuver expertly contrived by a ruthless VOC governor to remove a troublesome competitor has proved resilient is because it seems to fit so neatly with a wider view of Dutch triumph in this period. On the surface, this was a century of consistent success that made the Company the dominant European overseas enterprise in the seventeenth century and the United Provinces, itself in the midst of its famed Golden Age, a major European power in its own right. Beginning in 1602, when it was chartered, and ending in 1684, when it reached the zenith of its power, the VOC leapt, in this narrative, from success to success, establishing an imperial headquarters on the ruins of Jayakarta in 1619, taking possession of the spice-rich Banda Islands in 1621, planting its flag on Taiwan in 1624, wresting control of the crucial entrepot of Melaka (Malacca) from the Portuguese in 1641, defeating the powerful maritime kingdom of Makassar in 1667, and finally overwhelming the port polity of Banten in 1684.[71] And the Company was able to accomplish so much in part because it was a more rational, more coldly pragmatic, and effectively more modern organization than its Iberian rivals, which were forever trapped in premodern patterns of behavior that prevented them from competing successfully against this new Protestant challenger.[72]

In recent years, scholars have begun to cut away at the fabric of VOC triumphalism, showing the false starts, contained ambitions, and abject failures that characterized Dutch expansion in Asia while picking away at long-held assumptions about the uniquely rational nature of Company officials.[73] The Amboina trial presents yet more evidence of this, showing not an inevitable trajectory to VOC dominance in Asia but rather a precarious colonial outpost that seemed for long periods on the brink of its own demise and Company officials beset by real and imagined fears. As such it provides further reason to question dated Golden Age narratives of inevitable success in this period.

Moving away from notions of Dutch exceptionalism enables a better understanding of what is different about Amboina and what looks familiar. For centuries now, the 1623 case has been used as a rhetorical cudgel by English-language writers to beat the Dutch East India Company and its home government for what William Hunter called a "great wrong unredressed."[74] Beginning in 1624 with the first pamphlets produced in the aftermath of the trial, they have attacked the Amboina conspiracy trial as an event singularly without parallel. On one level, there is clearly some truth here. What happened in 1623 was, as this book shows, born out of a perfect storm, a conjoining of fears and crises that drove VOC officials in Castle Victoria to take actions that shocked even their superiors. And in the years after the case, Amboina generated an enduring political and diplomatic firestorm that was driven first by the outsized reaction of the English East India Company, which saw the trial both as an existential crisis that threatened its place in Asia and an unprecedented opportunity to force the VOC to provide compensation and concessions, but also by the efforts of the English state, which threw its resources, always unevenly and often with little effect, into prosecuting what it claimed was the judicial murder of its subjects. Together they worked to turn Amboina from a legal trial into some sort of original sin committed by the Dutch East India Company against the English nation. In their efforts, they were aided by the chaotic nature of De Bruyn's judicial proceedings, which opened up a space to reinvent a new version of the case that could be used to mobilize EIC investors, the court, and, to a degree, public opinion.

But in another way what happened at Amboina was also strikingly routine, a quotidian legal proceeding that could have happened in any one of a proliferating number of European colonial outposts. While English pamphleteers bemoaned the brutal techniques used by Dutch interrogators, they elided the numerous contemporary instances in which EIC agents used the same (or sometimes far worse) methods to uncover alleged plots. One of the clearest examples comes from Gabriel Towerson's own career. English pamphleteers worked with considerable success to turn Towerson into a stoic martyr wronged by an act of unprecedented cruelty.[75] In 1604, however, Towerson and a group of EIC officials had participated in the savage torture and execution of a Chinese goldsmith who they believed had been part of a plot to use the cover of an arson attack to steal some goods.[76] Like Van Speult years later, Towerson and his countrymen confronted a fearful landscape, a world of "murther, theft, warres, fire, and treason" crowded with dangers.[77] And they responded with the most brutal torture imaginable, burning the goldsmith "vnder the nayles of his thumbes, fingers, and toes with sharpe hotte Iron, and the nayles to be torne off." When this did not produce a result, they escalated the torture, tearing "out the fleshe and sinewes" and knocking "the edges of shinne bones with hotte searing Irons."

As such examples suggest, the underlying dynamic evident in Castle Victoria in 1623—the discovery of a conspiracy with what was probably a very limited grounding in reality, the torture of alleged plotters until a confession was extracted, and the final execution—was entirely unexceptional. As many scholars have noted, conspiracy thinking and the tendency to interpret events through a conspiratorial lens were pervasive across early modern Europe, and it is no surprise that Europeans transported such attitudes with them as they departed for colonial frontiers.[78] While each empire was driven by its own set of fears, one can find other trials complete with the same basic reliance on torture in isolated forts or outposts belonging to a range of European overseas enterprises in Asia.

Despite the protestations of English defenders, conspiracy thinking and the brutal, torture-dependent trials that it engendered were not the sole property of the Dutch East India Company or its employees. Instead, they were an endemic part of the European push into Asia and the anxieties and vulnerabilities that surrounded it. Finally, stripping away any notion of the Amboina trial as a carefully constructed strategy engineered by an emerging power destined always for imperial greatness shows it more clearly for what it was: a desperate, fearful, and brutal response by a group of offi-cials marooned on the edge of empire. The 1623 conspiracy case may have generated a uniquely durable controversy but it was also another episode in a much wider story, now in the process of being unearthed by scholars, about the uncertain and insecure nature of European empire in Asia.[79]

PART ONE
Amboina in 1623

CHAPTER I

With Treaty or With Violence

The Ternatans about two or 3 months before the discovery of the conspiracy began to rebel in the quarters of Luhu and Kambelo and murdered some Netherlanders.

—LAURENS DE MAERSCHALK, 1628

In February 1621, two years before the Amboina conspiracy case began to unfold, the governor-general of the Dutch East India Company, Jan Pieterszoon Coen, took command of an invasion fleet. Anchored in the harbor at Kota Ambon was the most powerful military force yet assembled by the Dutch empire in Asia. Crowded within the wooden walls of more than a dozen ships were 1,655 soldiers and sailors, virtually every fighting man the organization could muster, including 80 soldiers shipped from its distant outpost in Japan.[1] The fleet's target was the nearby Banda Islands, where local spice growers had persistently resisted VOC attempts to enforce its claimed treaty rights over nutmeg and mace. After years of frustration, Coen had decided that the Company's might would be brought to bear on Banda, wiping the slate clean and preparing the ground for a new population of settlers and slaves capable of funneling spices into the holds of VOC ships.[2]

From the walls of Castle Victoria, Herman van Speult, Coen's ever-dutiful subordinate, watched the fleet assemble. The campaign was to be a decisive moment not just for Banda but also for Amboina, where attempts to lock down the spice trade had faltered in the face of resistance by polities scattered across the Hoamoal Peninsula, which had begun to push back with increasing ferocity against their own treaties with the Company. Starting with the successful conquest of Banda, Coen's operation was designed to end in Amboina, securing Dutch dominion there and, with it, control over the flow of spices.[3] In fact, it had the opposite effect, sparking a descent into violent disorder that provided the backdrop to the 1623 conspiracy trial. Writing a year after the bloody pacification of Banda, Coen, who had nursed ambitious dreams of a single transformative campaign, painted a dark picture of the colony in Amboina, which was surrounded on all sides by enemies who worked in stealth to raise "our friends, vassals and subjects to rebellion."[4] This stark assessment was amplified by a string of violent clashes that took place across Amboina in the months before the 1623 trial, ending in the murder or flight of Dutch officials and the razing to the ground of a number of outposts.

This chapter explores Banda and Amboina together, showing how repeated attempts to exert control over the spice trade created a situation that VOC officials believed could only be resolved by force, and how a violent campaign launched against Banda in 1621 increased unrest across Amboina in 1623. At the center of this story are treaties—signed, ratified, but never observed. After its establishment in 1602, the Company had attempted to channel the flow of commodities in the Malukus by using restrictive agreements that required local signatories to deliver their crops of precious spices at a fixed price in return for protection against the Portuguese and the Spanish. Couched in the language of alliance against a common enemy, VOC treaties were intended to superimpose a reliable political template over an uncertain landscape. But even as they signed such documents, local spice producers had no intention of selling their crops exclusively to the Dutch at deflated prices, particularly when the presence of Asian trading powers like Makassar or European rivals like the English East India Company offered multiple opportunities to evade such restrictions. The result was that these treaties engendered rather than resolved disorder, creating what VOC officials viewed as false allies who were bound to the Company by signed documents but existed in a state of perpetual transgression.

The Company's administrators talked often in terms of opposing binaries, of control exerted either through "treaty or with violence."[5] Implicit in this was the notion that violence was the opposite of the treaty, something called into action only in the most exceptional of circumstances when all other mechanisms had broken down. In fact, as scholars like Martine van Ittersum and Arthur Weststeijn have shown, the two came bundled together in sites of Dutch expansion.[6] Treaties were not the antithesis of empire, an instrument of reciprocal recognition that ensured mutual sovereignty.[7] Rather, they became in many cases the very engine driving the expansion of VOC territorial control and with it the organization's transformation into an Asian power. Although expressed in the language of respect and recognition, such agreements created a problem that many Company officials came to believe could only be solved through violence.[8] Because of this, they came attached to a ticking clock counting down relentlessly from signing to the moment of violent resolution when the Company's false allies were either brought into line or, in some cases, simply erased from the landscape. It was this process that played out in the years leading up to the 1623 trial in Banda and which in turn triggered a rapid deterioration of political conditions in Amboina.

Spices and Treaties

Propelling the creation of the Dutch East India Company and running like a thread through its early operations in Asia was an overwhelming, insatiable lust for spices.[9] For Europeans, spices represented one of the great commercial prizes of the seventeenth century. While a number of spices could command high prices, an intoxicating triumvirate—nutmeg, mace, and cloves—stood at the top of the wider hierarchy.[10] Together, their capacity to generate the greatest profits meant that they assumed a prominent place in the European imagination. The value of these spices derived from their myriad properties that would, one writer assured his readers, take "too long to narrate."[11] Among other things, cloves could "strengthen the Liver, the Maw, and the hart, they further digestion, they procure evacuation of the Urine . . . preseveth the sight, and four Drammes being drunke with Milk, doe procure lust."[12] Nutmeg, just as potent, was said to "comferteth the braine, sharpeth the memorie, warmeth and strengthneth the Maw, driveth winde out of the body, maketh a sweet breath, driveth downe Urine, stoppeth the Laske (diarrhoea)."[13]

These potent attributes and the readily portable nature of precious spices combined to make them irresistible targets for commercial expansion. The great complicating factor, but one that also spurred dreams of absolute monopoly, was that these commodities were concentrated in the Malukus, a remote set of islands in modern-day Indonesia that was widely referred to as the Spice Islands.[14] Nutmeg and mace came primarily from the Banda Islands, and cloves from Amboina, located to the northwest within easy sailing distance.[15] Simply getting a ship thousands of miles from Europe to the Spice Islands was difficult; developing a reliable infrastructure capable of gathering, storing, and exporting these commodities year after year imposed a vast logistical challenge.

The first Dutch fleet to reach the Spice Islands arrived under the command of Jacob van Neck in 1599. It had been sent by one of the smaller trading companies, now known collectively as the pre-companies (*voorcompagnieen*), that combined to send fifteen such expeditions to Asia before the establishment of the VOC.[16] Van Neck's voyage was a stunning success, harvesting enough spices to generate a 400 percent profit and triggering a rush of copycat enterprises.[17] The arrival of so many competing fleets in a relatively short time drove down the price for spices and undermined the basis for profitable trade. It quickly became clear that one unified company would have a much better chance of exploiting this newly opened market. In December 1601, Johan van Oldenbarnevelt, the senior statesman in the United Provinces, convened a conference that brought together the directors of all the rival companies. The outcome of months of hard-fought negotiations was the Vereenigde Oost-Indische Compagnie, or United East India Company, which was formed by merging six of the pre-companies.

The VOC represented a significant improvement on the pre-companies. It was larger, more stable, and better equipped with a range of powers designed to allow it to compete effectively in Asia. The new organization drew on a vast initial capital of 6,424,588 guilders, which was raised from shares bought by 1,800 individual investors.[18] In contrast to its predecessors, which were capitalized for individual expeditions, meaning that all remaining funds had to be returned to the investors at the conclusion of these enterprises, the VOC's capital crossed voyages, lasting initially for ten years but later becoming effectively permanent.[19] At the same time, the 1602 charter gave the Company exclusive rights to a vast area of operations east of the Cape of Good Hope and west of the Strait of Magellan. This allowed the organization's directors, the famous Gentlemen 17 (*Heeren XVII*), to develop a long-term strategy for expansion in Asia, an option denied both to the pre-companies and to its English rival, which had been established two years earlier on the older model.[20] Finally, the States General gifted the VOC, which was created in part to carry the fight against Portugal and Spain into a new region, with an arsenal of privileges and powers that allowed it to wage war, conduct diplomacy, and plant colonies in Asia.

These powers were turned immediately toward the Spice Islands. Here, the fact that spice production was concentrated in a narrow geographical area located outside the boundaries of a major state, the very features that made it so difficult for Europeans to access the trade in the first place, seemed to create an opening for the Company.[21] Unlike other commodities that poured forth from disparate sources, the trade in nutmeg, mace, and cloves could, it seemed, be encompassed by a single organization equipped with a sufficiently aggressive strategy. The potential prize was enormous. If the newly formed Company could find a way to control the flow of spices in Amboina and Banda, it could ensure its long-term survival, make its investors rich, and deprive its Portuguese and Spanish rivals of access to a lucrative resource. But how to do this? How to stretch power across thousands of miles to control a commodity that had been available to the highest bidder for centuries, and to a territory where vessels belonging to a range of commercial competitors could simply land at any one of dozens of inlets along the coast to purchase spices? For VOC officials, the answer lay in a key instrument of the Dutch Empire, the protection/tribute treaty, which was used to stamp their influence over the spice trade.[22]

As the Company's expeditions pushed further into Asian waters, its captains and merchants moved to sign documents, which they described as "treaties" (*verbondt*) or "accords" (*accordt*), with local rulers and leaders.[23] These treaties were rooted in what seems at first a deferential attitude toward Asian rulers. From the beginning, VOC officials made no attempt to deny the essential sovereignty of local regimes as a prelude to ambitious claims. To the contrary, they insisted—and the point was reinforced by writers such as Hugo Grotius, who emerged as the Company's most effective legal champion—that European powers had no right to claim Asian territory on the basis of discovery, papal donation, the requirement for mass proselytism, or similar arguments. Instead, VOC officials carefully positioned themselves as the protectors of local rulers who had been threatened by the aggressive imperial incursions of Portugal and Spain. In Grotius's formulation, "When the East Indian princes and nations, suffering under the Spaniards' harsh injustice, saw the courage and strength of the Dutch, they implored our aid and alliance and were saved from extreme danger by our troops; for their own offered no protection."[24]

While Dutch agents reveled in their self-presentation as "the most valiant of men, defenders of their allies and subduers of their enemies; and . . . saviours of the Orient," the offer of protection came attached to a steep price tag.[25] The recipients of this protection were required to offer tribute in return for security, as "there can be no peace among nations without armies, no armies without pay and no pay without tributes."[26] The particular form this tribute took was the surrender of control over key commodities, most notably precious spices such as cloves, nutmeg, and mace, the sale of which dominated international trade in the region.[27]

The protection/tribute exchange was replicated in dozens of treaties signed between the Company and local rulers across Southeast Asia in the first decades of the organization's existence.[28] Such agreements enabled the Company to position itself as a sympathetic champion, but they came with far-reaching consequences. As Edward Keene has demonstrated, the VOC conceived of sovereignty not as a monolithic, indivisible whole but as a collection of rights that could be split up and parceled out to more than one party.[29] Because of this, protection/tribute treaties allowed the Dutch to slice off a set of key economic rights in exchange for a promise of protection against the Portuguese.[30] The result was that, once the treaties were ratified, local signatories no longer controlled the key commodity around which their economy was built. Instead, they gained an effective co-ruler in the form of Company officials determined to fence off their rights to spices.

Because they transferred rights, such documents also provided a malleable dispensation for violence. Once the VOC could show that it possessed a treaty conferring rights to a particular crop at a particular price, it could, equally readily, argue that it was entitled to use any means necessary to defend those claims. Almost as soon as the ink was dry on these documents, Dutch officials insisted that they were permitted to build forts to make sure that treaty clauses were being properly observed, to deploy their ships to exclude competitors, or to use force to punish violations of legally binding agreements.[31] When local signatories refused to hand over spices at artificially depressed prices, such treaties became a pathway toward direct control and the construction of a territorial empire in Asia. It was an outcome that some within the Company saw stretching out in plain view from the moment of signing. By "entering into a good alliance and treaty with the residents, the way was prepared," one official wrote in the most explicit of terms, "for the conquest and capture of the same lands."[32]

This was the case in the Banda Islands, where a string of treaties first signed in 1602 laid the groundwork for invasion and dispossession less than two decades later.[33]

Binding Banda

The Banda archipelago consists of ten islands, including Naira, Lontor or Bandar Besar, Gunung Api, Pulau Hatta, Ai, and Run, which produced the bulk of the world's nutmeg and mace in this period.[34] In the words of one early European visitor, this "place supplies the whole world with these products for they are grown nowhere else."[35]

Their role in the spice trade made the islands a key hub on regional circuits of trade. It also left them exposed, particularly as their inhabitants were dependent on imports to provide a range of basic goods including foodstuffs, all of which had to be transported by sea. Such vulnerabilities were compounded by Banda's turbulent internal dynamics. In contrast to more centralized polities like Ternate or Tidore, the Banda Islands were characterized by a fractious political environment. Lacking a single ruler or any sort or overarching state structures, the islands were administered

Figure 1.1 Nutmeg from the Banda Islands in 1599. Anonymous, c. 1619. Courtesy of the Rijksmuseum, Amsterdam. RP-P-OB-75.396.

by a loose confederation of elders called *orangkaya* (literally: "rich men"), whose position stemmed from their control over the nutmeg trade.[36] While they did occasionally cooperate, the *orangkaya* were divided into shifting factions that combined and recombined in an endless range of permutations and made it impossible to arrive at a single unified response to European incursions.[37]

For decades, Europeans had gazed covetously at the Banda Islands, which were worth, one observer explained, their weight in gold.[38] The Portuguese, the first European group to arrive in the region in strength, targeted the nutmeg and mace trade but failed to exert any significant measure of control over the archipelago's decentralized commercial networks.[39] Like the Dutch after them, they faced a problem on both ends: local expertise in the growing and preparation of nutmeg could not easily be duplicated or replaced, while there was, at the same time, a surplus of potential buyers willing to buy whatever spices the Bandanese were prepared to sell. Maritime polities like Makassar kept an agent permanently stationed in Banda to purchase spices, while a range of other Asian and European merchants, including by the early seventeenth century the "English, French, Javanese, Malays, Makassars, Botonese and other . . . nations," jostled for access to the lucrative crop.[40] The combination effectively insulated Banda from outside pressure, leading VOC officials to complain that the Bandanese were a "bunch of villainous, haughty, malevolent poor beggars who are always in arrears, no matter what their income. They rely on the fact that everyone needs them."[41]

When they arrived in Banda, the Dutch attempted to apply a standard protection/tribute template designed to secure rights to the nutmeg and mace trade. This commenced in 1602, when an expedition under the command of Admiral Wolffert Hermansz concluded a treaty with one group of *orangkaya*. It committed the signatories to "sell all their nutmegs and mace to their people [the Dutch] and not to anyone else" in return for a VOC "promise [that] by night or by day, they shall help as much as possible against whoever will hurt or damage the land of Banda."[42] These arrangements were confirmed in 1605, when a commitment by the Bandanese to deliver their entire crop to the Dutch was exchanged for a guarantee that "if it happens that some foreign enemies come from outside to war with or destroy the general lands of Banda, then the Hollanders will, as much as they can, help defend these lands."[43]

Why did the Bandanese sign such treaties, handing over expansive rights to the very commodities that they depended on for survival? One well-worn answer is that they simply did not understand the documents they were signing. Willard Hanna, who has written widely on the islands, describes VOC treaties as "alien, legalistic document[s]" that were entirely opaque to the Asian partner.[44] This approach assumes, however, that since it found expression in treaties prepared by the Dutch, the legal language of protection and tribute offered up to the Bandanese was foreign to Southeast Asian politics.[45] In fact, there were clear parallels with political practices across the region. The fluid nature of Southeast Asian politics, described by scholars as a mandala system characterized by multiple, overlapping "circles of kings," meant that protection was well established as a vital commodity of inter-polity exchange long before the first European ships arrived.[46] The available evidence suggests that the Bandanese, who had long been accustomed to finding security by playing off foreign powers, initially welcomed these treaties, in part because they were a continuation of past practices.[47] What was different was the Company's intent and, more important, its capacity to enforce these treaties.

Whereas Bandanese leaders clearly assumed that any concessions would only be sporadically implemented, leaving the way open for continued exchange, the VOC was prepared to commit significant resources to nailing down its claims.[48] As a first sign that things would be different, the Dutch moved quickly to establish a fortress in the archipelago so they could oversee day-to-day operations of the spice trade. This represented a new threat for the *orangkaya*, who had vigorously resisted any attempt by the Portuguese to gain a territorial foothold on their islands. By 1609, relations had deteriorated to the point that the Bandanese ambushed and killed a VOC admiral, Pieter Verhoef, and some forty of his men. The Company responded to this betrayal, which seared itself on the organization's collective memory, with force leading to another, even more expansive treaty pledging that all available spices would be delivered to the Dutch "without selling, trading or exchanging in the slightest to any other persons or nations other than the prescribed representatives."[49]

Predictably, the 1609 treaty was violated from the beginning. Writing from Europe, the Heeren 17 complained that the Bandanese traded freely with English merchants and other nations without any regard for the contracts they had signed.[50] In this way, the problem stemmed both from an unwillingness to abide by the restrictive provisions and from the active involvement of commercial rivals like the English East India Company, which worked to pull apart the fabric of the treaty regime.[51] As they would do in Amboina, EIC merchants targeted points of resistance where the widest gaps had opened up between spice producers and the Dutch. Their efforts were actively encouraged by Bandanese leaders, who, believing that the English company could offer military protection against the Dutch, sought to draw them in as guarantors of their territory by staging elaborate theaters of submission designed to bind their lands symbolically to the English king.[52]

The overall result was to create a state of permanent disorder, in which the Bandanese were in constant violation of the treaties they had signed. In the years after 1609, a number of high-ranking VOC officials became increasingly convinced that this problem could only be resolved through acts of violence that would bring the population into line while entrenching VOC control.[53] By 1612, Pieter Both, who had been appointed as the organization's first governor-general, suggested burning down Banda's nutmeg orchards. Since the Bandanese had "no other prosperity or wealth aside from the profusion of nutmeg trees," the destruction of those would force them into an acceptance of treaty provisions.[54] Other officials went further, declaring that the problem could be fixed only via the erasure of the local population. In 1612, Jacob l'Hermite, the chief merchant in Banten, suggested that the Bandanese should be "totally conquered or with proper guarantee brought to reason or entirely exterminated" (*gansch uitgeroyt*). If such steps were not taken, this "villainous monster could never be controlled as well as one would wish."[55] These comments were picked up and reinforced by the Heeren 17 in Europe, who argued in 1615 that the "Bandanese should be overpowered, the principals exterminated and chased away and the land repopulated."[56]

Such statements laid out a blueprint to move beyond the treaty framework to seize direct control of Banda. The process of final implementation was taken up by Jan Pieterszoon Coen, who had risen up within the ranks of the Company to become governor-general just as the Bandanese question was coming to its climax. Like many of his superiors, Coen was convinced that the Banda problem could only be resolved by a military operation that would entrench VOC control over the archipelago.[57] In 1621, he moved to put these plans into action when he sailed with an invasion fleet from Amboina to Banda. The deployment of such a large force was intended to be decisive, securing control over the archipelago and with it the flow of nutmeg and mace. For over a century now, scholars have debated whether Coen knew exactly how he would accomplish this goal—whether he believed a limited war followed by an even more onerous treaty and additional VOC fortifications would be enough to fulfill his aims or whether he anticipated the bloody campaign of pacification that would end in the death or exile of most of Banda's population.[58] For the purposes of this study, however, the question is less important than the campaign's devasting aftermath, which sent thousands of Bandanese refugees fleeing north into Amboina and Seram.

The invasion fleet that arrived off the shores of the Banda Islands in 1621 was unlike anything the Bandanese had encountered before. While the Company had mounted military campaigns before, this was something new.[59] On March 11, Coen launched his first sustained attack, assaulting the crucial island of Lontor from three different sides.[60] Faced with such overwhelming force, Bandanese leaders opted to surrender by signing a new treaty that recognized VOC sovereignty over the archipelago.[61] Elated by the quick victory, Coen wrote to his superiors that the Company had "conquered the spiteful, proud Bandanese."[62] In fact, the campaign was only just beginning. Rather than complying with their new obligations, the Bandanese were, the governor-general came to believe, settling in to resist, hoarding arms, and strengthening defensive structures. Suspecting that a revolt would break out as soon as the fleet departed, Coen and his council decided that the population on Lontor must be transported to Batavia, where they could be more readily controlled.[63]

Even as this mass transportation of Bandanese villagers was being set into motion, VOC officials claimed to have detected a set of conspiracies aimed squarely at them. Armed with the testimony of a single witness, Company agents proceeded to interrogate a group of forty-five surviving *orangkaya*, who had been held on suspicion of their "vile plans."[64] Tortured aboard one of the Company's ships, some died in the process while others leapt into the ocean to avoid further torment. Those who remained confessed, revealing multiple plots to attack the Dutch encampment and murder the personnel there, as well as three separate schemes to assassinate the governor-general in different locations. The *orangkaya* admitted under torture that they had deceived the Dutch with "pretty visage and feigned words" while secretly strengthening their redoubts in the hills, stockpiling weapons, and preparing for an all-out assault designed to throw the invaders back into sea.[65] On May 8, VOC officials decided to execute the accused, handing over the bloody task to a group of Japanese soldiers who had formed part of the original invasion force.

In the aftermath of the supposed conspiracy, VOC forces embarked on a campaign of brutal pacification designed to eliminate the possibility of further resistance. Those villagers who had fled into the hills or evaded control were starved out as the Company's forces cut the supply lines upon which the islands depended for food.[66] Such tactics had a catastrophic impact on the archipelago's population, which dropped from roughly 15,000 inhabitants prior to the invasion to just a few hundred.[67] As settlements were erased, the Company sliced the denuded islands into new divisions called *perken*, which were to be worked by a combination of European settlers and imported slaves. In those parts of the islands where the VOC did not intend to establish such estates, it simply extirpated the nutmeg trees to close down any possibility of clandestine trade. By the end of the process, Banda was unrecognizable—the population wiped from the map and the archipelago remade into a plantation economy.

While it took years to develop the expertise necessary to grow nutmeg successfully in its new plantations, the Company's Banda experiment was, by its own reckoning, spectacularly successful. In a few months of military operations, the disordered environment on Banda had been erased, the Company's untrustworthy allies eradicated and replaced with a new population of slaves working under Dutch masters. In his letters to his superiors, Coen reported triumphantly that the Company had become "master of all the islands of Banda."[68] But if the 1621 invasion seemed to resolve the organization's Banda problem, it had the opposite effect on nearby Amboina, where the campaign generated a wave of instability that rippled through an already turbulent environment.

VOC Rule in Amboina

For centuries, Amboina and Banda had been linked by physical proximity, their shared role in the spice trade, and a long history of contact and connection. After 1602, these connections multiplied as Amboina and Banda were wrapped up within largely identical treaties designed to control the spice trade. But, these were also very different places. In Banda, the VOC's aggressive strategy had been enabled by the territory's small size and the fractured nature of local authority, which meant that the

Company was able to muster an overwhelming military advantage that could be decisively deployed in a single extended campaign. By contrast, Amboina was far larger, with a total population that probably numbered around 70,000–80,000, or more than five times the inhabitants of pre-conquest Banda, and was characterized by a proliferation rather than an absence of armed political centers.[69] Because of this, it presented a far more difficult challenge for the Company, which found itself confronted by a territory that would take decades to master.

In February 1605, Steven van der Haghen accepted the surrender of a Portuguese fort on the island of Ambon, which was handed over without a fight. Although it became a locus of Dutch power in the region, Castle Victoria was poorly situated for the precise purpose it was intended for, that is, to control the flow of spices.

The problem was that the areas around the castle under direct VOC control produced few or no cloves. Instead, the center of spice production was

Figure 1.2 The fort at Ambon. Anonymous, c. 1644–1646. Courtesy of the Rijksmuseum, Amsterdam. RP-P-OB-75.450.

located in Hitu on the northern side of the island and on the Hoamoal Peninsula on the western edge of Seram.[70] This meant that VOC officials in Castle Victoria were engaged in a constant struggle to push their influence northward from Kota Ambon. Their chosen vehicle to do so was a familiar one, treaties, which were signed with a range of spice producers in Hitu and Hoamoal, promising that cloves would be delivered to the Company at fixed prices.

As in Banda, however, gaping holes opened up in the Company's treaty regime. For anyone looking to circumvent VOC prohibitions, there was a surplus of eager trading partners. The most sustained inroads were made by Makassar, which was willing to pay more for spices than the depressed prices offered by the Dutch, and Castle Victoria received a steady flow of reports about large quantities of cloves slipping through the net.[71] Traders from Makassar were joined by a range of other rivals, including English merchants who started to push aggressively into points of Company weakness in Amboina, sending ships to trade directly with settlements across the Hoamoal Peninsula.[72]

The Company's basic problem, that its authority was concentrated in places where there were comparatively few spices, was compounded by the warlike nature of early seventeenth-century Amboina, which Knaap describes as a "'contest state,' an arena in which the status quo between the most important players could rapidly change."[73] Home to a string of fortified centers, the area was defined by constant competition and warfare. VOC accounts from this period describe a militarized terrain dominated by a long list of settlements, each attached to a figure ranging from a few hundred to several thousand *weerbare mannen* ("fighting men").[74] Each settlement could match the Company's limited forces; if these thousands of warriors were ever combined, they would outnumber any army Castle Victoria could put into the field.

Alongside these challenges, VOC officials contended with a complex political environment in which their own influence seemed constantly under threat from a shifting combination of rivals. Large parts of the province fell under the nominal authority of the sultan of Ternate, which, alongside the nearby island of Tidore, maintained an outsized political influence in the region. Ternate claimed rights over a wide swath of territory that encompassed the Hoamoal Peninsula.[75] The Dutch East India Company had a long and frequently fractious relationship with the sultan of Ternate. The first expeditions from the United Provinces had been eagerly welcomed by Ternate's rulers, who saw in these newcomers a chance to secure a strong ally against the Iberian powers. After Spanish forces occupied part of Ternate in 1606, the sultan looked toward the Company to reclaim his territory, but in return for their military support VOC officials demanded exclusive rights to clove production in Ternate's sphere of influence.[76] In May 1607, Muzaffar (r. 1606–1627) concluded an agreement with the VOC in which he agreed to recognize the Dutch as his "protector" (beschermheer) in return for an oath "not to sell any cloves to any [other] nation or people," but rather to direct the full harvest to the Company at a set price.[77]

The VOC was willing to take action but it lacked the necessary troops to evict the Spanish, who were entrenched on Ternate. Because of this, it moved instead to establish a new fortress at Malayu, which became home to a relocated court.[78] The result was that Muzaffar owed his position directly to the Company's intervention. This fact convinced many observers that the Dutch could simply dictate terms.[79] In reality, successive sultans consistently pursued their own interests even as they continued to rely on VOC support.[80] In particular, Company agents worried that Ternate, even as it sheltered under the umbrella of their protection, was engaged in a process of creeping expansion designed to gather up support and undermine Castle Victoria's authority.

Such concerns played out most worryingly across the Hoamoal Peninsula, the so-called wicked corner [boosen hoeck] of Seram, which loomed large in the imagination of VOC officials.[81] A key clove-producing area, Hoamoal was home to a string of fortified polities each with their own military resources and each capable of exporting large quantities of spices.[82] There, the sultan of Ternate was represented by the kimelaha, a position sometimes likened by VOC observers to that of a regent or stadthouder.[83] Traditionally filled by members of the high-ranking Tomagola family from Ternate, the post was occupied in this period first by Hidayat from 1619 to 1623 and then by Leliato from 1623 to 1629. Both surrounded themselves with a small community of Ternatens, who were, VOC officials alleged, constantly plotting in secret to undermine or attack the Dutch.[84]

One reason the Company worried so much about the kimelaha was because these officials were based in the heavily fortified center of Luhu: the representative "of the king of Ternate lives here [in Luhu], along with 40 to 50 Ternatens that are the principal scoundrels of old. They have many strongholds in the steep mountains made of stone."[85] A "federation of village federations," Luhu was a formidable political and economic actor,

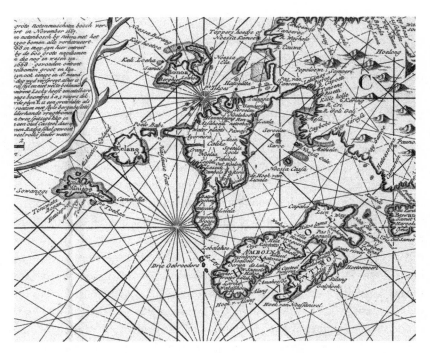

Figure 1.3 Map of Ambon and Hoamoal. From François Valentijn, *Oud en Nieuw Oost Indien.* Koninklijke Bibliotheek, The Hague, inv. nr. 185 A 5 part II, I. With thanks to the Atlas of Mutual Heritage (http://www.atlasofmutualheritage.nl/).

capable of mobilizing a large force estimated at some 2,500 warriors.[86] It had signed its own treaty with the VOC, committing it to turn over cloves to Castle Victoria, but, predictably, this was violated from the beginning. By the 1620s, Luhu had emerged as an important and largely autonomous node for the clove trade, capable of delivering a significant quantity of spices every year. The nexus between an increasingly anti-Dutch *kimelaha* and a hostile Luhu able to deploy thousands of heavily armed warriors preoccupied officials in Castle Victoria, who wrote frequently about the nature of this threat.[87]

VOC concerns about the *kimelaha* and Luhu more generally were sharpened by a wider fear of a process of creeping Islamization stretching out from Muslim areas on Hoamoal to Christian communities on Ambon that the Company relied upon for military manpower, labor, and support. A holdover from the period of Portuguese influence, these communities formed a crucial line of defense, buttressing Dutch power and providing

fighting men for VOC expeditions. But such settlements were also, officials in Castle Victoria believed, acutely vulnerable to an aggressive campaign of conversion. Looking nervously at their first line of defense, they
became convinced that the Ternatens and their allies in Luhu "were planning to bring our subjects, who we had conquered with the sword from
our enemies, with sinister ways and practices, to the Muslim faith, and to
alienate them from us."[88] If this happened, it would hollow out the local
structures upon which the Company depended, leaving the Dutch vulnerable. Because of this, VOC documents are filled with accounts of mosques
destroyed, preachers arrested, and whole villages transplanted, all in a desperate effort to halt the spread of Islam.

It made for an ominous picture. From their base in Castle Victoria, VOC
administrators described a far-flung territory populated by armed centers
and filled with false allies who had signed treaties with the Company but
were working in secret against the organization. While they pretended to
be friends, leaders across Amboina worked in the shadows to raise up rebellion against the Company.[89] And this dynamic seemed only to be getting
worse year by year. Writing to his superiors, the governor-general explained
that the "malice of the Amboynese not only continues but increases daily."[90]
In Banda, the Company had been able to suppress resistance through the
use of overwhelming military force concentrated in a single military campaign. No such option was available in this case. Instead, the task of grap-
pling with these problems fell to Herman van Speult, who had risen
within the organization's ranks to assume control over the VOC colony in
Amboina.

According to his own letters, Van Speult entered the Company's service around 1612.[91] Once he came to Asia, his career became bound up
with Amboina, where he rose quickly to the highest rank. First posted to
Castle Victoria as an upper merchant (opperkoopman) in 1615, Van Speult
was promoted in July 1617 to lieutenant governor under Steven van der
Haghen, a key figure in the history of VOC rule in Amboina but one who
was frequently absent. Just two years later, he became governor in his own
right and a member of the Council of the Indies.[92] It was a rapid rise for
an official—he had clearly impressed his superiors, most notably Jan Pieterszoon Coen, himself swiftly clambering up the VOC ladder—but it also
placed Van Speult at the center of an increasingly volatile situation.[93] By
1617, when Van Speult assumed a role as second in command, tensions were
clearly mounting. In its attempt to control the spice trade, the Company

had scattered its forces across a string of trading outposts in places like Kambelo and Luhu.[94] Rather than allowing the Dutch to actually police the treaties, these outposts, which were manned by a small number of soldiers operating in increasingly hostile areas, served mainly to open up additional vulnerabilities. Eager to go on the offensive, the Company instructed the captains of its vessels to attack junks from Makassar and other rivals that were trading secretly across the territory.[95] Such tactics, however, triggered ferocious protests from local spice producers that the waters around Amboina should be "free to all the world" and that the Dutch had no right to disrupt long-standing networks.[96]

Tensions threatened to burst into open conflict. Frustrated by a policy he had never fully endorsed, Van der Haghen, who had first taken possession of Castle Victoria in 1605, wrote that "if we persist in driving away the junks with violence, then we will come to great dispute here, reaching even to war."[97] It proved a prescient warning. The first significant conflict broke out in Hottomouri, a village lying in the narrow neck of land between Hitu and Leitmoir, which had been engaged in "piracy of the Company's subjects."[98] Forced to respond with his "small might," Van Speult gathered a force of just sixty European troops mixed with a thousand Ambonese auxiliaries to suppress what he described as a "rebellion" against Dutch dominion.[99] After storming a string of fortifications, he burnt the settlement and relocated its inhabitants, who were forced to work as captives.

In his efforts to secure VOC influence, Van Speult turned increasingly to Asian military manpower by expanding the use of *hongi* expeditions, which were comprised of fleets of swift local craft called *kora-kora* that were manned by a *corvée* type system of local mobilization.[100] Such fleets had been standard in Amboina long before the arrival of the Dutch but they were modified by the Company from a tool of raiding aimed primarily at gathering captives into an instrument of colonial control, designed to hold the province's different centers in check through a combination of threats and violence.[101] Settlements under Dutch control were required to supply a fixed number of *kora-kora* and men for these expeditions, with the heaviest burden falling on the Christian communities that the VOC was so determined to safegaurd.[102]

Under Van Speult's direction, the *hongi* expeditions became an all-purpose instrument designed to force compliance with the treaties that were designed to encircle the clove trade.[103] Like a mobile court, they provided a mechanism for the public display of authority, going out with the governor to "do the round with a great strength to hold our subjects in devotion."[104] But when such exhibitions failed, these fleets could also serve as a punitive instrument capable of attacking treaty violators, razing fortifications, and destroying settlements.[105]

Van Speult's use of the *hongi* to enforce control was praised by his superiors in Europe, who explained that "the method started by Governor Speult in Amboina to ensure the loyalty of the subjects of the castle and bring our enemies to reason is very good."[106] Although *hongi* expeditions gave the Company a valuable weapon in its efforts to hold the treaty regime in place, their effect was always temporary. If power traveled with the fleet, it also receded once it had passed, leaving the same problems to recur. Increasingly, VOC officials led by Jan Pieterzoon Coen became convinced that more drastic actions were needed to secure Amboina and the clove trade once and for all.

The powerful force assembled for the invasion of Banda in 1621 provided the opportunity to realize these plans. From the beginning, Coen intended the operation to consist of two parts. Writing to the Heeren 17, he explained that his intention was to secure not only Banda but also Amboina, where the Company's armies could be used to "erase the evil out of Amboyna."[107] While he did not lay out a detailed plan, Coen's writings suggest a violent campaign of pacification designed to remove or subdue rivals like Luhu. In this way, the governor-general believed that both territories could be dealt with together, thereby permanently securing the Company's hold over the Spice Islands.

The problem was that Coen had underestimated how long operations in Banda would take or how many men would be lost in the long campaign that followed the initial clashes as VOC forces surrounded and starved out the remaining inhabitants. In a letter dispatched to Europe, he complained that during "the expedition to Banda, we lost more time than we had wanted, and we had to leave many men there to exterminate [*eenemael uyt te royen*] the enemy finally."[108] To make matters worse, the onset of the monsoon season made conditions for a prolonged campaign in Amboina impossible. It was too much, the governor-general concluded reluctantly, to fight against "God's weather and wind and against the enemy and the sickness of our people."

Forced to abandon the second part of the campaign, Coen decided instead to summon local leaders to Castle Victoria to confirm the treaties signed with the Company.[109] It made for an impressive ceremony, but one with little staying power, particularly since the *kimelaha* and the leaders of Luhu and other settlements scattered across the Hoamoal Peninsula, where VOC resistance was concentrated, refused to attend. While this was happening, news of Coen's actions on Banda raced through Amboina, spreading a "very great fear" across that territory.[110] In a few bloody months, the Dutch had transformed a key part of an interconnected system that had existed for centuries, sending shock waves rippling through the wider region. Even more important, Coen's campaign had triggered the flight of a large number of "refugee Bandanese" [*gevluchte Bandaneesen*], who headed north to Seram and Amboina looking for safe haven.[111]

Rising Tensions

In Castle Victoria, the governor recognized immediately that the flight of hundreds of dispossessed Bandanese villagers into Amboina represented a significant threat. Determined to prevent them from joining up with anti-Dutch forces, he issued repeated warnings that any captured Bandanese should be brought to Kota Ambon at once.[112] The problem was that it was impossible to police the myriad sea routes leading into Amboina, particularly when local powers actively competed to "pull together the rest of the runway Bandanese."[113] Instead of halting the influx, new alliances appeared to be forming every day between the refugee Bandanese and a range of groups across Seram that found common cause in their opposition to Castle Victoria.[114] As was so often the case, the *kimelaha* in Luhu emerged, at least in the VOC imagination, as a central actor, leading Coen to write that the Ternatens in Luhu were "busy pulling those of Ceram and the rest of the refugee Bandanese to them."[115] Everywhere it seemed as if new and dangerous coalitions were in the process of forming between the "Ternatens, those of Luhu, the Cerammers, the refugee Bandanese and their followers."[116]

While the Malukus had been marked by conflict before, Coen's devastating campaign represented something of a different order, the decimation of a local society and the disruption of a trading system that had endured for centuries. Although some of the Company's worst fears about aggressive new alliances proved unfounded, the arrival of the Bandanese does appear to have marked a change in the nature of anti-Dutch resistance in Amboina. Looking back from later in the seventeenth century, writers like

Rumphius concluded that the refugee Bandanese had infected "the local population with bitterness, which caused much trouble in the later wars."[117]

In the aftermath of Coen's invasion of Banda, new flashpoints erupted across Amboina. For years, the Company had sought to secure the Christian settlements scattered across Ambon as a bulwark against Muslim strongholds in Hitu and Hoamoal.[118] In September 1621, however, Van Speult received disturbing news. In the village of Waai, located in close proximity to the center of Dutch power at Castle Victoria, "more than half of the village (Negrij) . . . had betrayed us and become Moors."[119] Working in secret, the villagers had constructed a mosque to complete the final conversion of the village. In response, the governor dispatched soldiers to destroy the mosque, burn the village, and relocate its inhabitants to a new settlement under the walls of the castle, where they would be watched over by a trustworthy chief. In Batavia, Coen applauded the move, writing that the decision to burn the "village of Way and transport the people to the castle because more than half of them have become Moors is well done, as long as it is ensured that they will not apostate again and will not start more evil."[120]

By 1622, it was clear to everyone that the Company had passed over into dangerous new territory on Amboina. Increasingly, VOC officials painted their situation in desperate terms. It "is difficult," Coen wrote, "to advise what place the Ternatens have actually set their sights on first, and in what way. But the one thing that is certain is that they . . . seek our ruin [onderganck trachten]."[121] A new front opened up on Manipa, an island west of Seram. Here the VOC had attempted to expand its sphere of influence by signing a treaty in February 1622 that offered a familiar exchange, promising to protect Manipa's inhabitants against all enemies in return for a promise to recognize VOC sovereignty.[122] The treaty triggered, however, an outraged response from the kimelaha in Luhu, who assembled a fleet to attack Manipa and reassert Ternaten influence.[123] Determined to prevent this from happening, Van Speult rushed his own troops to the island to defend the boundaries of VOC influence.[124] Although the governor's rapid response seemed to diffuse the conflict, such incidents signaled a further hardening of battle lines.[125]

By 1623, Van Speult's worst fears seemed to be coming true when survivors trickled into Castle Victoria bearing news of gruesome attacks.[126] Just weeks before Shichizō was discovered on the battlements of Castle Victoria, VOC officials posted in Kambelo, a polity located close to Luhu on the eastern side of the Hoamoal Peninsula, recorded a macabre discovery. Described by VOC officials as one of the "principal troublemakers" [*principale roervinken*] of Amboina, Kambelo was home to a small Company outpost planted there to monitor the spice trade.[127] Amid mounting tensions, the local chief merchant, Jan van Leeuwen, received warnings not to go out in the jungle. Needing wood to burn, he decided to send out a carpenter guarded by three soldiers. When they were ready to return, the carpenter stayed behind to finish the job. After hours had past, a search party led by Van Leeuwen himself was sent out to investigate. Looking through the dense vegetation, they stumbled across the carpenter's decapitated and mutilated body.[128] Although there were no further clues as to the perpetrators, the chief merchant was convinced that a bounty had been placed on Dutch heads by the Company's enemies. Fearful of further attacks, Van Leeuwen rushed back to Castle Victoria carrying news of the carpenter's murder. Once there, he would reemerge as one of the Amboina judges, sitting in judgment of a conspiracy that, VOC officials believed, could be tied directly back to Hoamoal.

More violence erupted on the other side of the peninsula, in Luhu.[129] To monitor the spice trade there, the VOC had placed a token garrison consisting of less than a dozen soldiers, with Pieter van Santen, another future Amboina judge, at its head. Marooned in an increasingly hostile environment, Van Santen received a warning that the wooden outpost was about to be attacked and burnt to the ground.[130] The prospect of arson attacks was terrifyingly real for European merchants in Southeast Asia, who slept uneasily in structures that could be torched in the night, burning or killing everyone inside. A contemporary account from Java highlights the depth of this fear as its author explained that even the mere mention of the word "fire" could jolt him violently awake: "Oh this worde Fire! had it been spoken neere mee either in English, Mallayes, Javans, or Chyna, although I had been sounde a sleepe, yet I should haue leaped out of my Bedde."[131] Outnumbered and fearful of being burnt alive, Van Santen resolved to flee. When he tried to escape, however, his entourage was "pounced on and raided by those of Lohoe on the road and they killed one of his suite and injured him."[132] It was a terrifying incident, with Van Santen just managing to escape with his life.[133] In Castle Victoria, Van Speult rushed into action. Fearful of losing Van Santen and his men, he dispatched a vessel, the *Eenhoorn*, crammed with soldiers to evacuate the

Luhu outpost. Three days after they had escaped, it was set alight and burnt to the ground.[134]

Although there is no evidence that such attacks were part of a concerted strategy, the return of Van Santen and Van Leeuwen in the weeks before the 1623 trial bearing reports of mutilated bodies and sudden ambushes had a devastating impact on Castle Victoria. Tensions were further inflamed by a third incident on Manipa, which had been at the center of an earlier confrontation with the *kimelaha*. There, another Company outpost was burnt to the ground, with men dead and valuable goods destroyed.[135] Such episodes seemed to signal a drawing in of VOC influence as far-flung outposts were attacked and razed, leaving the garrison in Castle Victoria increasingly isolated. More ominously, they pointed toward a wider onslaught that appeared to be gathering momentum in the shadows. The concentration of incidents seemed to mark a new stage in the history of the VOC presence on Amboina. Long hostile to the Dutch, the two polities of Luhu and Kambelo had at last discarded any pretense of friendship and were preparing for open war. If fighters tied to Luhu had already attacked the Company's men, there was nothing stopping them from mustering their fleets of *kora-kora* to eject the Dutch from Kota Ambon.

Such episodes, coupled with wider fears of a menacing new coalition between the refugee Bandanese and the Company's enemies, created a feeling of a settlement and a colony under siege. Coen's conquest of Banda, which had been intended to secure the colony in Amboina, had thrown it instead into disarray. For Van Speult, the very survival of the Dutch presence there seemed at risk. Looking out from the walls of Castle Victoria, where he had so confidently watched the invasion fleet assemble two years earlier, he saw dangers clustered all around him. And as the governor's imagination stretched nervously outward to Luhu and Kambelo, where he pictured fleets of *kora-kora* already mobilizing, it fixed as well on threats that might emerge from within the walls of Castle Victoria.

CHAPTER II

We Cannot Exist Well Without Slaves

There is nothing, I say again, that will do the Company more service and
profit than the purchase and collection of a large number of slaves.

—JAN PIETERSZOON COEN, 1623

In the weeks before the Amboina trial commenced, the cells in Castle
Victoria held a special prisoner. Confined in one of the fetid cells
first built by the Portuguese was Augustine Peres, the Company's
marinho—or captain of the slaves.[1] Before he had been jailed, Peres had been
tasked with managing the slave population in Kota Ambon, which had
swelled in the years leading up to 1623. It was a difficult and dangerous
role. As captain, Peres was charged with the impossible task of preventing
the steady flow of runaways, who escaped to seek shelter in the thick vegetation around the castle. And all the time he contended with the possibility, sporadically realized, of violent resistance as slaves fought back,
ferociously but usually without success, against their Dutch masters. Like
so many slave societies across the early modern world, Kota Ambon was
an arena for "an undeclared war, always likely to erupt . . . into sudden violence."[2] Peres's position put him on the frontlines of any such conflict, the
first target for defiance and the inevitable first object of blame.

What made the ground even more treacherous for Peres was his identity as a "Portuguese" from Bengal.[3] Despite this label, Peres had likely
never seen Portugal.[4] Instead he was almost certainly a member of the Lusified Asian communities that were scattered across the Portuguese Empire
and which formed such a visible artifact of the long Iberian presence in
the region.[5] But Portugal and its empire were at war with the Dutch East
India Company, which had been created in part to strike a blow against

[50]

Iberian possessions in Asia. Like so many of the other Portuguese speakers who are sprinkled through VOC muster rolls, Peres had been brought into the organization to work as a kind of middleman. The Company depended on such individuals to act as interpreters, overseers of slaves, and a range of other roles, but they were never fully trusted, and what precarious status they had could be stripped without warning. This was the case with Peres, who had been beaten by VOC officials for an unspecified offense in the weeks prior to the trial before being thrown into a jail cell. There he would remain until he was hauled into an interrogation chamber by the advocate-fiscal to be tortured until he confessed to a role in the plot.

The captain of the slaves has largely disappeared from the record of the Amboina trial. When he features in accounts of the case, it is simply as a minor addendum, just another plotter thrown in at the end of the judicial record with no real significance. And his imprisonment in the weeks leading up to the first interrogation has been missed in past studies.[6] In fact, the captain of the slaves matters for two reasons. First, his presence in Kota Ambon was tied up with the Company's growing embrace of slave labor from Asia in this period. In the 1610s, key members of the VOC hierarchy, with Jan Pieterszoon Coen included prominently among them, started to nurse far-reaching dreams of resettling the Spice Islands with thousands of Asian slaves imported into these territories to harvest the riches of the spice trade and provide a bulwark for VOC rule. In service of this ambition, they embarked on an aggressive and sustained push into the slave trade.[7] This experiment entered a new phase in the months leading up to the 1623 trial, as the organization's first successful large-scale slaving voyages started to bring slaves from the Coromandel Coast into places like Banda, Batavia, and Amboina. Such developments meant that Van Speult and Castle Victoria stood on the frontlines of a much larger turn to slave labor, which transformed the Dutch East India Company from a peripheral observer into a central actor in the Indian Ocean slave trade while permanently altering the demographics of key VOC settlements.[8]

Second, Peres's arrest before the trial matters because it was wrapped up with a wider unease centered on the population of coerced laborers held under Castle Victoria's control. The number of slaves held by the Company in Kota Ambon in 1623 was not especially large, probably numbering—the fragmentary sources suggest—around 150 men, women, and children. This was far fewer than in neighboring Banda, which Coen had moved to rapidly repopulate, or indeed compared to Kota Ambon later, in the second half of the seventeenth century, a period in which the port town was home to thousands of coerced laborers.[9] But this population should not be dismissed, particularly given how few European employees the Company had in Kota Ambon. It was also steadily rising as ships carrying slaves collected from distant ports dropped anchor in the harbor.

The presence of a significant group of slaves held within the walls of Castle Victoria just as the security situation seemed to be deteriorating added another element into an already volatile mix for VOC administrators like Van Speult or De Bruyn, who came to imagine what they saw as the nightmarish possibility of a slave uprising erupting in their midst. Indian Ocean slavery was not, as it has sometimes been presented, comparatively "benign."[10] Instead, it depended on the constant threat of extreme violence, and this violence, as was the case with other slave societies, generated a gnawing fear that it might be repaid at any point via resistance or insurrection. And the fact that Peres, the one person tasked most directly with holding the slave population in check, was imprisoned in the immediate runup to the case, his labor lost, his loyalties in doubt, only added to this anxiety.

This chapter aims to put Augustine Peres and the enslaved laborers held in Kota Ambon back into the record of the 1623 trial. It mirrors a wider turn in scholarship on the Dutch East India Company itself. Although specialists have long noted the prevalence of slaves in VOC colonial possessions, there has been no equivalent of the sustained rush of works focused on slavery in the Atlantic world.[11] The result is that the slave trade has not, with the notable exception of the VOC's South African colony, become a central theme in Company history.[12] In recent years, however, this dynamic has shifted decisively as a new generation of historians, including Markus Vink, Rik van Welie, Kerry Ward, Remco Raben, Henk Niemeijer, and others, have looked again at the wider intersections between the Dutch East India Company and the slave trade.[13] Together, they have called for an unsilencing of this aspect of VOC history.[14] Through their work, the picture that has started to emerge is of an organization deeply and intimately involved in all aspects of the slave trade, even while slavery was essentially eliminated in the United Provinces. The Company did not make vast profits from the slave trade—it was less than one percent of the organization's total trade—but it relied on slave labor to prop up its territorial possessions.

While slaves were pulled in greater numbers to Banda in this period, Kota Ambon had by 1623 started to emerge as a node for imported labor in its own right, and there the fears generated by a population of slaves held within the walls of the castle surfaced dramatically during the Amboina conspiracy trial.

"A Thousand Dutch or Whites Could Live Very Well"

When the Dutch East India Company first moved into Asia, its administrators displayed little interest in the slave trade, and there are few sustained references to schemes to import significant numbers of slaves in the organization's early correspondence. Instead, the push into the business of large-scale slavery was tied to the decline of a potent vision that had once captivated VOC officials, namely, that territories like Amboina or Banda could host large self-sustaining communities of European settlers that could be planted cheaply and, once there, flourish with minimal support.[15] As the Company set down roots in Asia, its administrators became convinced that they needed to populate their new possessions in order to secure them properly against a range of internal and external enemies and to guarantee Dutch control over the spice trade. Achieving these ambitions required a steady pipeline capable of supplying loyal colonists. But where were these settlers to come from? The obvious answer was that they would be brought from the United Provinces in the form of thousands of enterprising migrants, who would flock to the new colonies to work in the spice orchards.

In the first decade after the Company was formed, VOC officials sketched out grand dreams of overseas colonies populated by hard-working Protestant laborers who would pluck the very riches of the spice trade from the trees, thereby filling their own pockets, bolstering the organization's coffers, and entrenching its monopoly over spices. As the Company's oldest colony in Asia, Amboina was at the center of this vision. In 1608, just three years after taking possession of part of that territory, Cornelis Matelieff de Jonge advised his superiors that close links should be established between Amboina and Banda so that "a thousand Dutch or whites could live very well there."[16] His proposal hinged on an idea calculated to appeal to the Company's bottom line, that such settlers would quickly become economically self-sufficient. All that was required, Matelieff argued, was to set prices for spices high enough to ensure adequate income for these transplants, thereby relieving the VOC of the financial burden of supporting large number of settlers.

After the Company established a foothold on Banda, calls for large-scale European colonization gathered further momentum. In 1612, Jacob l'Hermite, the chief merchant in Banten, explained that the Company should colonize its new possessions with "our own nation."[17] Starting immediately, a "large number of families should be sent to the Indies to pluck the fruits there." Like Matelieff, l'Hermite was convinced that European migrants could prosper with only minimal support. Rather than draining VOC resources, these settlers could simply sell the spices they had gathered to the Company, using their profits to "richly support their wives and children, without receiving any pay or expense from the Company."[18]

For Jan Pieterszoon Coen, the establishment of European settler communities formed the natural accompaniment to his plans to remake the Spice Islands, and he insisted that permanent "colonies should be planted" in Amboina and Banda without delay.[19] Beginning in 1614 with a famous imperial blueprint, "Discourse to the Honorable Directors Concerning the State of the Netherlands Indies" (*Discoers aen de E. Heeren Bewinthebberen touscherende den Nederlandtsche Indischen staet*), submitted to his superiors, Coen issued repeated calls for large numbers of settlers to be dispatched from Europe. In his words, every ship leaving from the United Provinces for Asia must carry with it "a great number of people, seagoing people and soldiers . . . also men, women and children to plant colonies."[20]

So critical were such settlers that the Heeren 17's failure to send them in adequate numbers represented a clear dereliction of their duty. On Amboina and Banda, the fruits of the spice trade were, Coen berated his superiors, lying on the ground rotting:

> But why have Your Honors so far planted no colonies in Amboyna and Banda? For the conquered islands of Banda, the nutmeg and mace is being lost because there are no people to pluck them . . . Amboyna is extraordinarily good and suitable to plant colonies, and this will be the way we save excessive annual costs and secure these lands.[21]

In addition to harvesting the riches of the spice trade, such settlers could, once firmly in place, be mobilized to provide military support when VOC possessions came under threat.[22] As such, they could secure the Company's newly acquired territories and serve as a vital buttress for Dutch power in Asia.

With characteristic precision, Coen spelled out exactly how the Company should set about securing large numbers of European settlers. The organization should accept anyone it could get from the United Provinces: adults, families, single girls or boys, and even children. At the top of the list were "honest married folk" (*eerlijcke getroude lieden*) or "honest families," who should be shipped over in large numbers.[23] Their number should be supplemented, however, by the recruitment of single women, a group that became known as the "Company daughters," as well as boys and girls drawn from the "many orphanages of the United Netherlands," whose charges could be shipped over to provide a new generation of European colonists in Asia.[24]

From the beginning, however, such plans encountered problems on both ends. First, there was only a thin trickle of potential migrants willing to undertake the long and hazardous voyage to Asia. In 1610, the incoming governor-general, Pieter Both, could only assemble thirty-six women to travel with him to Asia, while a year later just twenty-five European families were settled for the first time in Amboina.[25] Once in Asia, such settlers failed to match up to the organization's oversized expectations. When they had sketched out their plans, VOC officials had pictured hard-working Protestant settlers loyal to the Company and ready to engage in the kind of backbreaking labor needed to turn places like Banda or Kota Ambon into prosperous, self-sustaining colonies. But rather than the enterprising migrants they had imagined, administrators like Coen described this first generation of colonists as the "scum of the lands" (*schuym van lande*), who created more problems than they solved, disrupting the Company's carefully laid plans and throwing its colonies into disarray.[26]

Although he continued to call for more settlers from Europe, Coen wrote a scathing indictment of the married couples who had arrived in Amboina. Instead of buttressing the Dutch empire in Asia, the newcomers had undermined the organization's prestige through their constant drunkenness and bad behavior. "Our honor (*eere*) is greatly damaged," he insisted, "and the Indians are absolutely scandalized by them, because they do nothing but live bestially."[27] Coen was equally critical of the "Company daughters," writing that there is "no slave or woman of this land that is so unsuitable and unmannered." "It seems," he concluded, "as if they were not raised by people but came out of a wilderness."[28] Such vociferous condemnations seemed to allow for little possibility that the situation would improve. "From such bad plants," Coen wrote dismissively at one point, "there is little hope of receiving good fruit."[29] Despite these complaints, however, small numbers of Dutch settlers continued to land in Asia. In 1622, VOC officials in Batavia noted the arrival of a new group of women split aboard three ships, while a year later a large party of more than eighty Dutch women was dispatched to Asia.[30] But it was increasingly clear that the grand schemes sketched out in the early years of the VOC's existence would not be realized, and by the 1630s they were abandoned altogether.[31]

As soaring dreams of colonies populated by thousands of European settlers foundered, new plans emerged to take their place. For VOC officials eager to populate newly acquired territories, one possibility was to look east toward a vast potential labor pool in China. Such plans were set into motion after the establishment of Batavia, which was envisaged as a regional entrepot where merchants from all over Asia could gather to trade under the protection of Dutch ships and soldiers.[32] Soon after the port town was conquered, the governor-general began to issue calls for Chinese settlers to be drawn there via incentives or, if these failed, through the use of force.[33] By July 1620, eight hundred Chinese were already resident in Batavia, which emerged over time as what Leonard Blussé famously described as a "Chinese colonial town under Dutch protection."[34] Chinese settlers were considered indispensable for a trading hub like Batavia, but Amboina and especially Banda, which required a host of workers for the spice orchards, presented a different challenge.[35] As ideas about European settlers faltered and fell away, Dutch officials began to argue that the solution to the Company's manpower problems lay in the import of large numbers of slaves.

"To an Unending Total"

In 1614, the serving governor-general, Gerard Reynst, declared in a letter to the Heeren 17 that "Amboina, Banda and Moluccas islands . . . must be provided with a good number of slaves."[36] The next year he returned to the same theme, explaining that "we cannot draw the work in these quarters from our nation, even if we were well provided with them. The heat is too great and the drink overflows in most all places. I have already found that one slave does more work than two of our nation. If I could obtain more slaves . . . I would know how to use these well in our service."[37] Reynst's comments were underpinned by two familiar ideas—that slaves were better suited physically than European recruits for the kind of labor required in the hot climate of Southeast Asia and that they would prove far more cost-effective than relying on European workers.[38]

By 1616, Coen, who would soon assume the top job within the VOC, had begun to argue as well that the Company must move aggressively into the slave trade. Writing to the Heeren 17, he insisted that "concerning the purchase of slaves, this should be done in any manner possible as this is a very advantageous matter for the Company." He explained the situation in stark terms, declaring that "we cannot exist well without slaves" (*want connen niet wel sonder slaven bestaen*).[39] Because of this, no limits should be placed on the Company's investment. Instead, the "purchase of slaves should go on to the number of many thousands, indeed to an unending total."[40] For Coen, large numbers of slaves were needed most urgently in a triumvirate of settlements—Amboina, Banda, and Batavia—which must be steadily populated. To achieve this, the Company should draw from "all the places of the whole Indies as many slaves . . . [as] can be obtained with reasonable prices and transported on ships to populate Batavia, Amboina and Banda."[41]

For Coen and others within the organization, the acquisition of large numbers of slaves would serve multiple functions. First, such laborers could replace the "bad rabble" (*quaet gespuys*), the recalcitrant inhabitants of places like Banda who refused to abide by their treaty obligations.[42] If the arrival of large numbers of slaves would give the Company the workers it needed to harvest the riches of the spices trade, it would also secure those territories under VOC control. Filling colonies like Banda or Amboina with bonded laborers would "create awe in our feigned friends, keep our enemies in fear, and hold the rebellious in obedience."[43] At the same time, Coen believed that a large slave population could serve as a first line of military defense for the Dutch empire in Asia. As evidence of this, he pointed to the Company's failed assault on the Portuguese trading port of Macao in 1622, which had been thwarted, he claimed, by loyal slaves who had forced the Dutch attackers to retreat.[44] Coen was convinced that VOC slaves could perform the same function, serving not only as compliant workers but as active guardians of empire. Finally, a turn away from

European colonists to slaves drawn from Asia presented one further advantage by shifting control more firmly toward VOC officials on the ground. For someone like Coen, who railed constantly against his superiors' failure to supply him with adequate resources, tapping new sources of labor offered a way to circumvent past frustrations. Whereas the flow of European settlers depended on the Heeren 17's recruitment efforts in the United Provinces, slaves were different. From their base in Asia, VOC administrators could personally direct the trade by sending ships to purchase slaves from selected hubs across the region.

Herman van Speult arrived in Amboina in 1615 just as one dream of compliant workers was foundering and a new one was taking its place. Landing in Kota Ambon, he confronted the human consequences of the Company's failed plans in the form of Coen's so-called bad plants, the first generation of European migrants brought to Amboina.[45] One of the earliest records with Van Speult's name attached to it is a resolution dated 9 January 1617, just as he was beginning his steady rise up the ranks in Amboina. On this day, the serving governor, Steven van der Haghen, sat down with his council to debate what to do with the "Hollander women" who had been brought in to settle the new colony.[46] Rather than the devoted wives and mothers of a new Dutch empire in Asia, they had become, the council lamented, a source of shame that contributed to the "disrepute and prejudice of the Company and our nation." Refusing to labor on the land, they had instead busied themselves dealing in arak, a powerful local spirit distilled from sugarcane. In his own letters, Van Speult echoed these complaints, writing that the Hollander women "lead very insolent lives with drinking, cursing and swearing, fighting and smashing."[47] On to the standard list of charges, he piled new accusations, blaming them for the death of their infants, who had succumbed not to tropical conditions but to the arak they had been given, he claimed, to suckle on. Eager to displace the problem, the council decided to remove the evidence of the Company's failed colonization plans from Amboina. The Hollander women would, they decided, be shipped to one of the Banda Islands to harvest the nutmeg crop there.[48] It was a striking repudiation from an organization that had aggressively sought out these settlers, recruiting and transporting them thousands of miles to a remote part of Southeast Asia. Although the individual fate of these women cannot be tracked, the difficult conditions in Banda probably ensured that many did not long survive the move.

Always the loyal subordinate, Van Speult embraced Coen's vision of an industrious population of slaves working across the Company's territories. In letters to his superior, he argued that European settlers were not only unsuitable for labor in Amboina but that using them for such work served only to invite "blame and derision" (*verwijt ende spot*) from the local population, thereby undermining the Company's prestige in the islands and producing only "tumult and rebellion."[49] These problems could only be remedied by a large slave population, and, mirroring the governor-general's language, Van Speult insisted that the Company could never have enough slaves in places like Amboina.[50]

But if officials like Coen and Van Speult agreed on the urgency of the need, it was far from clear where the Company, a newcomer to Asia still feeling its way through preexisting circuits of trade, would be able to acquire large numbers of captive laborers. Slavery was a well-established practice with a long history in Southeast Asia. Arriving in the region, the Company came into contact with a world populated by a vast range of coerced laborers extending from debt bondsmen and bondswomen, who retained the possibility of repaying their debts, to slaves, who could be bought, traded, and sold freely.[51] In Amboina itself, slave holding percolated down through different levels of society. The Amboinese were, one Dutch writer explained, "well inclined to the purchase of slaves," and the settlements scattered around Kota Ambon incorporated significant numbers of bonded laborers.[52] Even though slavery was commonplace, local circuits were, as Remco Raben has argued, never large or stable enough to service the Company's needs.[53] How then to translate Coen's calls for an "unending total" of slaves into reality?[54] It was a problem that preoccupied VOC officials in the decade leading up to the Amboina trial.

Circuits of Unfree Labor

Since its arrival in Asia, the Dutch East India Company had been in a perennial state of war with European enemies and local rivals. Such operations generated a continuous supply of what it called *kettinggangers* or "chained laborers," who flowed into places like Amboina.[55] Many were drawn from Portuguese and Spanish ships, which were regularly seized by VOC fleets.[56] Since such vessels were crewed by sailors pulled from across Asia, this meant that the Company drew a diverse array of captives into its net, including, for example, a group of Gujarati prisoners who were eventually dispatched to labor in Banda.[57] Chained laborers were drawn as well from the vessels of Asian competitors, such as Makassar, which attempted to exploit the holes that had opened up in the Company's treaty regime.[58] While VOC attempts at enforcing a blockade seldom succeeded in fully closing down clandestine trade, they did produce a steady flow of captives.

In addition to captives gained through war, the Company acquired significant numbers of slaves from a string of mass conspiracy trials involving the Bandanese. Some of these trials took place on the Banda Islands themselves in the aftermath of the invasion, others in Batavia, where the Company had shipped a large contingent of Bandanese villagers. In February 1622, VOC authorities discovered what they claimed was a widespread plot to murder the Dutch in Batavia and burn the city down. After Bandanese leaders were tortured by "water, cord and fire," they confessed to a remarkably ambitious conspiracy not simply to escape Dutch rule by running away but also to join with neighboring powers to raze Batavia to the ground.[59] In order to accomplish these ends, the conspirators had, VOC officials alleged, dispatched letters to hostile rulers across the region to seek firm alliances with them. After a perfunctory trial, a total of eight ringleaders were condemned to death and rapidly executed.[60] Although they did not believe that the vast majority of Bandanese in Batavia had any direct knowledge of the plot, Company administrators decided that the blame must be spread around, and 517 men, women, and children were designated "as slaves for the service of the Company."[61]

If such mechanisms could inject large numbers of slaves into the VOC system, they were also too irregular to fill the organization's needs. What the Company wanted was a reliable purchasing hub where it could dispatch vessels year after year. The problem vexed VOC officials like Van Speult, who offered up a range of possible solutions. One potential point of supply was Bali, which lay within easy sailing distance from Amboina. In 1619, Van Speult received reports that significant numbers of slaves could be purchased there for twenty to twenty-five reals.[62] Eager to take advantage, he dispatched a vessel equipped with 7 soldiers and 1,500 reals to purchase as many slaves as possible.[63] However, such attempts proved disappointing, and it was not until the second half of the seventeenth century that Bali emerged as a reliable hub for VOC slaving expeditions.[64]

A second, more distant possibility was to tap into African circuits. As early as 1614, VOC officials had suggested that the Company should look toward Madagascar, where "an abundance of slaves for little money" could be found.[65] This suggestion was picked up and amplified by Coen, who was convinced that slaves from Africa could be used to transform the demographic landscape of VOC colonies.[66] Mirroring his superior's language, Van Speult pushed for the same solution in Amboina, arguing in his letters that Africa and especially Madagascar represented the swiftest way to solve the VOC's slave problem. Not only could slaves be obtained there in great numbers, but they were "of a good disposition and can be had for little price."[67]

While it was easy to talk about such possibilities, sending ships to Africa represented a significant logistical challenge for an organization that did not maintain an outpost in Madagascar. The result was that bold declarations about the need to purchase large numbers of slaves ran up against the reality that the Company lacked any reliable mechanism to effect its plans. This began to change, however, in the run-up to the Amboina trial, when Coen's aggressive push into the slave trade succeeded in opening up a new circuit capable of delivering thousands of slaves to the Spice Islands.[68] For years, the governor-general had been badgering his subordinates in India to "send as many people as you can obtain and can be shipped" for in "all quarters, we are in need of people."[69] When their efforts did not yield adequate results, Coen intervened by dispatching a "large ship," the *Golden Leeuw*, to the Coromandel Coast in southeastern India for the purpose of buying up as many slaves as possible.[70] In his letters to VOC agents in India, Coen explained that the Company urgently needed 2,000 to 3,000 slaves, especially young boys and girls, for Batavia, Amboina, and Banda.[71] Although the voyage proved disappointing, yielding just 124 slaves, who were immediately dispatched to Banda, it established a template that was expanded in subsequent years.[72]

In 1622, Coen sent another large vessel, the *Nieuw Seelant*, to the Coromandel Coast with orders to purchase as many slaves as possible. This time its captain acquired more than a thousand men, women, and children "to strengthen our new colonies of Batavia, Amboina and Banda."[73] The success of the *Nieuw Seelant*'s voyage can be traced directly back to the cyclical famines that were sweeping through the area just as the Company started to target the subcontinent as a key staging point for its network of coerced labor. While there are no contemporary descriptions of the situation in Coromandel in 1622, an account of a later famine gives some sense of the devastation:

> The famine has worsened to such an extent that entire villages, hamlets, and settlements have been depopulated, leaving hardly anyone. Dead bodies are laying scattered in dry tanks, along common roads, indeed, even the streets of the city of Nagapatnam. Those who have survived until now more resemble lifeless corpses than living people, crying along the fields and roads for a single meal to fill their empty stomachs before dying.[74]

For the VOC, such desperate conditions opened up an unprecedented opportunity to expand its pool of laborers.[75] Determined to capitalize, the authorities in Batavia resolved to send vessels to "gather as many people as our ships can carry."[76] At the same time, Company agents located in Coromandel urged their superiors to dispatch more funds so they could take advantage of conditions on the ground.[77]

Departing the Coromandel Coast in 1622, the *Nieuw Seeland* carried 1,167 slaves crammed tightly below deck in terrible conditions.[78] Very quickly the ship's internal systems began to break down. The rudimentary cooking facilities available on deck collapsed under the strain of supplying so many people, meaning that only uncooked rice and a small amount of water were available to the more than a thousand men, women, and children locked below. The result was first starvation and then, very quickly, death. By the time the ship reached Batavia in December 1622, only 930 of its human cargo were still alive.[79]

With the *Nieuw Seeland*'s 1622 voyage, the Company morphed into a significant force in the Indian Ocean slave trade.[80] For Coen, it seemed as if he had at last stumbled upon the formula he had been looking for. Writing back to the Heeren 17, he reported triumphantly that this was the first time the organization had been able to obtain the slaves it needed in the desired numbers since he had first called for such schemes in 1614.[81] The next year a new ship was sent, and with it another thousand slaves sailed from Coromandel to Southeast Asia.[82] The success of such voyages established an enduring template that would turn the Indian coast into a key transit point for VOC slaving voyages for decades to come. Starting with the Coromandel Coast, the South Asian circuit later expanded to include

Arakan (in modern day Myanmar) and Bengal, which in total would deliver thousands of slaves to places like Amboina, Banda, and Batavia.[83]

In Kota Ambon, Van Speult received a steady stream of letters from Coen insisting that nothing was more important than having the territory "properly populated and well provided with slaves."[84] And in turn, he reflected back the governor-general's language about the need to rapidly increase the size of the slave population. Penetrating down from such comments, however, to count the number of slaves actually present in Kota Ambon in the years leading up to the 1623 conspiracy trial proves more difficult. For the second half of the seventeenth century, the question has been decisively answered via Knaap's painstaking investigation of a particularly complete set of *zielsbeschrijving* ("description of souls"), a kind of "proto-census," from 1671 to 1695. However, such records do not exist for 1623, which means that any attempt to count the population of Kota Ambon and the relative proportion of free to enslaved people requires combining a range of fragmentary sources.

Slaves in Amboina

The most detailed accounts derive from the archive attached to the Amboina trial itself. They come in the form of depositions recorded by the former judges in the aftermath of the case, who provided descriptions of who was living in Kota Ambon when the conspiracy was discovered.[85] There are reasons to treat the figures contained in these records with some caution. For one, they were set down years after the fact, in depositions recorded in 1628. At the same time, they include considerable variations, with discrepancies between the lowest and highest ranges provided by different judges. This can be explained in part by the elevated mortality rate in Kota Ambon in this period, which quickly rendered a precise count redundant. In his letters, Van Speult returned again and again to the disorienting scale of the death rate, which seemed capable of sweeping away a significant fraction of the garrison in a few short months. In July 1621, for example, he lamented that an outbreak of dysentery had caused fifty men in the garrison to die since March 1, while a 1623 letter recorded 115 deaths, a huge number for a relatively small settlement, in a single year.[86] If Kota Ambon's population was continually shifting, it is also possible that some of the judges may have offered deliberately depressed figures in an attempt to diminish Dutch strength and magnify the scale of the English threat. Even with these cautions, however, the judges' estimates, which are consistent with other sources from this period, provide the best picture of who was living in Kota Ambon in 1623.

Like Manila or Batavia, Kota Ambon was an artificial colonial creation planted in Asian soil. Engineered effectively "from scratch," it was a "city of migrants" that lacked any significant Amboinese population.[87] The former judges divided its residents into four groups: VOC employees, *Vrijburger* or free citizens, *Mardijkers* or free Asians, and slaves.[88] First were the Company's employees. These were the backbone of the Company's presence in Kota Ambon, the officials who governed the territory, the merchants who oversaw the trade in cloves, the soldiers who were tasked with defending it against any threat, and the dozens of artisans, stewards, and other support staff whose skilled labor underpinned the proper functioning of Castle Victoria. The judges were primarily focused on the soldiers, with most clustering their estimates between eighty and a hundred men.[89] That figure matches a 1627 description that states there were just eighty-four men in Castle Victoria's garrison.[90]

For other VOC employees in Kota Ambon, we have to rely on figures supplied by Coen in his communications to his superiors. In 1619, the governor-general wrote that there were just 194 Europeans spread across the whole of Amboina, while a year later he recorded that this number had only risen to 196.[91] By August 1622, that is, roughly six months before the trial, this figure had climbed to 345 "Netherlanders" scattered across the whole of Amboina province, in "castle Amboyna, Hitu, Kambello, on the coast of Ceram, and at the factories on different islands."[92] We know from a range of contemporary sources that the Company posted around 150 men to its outer outposts on Ambon, Hoamoal, and the scattered islands nearby.[93] Put together, this suggests that there were around two hundred Europeans in direct VOC service in Kota Ambon, with around half of those serving as soldiers.

Second were the *Vrijburger* or free citizens. These were settlers who had been shipped over to Asia or former VOC employees who had elected to settle in Kota Ambon after their contracts came to an end.[94] The former were the remnants of the VOC's grand colonization plans, the latter started to appear in Amboina after 1610 as the Company expanded its reach. With close ties to the territory, they typically married Asian women and set down deep roots in the new colony.[95] Neither group, however, provided a constant stream of new entrants, and the number of free citizens remained within a narrow band. According to the judges, there were around eighty or ninety free citizens and later sources suggest that such figures may have been inflated.[96]

Third were the *Mardijkers* (*orang merdeka* or "free man"), free Asians left over from the Portuguese period. The *Mardijkers* were not Amboinese. Instead, they were described by the judges as "Indians of other quarters, and strangers in Amboina" who had settled in Kota Ambon during the period of Portuguese control.[97] While the Company had expelled most of the colony's original residents, the *Mardijker* community had hung on, weathering the change of regime. According to the former judges, there were around a hundred *Mardijkers* capable of military service in Kota Ambon, although the judges believed they would be of little use in a crisis.[98] This figure matches Van Speult's own estimate from this period, which specifies that there were around one hundred "able-bodied" male *Mardijkers*.[99]

The final group consisted of slaves, who were further divided into two distinct categories. First were the so-called chained laborers who flowed regularly into Kota Ambon from a range of sources. In 1620, for example, Van Speult noted the arrival of close to a hundred prisoners captured in part from the Spanish.[100] Some were dispatched to man VOC galleys, a particularly brutal form of labor with a high mortality rate, but others stayed in Kota Ambon to work there. The most detailed description of this group in 1623 comes from one of the judges, Jan Joosten, who stated that they were around forty "Javans, Macasars and Portingalls or Spaniards" held together under guard at night.[101] The second contingent consisted of what one scholar has called work slaves.[102] It was significantly larger. In August 1622, Coen wrote that there were eighty-three "blacks," the usual designator for slaves, in VOC settlements in Amboina, and it is likely that most of these were concentrated in Kota Ambon. By February 1623, this figure had risen, the former judges suggested, to between 100 and 150, with most estimates clustered at the lower end.[103] Counting the two groups together suggests a total slave population that may have numbered as low as 140 or as high as 190.

In Banda, VOC slaves came to work in the spice plantations established after Coen's invasion. In Kota Ambon, by contrast, they toiled primarily as urban laborers engaged in a range of tasks related to the functioning of the port and the Company's settlement there. Whereas the *kettinggangers* were drawn from a predictable combination of Iberian enemies and Asian rivals, the sources tell us little about where the work slaves collected in Kota Ambon came from. The most obvious point of supply was the large number of Bandanese prisoners flowing out of Batavia in this period. We know that ships carrying Bandanese slaves periodically dropped anchor in the harbor at Kota Ambon on their way to Banda, but there is no clear evidence that they remained to work here.[104] Rather, the newly demarcated plantations in Banda functioned to draw in available laborers, even as Van Speult protested that using Bandanese slaves on Banda would serve only to generate new points of resistance.[105]

The second obvious point of supply was South Asia, where the ships dispatched by Coen had succeeded in opening up new circuits. Here there is evidence that the Company's Coromandel experiment had an immediate impact on Amboina. In late 1622, Coen wrote to his subordinate in Banda, Martinus Sonck, that "50 of the stoutest" slaves recently arrived aboard the *Nieuw Seeland* from Coromandel would be dispatched immediately to populate that territory.[106] A few weeks later, in January 1623, the vessel carrying these slaves, the *Eenhoorn*, dropped anchor in Kota Ambon.[107] Its appearance created a dilemma for Van Speult. While he had instructions to send the ship and the fifty slaves it carried on to Banda, the governor was also under sustained pressure from his superiors to cut costs in Amboina.[108] Carried aboard the *Eenhoorn* was a letter from Batavia instructing Van Speult that the territory under his control must become self-sufficient "without requiring one real of the Company's money."[109] The way to do this, Batavia insisted, was to make sure that Amboina was "properly populated and equipped with slaves," who could work in a range of occupations without damaging the VOC coffers. But instead of sending him the necessary labor force, the governor's superiors had ordered the *Eenhoorn* to travel on to Banda to discharge its human cargo there.

It made for an obvious and infuriating contradiction for a VOC official set on rising in the organization. Determined to follow one set of instructions, Van Speult decided to take matters into his own hands by seizing possession of the fifty slaves from Coromandel. In a letter to the new governor-general, Pieter de Carpentier, who had succeeded Coen in the role, Van Speult explained that he had "kept the slaves that came with the *Eenhoorn* for Banda," as they were needed to work in the colony and to compensate for the high mortality rate among the Company's existing slave population.[110] The logic was clear. If Batavia wanted to reduce expenses, then Van Speult had no choice but to take possession of any slaves he could acquire, even those destined for another territory. The arrival of the group from Coromandel tied Amboina tightly to an emerging node in the Company's network of unfree labor. After 1623, slaves from South Asia continued to trickle into Amboina, swelling the labor force even as VOC administrators complained that they succumbed too quickly to adverse conditions in the colony.[111]

Even in the absence of a precise census, it is clear that slaves constituted a significant share of the town's population and one that was on the rise. Unarmed and frequently traumatized by transportation or captivity, slaves did not present a conventional military threat. In contrast to the *ketting-gangers*, who were entirely male, the work slaves included women and frequently children, who were purchased in significant numbers in Coromandel. Held in chains or permitted limited movement under guard, they confronted a fortification manned by dozens of soldiers and with cannons dotting its walls. But for all the obvious military imbalance, the slaves gathered in Castle Victoria were also a source of fear. Like other slaveholders in disparate parts of the world, the Dutch in Kota Ambon worried about a sudden outbreak of violence as the terrors visited so routinely upon slaves were revisited on their masters. And in Kota Ambon, a combination of factors worked to sharpen this fear, which lay hidden just beneath the surface.

For one, the slave population contained a relatively large number of *kettinggangers*, who were viewed as the most dangerous of captives. In his letters, Van Speult complained that "we have a castle full of prisoners" imposing special demands on a perennially depleted garrison.[112] As enemies captured in war, chained laborers were the subject of especially harsh treatment. The 1617 General Instruction issued across the Company's empire stipulated that "captives of the enemy, without respect of quality or condition . . . shall be used as slaves in galleys and in other servile service . . . and they shall be treated as rigorously as we find best."[113] In this way, VOC officials believed that the safest place for such prisoners was on galleys and other vessels, where the chance of escape was limited and the harshness of conditions combined with the backbreaking nature of labor reduced the chance of an uprising.[114]

Some chained laborers were dispatched from Kota Ambon to crew galleys but other worked on land under a guard that fluctuated in number, depending on illness and whether the governor had sent out a *hongi* expedition. The severity of conditions meant that the chained laborers confined in the castle periodically erupted in spasms of violence. Three years before the Amboina trial there was a spontaneous uprising among the *kettinggangers* when a group of prisoners from the Aru Islands near Banda had fought back against their captors.[115] The incident started when Van Speult discovered that some of the prisoners had cut through their chains and were planning to escape. In response, he ordered the two supposed ringleaders brutally whipped. Such actions triggered a general revolt among the remaining prisoners, who killed a carpenter before attacking their guards. Desperate to regain control, the castle's musketeers fired into the captives. In the ensuing chaos, more than twenty people were injured, while eleven managed to flee. In the wake of the uprising, the governor decided that the principle instigators would have their right hands cut off before being hanged in the square in front of the castle. Such brutal punishments were common in the VOC empire, where any violent resistance, however short-lived, was always punished by death, but Van Speult was clear in his letters that such actions were especially needed here due to the large number of *kettinggangers* collected in the castle.[116]

While the Aru revolt showed just how quickly control could fray and break, the sources are also filled with far more quotidian acts of extreme violence inflicted by both masters and slaves. Alongside long accounts of trade, Van Speult's letters are sprinkled with terse descriptions of terrible violence unleashed by individual slaves, often *kettinggangers*, who responded with brutal means to a system that had brutalized them. In one, the governor described a gruesome murder and the retribution that followed:

A while ago a horrible murder was done by one of the captured slaves from Malacca [Melaka], running amok with the carpenter's boy without any words, he stabbed him murderously with a Kris [dagger], cutting himself in the stomach with same kris, but as he doubted the wound would kill him, he tore up his own intestines. This terrible act was reported to me and I have immediately informed myself on the case and inspected the delinquent, who we think could not have lived to the next day and should be punished for such an enormous deed. So we called the council together and orally sentenced him and executed him, cutting off his hands and dragged him to the tribunal, where he was hanged.[117]

It was, even in the brief sketch contained in Van Speult's letter, a shocking case: the sudden killing of a young carpenter's assistant followed by a failed attempt at suicide. Determined to punish the offender before he died from his wounds, the governor and the council ordered his hands amputated and the slave hung. Such episodes highlight the pervasive violence that underpinned VOC slavery in Kota Ambon. Although we cannot know what drove the unnamed slave from Melaka to act in this way, the incident gives lie to any notion of Indian Ocean slavery as somehow more benevolent than its counterparts in the Americas. Instead, "faced by the institutionalized barbarism of the slave regime," slaves responded, as Robert Ross has argued for the Company's South African colony, "with their own atrocities."[118]

If individual acts of violence could temporarily disrupt the system, far more worrying was the possibility of an organized insurrection rising up from within the slave population. In particular, the governor nursed his own fears about corrupting influences that might seep into the slave quarters. The problem was that the Company's net had swept up prisoners from across the region, making it difficult to know who exactly was confined within the walls of Castle Victoria. In 1619, Van Speult recorded a disturbing discovery that one of the slaves captured near Melaka and brought to Amboina was a "Moorish priest" (*Moors paep*), who might, he feared, incite fellow slaves to rise up against the Dutch.[119] Determined to stamp out a potential threat, the governor had the man tortured to discover where the "Moors were gathering" in secret. When this failed to dislodge useful information, Van Speult resolved to send him away, thereby removing any source of potential corruption.

Alongside the constant threat of uprisings, the governor was apprehensive about fugitive slaves who regularly escaped their bonds to flee into the thick jungle around Kota Ambon. It was a concern shared across the Dutch empire where rising numbers of slaves prompted new regulations designed to halt fugitives. In January 1622, just as it moved to open up the Coromandel circuit, the Company issued a fresh edict directed at runaway slaves. Prompted by the mass escape of twenty-four laborers, the order offered a large reward for runaway slaves or their dead bodies.[120] If the information came from one of the escaped slaves themselves, they would be gifted with money and freedom from punishment.

In Kota Ambon, the basic problem of runaways was made worse by the uncertain nature of the political environment. In particular, Van Speult worried that fugitive slaves could convey damaging information to the Company's many enemies, who would eagerly shelter them in return for such intelligence. In 1620, for example, the governor complained that a group of Portuguese captives had likely run away to Tidore, where they would find a ready welcome. Even worse, he dreaded the prospect of fugitive slaves returning at the head of a column of warriors from Luhu, Kambelo, or any one of Castle Victoria's other enemies. The regular flight of slaves forced the governor to increase security, which in turn meant that slaves were less productive. Angered by the number of runaways, Van Speult complained that keeping the prisoners in their chains would mean that the Company would only get "half the work."[121]

In this way, the presence of a significant contingent of slaves in Kota Ambon generated the kind of fears that were standard across slave societies in different parts of the world. All of this was typical enough for a relatively new colony transitioning into an increasing dependence on slaves, but in February 1623, VOC authorities in Kota Ambon confronted one further source of instability in the form of the captain of the slaves, Augustine Peres, who had been removed from his role and imprisoned in the weeks leading up to the trial. In later periods when almost all the slaves in Kota Ambon were held in private hands, the slave population was widely scattered in relatively small groups, making communication difficult and reducing the possibility of resistance. In 1623, by contrast, the Company owned the majority of slaves in Kota Ambon, who were locked up overnight in Castle Victoria under the watch of the captain of the slaves.[122] All of this made Augustine Peres a vital figure in the infrastructure of control.

Although the Company was at war with the Portuguese and frequently denounced Iberian treachery, it employed a significant number of Portuguese speakers. Many of these were former *kettinggangers* who had worked their way into positions of trust over years of backbreaking labor, transitioning, if they survived, from slaves to wage earners. Their backgrounds suited them to work as interpreters in a region in which Portuguese remained a key language of communication.[123] Other *kettinggangers* moved out of bondage into roles similar to that held by Peres. A typical example was Pedro Fernandus from St. Thome in India, who had spent thirteen or fourteen years as a chained laborer before becoming a slave overseer in 1618.[124]

Peres appears to have followed a different course, although we know very little about this individual who left only the shallowest of imprints on

VOC records. He first appears in 1621 as an "overseer over the blacks" (*maringe over de swerten*), earning a monthly wage of five reals plus rations.[125] Aged thirty-six in 1623, he was probably born around 1587 in Bengal, in one of the Lusified Asian communities that formed such an important support structure for the Portuguese empire.[126] As far as we can make out, Peres arrived in Kota Ambon with Coen's fleet in the immediate aftermath of the invasion of Banda in June 1621.[127] If he was a former *kettinganger*, there is no mention of it in the records, and it is more likely that he was a willing migrant whose arrival in Southeast Asia may have been connected with the opening up of new slaving circuits in the region.

From the beginning, however, Van Speult appears to have harbored suspicions about the new captain of the slaves. From one of only a handful of references to Peres, we know that the governor had presented him with a wife drawn from the slave population.[128] It makes for an intriguing detail that only found its way into the sources because of the Amboina trial itself, as Peres's execution meant that the governor had to decide what to do with his widow.[129] What exactly prompted this initial move remains unclear, but it was surely an attempt to bind the *marinho* closer to his Dutch masters, ensure his loyalty, and give the governor some sort of hold over him.

We do know that in the weeks leading up to the trial relations between the governor and the captain of the slaves declined sharply when Peres was publicly beaten for an unnamed offense. When he responded by abusing Van Speult, cursing and telling him to go to the devil, he was thrown into a cell in Castle Victoria by the advocate-fiscal, Isaaq de Bruyn, who would, just weeks later, haul Peres up to the torture chamber.[130] Although the origins of this clash are not clear, it probably stemmed from a combination of overlapping issues: problems with the Company's slaves, the governor's dissatisfaction with Peres's service, and, it seems safe to assume, a generalized suspicion of a perennial outsider.

Whatever the reason, it meant that the chief agent in charge of managing the slave population was placed in chains at the precise moment when the wider security situation seemed to be slipping inexorably into disorder. It was not simply that Castle Victoria had lost Peres's labor. Rather, the terrible fear that would come to swell up within the confines of the Amboina trial was that Peres retained some sort of sinister power over the slaves gathered in Kota Ambon and that it could be turned against the Dutch. In this fevered dream, the slaves would become a formidable weapon that could be expertly wielded by their former captain. It was something that the Amboina judges returned to again and again when they declared that Peres "could have used a considerable number of slaves for this treachery as the slaves did not refuse their services to his command."[131] In this way, Peres was transformed from an agent of VOC order into a kind of slave general who could use his charges to wage war against his former masters. And just as this combination of a rising slave population and an unreliable overseer seemed to present new perils, the governor looked nervously within the garrison to the Japanese soldiers tasked with defending the castle against attack.

CHAPTER III

Dangerous and Difficult to Govern

They are lambs [in Japan] and like devils outside their land.
—JACQUES SPECX, 1613

On May 30, 1622, less than a year before the Amboina trial erupted, Van Speult drew up Castle Victoria's garrison on parade. The occasion was the anniversary of Coen's conquest of Jayakarta three years earlier, which was celebrated annually throughout the VOC's expanding empire.[1] Formed up in front of the low-slung fort were less than a hundred European soldiers assembled in ragged lines. Van Speult's eye was drawn, however, to another group standing to one side. Lined up under the watchful eye of their captain was a cohort of a dozen soldiers, each armed with the distinctive twin swords that were their calling card.[2] The Japanese contingent in Kota Ambon was not large, but they were well armed and had a ferocious, if always vastly exaggerated, reputation for violence.[3] And in a small garrison with its ranks constantly depleted by illness, they were an important component of the castle's defenses, particularly as tensions ramped up in the aftermath of the invasion of Banda.

How did twelve Japanese soldiers end up in a remote fortress in Southeast Asia over two thousand miles from the nearest Japanese port and in the employ of a European chartered company?[4] They were not there by chance. These were not Japanese wanderers marooned by current or wind far from their homes. Instead, these men had been brought to Kota Ambon as part of an ambitious experiment launched by a small group of VOC officials to harness excess Asian military capacity and turn it to the organization's advantage.

Since its formation, the Company had used the powers granted in its 1602 charter to establish a string of colonies, forts, and outposts across Southeast and East Asia. These were, by its own account, perpetually undermanned. The core of VOC forces was made up of soldiers drawn not only from the United Provinces but also, in an effort to find enough recruits willing to make the hazardous journey to Asia, from across Europe more generally.[5] Although there was a steady and increasing flow of soldiers from the continent, it was never enough to fill the organization's insatiable appetite for men. According to one early estimate from Coen, the VOC needed between 2,500 and 3,000 soldiers to properly carry out its objectives in Asia.[6] Instead it listed fewer than a thousand men on its muster rolls, and this number was itself in constant decline due to the high mortality rate across the Company's scattered holdings. It was nowhere close to enough for an organization engaged in near constant warfare as it moved aggressively to enforce treaties, defend its possessions against outside attack, and wage extended campaigns in Banda and elsewhere.

In its search for labor, the Company had turned to Asian sources by opening up new slaving circuits in South Asia. It deployed the same template for military manpower by looking across the region for alternate points of supply that could relieve the burden on its European troops.[7] One way to do this was by pressing members of the free Asian *Mardijker* community into service, but their numbers were always limited. Another was to look toward local allies who could be mobilized, for example, via the *hongi* expeditions discussed in chapter 1, and the VOC came to rely on such fighters as an indispensable supplement to its core of European soldiers. But alongside such mechanisms, Company officials also nurtured ambitions of creating their own legion of Asian troops permanently under arms who in, Remco Raben's words, "recognized the VOC alone as master."[8]

The recruitment of Japanese soldiers, who were available in great numbers after the end of the bloody Sengoku or Warring States period (1467–1568), represented the first systematic attempt to tap into local circuits of Asian military manpower and bend these to the Company's will. Predictably, it was a familiar official, Jan Pieterszoon Coen, who emerged as the most aggressive champion of these soldiers, writing letter after letter demanding that his subordinates in Japan dispatch a steady stream of recruits.[9] While Coen's writings pictured long columns of Japanese mercenaries marching outward in service of the VOC, other officials within the organization were far less convinced of their utility. Japanese mercenaries were, they insisted, unruly, difficult to control, and required constant surveillance. Of "the Japanese we have," one early governor-general protested, "the bellyful already; it is an excitable and difficult race."[10] The most damning complaints came from those officials tasked with managing the recruits. They accused the Company's recruitment scheme of creating new dangers by adding further uncertainty to an already perilous landscape. The result was to open up a gap between the expansive plans put forward by Coen and the reality on the ground.

This was the case in Amboina, where concerns about the loyalty of Japanese troops flared dramatically during the 1623 trial. In contrast to his repeated references to slaves, Van Speult was far quieter when it came to the Japanese soldiers under his command in the months leading up to the first interrogation, and there were no eruptions of violence or sudden jailings of key personnel. But there are signs that the governor was uneasy about these recruits, whom he had barred from certain duties. Although there were just a dozen Japanese soldiers in Castle Victoria, they were, unlike the far more numerous slaves, heavily armed, with free movement throughout the castle. And in an increasingly turbulent political environment, it was all too easy to spin out dark visions that pictured these Asian soldiers, held to the Company by contract rather than loyalty, as a treacherous fifth column capable of opening the gates to their new paymasters.

In the end, the Company's experiment with Japanese soldiers was a limited one, just a few hundred soldiers shipped out before the scheme was eventually abandoned in the aftermath of the Amboina trial. But it was part of a wider shift, never total but always significant, to local military manpower that underpinned the expansion and longevity of the VOC's Asian empire. An estimated 100,000 Asian soldiers, whether allies, mercenaries, or vassals, served the organization across the course of its long existence.[11] Japanese mercenaries, who start to appear on VOC muster rolls just over a decade after the formation of the organization, may have represented a dead end but they were also a key milestone in the Company's long embrace of Asian military labor.[12] This reliance on Asian soldiers generated its own anxieties. As was the case with other European empires, Asian troops could and did prop up colonial rule and allow the expansion of European influence, but they were also a consistent focus of suspicion and dread. The nagging fear, always present and sporadically voiced in colonial documents, was that, armed and alone in their barracks, they would turn against their imperial masters.[13] And it was this fear that came to the surface in February 1623, when Shichizō first appeared to explain his conduct on the walls.

"Bold Men"

The first mention of Japanese soldiers in VOC services comes in a February 1613 letter sent by the head of the Japan trading outpost, Hendrik Brouwer, to the serving governor-general, Pieter Both:

> We regard here the Japanese under good command to be bold men. Their monthly pay is also low and moreover they can be maintained with a small cost of rice and salted fish. With the oral instructions that you gave me last time, we wanted to send 300 men with these ships, but so as to bring more provisions, only 68 heads were shipped, including 9 carpenters, 3 smiths and 2 or 3 masons, the rest sailors and soldiers. If you value the service of these, there will always be enough people here [to recruit] as his majesty [the shogun] has given us his consent to take out as many as we desire.[14]

As he makes clear, Brouwer had not conceived of the idea himself. Rather he was responding to an instruction delivered by his superiors to recruit large numbers of Japanese soldiers. The plan was ambitious. Three hundred men, the initial quota set for Brouwer to fill, may not seem like an especially large number, but it would have constituted a significant share of the Company's total military force scattered across its colonies, forts, and outposts.[15] Japanese mercenaries were not, in other words, intended simply as ancillary troops capable of making up the numbers around the edges. Rather, the governor-general clearly believed they could become an important part of the organization's fighting force.

It is not difficult to understand why Japan loomed so large in the Company's vision, for the archipelago seemed to offer an unique opportunity for recruiting soldiers. Highly militarized, it was also unexpectedly at peace after the violent excesses of the Sengoku period and Hideyoshi's vast, failed invasion of Korea in the last decade of the sixteenth century. It meant that Japan was brimming with experienced fighters with no obvious employment. In the Philippines, Spanish observers who feared these soldiers might be turned against them wrote that "about one hundred thousand men,

Xaponese soldiers, who were employed in the war with Corea, have returned to their own country, who are now idle and poor."[16]

There was also a clear precedent for recruiting Japanese soldiers. In the early seventeenth century, thousands of Japanese migrants and merchants had been propelled by a great surge in maritime connections into ports across Southeast Asia.[17] The result was the emergence of Japanese settlements (*nihonmachi*) that sprung up in places like Dilao in the Philippines, which had an estimated population of 3,000 Japanese residents, Siam, Cochinchina, and Cambodia. As these settlements grew, Japanese mercenaries started to make an appearance in armies across the region.[18] In the first decades of the seventeenth century, Japanese fighters found employment in Siam, where successive kings deployed a legion of these troops; in the Philippines, where they engaged in the bloody suppression of a Chinese revolt on behalf of their Spanish masters; and in Cambodia, where such recruits bolstered local forces gathered to resist a potential invasion. The largest group was active in Ayutthaya (Siam), where successive kings employed a formidable contingent of Japanese soldiers estimated at several hundred men. According to one contemporary observer, the king of Siam's power "by water and land, consists most of his own Vassals and Natives; he hath

Figure 3.1 The Japanese in Southeast Asia in 1600. Anonymous, 1601–1602. Courtesy of the Rijksmuseum, Amsterdam. RP-P-OB-75.407.

indeed some few Strangers, as Moors, Malayers and some five hundred Japanners, the most esteemed for their courage and fidelity."[19]

Although it was not the first foreign employer to look toward Japanese soldiers, the VOC did introduce a series of innovations that set it apart. Instead of hiring recruits in the *nihonmachi*, the Company opted to go straight to the source in Japan. The advantages of such a strategy were obvious. Signing on men in Japan removed any possible constraints brought about by the size of the existing Japanese community or the limited number of vessels sailing to Southeast Asia from Japanese ports each year. It also breathed new life into the Company's trading outpost in Hirado, on the northwest coast of Kyushu, which had struggled to turn a profit since its establishment in 1609. Now, VOC officials believed that a loss-making commercial hub could be transformed into a booming recruitment center from which a steady stream of experienced soldiers could flow.[20]

The second innovation was tied to the first. The Company did not want to recruit in the shadows, discreetly hiring soldiers via hushed transactions, but out in the open, with the explicit permission of the Tokugawa regime (Bakufu), which had consolidated power over the archipelago after the battle of Sekigahara in 1600.[21] Gaining this consent, and particularly the approval of Japan's preeminent political figure, Tokugawa Ieyasu, the first Tokugawa shogun, would, it was hoped, smooth over any potential difficulties and open the floodgates for recruitment. Surprisingly, the Bakufu agreed. Brouwer's boast that he had secured shogunal consent is supported by other sources confirming that he had asked for and received permission to recruit men in Japan.[22] The willingness of the Tokugawa regime to sign off on this request stemmed not from VOC pressure, for the Company was a minor actor in Japan that was in no position to demand concessions, but rather from a more general attitude toward the unruly activities of its subjects abroad.

While merchant ships carrying Bakufu-issued trading passes (called *shuinjō*) were guaranteed shogunal protection, Tokugawa representatives worked to sever links between the regime and Japanese merchants or migrants once they departed the archipelago. In letter after letter sent to Southeast Asia in this period, Tokugawa Ieyasu condemned the often violent conduct of his subjects, publicly renounced any claim to legal authority over their bodies, and insisted that all offenders should be dealt with according to local law.[23] Concerned officials were, the shogun stated repeatedly, fully entitled to order any punishment they deemed appropriate, including the execution of Tokugawa subjects. This cutting of any connection with those Japanese operating abroad and the insistence that all offenders be punished within the framework of the host state's legal system meant that the Bakufu effectively washed its hands of its subjects once they had departed Japan. As a result, Tokugawa officials showed little hesitation in approving Brouwer's requests, as long as the soldiers recruited by the VOC were deployed far away from Japan in distant lands.

The Company's last innovation centered on the nature of the recruits' service. In those parts of Southeast Asia where Japanese fighters were most active, the twin roles of merchant and mercenary blurred into each other, and there is little evidence of any sort of rigid dividing line. Merchants became mercenaries and then shifted back again, often holding multiple identities at the same time and deploying them according to the circumstances. In Cambodia, for example, recruitment of these soldiers was propelled by the eruption of crises that, once abated, allowed for a return to commerce. Even in Ayutthaya, where the Japanese claimed the long-term role of palace guards, there is no evidence that military duties took precedence over commercial interests. This was certainly the case with the most famous of all Japanese mercenaries, Yamada Nagamasa (d. 1630), who juggled his twin identities as violent soldier of fortune and prosperous merchant with apparent ease, engaging in successful military campaigns while building a highly profitable commercial network that saw him compete with the VOC for control of the lucrative trade in deer skins.[24]

In this way, Japanese migrants existed along a shifting continuum, transforming into mercenaries when it suited them but swiftly reclaiming their role as merchants when opportunities for profit emerged. They were, in other words, military and commercial entrepreneurs rather than professional soldiers, and it was this template with its blurred lines and overlapping roles that became standard across Southeast Asia. The Company, by contrast, had no intention of recruiting part-time military entrepreneurs who toggled back and forth between trade and violence. Instead, it wanted professional soldiers who would be docile in the barracks and ready for deployment anywhere their service was needed. As a result, the VOC attempted to engineer the figure of the professional Japanese mercenary constrained and controlled by strict contracts and recruited only for war.

The sixty-eight recruits referenced by Brouwer in his 1613 letter were shipped aboard the *Roode Leeuw met Pijlen*, which sailed in the company of a second vessel, the *Hasewint*. In addition to the recruits, they carried a swift galley (*barcque*) that had been constructed in Japan but broken into two pieces for transportation.[25] It was intended to police the waters around Banda, where it could do special service by enforcing the treaties designed to channel the flow of spices. Crucially, this could all be done, Company officials insisted, without requiring additional troops from Europe or diverting "the might of the Netherlanders."[26] In other words, Japanese fighting men could prop up VOC aims without placing further demands on the core of European troops. It was a clear summary of the logic behind the wider experiment as the Company sought to draw in Asian manpower to support its dive into the region's politics.

While Pieter Both had issued the first instructions to recruit Japanese soldiers, the driving force behind the Company's experiment came from another source, Jan Pieterszoon Coen, who was on his way to becoming governor-general. One year after Brouwer's letter, Coen laid out a series of far-reaching plans involving the use of Japanese soldiers in his expansive 1614 "Discourse to the Honorable Directors Concerning the States of the Netherlands Indies." Rather than being condemned to the defensive in its ongoing struggle against Portugal and Spain, which were both entrenched in Asia, the Company should, he argued, strike at the great Iberian centers of power in Asia: the bustling Portuguese entrepot of Macao and the heavily fortified Spanish city of Manila. To launch such an ambitious assault, the Company should look toward Japanese soldiers to bolster its armies in the region:

> [Through the conquest of Manila] the Spaniards shall be forced from the Moluccas, and indeed out of the East Indies . . . and along with this we shall get the riches of China. In executing such an important assault we can expect no small support from the islands of Manila as the poor subjects are weary of the Spanish yoke. For the execution [of the assault] we can with our money get great help from Japan . . . because the Japanese soldiers are as good as ours and the Kaiser [shogun] has given us his promise that we can take out as many people as we can get hold of. We can get enough as they are ready and willing, as we have found from our experience. These same Japanese soldiers can be used to do great service in the expedition to Macao, and with whom this expedition can be effected. With these victories, we shall not only capture a great treasure but also the rich Chinese trade.[27]

In this way, the recruitment of Japanese troops promised to help redraw the strategic map, allowing the VOC to evict the Portuguese and the Spanish from vital chokepoints and ensuring Dutch dominion over key trade routes.[28]

In his writings, Coen was clear that hundreds or even thousands of soldiers could be drawn from Japan, where the Dutch could "take out as many people as we can get hold of." In sketching out such an ambitious vision, he introduced a distinctively martial twist to a much older idea. For decades, the Jesuits and other European religious orders had seen Japan as a zone of unfulfilled possibilities, where dreams of mass conversions could be realized. One senior Jesuit official wrote that this "enterprise of Japan is without doubt the most important and beneficial of all being undertaken in these oriental parts and, indeed in all of discovery" and for these reasons "a very great harvest may be expected here."[29] For such writers, Japan represented uniquely fertile ground, a bountiful field waiting to be harvested by Jesuit missionaries. With minimal expense and only a small number of personnel, the archipelago could yield an army of converts. In his writings, Coen also presented Japan as a zone of possibility where outsized ambitions could be realized. Just as the Jesuits confidently predicted "a very great harvest" of souls, he anticipated a great harvest of willing bodies. But rather than an army of Christian converts able to carry the fight to the heathen, Coen saw the possibility of columns of Japanese mercenaries with Dutch officers at their head marching through Southeast Asia in service of the Company's aims. And just as was the case with his Jesuit counterparts, such visions were buoyed by a fantasy that never delivered on its promise.

In 1614, when he drew up his "Discourse," Coen was rising fast but was not entrenched in the top job. Not everyone within the organization, however, including some of his immediate superiors, shared his enthusiasm for Japanese troops.[30] But there was enough interest in the potential of these soldiers to spur new instructions for Jacques Specx, the VOC's long-serving chief merchant in Japan, to recruit a second contingent to be shipped aboard two vessels, the *Enckhuijsen* and the *Fortuijne*.[31] Although the sources are incomplete, this is the best documented of the cohorts transported from Japan to Southeast Asia. As such, it provides the clearest window into the recruits' experience of VOC service while exposing the persistent tension between Coen's soaring plans and the reality on the ground.

Serving the Company

Specx's new hires were to travel to Java aboard two ships that were anchored in the narrow confines of Hirado harbor. Blessed with good Dutch names, these were two very different vessels. The *Enckhuijsen* was a typical VOC workhouse, a cargo vessel built in the United Provinces and estimated at some 300 *last* or roughly 600 tons, which had made the long voyage from Europe to Asia in May 1614.[32] By contrast, the *Fortuijn* was a local junk that had been purchased by the Company in order to make up for its shortage of available vessels, and then outfitted with new rigging.[33] It was far smaller than its sister vessel, just 140 *last* or roughly 280 tons, making it less well suited for long ocean voyages with large numbers of men.[34]

By the end of the year, Specx had finished recruiting and he recorded the names of fifty-nine men alongside their wages in an official document. With this done, he moved to bind the recruits to the Company with a contract dated the "year and age named Iewa guannien [first year of Genna] in the 11th month and 11th day," or December 31, 1615.[35] Writing to his superiors, he explained that the recruits had been placed "under an appropriate oath and articles that I put together and translated in the Japanese language and writing."[36] The contract itself was to last for three years, but crucially this started not from date of signing but rather from the commencement of service, once the recruits had reached Southeast Asia. If one added in waiting times and the long sea voyage itself, the result was a far longer period of obligation to their new employer, lasting usually between four and five years.

The 1615 contract was designed to convert unruly recruits into dependable soldiers who could be relied upon to defend isolated garrisons or to carry the fight to the enemy's walls. Such documents were standard for VOC soldiers or sailors hired in Europe, but Specx, who was clearly concerned about how to maintain order on the long voyage to Southeast Asia, moved beyond conventional templates in an effort to ensure compliance. The 1615 contract begins with a set of unexceptional provisions that would have been immediately familiar to any one of thousands of Dutch sailors or soldiers. The recruits pledged never to start brawls or engage in fighting, gamble, "drink to intoxication," or "harass or attack married women and girls." They were to obey the captain, the helmsman, or "any Dutch authority" at all times, both on the ship as well as ashore; never to "speak back when given orders"; and, above all, never to oppose their superiors or to take any violent action toward them. Violation of these final provisions would lead to the swift application of capital punishment.

But it was not simply their own bodies that were subject to punishment. Diverging from comparable agreements signed with European recruits, the contract pulled in not only parents, wives, and children but also the guarantors standing security, who were also listed in the document. The inclusion of a collective punishment provision means that the contract represented, at least in theory, a striking expansion of VOC jurisdiction, giving Specx, the head of a minor European trading outpost, the ability to draw the families of his recruits into a VOC juridical web and punish them accordingly. It was by no means clear if the Company had any basis for such a significant extension of its authority, but the question of actual enforcement was always less important than the psychological impact of the clause, which was designed to force the recruits into obedience by pegging outsized consequences to their actions.

Despite the harshness of the contract, Specx does not seem to have struggled to find enough men willing to attach their names. The handful of recruits who listed their hometowns in the 1615 agreement were overwhelmingly local, drawn either from Hirado itself or from Nagasaki, a bustling port city less than a hundred miles down the coast. Some were surely Christians looking for a way to escape the increasingly fierce persecution of the Tokugawa state—the list included two Miguels and one Pedro, who were probably either baptized in their youth or born to a Christian family. But the majority showed no obvious Christian connection, and the bulk of the recruits were probably seeking economic opportunity, and hence intended to return to Japan once their contracts had expired. Given the difficult economic conditions in Hirado and Nagasaki, where the wealth from trade networks was concentrated in the hands of a relatively small number of local officials and rich merchants, the fact that regular wages would attract so many is not especially surprising. Hirado, the most important site for recruitment, was flooded with unemployed men looking for work. An English observer writing in 1613, when the Company commenced its program of recruitment, described a town filled with "base people or Renegados . . . loytering vp and downe."[37]

The presence of a large population of what was described as "diuers [diverse] vagrant people" was tied to the progressive closing down of long-serving avenues for employment that had once sucked up available labor in places like Hirado.[38] During the Sengoku period, when Kyushu was periodically convulsed by conflict, local warlords had displayed a boundless appetite for fighting men, but such opportunities had largely disappeared after the battle of Sekigahara in 1600. At the same time, large-scale piracy, which had drawn in thousands of Kyushu inhabitants at its peak, was finally suppressed. Although Toyotomi Hideyoshi, the second of Japan's three great unifiers, had officially banned piracy in 1588, these practices had simply mutated into a different form. During the first decade of the seventeenth century, ports like Hirado continued to play host to a range of pirate groups, and European vessels sailing through Asian waters regularly encountered such ships on the busy sea-lanes of early modern Asia.[39] By the time Specx began hiring, however, little trace of a once thriving pirate hub remained, and the Company probably drew at least some of its recruits from the maritime communities that had once participated in Japan's great wave of seaborne predation. As further evidence of this, the 1615 contract listed a handful of specialized roles, including mast climber and master of the anchor, while the remainder of the recruits were expected to crew the *Fortuijn* on its voyage to Southeast Asia.

The lack of economic opportunities made Hirado a fertile ground for recruitment, with the head of the rival English factory noting that there was an abundance of "dasparate, warlike people & ready to adventure for good pay."[40] But Specx was probably aided as well by the development of a specialized class of recruiters who had sprung up to cater for the Company's needs. Evidence of this can be found in the 1615 contract itself, which lists a handful of guarantors who stood in for multiple recruits. Sakino Matsy Sejusteroo, for example, offered himself up as security for eight individuals, while another, Amia, put himself forward for five. If these were indeed recruiters, then such practices were a parallel of the system that had emerged in the United Provinces, where a specialized class of agents, the *zielverkoopers* or "soul sellers," worked to supply the Company's inexhaustible demand for labor.[41] They did so in part by simple entrapment, effectively imprisoning vulnerable recruits in sealed-off boarding houses, but also by selling wondrous dreams of unlimited riches that extended to putting "a Hammer into [the recruit's] Hands to knock the Diamonds out of the Rocks they shall meet with."[42]

VOC schemes hinged in part on a widely shared conviction that the Japanese were, to use the language of a later empire, a peculiarly martial race. One European observer called the Japanese "the most warlike people in this part of the world."[43] They were thus set apart from the Chinese, for example, whom the VOC viewed as compliant settlers suitable for populating colonial settlements like Batavia or Tayouan.[44] The problem was, however, that the Company did its actual recruiting in two cosmopolitan ports, Hirado and Nagasaki, that had a deep history of long-distance trade and an accordingly diverse population. The result was that even if the Company thought it was hiring Japanese mercenaries, it is far from clear if that was always the case.

One clue to this messier reality comes in the last name of one of the soldiers caught up in the Amboina trial itself, Thome Corea. If, as Iwao Seiichi suggests, he had a Korean connection, this was not unusual in Hirado, where the local lord had brought back hundreds of Korean captives, who had been instrumental in the creation of the famous Mikawachi porcelain industry.[45] We know from the records associated with the trial that Thome Corea was aged fifty in 1623, meaning that he was born around 1573. He was thus probably brought to Japan in the turbulent aftermath of Hideyoshi's invasion. His unlikely career suggests that the Company's recruitment plans opened up an unexpected space for reinvention, one in which Korean captives could morph, in search of a stable wage, into Japanese soldiers. If so, Corea was not alone in making this change. VOC records include multiple references to "Japanese" soldiers with names that suggest external origins but who were able to take advantage of new opportunities afforded by the Company's martial visions.[46]

Of Specx's fifty-nine new recruits, the most important was the captain or *overhooft*, Kusnokij Itsiemon (likely Kusunoki Ichizaemon), who was tasked with managing the Company's new soldiers. In return, he was given a generous salary of eight taels (which was more than three times the standard pay for one of his charges), a generous advance of twenty-five taels, and the right to bring a servant, Rockoso, who was described in the contract as a *jongen* or "boy." Unlike most of his subordinates, Kusnokij was from the distant commercial metropolis of Osaka rather than Kyushu. It is not clear how he came to be in Hirado or why Specx felt that he was the right person to take charge of the contingent. In any event, Kusnokij proved a disastrous choice, and his inept leadership produced a string of problems once the *Fortuijn* departed Hirado.

The purpose of these recruits was to strengthen the Company's forces, and Specx set about equipping them with a small arsenal of weapons "that were needed to arm the Japanese."[47] These included forty Japanese firearms (*Jappanse roers*), eleven Japanese bows, and forty-five Japanese spears of different lengths. The muskets were not cheap, costing a total of seventy-two taels, but they packed a powerful punch. Musket technology had advanced in leaps and bounds in Japan through the sixteenth century, driven in large part by the prolific use of these weapons in the endless conflict that characterized the Warring States period. Like other muskets from this time, these weapons were slow to reload but in the hands of well-trained troops they could be lethal.[48]

But if the recruits were armed to the teeth, there was a problem: the vessels designated to transport them to where they were needed in Southeast Asia were in no state to undertake the long voyage to the trading port of Banten, on the island of Java. In fact, it took months before the *Enckhuijsen*, which had made the long voyage from Europe, was overhauled and ready for departure. This long delay earned Specx a sharp reprimand from his superiors, who accused him of disrupting the Company's wider trading schedule through his incompetent management.[49] For the recruits, however, the delay was probably welcome, as it left them with money in hand and few responsibilities.

By 1615, Hirado had established its reputation as "a second Sodamye," where dozens of brothels and taverns clustered along the shoreline, offering their services to incoming mariners. There was, one visitor explained, "never a house in the towen butt the bassest swabber in the fleete may have wine and a hoore."[50] Not surprisingly, the combination of alcohol and idle men created ample opportunities for violence as groups of mariners were seen "stagring drunk up & downe the st[r]eetes, slashing & cutting ofee each other w'th their knyves, lyke mad men."[51] To restore order, local authorities took drastic measures, including executing a number of offenders.[52] The long period of inactivity also gave time for rivalries to fester within the contingent itself. The most dangerous emerged between Kusnokij and a charismatic rival, Ceyemon, who, clearly covetous of his superior's position and privileges, worked to undermine these. Their rivalry simmered for months in Hirado before exploding into violence when the recruits finally arrived in Southeast Asia.

At last, after months of preparation, the *Enckhuijsen* and the *Fortuijne* departed Japan on March 5, 1616. Most of the Japanese recruits, perhaps forty or fifty men, were to travel aboard the smaller junk, which was placed under the command of Jacob Joosten van Lodensteijn. Van Lodensteijn was the brother of one of the original *Liefde* mariners who had been shipwrecked on an early Dutch expedition to Japan in 1600, but unlike his sibling, who had established himself as a successful merchant, he had little experience of Japan and no facility with the language.[53] The result was that he had to rely on Kusnokij, who was posted on the *Fortuijn* to maintain control of the new recruits. Clearly aware of the brewing conflict, Specx elected to place Ceyemon on the *Enckhuijsen*, to take charge of the handful of Japanese soldiers there and to keep out of Kusnokij's way. In total, the two ships spent fifty-one days at sea before arriving in the port of Banten on April 24. For the larger *Enckhuijsen*, the voyage seems to have passed without incident, in part because of Ceyemon's leadership but also because the ship was (in relative terms) far larger and more spacious. Aboard the *Fortuijn*, however, things quickly deteriorated.[54]

The life of a VOC mariner, whether European or Asian, was a stunningly harsh one. Likened by one observer to a "subservient slave," a sailor aboard a Company vessel had to be ready "on the slightest nod or command of any superior, to do everything he is told without grumbling. At any show of reluctance, he is threatened and beaten with the rope's end."[55] To keep its sailors in line, the Company relied on harsh discipline. For minor lapses or wrongdoings, the VOC enforced a comprehensive system of fines and levies that seemed calculated to strip sailors of their earnings.[56] For more serious violations of a ship's regulations, the punishments rapidly escalated. The captain of the *Enckhuijsen* stipulated that anyone found bringing unauthorized alcohol onto the ship or buying it illicitly would be dropped from the yardarm three times and then lashed before the mast.[57] This involved hoisting the culprit up in the rigging, tying his arms and then dropping him, usually around forty or fifty feet, thereby either dislocating or breaking his arms. For graver offenses, there was, one firsthand observer wrote, "a very great severity exercised over the Malefactors."[58] This extended to punishments such as keelhauling, in which the offender was thrown overboard and dragged under the keel of the ship to the other side, ripping his flesh away on the encrusted hull of the vessel.

Such systems held the vast majority of VOC crews in check for far longer voyages. On the *Fortuijn*, however, a combination of the small size of the vessel, unfamiliarity with the ship's routines, and inept leadership pushed the recruits close to mutiny. When he came to assess what had happened, Specx wrote first that shipping out recruits on smaller vessels invariably created more problems. We are, he declared, "always apprehensive that more discontent and troubles will take place on the junk as the ship."[59] On smaller vessels like the *Fortuijn*, the crew would probably have been divided into two four-hour shifts, giving them at most four hours of sleep at any one time. The result was that most sailors slept in wet clothes, tumbling into their hammocks as soon as they finished their duties only to have their sleep cut short when the watch changed again.[60] In such conditions, illnesses like dysentery spread quickly, and there was little prospect of medical attention.[61] If conditions were already poor in fair weather, they became appalling during storms. When the weather turned, the hatches were battened down, sometimes for days or even weeks on end. Water seeped into everything, and the smell of rotting mixed with the general stench created by crowding large numbers of people into small spaces with inadequate ventilation. With sailors unable to access the primitive toilet facilities, which were usually located in the open on the bow of a ship, the cabin quickly became fouled with excrement and vomit.

To this must be added the inevitable terrors of an ocean voyage in the age of sail. For those unused to the open ocean, the experience was, in the words of one equally unprepared voyager, "altogether unconceivable." Conventional bravery counted for nothing: "tho' I have been oftentimes in great dangers [. . .] and upon many occasions have, with Courage enough, stood before the Enemy; yet did none of these dangers ever terrifie me comparably to this [experience of a storm]." In these moments, "death doth not only seem sure and inevitable, but comes attended with all the Horrour imaginable, and drest in its most hideous and terrifying shapes."[62] Such fears were of course justified, as VOC ships did periodically disappear without a trace. This was the fate of the *China*, which departed Japan in 1620 with a contingent of close to a hundred Japanese passengers, but which was lost somewhere along the sea lanes, with all lives lost.[63]

Such desperate conditions would have been immediately familiar to the thousands of sailors and soldiers who departed the United Provinces each year. Crucially, however, the Japanese contingent shipped aboard the *Fortuijn* lacked the rigid hierarchies that worked to compel obedience in such circumstances.[64] The task of maintaining order fell to Kusnokij, who was now required to justify his wages and privileges. He proved, his superiors concluded, entirely "unsuitable for command," an idle and unreliable captain with no capacity to exert control over his already fractious charges.[65] The resultant breakdown in authority seems to have brought the recruits to the very edge, if not actually over the brink, of mutiny. They were, VOC officials declared, nothing more than a "mutinous rabble," who had "behaved very maliciously," endangering the safety of the ship and coming precariously close to armed resistance.[66]

A rigid disciplinarian, Coen was understandably disturbed by what had happened on the *Fortuijn*, but it did not shake his basic belief in the value of Japanese troops. On May 14, just a few weeks after the junk dropped anchor at Banten, he addressed the near mutiny in a letter to the head of the Japan factory. In the future, Specx must "inspect" (*monsteren*) his recruits more carefully and make sure that any potential troublemakers were weeded out before leaving port.[67] In this way, the problem could be solved simply by better hiring practices and proper diligence by officials on the ground. Specx should simply line up the recruits on the shore, remove any bad apples, and dispatch the rest. It was, Coen insisted, not a problem with the recruitment plans as a whole but simply a matter of finding the right disciplinary formula. Furious at such a blithe dismissal, the Japan chief responded that "such rabble [*geboeften*] can often, as long as they are on land, remain quiet so that they are difficult to recognize and be weeded out."[68]

Instead of an isolated incident, the mutiny provided a taste of things to come. Even after his inept performance on the *Fortuijn*, Kusnokij managed to retain his position as head of the Japanese contingent, which had swelled again with the arrival of the *Enkhuijsen* to include his longtime rival, Ceyemon. Their rivalry was swiftly renewed; on March 2, Kusnokij decided to take action by ambushing Ceyemon as he lay in his bunk with his fellow mercenaries, talking and smoking. Stabbed without warning from behind, Ceyemon died immediately. It was a bloody climax to months of simmering tension, and the perpetrator was seized immediately for punishment. But if Kusnokij was an incompetent leader, he proved far more ingenious when it came to legal maneuvering. When he was arrested, he insisted that his actions had been entirely legal and that he was simply fulfilling his role as commander of the Japanese, a charge that had been given to him, he maintained, both by Specx and the lord of Hirado. Since Ceyemon had been "mustered under his command," Kusnokij was entitled to punish him for insubordination and his repeated attempts to "belittle him and make himself master."[69] In other words, when he stabbed his rival, he was acting as a properly constituted officer rather than carrying out a private vendetta.

It was a shrewd and essentially plausible defense as the recruits were indeed bound by a contract that stipulated harsh punishments if any of them attempted to subvert or oppose the officials placed in charge of them. It did not, however, satisfy the VOC tribunal convened to issue judgement. Lamenting the loss of Ceyemon, who had been marked for greater things, the tribunal concluded that such actions were an affront to "godly law and . . . Christian justice and also Japanese custom." There could only be one punishment, and, despite repeated protests about his authority, Kusnokij was swiftly executed. With the murder of Ceyemon and the execution of Kusnokij, the *Fortuijn* contingent had already lost two leaders before it had even started its duties. Company officials moved quickly to make a new appointment. On June 10, just a week after the murder, a new captain, Gonssen, described as "an expert at war of their manner and otherwise qualified and competent," was handed responsibility for the contingent.[70] He might have wondered what he was taking on but he was at least spared the prospect of another extended sea voyage.

When Coen had announced the need to recruit large numbers of Japanese soldiers, he had envisaged them in the vanguard of attacks against Portuguese and Spanish strongholds. The reality was less impressive, however, as the soldiers transported aboard the *Fortuijn* were thrust into a series of minor marketplace skirmishes that erupted between the English and Dutch companies in Banten.[71] Such engagements won them praise for their reckless courage, but a steady string of disciplinary issues persisted.[72] One member of the *Fortuijn* contingent, Pedro, was found sleeping when he should have been patrolling the walls of the fortress. He was promptly executed by firing squad. Another, Saemon, was sentenced to hard labor for a similar offense, with VOC officials insistent that he would have been killed if they had been able to locate at least one proper witness.

Such episodes prompted a continued search for the right disciplinary formula to turn the recruits into obedient servants of the Company. Back in Japan, Specx weighed in. The problem was, he insisted, that the Dutch commanders were not being harsh enough with the recruits. The "Japanese sabre" was the only medicine that they could understand and it must be ruthlessly used to ensure compliance.[73] In the months after they arrived in Banten, the *Fortuijn* contingent was broken up and scattered around the Company's various outposts, wherever they were needed. They start to reappear in the records around 1619, at the point when their initial three-year contracts came to an end. Some, like Tombe, Schoyts, Itsico, Thosoo, Groboo, Johan Fanso, and Joan Maccau, opted to reenlist at slightly elevated wages in July 1619.[74] Others, seeing their numbers diminished by sickness or death in battle, decided they had had enough of Dutch service and resolved to return to Japan. Predictably, this prompted yet more problems. As soon as they reached Japan in 1620, they demanded back wages extending not to March 1616, when their ship had actually departed Japan, but rather to November 1615, when they had first signed their "letters of article" (*articjkelbrief*). It was almost too much to bear for Specx, who wrote furiously that the recruits' demands for an extra three months of back pay went "against reason and Japanese custom."[75]

The experience of the *Fortuijn* contingent encapsulates some of the tensions embedded in the Company's recruitment scheme. Despite these problems, Coen continued to write letter after letter requiring his subordinates to pick up the pace of recruitment.[76] On March 30, 1618, he demanded that Specx immediately dispatch "25 Japanese of the most suitable, brave young men that can be found."[77] In 1620, he wrote to his superiors that "for the strengthening of all the garrisons we have sent for a good number of Japanese . . . up to 3 or 400 will be sent this year."[78] He followed up that year with another, even more urgent missive, insisting that Specx "send here as many brave Japanese as time and circumstances permits. They will not be used for labor but for war."[79] In response, the Hirado factory dispatched at least two and probably more contingents of recruits: ninety sailed aboard the *Nieuw Bantam* and *Galiasse* in 1619, and in 1620 another group of roughly one hundred men was sent out aboard the *China*.[80] It was not enough for Coen, however, who took every opportunity to urge his agents in Japan to send more soldiers.

Remarkably, these instructions endured even as the Tokugawa regime moved to clamp down on the steady flow of soldiers out of the country. In 1621, the Bakufu, alarmed at the expanding scale of the mercenary trade, barred the Dutch from further recruitment of soldiers in Japan. The edict, dated Genna 7, fifth month, twenty-second day, or July 11, 1621, was issued to the lord of Hirado and prohibited the "taking of purchased men and women to foreign countries," as well as the "sending out of swords, daggers and other weapons."[81] For Specx, this shift in policy stemmed from an increasing Bakufu concern that its subjects would "become involved in foreign wars," thereby drawing the regime itself, which valued stability above all else, into an unwanted conflict.[82] For Coen, however, the ban represented nothing more than a temporary stumbling block and he ordered his subordinates in Japan to spare no effort in overturning the edict: "It is necessary that you work with discrete diligence to once again gain the previous license to ship Japanese and weapons from the kaiser [shogun]."[83] In another letter, he was even more insistent, instructing his subordinates to "spare no cost or trouble" in overturning the shogun's ban.[84]

But for all of Coen's bold statements, Japanese soldiers struggled to find a place within the Company. While the records are peppered with praise for their bravery in combat, this was balanced by a string of ongoing disciplinary issues.[85] In the end, these men, for all their success in battle, did not fit neatly into the Company's rigid structures, where everything had its proper place. Transported across great distances, marooned in isolated barracks in feverish, unwelcoming places, and forced to accommodate an unfamiliar culture and organization, the recruits jostled against VOC control. The problem was made worse by the absence of the routines that had ordered life in Japan, creating a vacuum not easily filled. The concern was voiced most clearly by Specx, who explained that the Japanese "are dangerous to govern outside their land. If it does not go to their liking or when badly treated, they at once take a desperate attitude, which in their land would be prevented by rigorous justice or rather by tyranny. In this way they are lambs [in Japan] and like devils outside their land."[86] The result was a constant friction between the organization and its new employees. While Coen remained convinced of the value of Japanese recruits, his subordinates protested a group forced into their midst who were, they insisted, "not so useful or trustworthy."[87] In Kota Ambon, Van Speult seems to have shared these concerns, but, in a political environment seemingly spiraling out of control, the governor came to see something far darker: that these soldiers might become a weapon turned against their supposed masters.

Japanese Mercenaries in Amboina

Perpetually depleted by illnesses that swept through the town, the garrison in Kota Ambon required continual injections of fresh soldiers. Given this fact, it is not surprising that the Company would use Japanese arrivals to fill its diminished ranks. From the beginning, VOC officials had planned to use Japanese soldiers in Amboina, suggesting that the kind of swift Japanese craft shipped aboard the *Roode Leeuw met Pijlen* and the *Hasewint* in 1613 could, once manned "with rowers and fighters," do good service in Hitu, Luhu, and Kambelo.[88] With the Company's consistent focus on nearby Banda, however, such plans were delayed and the first Japanese recruits seem to have arrived in the territory around 1620. They came from two distinct sources.

One was connected to an ambitious scheme proposed by a Japanese soldier called Saquemonne, recently arrived from Hirado, who had supposedly obtained proof of a rich silver deposit in Amboina.[89] Coming before the governor-general, he had persuaded the Company to release not only himself but more than twenty other Japanese recruits to investigate the reports firsthand. It was an appealing proposition for VOC officials: if the deposit was located and successfully mined, it would boost the Company's fortunes in the territory; if not, the recruits could simply be relieved of their mining duties and returned to their role as soldiers.[90] In Kota Ambon, Van Speult recorded the arrival of the miners in Amboina. Supportive of any effort that might increase the revenue coming into the territory, he supplied the newcomers with all necessary tools, including hammers, chisels, and levers.[91] The work started quickly, with Van Speult registering his amazement at the miners' impressive speed in excavating vast quantities of soil.[92] At first, it seemed as if they had have been successful, and a rich sample of silver was brought for the governor's inspection. But the next visit produced a far inferior mineral, leading Van Speult to suspect that he had been deceived by a sample specially transported for the purpose.[93] When no vein of silver was in fact discovered, the scheme was shelved and the miners enlisted for service in Amboina.

The second point of supply stemmed from Coen's invasion of Banda. Two cohorts of Japanese soldiers, with more than eighty soldiers divided between them, had participated in the campaign.[94] Thrust into combat, they had distinguished themselves in the fierce fighting that had taken place at the beginning of the invasion. Coen was so impressed by their performance that he decided to reward some of the recruits with a personal gift for their bravery in storming the well-defended heights of one of the islands.[95] After hostilities ended, these soldiers were handed a new role. On May 8, 1621, when VOC officials decided to execute forty-four *orang-kaya* for supposedly plotting to renew hostilities against the Dutch, the bloody work of execution was passed over to six Japanese soldiers, who were ordered "with their sharp swords," to cut the eight ringleaders through the middle, then cut off their heads before finally quartering their bodies. The remaining thirty-six were then beheaded and quartered in a gory scene that has been widely depicted in text and image.[96] While VOC forces were still engaged in the final pacification of Banda, Coen traveled to Amboina in June 1621. Once there, he assigned a number of troops, including, we can assume, one part of his Japanese contingent, to strengthen the garrison under Van Speult's command.[97]

In contrast to his far more detailed comments about the slave population in Kota Ambon, Van Speult was largely silent about the castle's Japanese recruits, at least until they were thrust into the spotlight after the Amboina trial erupted. In part this was probably because of the relatively small size of the contingent, but it was also the case that much of Van Speult's correspondence, particularly in this period, was directed toward Jan Pieterszoon Coen, his immediate superior and most effective patron, who had little interest in hearing criticism of a scheme that he had personally championed for years. Despite this, there are traces in the records that Van Speult nursed his own doubts about these troops, and that these laid the ground for his rapid actions when Shichizō was first brought before him.

These suspicions derived partly, we can assume, from his experience with Saquemonne, who had, Van Speult believed, attempted to trick him into supporting his mining scheme with a fake sample. But his attitude was likely also informed by the views of Steven van der Haghen, who had been Van Speult's direct superior for a number of years. Of all the VOC officials to confront the Company's recruitment scheme, Van der Haghen was the most critical. In 1616, the VOC veteran had penned a scathing indictment of Japanese soldiers that extended far beyond the usual complaints about poor discipline. For him, such recruits presented an unacceptable risk: the "soldiers from Japan are of no service to us, because they are very dangerous (*seer dangereus*) and difficult to govern."[98] In this way, he concluded that the entire scheme was ill-fated. It would have been better, he declared, "to leave these people in their land." It was a belief that Van Speult seems to have adopted, and which underpinned his actions when Shichizō was hauled into the interrogation chamber to be questioned.

The advice from Specx in Japan was always to use the Japanese in the "most dangerous places," thereby reducing the possibility of discipline issues breaking out in the barracks.[99] In Amboina, Van Speult seems to have heeded these words. According to one of the judges, these soldiers were "used in the Corrocorres [kora-kora] . . . and other perilous exploits."[100] Sending Japanese soldiers out on the *hongi* expeditions, which served as the primary vehicle for clashes with rival polities across Amboina, kept them in the heat of battle and away from trouble, but at some point they had to return to Kota Ambon, and their presence within the castle appears to have weighed on the governor. Uneasy about the situation, he took some concrete steps to wall off his Japanese troops. According to English observers, the Japanese did "serve the Dutch as Souldiers, yet were not of their trusty band."[101] As a result, they were not provided with firearms except on special duties, and it was "forbidden to all the Dutch, upon great penalty, to sell and hand-gun, powder or bullets, to the Japons."[102] They were also barred from key duties, including serving on the walls of Castle Victoria as the first line of defense against outside attack. In this way, the Company's Japanese recruits occupied a familiar position. Like so many other Asian soldiers in the employ of European empires, they were both indispensable and dangerous at the same time. Trusted with arms and yet never fully trusted, they were an inevitable focal point for suspicion.

In the aftermath of the Amboina trial, Van Speult would claim that some of the Japanese soldiers under his command had become too close to the English, raising his suspicions weeks before Shichizō was apprehended. They had, he wrote in June 1623, shown a disturbing "familiarity" with those English merchants resident in Kota Ambon.[103] This was compounded by the fact that at least one of the recruits had previously served the English East India Company before entering VOC ranks, making him a potential turncoat.[104] Assessing the truth behind such statements is difficult. While it is likely that Sidney Miguel, a Japanese soldier who will be discussed in more detail in chapter 5, had worked either in one of the English factories in Asia or served aboard an English company vessel before joining VOC ranks, there is no sign that members of the Japanese contingent in Kota Ambon were in close contact with Towerson or his fellow merchants. Rather, what Van Speult probably witnessed was a casual interaction in the castle, where English merchants came daily, but one that morphed in the deteriorating environment into something more ominous.

In the end, gaps in the record leave some details concerning the Japanese contingent in Castle Victoria unknowable. What does seem certain, however, is that like the "Portuguese" captain of the slaves, the Japanese soldiers in Kota Ambon held a precarious status that could be pulled away at any point, leaving them open to the full weight of suspicion. And in the weeks before the trial, as tensions mounted, it was all too easy for these doubts to come spilling out.

CHAPTER IV

The English Serpent

We fear them more than the enemy.

—"DISCOURSE TO THE HONORABLE DIRECTORS CONCERNING
THE STATE OF THE NETHERLANDS INDIES," 1614

I n September 1622, Gabriel Towerson bought a house. He had been
agonizing over the purchase for weeks. A house was a big investment,
one of the largest he was likely to make as chief-merchant of the English East India Company in Kota Ambon, and it would place new strains
on the outpost's already precarious finances. But for Towerson, a permanent structure was essential to provide accommodation for the merchants
under his command and a safe storage space for cloves and other goods,
away from the monsoonal rains that lashed down on Kota Ambon for
weeks on end. And, as he declared confidently in one of his letters, this
was "as fyne a howse as any in these parts of the Indies."[1] Built solidly of
stone, it would provide a secure haven and a lasting base that would guarantee the English company's fortunes in Amboina.

In the final negotiations, Towerson came to rely more and more on the
governor, Van Speult, who had intervened personally to facilitate the sale.
In one of his last letters back to his superiors before the 1623 trial, Towerson praised the governor's conduct, writing of the "love shewed to mee in
dyvers curtisies," while requesting special gifts to properly thank him for
his assistance.[2] Such comments reflect the intimate relationship that existed
between the Dutch and the English at Amboina.[3] Until Towerson's purchase of a house, English merchants had leased space inside Castle Victoria.
This meant that Towerson and Van Speult were in constant contact, sharing frequent meals and drinking arak, the powerful local spirit, together. In

many ways, such close relations are unsurprising. After all, England and the United Provinces were close allies, bound together by their Protestant faith as well as a long, shared history of struggle against Spain. While the two companies had been fractious rivals in the past, including a brief phase of open war, they had been converted into partners after the conclusion of the Treaty of Defense in 1619, which had committed them to profit sharing and joint military operations. And for two groups of strangers in an unfamiliar landscape, there was a natural impulse for English and Dutch merchants in Amboina to draw together.[4]

But whereas Towerson's correspondence reflects a belief that he had found a reliable ally, the letters coming in and out of Castle Victoria reveal a very different picture. Writing of the English merchants scattered across Amboina, Van Speult lamented the "fraudulent malice [*frauduleuse malicie*] that they seem to be born with."[5] Even as he toasted Towerson, the governor believed that he would inevitably be betrayed by him. It was only a question of when the English would strike, and Van Speult assured his superiors that he would act swiftly to prevent any encroachment on Dutch sovereignty. Such comments did not make the governor an outlier. Instead, they reflect a powerful suspicion of the English that runs like a thread through VOC letters from this period, especially those penned by its most powerful official in Asia, Jan Pieterszoon Coen, who displayed what M. A. P. Meilink-Roelofsz described as an "almost pathologically anti-English attitude."[6] Instead of allies or friends the English were secret foes intent always on "undercutting" (*ondercruypinge*) and hollowing out the Dutch empire from within. There was "no place in the Indies," Coen explained, "that the English do not try to undercut and taint."[7] The result was a potent declaration that the English were to be feared more than any enemy. Repeated again and again, it spurred a powerful feedback loop of anxiety and distrust that was continually magnified and reinforced with the arrival of every new letter.[8]

Why were the English the subject of such intense anxieties, of hyperbolic warnings that "in the whole of the Indies there is no more harmful party"?[9] Certainly the merchants attached to the EIC were fierce commercial rivals, who had pushed aggressively into areas in which Dutch control was weakest while working to undermine the treaty regime. At the same time, however, the English company was poorly funded, badly organized, and consistently outmaneuvered by its Dutch rival, which had, in a brief phase of open war, brushed aside the EIC threat. Why then did the English loom so large in the VOC imagination, particularly when the Company contended with so many other rivals and enemies in the region? As recent work by Jennifer Gaynor and others has shown, the war over spices, long described as an Anglo-Dutch struggle, was in fact a far more expansive conflict, drawing in maritime powers like Makassar, which presented a more sustained challenge to Dutch hegemony in the region than the English company with its limited resources.[10]

The answer lies in the peculiar role of the English as "feigned friends" (*geveynsde vrienden*), a formulation that recurs again and again in VOC documents from this period.[11] Living close or sometimes within the walls of VOC factories and forts, English merchants were the constant companions of the Dutch. And from this privileged position, sheltered beneath the umbrella of the VOC's military might, they hatched, Dutch officials alleged, secret plans to strike at their protectors, identifying weak points that, once targeted, could bring the Company's empire in Asia crashing down. It was the subtle, insidious "creeping of the feigned friend" (*ondercruypinge van de geveynsde vrienden*), always close by, always working against the Company's plans but always in the shadows, that made the English so dangerous.[12]

While Dutch anxieties about the English were present from the beginning, they ramped up in the years leading up to the Amboina conspiracy trial. Paradoxically, the catalyst was the Treaty of Defense, which was designed to reconcile the two organizations and end their long rivalry. Forced upon the companies against the wishes of Asia-based administrators like Coen by two home governments eager to ensure that the conflict in Asia did not disrupt a key military alliance in Europe, this agreement pushed the two organizations into a tight embrace while opening up territories like Amboina to EIC merchants. The treaty did not, however, usher in a golden age of cooperation. Instead, it placed, in the view of many VOC officials, a deadly "serpent in the Company's bosom," one capable of striking at the heart of the Dutch empire in Asia.[13]

The English in Asia

For pamphleteers writing in the aftermath of the Amboina trial, it was common to begin with a brief prelude lamenting the betrayal by one or other party of the "ancient amity, and good correspondence, held between . . . [England] and the Netherlands."[14] Although such references were inserted mainly to give weight to subsequent charges of perfidy, they reflected a long and genuine history of alliance between the two countries that stretched back to the chaotic first decades of the Dutch revolt against Spain, when England had emerged as the new republic's most important international ally. Successive English monarchs provided consistent support across the Eighty Years' War with Spain, while large numbers of English soldiers fought in the Netherlands, which became a kind of military apprenticeship for many.[15] It was a point that was regularly thrown in the face of Dutch merchants in Asia, who were reminded by their EIC interlocutors that the English had played an essential role "in driving the Spaniardes out of the Loe Cuntries & making the Hollanders a free state."[16]

As the threat of Spanish conquest diminished and Dutch power grew, it was clear that before long England and the United Provinces would become locked in a fierce commercial competition. The English East India Company was born into a state of rivalry with Dutch efforts in Asia. Formed in 1600, that is, two years before the VOC, the new organization was created in response to the voyages initiated by the Dutch pre-companies to Asia. The first petition presented to the English monarch, Elizabeth I, to obtain rights to charter the new company made specific reference to the "successe of the viage pformed by the Duche nation." Since English merchants had "noe lesse affection to advaunce the trade of ther native Cuntrey," they had resolved to ask the crown to provide them with a charter granting exclusive rights to Asia.[17]

Although it was designed to rival Dutch efforts, the EIC, which was chartered on December 31, 1600, was, in its early iteration, a weak organization that proved unable to compete effectively with the VOC when it was established in 1602. Unlike its Dutch counterpart, which received its initial capital for a full decade, the EIC was originally capitalized only for individual voyages. As a result, it had a relatively small capital, which had to be disposed of at the conclusion of each voyage, thereby bringing the expedition to a close and providing a platform to raise funds for the next voyage.[18] The system rendered long-term planning difficult, as each voyage was in effect a separate, individually capitalized endeavor required to turn a profit. After 1608, when the EIC began to send out more frequent expeditions, these individual voyages came to overlap, generating direct competition between what were after all financially separate enterprises. Recognizing these problems, the organization decided to raise its first joint stock in 1613. The move served to stabilize the English enterprise in Asia but its limited duration meant that the EIC continued to lag behind the Dutch company, which by this point had made its capital permanent.[19]

Unlike the VOC, which was able to build directly on the experience gained during the experimental pre-companies phase, the EIC was in effect a newcomer to Asian trading circuits. This meant that its early operations were tentative, as English merchants sought to probe the contours of the vast Asian market. In the first decade of its existence, the new organization managed to equip just fourteen ships.[20] This uncertainty about Asian trading circuits meant as well that EIC merchants in the region tended to travel in the wake of the Dutch. Whether in established entrepots or isolated port cities, it was common for Dutch merchants to watch in frustration as their English counterparts set up shop in close proximity to them. One example of a much wider pattern took place in Japan, where the Dutch had established their factory in Hirado. The choice, which had been heavily influenced by the exaggerated promises of an enterprising local lord, made dubious commercial sense as it marooned VOC merchants hundreds of miles away from Japan's sprawling commercial metropolises of Edo and Osaka, where the greatest profits could be made. And yet, despite these factors, an EIC expedition under the command of John Saris, elected to set up their own trading hub in the same port four years later, thereby ensuring that there were two European factories in an isolated town with just a few thousand residents.[21]

Enraged by such practices, Coen wrote long letters to his superiors complaining that in "Jaccatra the English have now also taken up residence . . . In Jambi they have followed us with a yacht. The same also in Patani, Siam and Japan."[22] He concluded angrily that "there is no place in the Indies that they do not follow us."[23] Such a high degree of overlap was in part the product of an EIC belief, often mistaken, that the Dutch had planted their flag at the points maximally designed to produce profit. It was also a function of another difference between the two organizations. Unlike the VOC, which had been chartered in part to carry the war against Spain into Asia, the EIC had far more limited military capacities. Whereas the Dutch were able to seize Portuguese strongholds and settlements such as Kota Ambon, the English had no choice but to move into established ports. In practice, this meant that EIC merchants were invariably interlopers into markets the VOC had either claimed for itself or in which it had already established a foothold.[24]

The close proximity between their factories could produce strikingly intimate relations, and the records of both companies are filled with examples of shared meals, celebrations, and other such interactions.[25] There was no shortage of things to bring them together in an uncertain landscape. Many EIC employees had a long familiarity with the Netherlands, including direct experience fighting alongside Dutch soldiers in the war against Spain.[26] At the same time, and despite the apparently fixed nature of their national identities, the boundaries separating these organizations were far less distinct than they appeared at first. In their efforts to secure enough recruits willing to make the hazardous journey to Asia, both companies were compelled to look far beyond their national borders. What we know as the English East India Company was filled with employees drawn from across the British Isles and Europe more generally, while many of the VOC's servants had only the most limited connection with the Dutch Republic. In Amboina, for example, the "English" merchants identified in the sources included recruits drawn from places like Scotland and Wales or cities like Hamburg, while the VOC employed a Scottish steward and at least one musketeer who had been born in England.[27]

And yet, despite these connections, there was for every instance of genial cooperation an equal number of episodes marked by fierce rivalry or violent clashes as the two organizations waged what one prominent historian has characterized as an "existential and ideological" battle.[28] This rivalry played out in multiple ways. Across Asia, the companies jostled for prestige and standing, the English arguing that they were representatives of an older and more distinguished nation still headed by a monarch, the Dutch that they worked for a far more powerful organization that deserved a commensurate level of respect. Both sides complained incessantly about slights leveled against them or their home governments.[29] The result was repeated scenes, sometimes verging on comedy, in which the two sides bristled against each other, demanding that their counterparts show more deference.

The fiercest clashes, however, centered on VOC attempts to lock English interlopers out of the spice trade using the protection/tribute treaties they had signed with local spice producers in places like Amboina or Banda. The same scenes repeated year after year as English merchants intent on purchasing spices confronted Dutch officials who refused them access on the basis of monopoly rights contained within the treaties they presented helpfully for inspection. The result was a string of clashes over the nature and limits of these treaties as calls for free trade were met by an absolute insistence that such agreements closed off any possible space for English participation. Both sides quickly settled into positions from which they refused to shift. English merchants argued that the treaties themselves were invalid because they had been forced upon local signatories, while the Dutch replied that these were legally binding documents that would be enforced by violence if necessary.

Banda, where EIC agents where highly active, became one site for this clash. Amboina, where the English could find trading partners in Hoamoal and Hitu eager to evade Dutch prohibitions, was another. There, the two companies collided in 1605, 1610, and again in 1613 as EIC ships attempted to force their way into the clove trade.[30] In March 1613, for example, John Jourdain, an EIC commander, arrived in Hitu aboard the *Darling* determined to purchase cloves.[31] His initial attempts at doing so were met by a sustained protest from Steven Coteels, the VOC chief merchant. Since the Dutch were, by virtue of signed treaties, the "protectours of the countrye and people," any attempt to "reape the fruit" of Amboina was, Coteels insisted, nothing more than an act of burglary.[32] Given this, he would do whatever was necessary to prevent English incursions into the spice market, even if it required the use of force.[33]

Faced with these assertions, Jourdain counterattacked, taking aim at any notion that VOC protection was necessary or desirable. The Dutch made use, he argued, of false claims of protection in order to subjugate the local population. Their insistence on "buildinge and mayntaineinge castles in other countryes where you have little thanke[s] for your proteccion which you alledge" was nothing more than an excuse to "bringe these people to bee your subjects against their wills." If local leaders possessed the power to do so, they would have refused such offers and dismissed any talk of a treaty.[34] At the same time, Jourdain insisted that the VOC had no right to use the promise of protection to exclude outside merchants from accessing the spice trade. Amboina was a "countrye free for all men," an essential fact that no treaty could alter.[35] If the threat of Dutch retaliation was removed, local leaders and inhabitants would deal freely with the English.[36]

Similar clashes were repeated whenever the English attempted to push into areas governed by VOC treaties. In response, Dutch officials like Coen came to articulate a series of damning charges against their rivals. They argued, first, that the English were unfair competitors who had taken advantage of the security environment provided by VOC forts and fleets to profit. The fact that the English traded in the Company's area of operations allowed them to shelter beneath the peace imposed by the VOC's vast military expenditures, effectively giving them a free ride. Rather than investing in forts or troops of their own, the English operated under "the favor of our weapons," while the Dutch were forced to waste the hundreds of thousands of guilders necessary to provide security.[37] In this way, VOC officials charged that their competitor was an essentially parasitic organization that prospered only by leaching off their strength.

But it was not simply that the English took unfair advantage of VOC expenditures on defense. Rather, they worked as well to undermine Dutch power in the region. Increasingly, English merchants were painted as sinister agents that provided succor and support to the VOC's enemies while attempting to turn allies and subjects against its rightful authority. In this view, EIC officials were engaged in a vast and sprawling conspiracy designed to target the most vulnerable parts of the Dutch empire. They did this first through a prolonged campaign of "insolence, violence and vileness" (*insolentie, violentie ende vilipendie*).[38] Using deception and lies, EIC officials aimed to disrupt their rival's operations in Asia by undermining the Company's prestige, destroying its credibility, and turning local rulers against it.[39] At every opportunity, they attacked relentlessly, condemning Dutch operations in terms as "scandalously vile and villainous as they could think up."[40] The result was that English slander and lies followed the Dutch wherever they went in Asia.

At the same time, the English struck with unfailing precision at those places where the VOC was most vulnerable. "It's not enough," Coen charged, "that the English incited the war in Banda, but they also stirred up those of Amboyna against us, and helped the Spanish in the Moluccas against us." Daily, he continued, "they do their best to provoke war between us and Bantam with their false techniques and public lies."[41] It was a long list of charges: the EIC aided open enemies like the Spanish, incited revolts among local allies, attempted to provoke conflict with Asian powers, and sought everywhere to subvert Dutch influence. VOC officials were particularly incensed by what they saw as dangerous meddling in places like Amboina or Banda, where English merchants first roused up indigenous partners to revolt and then supplied them with arms when they did. In Amboina in the years prior to the Treaty of Defense, the Company accused the English of inciting Luhu to "civil war" while aiding Kambelo with weapons.[42] The last charge was particularly troubling, as cannons and muskets supplied by the English could be carried up to mountain redoubts and used to rain fire down on VOC vessels, thereby tipping the military balance against the Dutch.[43]

As he looked out across Asia, Coen concluded that there was nowhere that the English were not engaged in disrupting the Company's plans and undercutting its position.[44] At the heart of the charge against the English was the notion, repeated constantly in the sources, that the English were "feigned friends," who pretended friendship while plotting in secret. Aware of every weakness and every opening in the Company's defensive armor, they could target its vulnerabilities with pinpoint precision. While the VOC feared enemy powers like the Portuguese or the Spanish, anything they might do was at least out in the open and could be repulsed by force of arms. By contrast, the English could not be fought directly with weapons, a fact that made them doubly dangerous.

Alongside their broad-based campaign to undercut authority and influence, the English were also, VOC officials charged, the originators of strikingly intimate conspiracies to murder the Dutch within the confines of their ships, lodges, and forts. Again and again, the Company detected evidence of English plots designed "to murder all the Netherlanders" in precisely those spaces that should have provided security in an unsafe world.[45] In 1618, for example, the Dutch discovered a deadly plot orchestrated by the English on Java. The plot came to light after Manuel, another migrant (like Augustine Peres) from Portuguese-controlled territories, was overheard making suspicious comments.[46] After torture, Manuel, who was described as a "black born in Goa, Japanese interpreter," confessed that he had schemed with two accomplices "to run away together and commit some villainy or murder."[47]

Uncertain what to do, the conspirators resolved to seek help from an English merchant, Nicholas Uffelet, who met with them on multiple occasions. Rather than alerting the authorities, Uffelet encouraged Manuel and his accomplices to rise up and slaughter their Dutch masters. In taking such actions, they would, he promised, receive support from the English but should make sure only to strike when the Dutch were at their most vulnerable.[48] In this way, the impetus came in part from Uffelet, who had given direction and shape to a previously formless plot.[49] From the security of the English factory, he had encouraged Manuel to rise up against his masters and had pushed him to carry out a "gruesome act" that would strike directly at the Dutch. His guilt, moreover, seemed clear. When confronted with Manuel's testimony, Uffelet was, VOC officials declared, visibly shaken by the damning description of his conduct.[50] But, as was so often the case, nothing could be done against the Company's "feigned friends," who lay beyond the "compass of [Dutch] justice."[51] Whereas Manuel was condemned to be executed and then dismembered, his head placed on a stake, his body quartered and then hung from a cross as an example to others, Uffelet was allowed to walk free, unrepentant, unpunished, and with space to continue his scheming.[52]

Assessing the veracity of the multiple charges leveled against the English is difficult. Certainly, EIC agents took every opportunity they could to disrupt the treaty regime and to hinder VOC operations in Asia, including spreading rumors and colluding with anti-Dutch forces. But it was also the case that VOC officials assumed patterns and a wider coherence of action that did not exist. For Coen and others like him, every setback, however slight, formed part of a pernicious chain initiated by the English and designed to undercut Dutch plans in Asia. In fact, the English company, which never had enough ships or men, was often far more passive than the Dutch believed, and local actors more independent. Where the EIC did intervene, it was frequently on someone else's initiative. In places like Kambelo or Luhu or Banda, it was local partners who aggressively sought out the English in an effort to find a protector capable of serving as a counterbalance against the Dutch.[53]

What is clear is that such charges bred a corrosive combination of anger and fear that seeped through the Dutch East India Company. The capacity of the English, the internal enemy, to act in secret beneath a veneer of friendship made them more menacing than external foes such as the Portuguese or the Spanish. Writing from an isolated outpost, one VOC official explained simply that the "inner (innerlijcke) enemies causes the Company more hindrance and damage than the external (uijtwendige), which we can protect against with weapons."[54] The feeling was shared by Coen, who declared to his superiors that EIC "insolence, villainy and hindrance" was responsible for more damage to the Company "than the strength of all your enemies."[55] The result was that outrage about the English cascaded through the records, consuming page after page until even Coen himself felt required to apologize: "I am sorry to blot so much paper on the matter of the English."[56] Given this tension, it is not surprising that there were sporadic outbursts of violence as the two sides took up arms against each other. In Banten, for example, a neutral port city that played host to both organizations, frictions erupted into armed clashes in 1617.

War and Peace

In July 1617, the most banal of disputes, a disagreement over the purchase of fish, turned violent. Both sides quickly joined the fray, with predictable consequences.[57] A second incident occurred a few months later when a group of Spanish and Portuguese captives found shelter in the English lodge. The English company's willingness to provide a haven for runaways was a common source of complaint, with VOC officials alleging that their rival's factories operated as sanctuaries for "our criminal and civil offenders, betrayers, conspirators, captured Spanish, Portuguese, soldiers, sailors, blacks and other troublemakers."[58] In this case, the Iberian runaways made the mistake of leaving the shelter of the lodge and they were seen on the street by a VOC merchant, who attempted to capture them. The situation soon escalated, and a large mob of English merchants mixed with local allies and heavily armed with pikes and firearms marched on the VOC warehouses intent on violence. The Dutch merchants based there wisely opted to flee, seeking shelter in the house of one of the Chinese merchants operating in the port city.[59] This left a small group of the VOC's Japanese recruits to defend their employer's goods against a force estimated at some 250 men. They resisted ferociously, causing the mob to retreat but suffering a number of casualties in the process.

Episodes such as these, combined with persistent feuds over trading rights, convinced influential parties within both organizations that only a show of overwhelming force or, more likely, open war would improve the situation. Since the English were already engaged in a campaign aimed at undermining the Dutch Empire in Asia, it would be better, Coen argued, to "announce the war and go to war."[60] War would provide clarity, replacing "feigned friends" with open enemies who could be combated with force. This sense of approaching conflict was matched on the English side by an increasing belief that something had to be done to stop the repeated encroachments on their rights in Asia. Matters came to a head in November 1618, when a large EIC fleet arrived in the harbor at Jayakarta under the command of Martin Pring and Thomas Dale.[61] With the military balance for once tilted in their favor, the English decided to strike first against VOC "Iniuries and Insolencies" by seizing a richly laden vessel, the *Zwarte Leeuw*.[62]

The attack marked the start of a brief phase of open conflict between the two organizations. Although initially limited to Jayakarta, it spread quickly to those ports across Asia where VOC and EIC merchants clustered together. In Japan, for example, EIC officials watched as "these Hollanders haue, by sound of trvmpet, abord all their shipps in the harbor . . . procleamed open wars against our English nation, both by sea & land, w'th fire & sworde."[63] Although Coen was initially forced to retreat with his forces to Amboina, the eruption of war soon worked in favor of the larger company.[64] For years, Dutch officials had protested English incursions. Now at last they were free to deploy their superior military resources to expel these rivals. In the harbor at Kota Ambon, Coen assembled a powerful fleet before returning to Jayakarta, where he ejected the English and razed the town to the ground.[65] The victory gave the Company what it had long sought, a permanent headquarters under its direct control on Java, while strengthening its position across the region by sending, Coen gloated, "a great fright through the whole of the Indies."[66]

But almost as soon as it had started, this phase of open conflict was brought to an end by the intrusion of European politics. If war between the companies simplified things in Asia, it was far less welcome in Europe, where both governments depended on a working alliance against Spain. The outbreak of war in Asia came just as the twelve-year truce between Spain and the United Provinces, which had been signed in 1609, was winding down. Faced with the prospect of renewed war with Spain, the Dutch and English governments pushed for a settlement to halt any further escalation of the conflict in Asia. Beginning in 1619, Dutch representatives traveled to England to negotiate a new agreement that could end the war between the companies.[67] Driving talks behind the scenes were two powerful actors—King James I and Prince Maurits, the *Stadhouder* and commander of the United Provinces' military forces—both of whom prioritized a firm military alliance between the two countries over any differences between the companies.[68]

After six months of negotiations, the Treaty of Defense was signed in June and then ratified in July 1619.[69] It was intended to eliminate the possibility of future conflict between the two companies by binding them together as formal allies committed to sharing the profits of the spice trade. The treaty began by affirming a new beginning, stipulating that "all irregularities, offences and misunderstandings shall be forgotten and buried."[70] War was to be replaced by "assistance, friendship, and reciprocal correspondence" as the two parties were transmuted from enemies into trusted allies. In order to avoid any future disputes, the companies would simply divide up the spice trade, with two thirds going to the VOC and the remaining third swallowed up by its English rival.[71] With the looming deadline of renewed conflict with Spain, the treaty also required the two companies to cooperate by assembling a joint Fleet of Defense comprised of twenty ships split evenly between them, and designed, despite its name, to strike at Iberian possessions and sea routes. As part of the wider agreement, the English agreed as well to contribute to the cost of maintaining the VOC's forts and garrisons spread across the Spice Islands.

The sprawling agreement transformed the two feuding organizations overnight into partners with a shared budget and a joint military establishment. In Europe, the news was generally welcomed, but in Asia, where the first reports of the treaty arrived around March 1620, the response was far more mixed. While some within the English company celebrated the suspension of conflict, many others believed they had been boxed by the king's eagerness to secure an alliance with the United Provinces. Although the EIC had at last gained a share of the spice trade, it was also required to contribute an unspecified sum to the VOC's bloated military establishment in Asia.

In Batavia, the news of the treaty was greeted by many with frustration.[72] The most vociferous reaction came predictably from Coen, who recorded his shock at hearing the news.[73] While he acknowledged the realities of European politics—"we are aware of how much the state of the United Provinces depends on the good friendship, correspondence and honor of the crown of England"—he did not believe they justified such a one-sided agreement that was concluded just as the VOC was poised to expel the English from the spice trade.[74] Their great rival had been let back in, he protested, at the precise moment that the Dutch seemed capable of excluding them from the region once and for all. Why should the English be allowed a fixed share of the spice trade, something VOC officials had been arguing for decades that their rivals had no claim to? Outraged, Coen declared that "I cannot understand why the English should be allowed one third of all the cloves, nutmeg and mace. They cannot pretend to one grain of sand . . . of the Moluccas, Amboyna or Banda."[75]

In addition to deriding its strategic logic, Coen was convinced that the Treaty of Defense was fundamentally unworkable. For him, the English nation was simply "incompatible. They do as much wrong to us as they can and they are always first to complain. The jealousy, the distrust, the ill favor . . . shall not be taken away by rules, accords and orders."[76] Back in Europe, the Heeren 17, caught in a difficult position between the complaints of their subordinates and the priorities of their government, urged patience and friendship. Instructing the governor-general to curb his reckless statements, they reached for a bizarre marital analogy, suggesting that the EIC was like a difficult spouse who must be won over with time and patience.[77]

Despite all of Coen's protests, the treaty took immediate effect, pushing the two companies into a tense embrace.[78] For its drafters, the treaty was designed to give both sides what they wanted, removing longstanding points of contention and laying the basis for cooperation. Instead it inflamed the situation, reanimating and giving new urgency to the old charge, buried since the commencement of open hostilities, that the English were "feigned friends" who pretended alliance while working in secret to undercut the Dutch. If anything, the dangers seemed even greater now, as the treaty gave the English access to territories like Banda or Amboina that had been previously closed to them. Under cover of their new status as allies, the English were free, Dutch officials believed, to go wherever they wanted, spreading poison, undermining alliances, and inciting rebellion. One VOC merchant explained that the "English seeing that they can no longer harm us with weapons, have put their tongues to work" in a way guaranteed to damage Dutch interests.[79] In this way, the Treaty of Defense had inserted a "serpent" close to the Company's heart, one whose "hard bite" could prove fatal this time.[80]

In Amboina, the Treaty of Defense opened up a new space for English operations. On February 27, 1621, an EIC veteran, George Muschamp, arrived in the bustling port of Kota Ambon to take up his position as chief merchant of the newly established English outpost there.[81] His appearance marked a dramatic turnaround for the colony. Just a year earlier, the governor had been ready to defend Kota Ambon against a potential assault from an EIC fleet. Now he was required to open the port city to his former enemies and to share the profits of the spice trade.[82]

Opening Amboina

On February 23, 1621, as Muschamp was nearing Amboina, Coen penned a remarkable letter addressed to the governors of Banda, Amboina, and the Moluccas, the key territories for the spice trade. Entitled "The Particular Advice and Orders of General Coen," the document set the tone for the implementation of the Treaty of Defense in Asia.[83] The governor-general began by acknowledging the absolute need to obey the treaty's clauses by maintaining "good friendship, correspondence and unity" with the English while ensuring they received one third of all the cloves, nutmeg and mace. In this way, Coen was insistent that the treaty must be obeyed and there could be no attempt by his subordinates at deliberate sabotage of its provisions. His message was tempered, however, by a set of ominous warnings.

For Coen, there could be no question that the English would use their new position to plot against the Dutch. Armed with deception and lies, they would attempt, as they had done in the past, to "usurp our authority, make a fortification, gain followers, cause separation among the subjects or limit the Company's justice."[84] It was a long list filled with perils. The Company's new allies would, the governor-general argued, use the cover supplied by the treaty to construct a "fortification within our limits"—that is, within the boundaries of established colonies—from which they could defy VOC orders. To stop this from happening, the governors of these territories must, he insisted, prohibit the English from transporting cannons or other heavy weapons onto land, where they might be used to convert innocuous structures into strongholds. In addition to erecting physical fortifications, English merchants would seek to create new followers, their own "creatures" (*creatueren*) within Dutch forts and settlements, raising up a fifth column that could be relied upon to support EIC interests. In order to prevent this from happening, Van Speult and his fellow governors must make sure that their subjects and allies were not misled by English promises. Even seemingly innocent acts could be used as a conduit to spread influence, and the English must not, Coen insisted, be permitted to "baptize or marry any of our subjects, natives of these lands, free people or whoever it may be, their children or slaves." It was a reminder that the English would work through the groups most vulnerable to their influence, including Asian employees, subjects, or slaves.

Such letters from the Company's chief official in Asia sketched out the ways in which the English could use subterfuge and trickery to hollow out the Dutch presence in Asia. On the surface, however, Anglo-Dutch relations at Amboina seemed warm. With no home of their own, the small group of English merchants who arrived with Muschamp had no choice but to live on top of the Dutch. On July 17, 1621, Van Speult recorded that Muschamp and his countrymen would either be housed directly in Castle Victoria or allowed to lease space in VOC outposts scattered across Amboina.[85] It meant that the two sides crowded together, sharing a roof, food, and, in the more isolated outposts, even the same bed. Muschamp, the new chief merchant, had his own reasons to distrust the Dutch. His right leg had been shot off by a cannon in naval battle with the VOC in 1617, but, encouraged by Van Speult's welcome, he seems to have warmed to the governor.[86] Relations improved still further when his successor, Gabriel Towerson, reached Amboina in September 1622.

Aged forty-nine when he landed in Kota Ambon, Towerson's career was bound up with the steady expansion of English trading horizons in this period. His father had led three voyages to West Africa in the sixteenth century, while his brother, William Towerson, had served as a director of the East India Company before standing for the position of deputy governor. Gabriel Towerson's own career maps smoothly onto the early development of the organization. He had sailed aboard the EIC's first voyage to Asia before opting to stay on at Banten as the head of the factory from 1605 to 1608.[87] There he had, as referenced earlier, prosecuted his own brutal and improvised trial characterized by a rush to torture.[88] The primary suspect, a Chinese goldsmith called Hinting, was terribly burnt with "sharpe hotte Iron" over a long interrogation before he was shot "almost all to peeces" as punishment for what was in fact little more than a failed act of theft.[89] In 1617, less than a decade later, Towerson reappeared in India, where he encountered Thomas Roe, the famous ambassador sent from London to negotiate with the Mughal emperor, who complained that Towerson had "arrived with many servants, a trumpet, and more show than I use."[90] By 1620, he was back in Asia, where two years later he received instructions to take over responsibility for the English factory in Amboina.

Muschamp departed Amboina in September 1622, transferring authority to Towerson.[91] Unlike his predecessor, who had been wounded in an earlier clash, the new chief merchant had missed some of the worst conflicts with the Dutch and he seems to have quickly struck up a close relationship with Van Speult. They were together frequently at meals, ceremonies, and a range of celebrations, including the baptism and christening of children born to VOC officials and local women.[92] Such encounters seemed to convince the chief merchant that he had found in Van Speult a sympathetic collaborator who would support the English presence in Amboina.[93] In his last letter to his superiors before the outbreak of the trial, Towerson lavished extravagant praise on Van Speult, lauding his conduct, "extraordinary curtisie," and generosity toward the English.[94] The governor belongs, Towerson declared, in "the first ranke of all the Dutch that I have bin acquainted with for an honest and uppright man."[95] Such generous comments generated a predictable response from Towerson's superiors in Banten, who cautioned him to be wary of Van Speult's "desembling friendship."[96]

While Towerson's letters painted a rosy picture of former enemies transmuted by the Treaty of Defense into new friends, Van Speult's correspondence looks very different. A stream of letters coming in from Batavia reinforced and amplified Coen's earlier warnings. On March 15, 1621, in a letter dated just a few weeks after his advice to the three governors, Coen explained that "you are recommended not to trust the English more than the certainty of the forts and our wellbeing allows. Their tongues shall be allowed no more freedom than the others and will be punished as mutiny if they disturb the general peace and well-being."[97] On November 23, 1621, he instructed Van Speult to watch closely for English "creeping" (*cruypen*) that threatened to undercut the Company's control over Amboina.[98] And on October 28, 1622, just a few months before Shichizō was discovered on the walls of the castle, Coen was insistent that the English, along with hostile local powers, sought the downfall of the Dutch.[99] If they used violence, Van Speult must, Coen insisted, be ready to fight fire with fire, authorizing any measures necessary to preserve the Company's hold over the territory.

Such letters raised fears about future plots. Others functioned to circulate news about terrifying conspiracies, invariably involving English merchants lurking somewhere in the shadows, that had been uncovered in nearby parts of the VOC empire. In September 1622, for example, Van

Speult received word of another chilling conspiracy that had supposedly been discovered in Banda just a month earlier. It had been detected by Van Speult's fellow governor, Martinus Sonck, among a few hundred Bandanese survivors of the invasion living beneath the walls of the VOC fort there.[100] Subsequent events followed a predictable pattern, with the use of torture leading to the confession of a sprawling conspiracy involving multiple external parties. According to their confessions, the Bandanese had plotted with the Company's enemies on Seram, who were planning to dispatch a large fleet filled with warriors in order to murder as many of the Dutch as possible.[101] Hiding in the background were of course English merchants who, VOC officials presumed, "had knowledge of the aforesaid conspiracy" and had lent their support.[102] Although the conspiracy had been averted just in time, it was an ominous warning. If such plots could form in Banda, which had been conquered by the Company, its population decimated or resettled beneath the walls of a fort, they were surely hidden beneath the surface in Amboina, where the VOC faced far more dangerous rivals.

Such letters describing plots and conspiracies discovered in other territories served to create a continually reinforcing fear loop for officials like Van Speult. The Dutch East India Company was an organization that relied upon and was sustained by correspondence. Its scattered forts, factories, and outposts were held together by a steady stream of letters with each missive constantly referencing and reinforcing the last. But the same correspondence that acted to circulate information about prices and trading patterns so efficiently also served to spread fear. Opening each new letter in Castle Victoria, the governor seemed to find more evidence of murderous plots that had been uncovered at the last minute, just as they were about to be set into bloody motion. The result was to create a world brimming with inevitable peril.

In his own letters written in the years leading up to the Amboina trial, Van Speult returned repeatedly to the treacherous nature of the English. In 1621, even as he welcomed Muschamp, he wondered at the "faithless and false dealings of the English that is a truly scandalous matter."[103] As he scoured the landscapes for signs of an inevitable plot, the governor assured his superiors that he would act immediately to shut down any such conspiracy, writing: "We will here following Your Honor's command (with God's help) take steps to make sure the English do not take advantage of us. If we discover anything untowards, we will punish according to its merit."[104] In another letter written in June 1622, he was clear that he would take whatever action was needed to make sure that the "the sovereignty [of the Company] is not reduced or harmed" by an EIC conspiracy.[105] The result was that by early 1623 Van Speult was in a state of expectation, convinced that a plot must inevitably emerge from the small group of English merchants clustered in Kota Ambon. It was only a matter of time before the English snake, forced by a misguided treaty within the walls of Castle Victoria, gave into its nature. And, primed by warnings from his superior, the governor would be ready to act, hacking off the head of the serpent before it could strike.

CHAPTER V

The Trial

Protect us from such perfidious assaults.

—HERMAN VAN SPEULT, JUNE 5, 1623

B y February 1623, the garrison in Kota Ambon was in state of high alert. VOC merchants in Manipa and across the Hoamoal Peninsula had been forced to flee from a string of attacks, only narrowly escaping with their lives, and had watched as the outposts that had sheltered them were razed to the ground. They had arrived in Kota Ambon carrying news of mutilated bodies and murderous ambushes. Rumors of more to come flashed through the town, morphing and growing as they spread from person to person.[1] The fear of an attack from the outside combined with a terrible suspicion of other dangers hidden within the settlement itself. Everywhere it seemed as if the Company's hold over Amboina was under threat. Barraged by letters warning him to aggressively root out the inevitable conspiracy and watching nervously as the boundaries of VOC influence appeared to be contracting before his eyes, the governor waited for the next sign of peril.

It came in the form of a report delivered at dawn on February 23 by the lieutenant of the guard, Carel Huel.[2] The previous night Shichizō, a soldier from Japan, had been observed walking the battlements of Castle Victoria, stopping to ask questions of the youngest and most inexperienced soldiers he could find about the defenses of the castle and how often the guard was changed. Huel's report sparked an immediate and fevered response. Shichizō should not even have been there in the first place. Japanese soldiers were barred by the governor's own orders from serving on the walls of the castle. And Shichizō's line of questioning, at least as it was reported back, seemed too insistent and too precisely targeted to be innocent. For the governor, everything seemed suddenly to lock into place as the rising suspicions and fears of the past months coalesced into a terrible certainty: here was the conspiracy he had been expecting for so long.

In the rough barracks where the Japanese contingent was housed, Shichizō was sleeping, unaware of the discussion going on above him.[3] He awoke when armed soldiers burst into the room. They seized him roughly, hauling him half-dressed before Van Speult and the members of the council.[4] The interrogation commenced immediately. Why had he been asking such questions? What was he trying to find out? And always in the background: who was he really working for? When he denied everything, Van Speult summoned the watchmen, who confirmed that Shichizō had questioned them during sermon times, when there were fewer witnesses present.[5] Why, the governor pressed on, had he asked such questions at such a time to these soldiers? Struggling to respond, the young soldier explained that he had asked these questions for his own "amusement and pleasure" (*uyt vermeyen en om plaisier gedaen*).[6]

There was no shortage of better, more calculated answers that Shichizō might have given. He could have insisted that, like his superiors, he was worried about a possible attack, that he wanted to make sure the castle was properly secured against a sudden assault, that he was simply doing his duty as a loyal soldier of the Company. But given the heightened atmosphere of suspicion, it is not clear if any of these would have served to slow the rapid escalation of events. If Shichizō refused to reveal his true motivation, Van Speult decided that he must be brought immediately "to torture" (*ter torture dede brengen*) until he confessed. The young soldier was tied roughly to a door frame and, with a gesture, the "torture of water" commenced.

Torture was a familiar part of the early modern world, an integral and largely uncontroversial component of judicial procedure. But unlike other state-sanctioned torture techniques from the period, such as the rack or the thumbscrew, which have largely faded from use and view, we know a great deal about the physical experience of the "torture of water." This is because of the extended controversies that played out during the Bush administration over the use of so-called enhanced interrogation techniques, which generated a vast pool of information documenting their effects. While there is a danger of injecting modern sensibilities into a seventeenth-century world in which brutal violence was far more common, these descriptions are nonetheless valuable as they convey something about the actual experience of waterboarding.

Comparing VOC descriptions of what happened in Castle Victoria with contemporary accounts of waterboarding reveals an almost word-for-word match between the methods used close to four centuries apart. For defenders of waterboarding, either officials within the Dutch East India Company or their modern counterparts in the Bush administration, it was a terror grounded in perception rather than concrete reality. The flow of water into the victim's mouth created the sensation of drowning, a false panic that dissipated as soon as the interrogation ceased. As one of the Amboina judges explained, "so long as the water is poured over the

Figure 5.1 Imagined illustration of waterboarding at Amboina in 1623. Anonymous, 1673. From W. Stubbe, *A Further Justification of the Present War Against the United Netherlands* (London, 1673). Courtesy of the Rijksmuseum, Amsterdam. RP-P-OB-68.279.

face, it causes a great oppression [of breath] in the patient but as soon as the pouring of water stops all the pain and torment ceases, leaving no trace or sign of any harm, and restoring the person to their previous state and disposition."[7]

Anyone who has experienced the technique even for a few seconds describes it very differently: "[you] feel that you are drowning," one journalist briefly subjected to the method explained, "because you are drowning—or, rather, being drowned, albeit slowly and under controlled conditions and at the mercy (or otherwise) of those who are applying the pressure."[8] It is not, in other words, simply the sensation of drowning. Rather, interrogation via waterboarding was a "series of near drownings" that had a catastrophic effect on the human body, resulting in spasms that resembled protracted convulsions.[9] The traumatic nature of the experience means that the average subject's endurance is measured in seconds rather than minutes. CIA officers subjected to the technique lasted on average just fourteen seconds, while interrogators at Guantanamo and other sites were set a maximum length of forty seconds per waterboarding session, a limit that was only rarely met.[10] Shichizō seems to have endured the torture for much longer. In a confidential letter to Pieter de Carpentier, who had replaced Coen as governor-general, Van Speult explained that the young soldier had "resisted for quite long" (vry wat wederhielt) as huge pots, each containing sixteen quarts of water, were carried to the interrogation chamber.[11]

Some picture of the scene can be formed from a modern document that breaks down a single cycle of torture and interrogation into its constituent parts. Each round of the "watering cycle" escalated through four stages. First, "demands for information [were] interspersed with the application of the water just short of blocking his airway," then an increase in the amount of water "until it blocked his airway and the subject started to have involuntary spasms," then a pause to clear the victim's airways before a return to further demands for details.[12] In this way, the key questioning phase came as the body was shaking and spasming, attempting to suck in oxygen.

In Shichizō's case, the situation was rendered still more difficult by the unfamiliar language in which he was questioned. In the trial record prepared by the advocate-fiscal, the young recruit's exchange with his interrogators is presented as a straightforward exchange in Dutch. But, like the bulk of the Japanese contingent, Shichizō did not actually speak Dutch, nor did any VOC official in Castle Victoria speak Japanese. Deciphering what language he was interrogated in proves surprisingly difficult because, in one of its many omissions, the trial record makes no mention of language. Instead we have to rely on the depositions produced in the years after the trial, which reveal that the interrogation took place in a third language, Malay.[13] For the VOC and its Asian servants, Malay acted as a vital lingua franca that was used in the Company's garrisons, ships, and trading outposts across Southeast Asia. It did not, however, have the same currency in East Asia, where it was rarely spoken even in cosmopolitan port cities like Nagasaki or Hirado, where the Company did its recruitment. Because of this, most Japanese recruits in VOC service would have had little familiarity with the language. It was for this reason that the Company employed Japanese interpreters (*Jappanse tolck*) like Manuel of Goa, who had been implicated in an earlier conspiracy trial.[14] Shichizō could probably speak some Malay, for this was the language of daily interactions in a place like Kota Ambon, but there is no sign that he was either proficient or even particularly competent in the language. This added a nightmarish quality to the interrogation as the young soldier, gasping for air, struggled to find answers in an alien language.

At some point as the day wore on, he did confess. In the same letter to De Carpentier, the governor explained that Shichizō declared under torture that the Japanese intended to make themselves masters of the castle.[15] It was a clear answer. The Japanese had been plotting to seize Castle Victoria, to rise up against their superiors, and take possession of the fortification for their own ends. But it was not what Van Speult was looking for. In his account of the interrogation, the governor explained that the Japanese were "not powerful enough" to carry out such a plot.[16] They could not, therefore, be acting alone. And Van Speult was sure that the Company's "feigned friends," the subject of warning after warning from Batavia, were somewhere in the shadows. Only the English had the necessary combination of motivation to eject the VOC from Amboina, access to the Company's Japanese troops, and the resources to carry out a conspiracy against the Dutch. At last, under the relentless burden of interrogation, the young soldier made the necessary jump to the English. It was a pattern that would repeat again and again over the course of subsequent days, as prompting from VOC interrogators convinced there were more parties waiting in the shadows functioned to stitch new conspirators onto a plot that grew ever outwards.

Shichizō confessed that he been approached by Sidney Miguel, another Japanese soldier, who had once worked for the English in an unnamed capacity. Miguel had asked him "whether he and the other Japanese would deliver the castle to the English." Willing to betray his masters, he had answered that he would, if he received "good payment." Shichizō named two English employees including Abel Price, a barber/medic, who had supposedly met secretly with the Japanese to plot the assault. Price, a volatile drunk who had been punished repeatedly by Towerson, seemed the one member of the EIC factory least likely to be entrusted to such a role, but his proclivity for public gambling and drinking meant that he was also widely known around the castle.[17] The conspiracy itself would be set into motion when an English ship arrived in Kota Ambon's harbor, at which time two Japanese soldiers would seize control of each of the four bulwarks of the castle, while the rest would wait in the central hall to capture Van Speult. Anyone who resisted would be killed, cut down with the long swords that each of the Japanese soldiers carried.[18]

Although he had been pushing relentlessly for it, the confession, when it finally came, seems to have stunned the governor, who was, he wrote later, "exceedingly astonished" (*boven maeten verwondert*).[19] Understanding the nature of Van Speult's reaction to the discovery and his subsequent conduct helps explain why this most controversial of cases was handled so badly. The governor was, both sides agreed, the exemplary Company man. Highly competent and hugely experienced, he was repeatedly singled out by Coen, the hardest of all possible taskmasters, for praise. Although he had never dealt with a conspiracy case on this scale before, Van Speult, who had sat as the foremost authority in Amboina for years, was no stranger to legal proceedings. Why then did he preside over a ramshackle case that violated some of the most basic rules of VOC justice and that seemed as if deliberately designed to provoke controversy?

The most persuasive answer lies in the governor's reaction to Shichizō's confession, which confirmed all of his most terrible fears. For months, Van Speult had been struggling with rapidly mounting tensions across Amboina. From Castle Victoria, he had watched as the Company's hold over the already volatile province seemed to be unraveling before his eyes. Now, in an instance, the terrifying plot he had feared for so long flashed into view. Crucially, it was aimed not only at the ruin of the Dutch presence in Amboina but also far more directly at his person. His own soldiers, armed and equipped by the Company, would lie in wait within the walls of Castle Victoria to seize him. If he surrendered without a fight, he would be imprisoned in the cells beneath the castle; if he resisted, he would be killed.

In his letters to his superiors recounting what had happened, Van Speult largely skipped over his response to the discovery.[20] Instead, the most detailed description was provided by an unlikely witness, George Forbes, a Scottish steward who had served the governor during the trial, before turning up in Britain in 1627.[21] Forbes's account suggests that the discovery of the plot triggered something close to a psychological breakdown in Van Speult. According to his description, the governor retreated from the case. When his subordinates came to him for instructions, he "gave them no answer, but in a fury did send them away discontented."[22] This withdrawal was prompted in part by the onset of physical symptoms, with Van Speult experiencing, Forbes explained, "such an extreme pain in his head that he was almost frantic, and was not able to lie upon any bed." If accurate, and there was no obvious reason for the steward to fabricate the episode, such descriptions suggest that the discovery of the plot plunged Van Speult into a state of shock, triggering physical symptoms and an extended attack of panic.[23] Either way, it is clear that the governor ceded effective control of the case, transferring authority to Isaaq de Bruyn, the chief legal officer, or advocate-fiscal, who assumed total charge of the next stage of the proceedings.[24]

In accounts of what happened in Kota Ambon in 1623, especially those attacking the conduct of the Dutch, Van Speult typically appears as the central figure directing matters from the first investigation through to the bloody end in front of Castle Victoria. In fact, although he initiated and oversaw the first interrogation, the governor largely retreated from the stage for a crucial period in the middle of the proceedings, retaking control only in the closing days in a failed attempt to limit the political repercussions that he recognized would flow inevitably from a mass execution of English merchants. Far more than Van Speult, therefore, it was De Bruyn who shaped the course of the Amboina trial. Despite his central role, there has been surprisingly little discussion of the advocate-fiscal's background and the particular training and skills he brought to the case.[25] Looking more closely at De Bruyn, however, helps explain the chaotic nature of the case, for he was, by any assessment, utterly unequipped to manage a trial of this kind.

It is difficult to imagine a VOC employee more different from the governor than De Bruyn. While Van Speult had a long experience of Asia and
Amboina, the advocate-fiscal had arrived less than a year earlier; while Van
Speult had risen through the ranks of the organization, succeeding at all
the roles he had been given, De Bruyn had failed at everything he had tried.
And while Van Speult was ruthlessly competent, the advocate-fiscal was,
as his own superiors later acknowledged, a fraud whose claims vastly out-
matched his abilities.

"Passed Himself Off as a Jurist"

Isaaq de Bruyn was a man on the move, part of a new generation of VOC
employees that reflected the organization's rapid transition from a commercial interloper into an Asian power with colonies and trading outposts
scattered across the region. After the establishment of Batavia in 1619, the
Company's hierarchy had made an attempt to move away from the rough
merchant adventurers who had driven the first push into Asia in favor of a
new cadre of highly educated men with the proper background and training to administer an emerging empire. This experiment was made possible by a supply of candidates increasingly willing to undertake the long
and perilous sea voyage to Asia, where they believed they would be able to
translate their education and talents into riches. Some of these new recruits
proved highly competent but, as the Company would learn to its cost, an
education in Europe did not automatically translate into success in Asia,
and its attempt to shoehorn well-credentialed novices into high-ranking
positions sometimes ended in disaster.[26]

One example of how badly the Company's experiment could go wrong
is evident in the career of Pieter Nuyts, who arrived in Batavia after a
number of years at Leiden University. Although he had no experience of
Asia, Nuyts was promoted immediately to the elevated position of coun-
cilor of the Indies and assigned two senior roles: ambassador to Japan and
governor of the VOC's new colony on Taiwan. Arriving in Japan in 1627,
he managed to offend everyone, including his fellow Dutch merchants,
local officials, and high-ranking Tokugawa officials in Edo, who refused
to have anything to do with him. His second posting as governor of Taiwan proved equally disastrous, resulting in a full-blown regional crisis when
he attempted to arrest a pair of Japanese merchant vessels. Faced with a

deteriorating situation in Taiwan and Japan, the Company gradually came to realize just how poorly its new recruit had performed. So incensed were VOC officials that they ordered Nuyts detained in Batavia Castle. He remained there for a number of years before, in an unprecedented step for the organization, he was extradited to Japan in an attempt to persuade the Tokugawa regime to reopen relations with the Company.[27] The experience with such "tart and overrated sowers of confusion" persuaded some within the Company that they would do better to stick with humbler recruits.[28] Exasperated with the conduct of men like Nuyts, one governor-general concluded that such learned experts were not needed. Instead, the Company would be better served by "experienced merchants with alert mind and vigilance."[29]

Years before Nuyts's career came to a crashing end in a cell in Batavia, Isaaq de Bruyn arrived in that city to an enthusiastic welcome. Like Nuyts, De Bruyn had also passed through the gates of Leiden University, but in contrast with the ambassador to Japan, who could at least boast of a distinguished university career as a teenage protégé, De Bruyn's tenure had been marked only by failure.[30] Born in Middelburg in 1591 or 1592, De Bruyn was written in as a student at Leiden University in March 1612, at the age of twenty. By late 1613, however, he had abandoned his academic training and was back in Middelburg, where he married Johanna Junius in late 1613. The daughter of Francois Le Jon, better known as Franciscus Junius, De Bruyn's new wife belonged to a prominent academic family, and the marriage brought him a raft of connections. The marriage did not, however, signal an improvement in his fortunes, and he continued to jump sporadically between careers. In 1615, De Bruyn attempted to study theology in Saumur in France but a year later he was back in Middelburg, where he had reinvented himself as a businessman with a weaving mill. By 1617 this venture had proved too difficult, and he announced his intention to return to studying. Predictably, this worked out no better. In desperation and perhaps encouraged by his family, De Bruyn resolved to remake himself as a Dutch East India Company employee. He entered the organization's service in 1621, eager for a new beginning in Asia.

Arriving in Batavia gave De Bruyn a chance to slough off these disappointments and reinvent himself as a man of substance.[31] His sprinkling of learning would be enough, he was convinced, to secure a high rank and the success that had eluded him so far. Landing in the Company's bustling new headquarters, De Bruyn presented himself as a "doctor and jurist" (*doctor ende rechtsgeleerde*), capable of taking on a senior position in the organization's expanding legal bureaucracy. As with Nuyts, De Bruyn was quickly marked for greater things.[32] His appearance in Amboina was, however, entirely an accident. After landing in Batavia, De Bruyn had requested a transfer to the post of bailiff in the Moluccas, which would become, he hoped, the first step in a rapid ascent through the VOC hierarchy. On his way to take up his new assignment, the vessel he was travelling on, the *Eendracht*, was shipwrecked near Kota Ambon, on May 13, 1622.[33] Of the roughly 120 crew and passengers, only around 40 made it to shore. The remainder were killed by the pounding sea and the debris of the shattered vessel. De Bruyn was one of the lucky ones, although he was sufficiently injured in the wreck to require an extended period of recuperation.[34]

Although he had arrived in Kota Ambon by accident, De Bruyn clearly decided to make the best of things. Determined to make up for lost time, he quickly made an impression on the governor. For all his experience and obvious competence, Van Speult lacked De Bruyn's apparent credentials, and, like his superiors, he was quickly seduced by the new arrival's veneer of learning. Eager to secure De Bruyn's services, the governor wrote to Batavia, begging for him to be reassigned to Amboina. "It is very necessary," he explained, "that I have such person with me to assist, as the matters to attend to always increase every year and there is no-one qualified if I'm absent that I can rely on."[35] When permission arrived, De Bruyn was appointed as advocate-fiscal, a position sometimes described as roughly equivalent to a public prosecutor.[36]

On February 23, as the governor retreated, De Bruyn seized control of the proceedings, wielding, his superiors in Batavia concluded, the "prestige of [his] title" like a weapon to silence any possible objections.[37] In this, De Bruyn was aided by the unwillingness of anyone else on the council to challenge him. This included Laurens de Maerschalk, a VOC *opperkoopman* or upper merchant who was described as the "second man of the Councell of Amboyna."[38] That VOC officials like De Maerschalk, who later came to regret the decision, were content to step aside stemmed in part from De Bruyn's supposed qualifications but also from the fevered environment within the castle. The uncovering of one corner of the conspiracy had not brought relief with it. Rather, the discovery of a plot aimed directly at Kota Ambon had served only to heighten tensions. Until the plotters were all rooted out, they might, in a desperate attempt to carry out their designs, attack at any point. This combination of factors allowed De Bruyn to claim absolute authority to hunt down the rest of the conspirators.

The problem was that his ambitions far exceeded his actual capacities. While he could put on a good show, the advocate-fiscal was wholly unprepared for the case he now took charge of. Given his stuttering career, De Bruyn had accumulated only the thinnest patina of legal knowledge. Equally important, he had no experience of running large-scale trials and no apparent understanding of the standard protocols used by his counterparts in Batavia and elsewhere. This uncomfortable fact was recognized by his own superiors, who were appalled at the level of legal ineptitude displayed by their subordinate. Incensed by how badly he had botched things, they condemned him as a fraud who had simply "passed himself off as a jurist" [*voor een rechtsgeleerd uitgeeft*].[39] The result was to inject a lethal combination of ambition and incompetence into an already volatile case.

The bedrock of the case at Amboina, but also the clearest evidence of De Bruyn's incapacity to manage a trial of this kind, is the legal record "The Confessions and Sentences of Mr Towerson and his accomplices for the murderous conspiracy at Castle Amboyna" (*Confessien ende Sententien van Mr. Touwerson ende Complicen over de Moordadige Conspiratie op t' Casteel Amboyna*) that De Bruyn personally prepared.[40] When he came to assess the trial, the governor-general concluded that the governing council at Amboina with Van Speult at its head had ceded total control, leaving "him [De Bruyn] to make the draft of the documents and none of them has dared to add anything to it of their own, but all have fully trusted the title of advocate."[41] Sixty-three manuscript pages in length, *The Confessions and Sentences* includes a brief preamble, the signed confessions of all the alleged conspirators, the charge, and the final verdict. At first glance, the document looks reassuringly substantial. It consists of more than twenty confessions, each signed by an alleged plotter and witnessed by the fourteen Amboina judges—merchants, military officers, and other VOC employees pressed into service to rule on the charges. Scratching just below the surface, however, reveals a document riddled with inconsistencies, gaps, and outright errors.[42]

Frequently lacking qualified personnel, and with a legal system still in the process of forming, the Dutch East India Company administered justice in a rough, brutal, and often irregular way.[43] In assessing De Bruyn's work, therefore, we cannot rely on the outraged proclamations made by English pamphleteers in the aftermath of the case, as they sought to attack what had happened, or any sort of textbook standard of Dutch justice in this period. Rather, the most reliable and revealing appraisal came from De Bruyn's own superiors in Batavia in confidential letters intended for internal VOC consumption. Here, they condemned the advocate-fiscal's work for not following the "appropriate style of justice."[44] Without a "deeper investigation into the important circumstances" of the case, it lacked, they asserted, the "proper vigor and strength."[45]

The problem was, first, that *The Confessions and Sentences* lacked some basic components. Although there were exceptions, VOC trial documents, especially those generated by more high-profile cases, typically included a series of questions drawn up by the *fiscaal*, with the accused's answers written next to them.[46] These provided what were in effect cross-examinations that were designed to produce an admission of guilt. In the case of *The Confessions and Sentences*, these are simply missing. Instead, De Bruyn provided a brief summary of each confession, some a few paragraphs, others just two or three lines, indicating that the accused knew of and agreed to participate in the plot. The absence of a more detailed record was criticized by De Bruyn's superiors, who lamented the advocate-fiscal's failure to include the correct "matters of criminal process"—that is, "cross-examinations" (*Iterative Examinatien*) and "interrogations."[47] The problem was compounded by the fact that many of the short confessions presented by De Bruyn were filled with a range of basic discrepancies that a more complete accounting might have provided some way to resolve. A number of the accused directly contradicted each other on the most fundamental points of the case, some explaining, for example, that the plot would be put into motion when the governor was present, others insisting it would be initiated only when he was absent.

In his assessment of the case, the governor-general pointed as well to a second missing component also standard in Dutch judicial records from this period. These were the confrontations (*confrontatien*), in which those witnesses who had already admitted involvement were brought before the other accused in order to prompt a spontaneous confession without the use of torture.[48] *The Confessions and Sentences*, however, includes no mention of these, and there is no indication anywhere in the record that such confrontations actually took place. At the same time, there are strange holes in the document, with some individuals confessing their involvement but then disappearing entirely from the record, leaving no indication as to whether they were executed or spared.[49] Such lapses are striking enough, but even what little information is included is often deeply misleading. This is the case with the list of fourteen Amboina judges who supposedly witnessed and signed off on each confession. On closer inspection, some of the judges whose names appear were not actually present in Kota Ambon when the interrogations took place.[50] Jan Jacobsen Wyncoop, for example, declared in a later deposition that he had arrived in the port town only three days before the execution and had thus missed all the interrogations, even though his name appears beneath each of them.[51]

Viewing the record as a whole, De Bruyn's superiors were forced to conclude that the advocate-fiscal had failed to produce something that would stand up to sustained scrutiny.[52] While such omissions and errors undercut the proceedings, the case orchestrated by De Bruyn also violated some of the most rudimentary conventions related to the use of torture. As across much of continental Europe, Dutch legal practice endorsed the use of torture but erected certain limited safeguards around it. These were derived in part from the 1570 Criminal Ordinance, which, although not officially in force, was widely followed in the United Provinces.[53] First, torture generally required additional pieces of evidence—what is sometimes known as half-proof—before it could be used. As the term suggests, half-proof was a level of evidence that existed between a general suspicion and full verifiable proof, which generally meant the testimony of two eyewitnesses. John Langbein, who has written an important study on the law of torture, gives the example of a subject caught running away from the house of his victim with the bloody dagger and stolen goods.[54] In such cases, torture could be authorized because, to quote the 1570 code, "the thing is so clear, and the proof so apparent, that nothing seems to be wanting but the confession of the prisoner to convict him without doubt."[55]

In 1623, however, there was a conspicuous lack of any corroborating evidence beyond the initial reports of Shichizō's questions to the guards. Defenders of the Amboina trial argue, quite rightly, that such standards were not always observed even in Europe itself, let alone in isolated outposts in Asia.[56] In the Dutch Republic, the standard judicial instrument, the so-called extraordinary process, created an expedited legal procedure that made it far easier to use torture to force a confession.[57] For this reason, critics like Bavius Voorda (1729–1799) characterized the extraordinary criminal trial as something closer to a "deformed monster . . . than a well-arranged judicial procedure."[58] Even supporters of the system acknowledged that the extraordinary process meant that torture was too readily used either when there was too little evidence or too much, that is, in situations in which a coerced confession was not required.[59] But while the bar was often set low, this was in the context of domestic Dutch justice, where there was little possibility of prolonged controversy involving external powers. By its nature, the Amboina case, which involved the torture of a large number of English merchants, who stood outside the traditional parameters of the VOC legal system, was different. It was for this reason that De Bruyn's superiors were adamant that "the rigor of justice might have been tempered a little with Netherlands [Dutch] clemency (for such a neighboring nation)."[60]

Setting aside the question of half-proof, De Bruyn made no effort to follow the most rudimentary of protocols around the use of torture. Dutch legal practice required a *fiscaal* to note in a trial record when torture was being used and to clearly differentiate between statements that were extracted via the use of torture and those that were freely given. *The Confessions and Sentences* did none of this. Because of this, the governor-general complained, it was impossible to know whether the accused "made their confessions before or after torture."[61] In fact, for a trial built almost entirely around the use of torture, *The Confessions and Sentences* was strikingly silent on the question of torture, making only two references to its use in more than sixty manuscript pages. It created a significant gap in the record that enabled English propagandists to make sensational allegations about the use of even more brutal interrogation techniques.

The 1570 criminal code insisted as well that any confessions extracted via torture had to be confirmed by the accused at least twenty-four hours after the initial confession, at a moment when they were unbound and not being tortured.[62] The provision was designed to provide some guarantee against an overreliance on torture, but in reality it imposed the lowest possible hurdle, because if the accused refused to confirm the truth of his or her statement, they could simply be tortured again until they were willing to do so. The existence of this practice meant that VOC trial records invariably included a standard formulation indicating that the original confession had been confirmed by the accused "without being tortured or bound in irons" (*buyten pijne ende bande van ysere*). By contrast, *The Confessions and Sentences*, which laid out a case that hinged on the use of torture, included no such formula or, indeed, any reference to indicate whether these confessions had been confirmed.[63]

In this way, and even in the rough world of VOC justice, the case orchestrated by De Bruyn and the record it produced stand apart. Given total freedom to root out the plot by an absent governor and a fearful council, but completely unequipped to manage a trial of this nature, De Bruyn drove forward the most disorderly of cases. From the beginning, he proceeded to set a blistering pace, cramming more than twenty interrogations into just five days. This commenced on Friday, February 24, with the interrogation of Sidney Miguel, whom Shichizō had named in his confession as the key mediator between the Japanese and the English.

Friday, February 24

Sidney Miguel was just twenty-four when he was dragged into the interrogation chamber. This made him one of the youngest members of the Japanese contingent alongside Shichizō, who was twenty-three, and this fact may have drawn them together. But in other ways Miguel was very different from his fellow soldier. First, he came from Nagasaki, which had been a hub for Portuguese and Jesuit activity for decades.[64] His name suggests that he was either born into a Christian family or converted when he was younger. If so, he joined many other Japanese Christians who ended up in Southeast Asia on the run from Tokugawa persecution. Second, he had once, VOC officials alleged, worked for the English. If this is true, he most likely either departed Japan aboard an EIC trading vessel, which periodically recruited new crewmembers in Hirado, or found his way into the employ of an English factory in Southeast Asia.[65] At some point, however, he decided, presumably because of the promise of a regular wage, to enter VOC service as a soldier.[66]

Such facts suggest that Miguel, like many of the Japanese migrants who ended up in Southeast Asia, came to straddle different worlds. Further evidence of this can be found in his signature. All eleven Japanese mercenaries signed *The Confessions and Sentences* in some way. Although the original signatures are lost, the facsimiles made by an unnamed VOC scribe tasked with copying the entirety of De Bruyn's original record survive. Some of the Japanese soldiers interrogated at Amboina used Chinese characters. Shichizō, for example, wrote his name as 七蔵 creating a challenge for the scribe who attempted to duplicate the intricate and unfamiliar kanji. Others

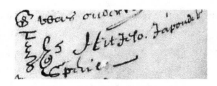

Figure 5.2 Copy of Shichizō's signature. Copie autentycq van de confessien ende sententien, NL-HaNA, VOC 1080.

Figure 5.3 Copy of Sidney Miguel's signature. Copie autentycq van de confessien ende sententien, NL-HaNA, VOC 1080.

were clearly illiterate, marking the record with a cross. Miguel's signature stands apart, a sweeping, Europeanized scrawl that looks very similar to the extravagant signatures preferred by VOC officials.

If Miguel's background made him better placed than Shichizō to respond to the demands of his interrogators, it did not help him in the end. Like his countryman, he proved unable to halt the rapid jump from initial questioning to torture. When Miguel denied any knowledge of the plot, the advocate-fiscal ordered the young soldier bound to a doorframe and waterboarded until he was willing to admit his involvement.

The subsequent confession confirmed the outlines of the plot and added some new details. Like Shichizō, Miguel named Abel Price and said that the barber had approached him two or three months earlier to convince the Japanese to join a plot to hand over the castle. In return for their participation, they had each been promised 1,000 reals, a huge sum more than a hundred times what the recruits were paid each month, in addition to whatever loot they could take from the castle.[67] More importantly for De Bruyn's purposes, Miguel named Gabriel Towerson, the EIC's chief merchant in Amboina, as the author of the conspiracy.[68] Compared to someone like Nicholas Uffelet, the supposed plotter discussed in the previous chapter, Towerson was a far bigger prize, a senior EIC administrator with close ties to the organization's upper hierarchy. With no record of the interrogation, it is impossible to know how much De Bruyn prompted Miguel for this detail as he gasped for air, but it was precisely the connection that the advocate-fiscal was looking for.

With this confession, the outlines of the conspiracy locked into place. Eager to take action against the English, De Bruyn raced through eight further interrogations of the remaining Japanese soldiers in a single day. Things settled quickly into a numbing routine: the suspect called in, the inevitable denials (all eight denied any involvement) followed by the binding of their limbs and then the four stages of the "watering cycle"—the demand for confirmation, the application of water until the subject began to convulse, the loosening of the bonds so he could vomit up the liquid, and a return to questioning. The shrinking nature of the individual confessions suggests that De Bruyn had little interest in what was being said beyond the confirmation of involvement. Whereas Shichizō's and Miguel's confessions stretch for close to a manuscript page (roughly three hundred words for Shichizō, two hundred for Miguel) in *The Confessions and Sentences*, the subsequent confessions consist of just a few lines: yes, he knew of the plot, yes he had confirmed his willingness to participate. The confession of Soysimo, a twenty-six-year-old mercenary from Hirado, recorded only that he "knew of the discussion with the English and had promised his assistance to help capture the castle." It was just over thirty words, with no details or real content. For Zanchoo, the youngest of the contingent, De Bruyn was even more perfunctory, with the entry noting simply that he "confessed as above" (*bekent als de vorige*).[69]

Even in these truncated confessions, however, there are surprising inconsistencies. Quiondayo confessed, for example, that it was the Japanese who, with the help of the English, sought to make themselves masters of the castle. It was an ambitious rewriting of the conspiracy that pictured the Japanese as the central conspirators, but in his rush forward De Bruyn made no effort to square it with the English-led plot he was sketching out. Reading closely through the confessions reveals another striking discrepancy. Although De Bruyn included confessions from eleven soldiers, a number of the accused declared that in fact twelve Japanese soldiers had been involved in the plot.[70] What happened then to this mysterious twelfth man, who managed to thread his way through the trial?

As is the case with so many other questions, *The Confessions and Sentences* gives us no answer. Instead, his identity only comes into view in the depositions provided by the Amboina judges, who explained that there were twelve Japanese, and "one of them was their Captain."[71] In some ways, this is not particularly surprising. Japanese contingents in VOC service were typically led by a captain, who received elevated wages in return for maintaining order, and there is no reason why the Amboina contingent would have been any different. But the captain's escape from punishment, even when he was identified by some of his countrymen as a fellow plotter, and his erasure from the record raise new questions. Part of the answer is provided by George Forbes, the Scottish witness, who explained that he had seen the "captain of the Japons" brought into the interrogation chamber "by the heels in a great bolt of iron by one leg."[72] Unlike his subordinates, however, who were tortured until they confessed, the Japanese captain "was let loose and nothing done to him." It raises yet more questions. What had he said to escape torture, especially when at least three of his subordinates were emphatic that the whole contingent of twelve mercenaries, that is, including the captain, had committed themselves to the plot?[73]

The most likely explanation is that he did so by offering De Bruyn something, diverting attention from his part in the supposed plot by helping condemn the soldiers under his command. Some evidence of this is provided by the testimony of one of the Amboina judges, who explained that the remainder of the Japanese were interrogated in the "presence of the captain of the Japanese."[74] This suggests that the captain may have acted as an interpreter between De Bruyn and his charges. He was well placed to do so. Of all the Japanese soldiers based at Kota Ambon, the captain was the only one in regular communication with VOC officials. Given his function as the key conduit between the Company and his charges, his language abilities were surely superior to the soldiers under his command. Taking on a role as interpreter would have given the Japan captain some room to maneuver. It meant that he could have effectively controlled these interrogations, feeding De Bruyn the answers he was looking for and eliding information that did not fit. If so, it was the same tactic adopted by Edward Collins, one of the English merchants accused at Amboina, who made the same calculation that it was better to denounce his countrymen than to deny all knowledge of the plot.

For the advocate-fiscal, the willingness of the Japan captain to condemn his own men suited his purposes. In the captain, De Bruyn found a source capable of confirming the details of the plot while enabling the advocate-fiscal to leap forward.[75] After all, the Japanese conspirators were never the main prize. Instead, their confessions were simply useful stepping stones to the English merchants gathered in their newly purchased house. The first to be hauled in for interrogation was Abel Price, the crucial go-between named by Shichizō.[76]

Saturday, February 25

It was all too easy for the advocate-fiscal. At the moment Abel Price was accused, he was lying in a cell of Castle Victoria, isolated from his countrymen and available for immediate questioning. He had been arrested for setting fires and committing "violence in other people's houses."[77] Remarkably, this was not the result of action taken by the Dutch. Instead, he had been locked up in a Company cell at the request of Gabriel Towerson, the chief plotter, who had supposedly entrusted Price with the vital task of making contact with the Japanese mercenaries. Critics of the case picked up on this fact, ridiculing the idea that Towerson would rely on a figure they described as a "drunken debauched sot" to suborn the VOC's Japanese troops, or that he would request the imprisonment of a key agent just as the plot was about to be put into execution.[78]

Brought to the interrogation chamber and confronted with the evidence, Price denied everything. His refusal to confess presented the advocate-fiscal with a dilemma. Even if the standard of half-proof was not reached, there was no real impediment to using torture techniques on Company employees like Shichizō or Sidney Miguel, who were constrained within the VOC legal system and bound by a strict oath. Doing the same, however, with someone like Price who stood outside the traditional bounds of VOC justice presented a Rubicon that would have to be crossed.[79] Although Dutch officials had long detected the existence of English plotters, they had hesitated to take direct action through fear of the political consequences that might follow. De Bruyn, however, never hesitated. Price was roped up to the doorframe and subjected to the same torture by water. He broke quickly, confessing that he had been charged by Towerson to induct the Japanese into the plot.

With this confession in hand, the advocate-fiscal decided that it was time to arrest the remainder of the EIC merchants not only in Kota Ambon itself but also in the attached outposts in places like Kambelo that came under Towerson's control.[80] He would do the first job himself, at the head of a small column of musketeers, while sending out soldiers to arrest the others.[81] By the end of the process, eighteen EIC employees were imprisoned and held under guard. With not enough space to hold them in the castle, they were placed in chains below deck in the bilges of anchored ships until they could be summoned for interrogation.[82]

In addition to locking up the accused, De Bruyn proceeded to search the English house in Amboina for incriminating evidence. He turned up nothing—no plans of the castle, no incriminating letters, no weapons caches or evidence of any kind. English writers honed in on this point, writing that there was "not a letter or other paper to be found in all the Chests and Boxes of the English . . . to discover this treason."[83] It did not matter, however, if the remaining English merchants could be pulled into the interrogation chamber to confess their crimes. And although the day had been consumed with the long process of arrest and imprisonment, De Bruyn ordered one further prisoner, Timothy Johnson, a twenty-nine-year-old merchant from Newcastle, to be brought up to the council chamber for interrogation.

Tortured, Johnson confirmed the now familiar outlines of the plot but he also produced a new detail, describing a meeting called by Towerson on "New-year's-day last."[84] Very quickly, the New Year's Day meeting came to assume a central place as the sinister fulcrum of the plot. It began, in the final retelling, with a large group of English merchants gathered secretly in Towerson's own chambers, where he made them swear a blood oath on the Bible to be "secret and faithful," for if the discussion became known, "it would cost them all our lives."[85] Seething with pretended injuries, Towerson "proposed to them that the Hollanders did great injustices to the English" and asked "if they did not have courage to avenge these."[86] When his subordinates protested that they were too weak to consider such an action, the chief merchant responded that he had secured the means to overcome their deficiencies in numbers "with the help of some Japanese soldiers that were inside" the castle. The response was eager and overwhelming. Every single merchant present at the meeting swore his allegiance, pledging to carry the plot forward to its bloody end until all those who resisted had either surrendered or were slain and the castle was firmly in Towerson's hands.

For once, both sides agreed that such a gathering had indeed taken place, but English survivors of the trial explained it very differently. For them, it was simply a matter of good accounting. Recently arrived as chief merchant, Towerson had taken the opportunity to summon his subordinates so he could check the account books of all the outlying factories and outposts.[87] The New Year's Day meeting presents an obvious point of focus for any assessment as to whether or not VOC interrogators had in fact uncovered some kernel of an actual conspiracy. If a group of English merchants had indeed speculated about finding a way to overthrow the Dutch in Kota Ambon, then this meeting, which pulled together personnel usually scattered across Amboina, was the most likely forum for such a conversation. While De Bruyn's theatrical version of events complete with blood oaths and pledges to lay their lives down is not persuasive, it is impossible to know what was discussed or whether English frustration took a dark turn, transitioning from complaint to whispered speculation about doing something about it. But even if De Bruyn did stumble upon some trace of a plot, it does not alter a trajectory of events that was already set. By 1623, VOC authorities in Amboina were primed to see conspiracies gathering in the shadows. This meant that from the beginning, they detected the outlines of a sprawling plot stretching out from Shichizō's suspicious questions on the walls of Castle Victoria to encompass an array of faithless friends, unreliable servants, and local enemies who must, they insisted, be tied together.

De Bruyn's fixation on the New Year's Day meeting came with one unexpected consequence. If this was the moment when the plot assumed its concrete form, everyone who was present was automatically guilty. It also meant that those few EIC merchants who could prove they had been absent for the New Year's Day meeting could show they had not been inducted into Towerson's plot. It was a narrow route out of the torture chamber, but one that was seized upon by a handful of English merchants.

The next day, February 26, was a Sunday, and even De Bruyn seems to have been hesitant to embark on another round of interrogations on the Sabbath, which had officially been decreed as a day of rest by Batavia.[88] Still, he was reluctant to allow the day to pass without at least one additional confession, and Robert Brown, a twenty-four-year-old from Edinburgh, was brought to the interrogation chamber and tortured until he confessed. Early the next morning, as if determined to make up for lost time, the advocate-fiscal resumed his frenetic pace, interrogating nine suspects over one marathon day, including two key witnesses—Edward Collins and John Beaumont—who, like the Japan captain before them, managed to find a path out of the torture chamber.

Monday, February 27

By the time he was hauled into the interrogation chamber on February 27, 1623, Edward Collins was a tarnished figure. In the weeks leading up to the trial, his undistinguished career had reached a new low. Based in Amboina for roughly a year, he had run out of funds and had responded by deceiving "severall men of good sommes of money."[89] Their subsequent complaints earned him the ire of his superiors in Banten, who instructed Towerson to confiscate all of Collins's goods and to send him away on the next ship. He was to be dismissed from the EIC, which had no desire to provide "imploiment to such untrustie unthrifts."[90] Before this could happen, however, the trial erupted, transforming his fortunes.

Two opposing versions exist of what happened to Collins in the interrogation chamber. According to his own much-publicized account, he was extensively and brutally tortured. In his testimony to an admiralty judge in 1624, he explained that he was brought to the "bloody stage" of the interrogation chamber, where he had vehemently denied everything, using "as many oaths and protestacons as hee could devide to make them sensible of his innocency."[91] When his interrogators declined to accept this, Collins was tortured "with water most greiveously." Even after this torment, Collins would not admit his involvement in a fabricated conspiracy. Predictably, he was strung up again so the watering cycle could be renewed. This time, however, the torture proved too "heavy for Flesh and blood to indure," and Collins followed De Bruyn's prompts by sketching out an imagined plot.

VOC officials, by contrast, explained Collins's experience very differently. Whereas they freely admitted the use of waterboarding to elicit confessions from the rest of the accused, the Amboina judges were adamant that Collins had not been tortured. Instead, they insisted that he alone had freely confessed, "saying to the Secretary write what I shall say unto you I will tell you the truth."[92] Because it is silent on the key issue of when torture was or was not used, *The Confessions and Sentences* provides no way of distinguishing between these two conflicting accounts, but it is the Dutch version of events that seems more likely. This is in large part because when it came time to explain what the Dutch had done, Collins identified the wrong kind of torture technique. When pressed by the Admiralty judges to recount his version of events, he described not waterboarding—that is, simulated drowning—but rather "the water cure," a torture technique in which interrogators poured vast quantities of water into the suspect's mouth until their organs swelled, causing unbearable pain.[93] It was an account that would reverberate out, coloring descriptions of the trial for centuries, but which also seems to have been wholly invented by Collins as he sought to convince his former employer of his value as a witness.[94]

It seems most likely that, faced with the threat of torture, Collins opted to give De Bruyn what he wanted to hear. Collins was exactly what the advocate-fiscal was looking for, a witness based inside the EIC outpost in Kota Ambon who was willing to confirm his suspicions about the emerging plot. In fact, the one part of Collins's account that does seem persuasive centers on his interactions with De Bruyn. Unable to make the necessary connections, he faltered again and again under the advocate-fiscal's aggressive questioning. But each time he did so, De Bruyn was there, ready to prompt him with an answer. So obvious were these interventions that they earned De Bruyn a rebuke from another interrogator also present that he should allow the witness to speak for himself.[95]

Collins's strategy proved spectacularly successful. As with the Japan captain, his willingness to confess would ultimately save him from execution. But, more than this, he emerged over time as the star witness for both sides. For the EIC, he had confessed after enduring the most terrible of torture; for the Dutch Company, he was the only one of the accused to admit his guilt freely without the need for torture. It made him a central character in the controversy, giving him an indispensable status that he proceeded to exploit ruthlessly for decades. For Collins alone the involvement in the case proved a windfall, rescuing him from dismissal and giving him a firm basis of financial support—from the very organization that had once been so eager to eject him from its ranks—that he drew on for the rest of his life.

Like Collins, John Beaumont, who was interrogated on the same day, was able to navigate the maelstrom of the trial but he did so in a very different way. At age forty-eight, Beaumont was one of the oldest EIC employees in Amboina. Posted to Luhu on the Hoamoal Peninsula, he had established a close relationship with one of the Amboina judges, Pieter van Santen, who would eventually intervene on his behalf. When he came to be interrogated, Beaumont pleaded infirmity. After a brief experience of the "torture of water," he quickly confessed but attempted to draw a clear line separating him from the other conspirators. Having "been sickly and weak of memory and old," he had agreed to Towerson's demand but had not properly understood what he was signing on to and was too feeble to have taken place in the planned assault on the castle.[96] When he returned to England, however, he would miraculously regain his faculties, emerging as a key witness who was willing to travel to the United Provinces to condemn the very officials who eventually decided to pardon him.

If Collins and Beaumont escaped the worst excesses of the torture chamber, John Clark, a thirty-six-year-old assistant interrogated on the same day, was not so fortunate. Subjected to waterboarding, he refused to confess. Frustrated, De Bruyn ordered Clark hauled up again. The torture seemed initially to produce results, as he pleaded to be cut down, but as soon as Clark regained his breath he "began to sing his old song of having no guilt."[97] With this, the torture went on, and new pots of water were hauled to the interrogation chamber. The repeated drownings had a catastrophic effect on Clark's body. One judge testified that he made strange faces and seemed "to play the fool or to be frenzied in order to abuse the council with this method."[98] The description matches accounts provided by modern observers who reported that subjects responded to prolonged sessions of waterboarding with "involuntary leg, chest and arm spasms."[99] It was most likely these spasms that made it seem as if Clark was playing "the fool" as his body shut down in response to oxygen deprivation.

Frustrated with this resistance, De Bruyn decided that Clark's long hair was preventing the torture from working effectively by impeding the flow of water.[100] It must be cut, he decided, to force a final confession.[101] Even with his hair shorn, however, Clark still refused to admit his involvement. It created a problem for the advocate-fiscal, who was determined to secure a confession from all the English merchants present at the New Year's Day meeting. If waterboarding proved "too soft for the hardness of his nature," De Bruyn resolved, we know from later depositions, to escalate by ordering Clark's flesh burnt with a candle.[102] Predictably, *The Confessions and Sentences* makes no mention of this second method of torture, leaving another opening for two very different accounts to emerge. English pamphleteers insisted that the burning was savage and extensive, leaving terrible burns on Clark's flesh that were so gruesome that "his Intrales might be seene."[103] So terrible was the torture that the candle was extinguished several times by the fat dripping from his body. In contrast, the Amboina judges claimed that the candle was moved back and forth across the flesh so that there was no disfigurement or burning.[104] If it was extinguished at any point, it was simply because the candle flickered out naturally. Although English charges were clearly exaggerated, the combination of the twin tortures of fire and water did succeed in breaking Clark, who admitted that he joined with Towerson in their resolution "to kill all those that should resist them."[105]

In addition to Collins, Beaumont, and Clark, six other English merchants were interrogated on this marathon day. For four of them—Ephraim Ramsey, John Sadler, William Webber, and George Sherrock—the focus on the New Year's Day meeting gave them an opening to escape torture. Posted to the isolated outposts scattered across Amboina, they could show that they had been outside Kota Ambon when Towerson had supposedly convened the plotters. Two others, John Fardo and William Griggs, were less fortunate. A twenty-eight-year-old merchant, Griggs began by confessing that he had been present at the crucial New Year's Day meeting, where he offered his service to the plot. This much was standard, but Griggs went further, declaring that the English would receive aid from the "Japanese, slaves and Spanish captives" held in Castle Victoria.

This was something new. Whereas other confessions had indicated that Towerson would use those slaves held by the English to bolster his forces, this was the first time the VOC's own slave population—seemingly both the *kettinggangers* and the work slaves—was included in the ranks of plotters. With no record of the questions asked or the answers given, there is no way to know if this detail came spontaneously from Griggs. It seems more likely that it followed a prompt from De Bruyn, who was convinced that Augustine Peres and the growing number of slaves housed in Kota Ambon must be involved somehow. If so, it was another example of the plot's capacity to stretch outward, this time by tapping into a different set of colonial nightmares of slave rebellions bursting out from within. What we do know is that even if this detail remained unconfirmed by any other confession, it was swiftly embraced by VOC officials, who added a new party onto an already capacious plot.

By nightfall on February 27, the advocate-fiscal had worked through a large share of the plotters, but the ringleader—Gabriel Towerson—remained. Before Towerson could be questioned, De Bruyn hauled Samuel Coulson, a twenty-six-year-old English merchant based at Hitu, into the interrogation chamber.

Tuesday, February 28

Tortured, Coulson made a familiar confession. He had been present at the crucial New Year's Day meeting, where he had agreed to join in Towerson's conspiracy to seize control of the castle. This much was familiar, but as he lay in chains imprisoned on one of the ships in the harbor, awaiting execution, Coulson scrawled an impassioned declaration of innocence across five unprinted pages of a child's book, *The Catechisme Or Maner to Teach Children the Christian Religion*, an English translation of the famous Heidelberg Catechism. Coulson's psalm book, as it would come to be known, eventually ended up in London, carried by the English survivors of the trial, where it was presented as explosive evidence of their innocence. Dated March 5, that is, just three days before his execution, Coulson's message explained that he was "clear of all such conspiracy." Forced to "confess that I never knew, or else go to torment," he declared that his confession was entirely fabricated, for he knew no more than a "child unborn of the business."[106]

It was a powerful piece of evidence that seemed to call into question the basis of the case. Not surprisingly, therefore, the meaning and veracity of Coulson's declaration was fiercely contested from the start. Defenders of the case argued that there was no way to prove definitively that it had been written by Coulson or that it had not been forged or somehow altered during the long voyage back to London. Equally, Coulson might simply have been faking. It was perfectly possible, VOC pamphleteers declared, for even the most guilty of parties to "faine and dissemble at the houre of [their] death."[107]

Even with such objections, Coulson's psalm book became a potent exhibit for the English case that seemed to open an unexpected window into the mind of an innocent man awaiting his own execution. The result was that it persuaded some writers otherwise convinced of English guilt that Coulson at least must have known nothing about the plot.[108]

With one more confession added to the list, it was time to interrogate the putative ringleader, Gabriel Towerson. Since his arrest, the chief merchant had been secluded, held at his own request apart from his countrymen. Presumably, Towerson believed that his rank and apparent friendship with the governor would be enough to shield him, but De Bruyn showed no hesitation in ordering the use of torture. The chief merchant broke quickly, confirming the familiar outlines of the conspiracy, including the secret meeting on New Year's Day. Driven by an overwhelming desire for

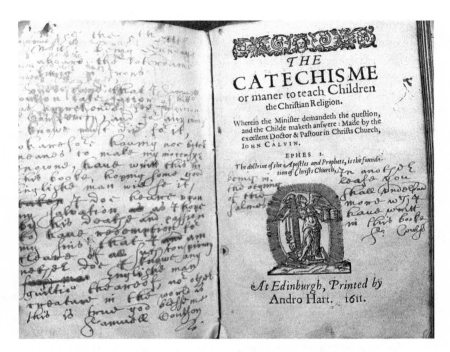

Figure 5.4 Samuel Coulson's psalm book. NL-HaNA, Staten-Generaal, 1.01.02, inv. no. 12551.62.

"honor and profit," he had intended to make himself master of the castle.[109] Once the fortification had been seized, he would have informed his superiors in Banten. If they agreed to provide support, he would hold the fortification for the EIC, but if they refused, he "would have kept it for his own self," setting himself up as a kind of white Rajah by finding local allies capable of supporting him. Like Coulson, however, Towerson contrived to proclaim his innocence in a note hastily scribbled on the back of a bill of debt that later ended up in London. On this, the chief merchant insisted that he was "guiltlesse of anything, that can be justly laid to me charge," thereby further muddying the waters of the VOC case.[110]

If Towerson was the great prize, one element of the plot was still missing. Although the involvement of the English, the Japanese, and the slaves had all been confirmed, the advocate-fiscal was certain that the conspirators must have had local allies whose thousands of fighters would have been mobilized in tandem to eject the Company from Kota Ambon. Luhu and Kambelo's recent attacks on Company personnel and outposts could not simply be isolated episodes; rather, they must be part of a wider campaign. De Bruyn, we know for once from *The Confessions and Sentences*, pressed Towerson again and again: Didn't he have allies in Luhu, Kambelo, or Hitu who had agreed to dispatch warriors to support the attack on Castle Victoria? But having already confessed to his involvement in the plot, Towerson refused to admit any such action. He had, he insisted, "not given any order to any person to discuss the matter with Loehoe, Hittoe or Cambello, concerning this matter."[111] If Towerson would not confirm their involvement, corroboration must come from another source, and as the sun rose on March 1, De Bruyn hauled Emmanuel Thomson into the torture chamber.

Wednesday, March 1

Thomson stood apart from his fellow EIC employees. For one, he did not come from the British Isles.[112] Instead, he was a German born in Hamburg who had entered EIC service via a circuitous route. At age fifty, he was two years older than John Beaumont, who had used his supposedly infirm condition to argue that he could not be considered alongside the other plotters. Unlike Beaumont, however, Thomson refused to confess, setting in motion a marathon day of interrogation and torture. Waterboarded again and again, he denied any knowledge of or involvement in the plot. As had happened with Clark earlier, De Bruyn determined that Thomson must be subjected to further torture to produce the necessary admission of guilt.[113] When lit candles were placed under his armpits, he still refused to confess. According to English accounts, which seized upon Thomson's interrogation as another example of VOC brutality, "his body was burnt in 7 or 8 severall places miserable," and even Dutch sources, which are far more muted, acknowledge that he resisted torture for hours.[114]

One reason the torture may have lasted for so long was because De Bruyn was determined to secure final confirmation that Luhu, Kambelo, and Hitu had been involved somehow.[115] Eventually, after repeated applications of the torture of water and fire, Thomson broke, confessing that "those of Loehoe would come to help with some corcoreen [*kora-kora*]."[116] It was not what De Bruyn had pressed for—just Luhu rather than a wider coalition that included Kambelo—and it directly contradicted Towerson's own testimony, but it was enough for the advocate-fiscal. With this confession the sprawling conspiracy joining the English, the governor's

Japanese soldiers, the slaves held within the castle, and rival polities on the Hoamoal Peninsula had emerged into final view.

With De Bruyn's prize secured, the pace of the interrogation slowed. No one was interrogated on March 2, and it was not until the next day that De Bruyn moved to wrap up the remaining loose ends. His attention turned to Augustine Peres, still languishing in a cell in Castle Victoria. Peres had not been named directly by any of the other conspirators, but he was the obvious link between Towerson and the slave population. Equally important, his imprisonment in the weeks before the trial meant that his loyalty was already in question. Tortured, Peres confessed that he had been inducted into the plot by Shichizō, who had approached him on behalf of Towerson. It made the young Japanese soldier a far more significant actor than he previously appeared, handing him a new role as broker between different parties.[117] Although Peres's place in the conspiracy was not confirmed by any other confession, he came to assume an outsized role in the imagination of the Amboina judges, who pictured him as the master of a ferocious slave army. His hold over the slaves gave him, they declared in later depositions, a terrible power. Because the slaves would never dare to refuse an order, he could, one explained, direct them at will, throwing their bodies at VOC defenses in a determined attack.[118]

By the time Peres admitted his guilt, the advocate-fiscal had secured twenty-six confessions of guilt—from eleven Japanese mercenaries, fourteen EIC merchants, and Augustine Peres—in just nine days. It brought the first stage of the proceedings to a close. With these confessions in hand, it was now necessary to decide what to do with the plotters, who were scattered in chains through the castle and in the bilges of the Company's ships clustered in the harbor. Although De Bruyn had been driving the case relentlessly forward, he did not have the authority to take the next step. Instead it was up to Van Speult, who now returned to the cockpit of the case, to decide if the accused should be tried and hence surely executed in Kota Ambon, or whether a case of such obvious importance should be referred up to Batavia for the governor-general to decide.

The Verdict

There were powerful arguments on both sides. The case for immediate action was strengthened by the fears still swirling through the settlement.

Kota Ambon remained, its residents believed, acutely vulnerable. The plotters had been arrested and the castle's defenses placed on high alert, but the fear of a sudden attack had not subsided. There was no guarantee that the advocate-fiscal had been able to catch everyone, and there might be more conspirators hiding in the settlement who could still carry out the plan. Even more worrying—each day they waited gave more time for Luhu or Kambelo to assemble their forces in preparation for a final desperate attempt to rescue Towerson and drive the plot to its final end. Any delay presented, therefore, an unacceptable danger.

On the other side, however, were the potential repercussions. While the governor had instructions to watch out for conspiracies that might include the EIC, no one had authorized him to execute even one English merchant, let alone a dozen, including a senior administrator. The potential consequences of such an inflammatory action were obvious. They would drive a wedge between the United Provinces and its oldest ally, ripping apart the Treaty of Defense and sparking uproar in Asia and Europe. And equally important, there was a clear path out of such controversy. Van Speult could simply execute the Japanese soldiers, who were bound by oath and contract, but ship the English plotters under close guard to Batavia, thereby turning over the whole case to the governor-general to resolve.[119] As he debated what to do, Van Speult become increasingly aware that the advocate-fiscal was not in fact the learned "doctor and jurist" that he had so convincingly presented himself as. This expert in the law whose services the governor had worked so hard to secure had in fact bungled the job. According to Forbes, who saw this all firsthand, Van Speult "was exceedingly displeased with the Fiscal by reason of the interrogatories and responses."

The circumstances presented Van Speult with the most difficult decision of his career. The governor was unsure whether De Bruyn's rushed proceedings would stand up to scrutiny "if these matters should come to be examined and sifted."[120] But in the volatile environment of Kota Ambon it was unthinkable to redo the whole case, to tear up De Bruyn's work and start again. Deciding what to do seemed to paralyze the governor, and a strange lull settled over Kota Ambon after the frantic pace of the first nine days. Hours and then days passed without action as everyone waited, the garrison still on the walls expecting an attack, the prisoners locked in their cells or in the fetid bilges of ships awaiting their fate. By March 8, it was clear that something had to be done. With no easy way out, Van Speult resolved to turn the decision as to whether the suspects should be sent to Batavia or tried in Kota Ambon over to the council of Amboina judges, which consisted of thirteen merchants, captains, and officials.[121] Even as he did so, however, the governor, if we believe his own letters, set his finger firmly on the scale by recommending that the case be referred up to Batavia on "account of its importance and considerations."[122]

It was a clear push from a powerful official who was used to being obeyed, but weighed against it was the fear that crackled through the settlement, driving action forward. The Amboina judges were not neutral arbiters. Instead, their numbers included two merchants, Jan van Leeuwen and Pieter van Santen, who had been forced to flee the Hoamoal Peninsula. Having reached the safety of Castle Victoria, they were, it seemed, still pursued by a vengeful coalition determined to throw the Dutch into the sea. In the end, there was no contest, and the council resolved immediately that the "affair should not be deferred or delayed." Instead, punishment must follow at the place where the crime had been committed.[123] With the decision at last taken, the case sped up dramatically.

On the same day, March 8, De Bruyn was given the go-ahead to draw up a final charge. He responded with a ferocious denunciation of Towerson and his accomplices.[124] They were, he thundered, "creatures and accomplices [who] perpetrated high treason and tried to undermine the state of the United Netherlands East Indies Company in Amboyna" through "terrible murder and bloodspilling" (*schrickelijken moort en bloetstortinge*). The punishment must match the crime, and all fourteen English merchants who had declared some knowledge of the plot should, De Bruyn insisted, be executed alongside the Company's Japanese soldiers.[125] Towerson was to be singled out for especially gruesome punishment. The chief merchant should be beheaded, his body quartered, his head placed on the gate, and the four segments put on display in individual gibbets hung on the corners of the castle.

The council agreed, declaring that the plotters had conspired to commit "a horrible massacre and treason," but whereas De Bruyn had demanded the execution of fourteen English merchants, they resolved to exempt two, William Webber and George Sherrock, who were cleared as not being full participants in the plot. Although there is no mention of it in the trial document, it is also likely that one Japanese soldier, Sacoube, who had confessed that he was too "old and sickly" to have participated in the plot, was also spared.[126] While they had condemned Towerson as the ringleader, the council decided that his body would not be quartered in the gruesome way demanded by De Bruyn. Instead, they were more concerned with making a public demonstration of the consequences of the Company's Asian servants betraying their masters, thereby ensuring that such treachery would not be repeated. Alongside Towerson, three Japanese soldiers—Sidney Miguel, Shichizō, and Pedro Conge—were to be decapitated and their heads set on poles so they could be visible to observers both in and outside the castle.[127]

Although the verdict had been issued, Van Speult was acutely aware of the political consequences that might flow from the execution of such a large group of EIC merchants. In a surprise final intervention, he decided that two of the twelve English merchants awaiting execution would be granted a last-minute reprieve because of "the grace and pardon" of the governor-general, so that they might take care of EIC goods left in the organization's outposts across Amboina.[128] It was the flimsiest of possible justifications. There was little precedent for such last-minute pardons of convicted conspirators, and there were already six other English merchants who, having been found innocent, were perfectly capable of fulfilling this role. Instead, it seems likely that the governor hoped that this last-minute show of benevolence might serve somehow to dampen the inevitable controversy that would erupt when the English company learned of the fate of its employees.

But who was to be spared? John Beaumont, who had pleaded his age and infirmity, was an obvious candidate.[129] He had, he argued, never been fully inducted into the plot, and his case was further strengthened by one of the judges, Pieter van Santen, who intervened on his behalf. For the second candidate, however, things became far murkier. According to the record, the governor decided that lots must be drawn but that only three of the accused, Emmanuel Thomson, Samuel Coulson, and Edward Collins, would be permitted to participate. No reason was given for why these three—all of whom had confessed to some knowledge of the plot—should be given an opportunity to escape execution, but it is impossible to shake the suspicion that the whole thing was rigged in Collins's favor. Alone among the accused he had confessed freely, emerging as a key informant and ally of the advocate-fiscal. Now he was saved at the last moment as he prepared to march out to his death.

The execution was scheduled for the next day, March 9, on the open ground in the front of the castle. As night fell, Dutch ministers (*predikanten*) were brought in to tend to the condemned. The next morning, the accused were led out of the castle, through the silent ranks of gathered soldiers, sailors, and free citizens. As they approached the place of execution, rain fell steadily, drenching their clothes. Some went to their death with a show of piety, others pleaded desperately for mercy, but very quickly it was all over, and the blood of twenty-one men mingled with the packed dirt of the ground. The controversy and the fight for control over the Amboina narrative, however, were just getting started.

PART TWO

Remaking a Conspiracy Trial

CHAPTER VI

The War of the Witnesses

The punishment was lawfully inflicted, with moderation of the rigour of Justice and with clemency.

—*A REPLY TO THE REMONSTRANCE OF THE BEWINTHEBBERS*, 1632

It is impossible to maintain that Speult acted hastily or in a moment of panic. The Amboina "process" . . . was very methodical, carefully planned and prolonged.

—D. K. BASSETT, "THE FACTORY OF THE ENGLISH EAST INDIA COMPANY AT BANTAM, 1602–1682" (1955)

Assessed by the Dutch East India Company's own standards, the Amboina conspiracy trial was a legal mess crammed with errors, strange gaps in the record, and omitted procedures. Given shape by an incompetent advocate-fiscal operating in an environment of crisis, the proceedings and the trial document that they generated seemed capable only of raising new questions, and with them more controversy. Even before the trial's final act was complete, VOC officials in Kota Ambon, led by Van Speult, realized just how badly De Bruyn had botched the job. In the weeks after the mass execution of the alleged conspirators, they started to gather new evidence in an effort to prop up the case and justify its outcome.[1] While the Company's leaders in Batavia were convinced that their subordinates had acted decisively to prevent a dangerous conspiracy, they too were appalled by the conduct of the advocate-fiscal and the shoddiness of the trial records that were dispatched for inspection.

Given this initial response, it is remarkable how quickly and how completely such a chaotic case came to be transformed into a "methodical, carefully planned" legal process deliberately executed by VOC officials and how enduring this view of the Amboina trial has proved.[2] This transformation stems, I suggest here, from a convergence of the strategies adopted by the two warring companies in 1624, after news of the trial first reached Europe. The key actors in this story were two clashing groups of witnesses, each with a personal stake in the case and each determined to rewrite it for their own ends. They arrived in Europe around the middle of 1624 armed with explosive testimony, much of it clearly fabricated, and were immediately embraced by a sprawling infrastructure of first company and then state officials determined to make use of their claims to push back against allegations of misconduct.

On the English side, these were the six so-called Amboyna men led by Edward Collins, who landed in Plymouth around the middle of 1624.[3] Called before the Admiralty Court, they described the trial as a calculated act of judicial murder that formed the final step of an overarching conspiracy engineered by the Dutch against the English. Their testimony was collected, refined, and shaped into an even more potent form by John Skinner in a new narrative evocatively titled *A True Relation of the Unjust, Cruell, and Barbarous Proceedings Against the English at Amboyna in the East-Indies, by the Neatherlandish Governour and Councel There.* In this, he depicted the trial as a "cruell treacherie" deliberately set into motion in order to eject the English from the rich spice trade.[4] Such was the success of Skinner's retelling that it embedded a new version of the Amboina proceedings into the record that has remained influential ever since.

Part of this story has been told by scholars such as Alison Games, Anthony Milton, Rupali Mishra, Miles Ogborn, and Edmond Smith, but less well known is a similar process that played out on the Dutch side.[5] The key witness here was Laurens de Maerschalk, who emerged from an undistinguished VOC career that had been cut prematurely short to become the indispensable agent of a campaign designed to remake De Bruyn's trial. Armed with De Maerschalk's testimony and a new interpretation of waterboarding as a uniquely moderate torture, VOC officials produced a revised account of the trial that was presented to the States General in late 1624, before being handed over to EIC representatives and subsequently published in English translation as a pamphlet.[6] It depicted a textbook legal case filled with multiple checks and built around an interrogation technique that could not properly be labeled as torture.

Crafting these new accounts of Amboina required the active collaboration of witnesses, company administrators, and frequently state officials. The 1623 trial was one of the first legal cases of its kind—that is, involving a combination of Asian and European protagonists all operating far from their home states.[7] In Japan, the execution of a group of Tokugawa subjects on what appeared to many observers to be trumped-up charges excited no response. While the Tokugawa regime made no statement regarding this case, there can be little doubt as to its position. In letter after letter, the shogun had made it clear that local legal authorities had jurisdiction over Tokugawa subjects abroad and were free to punish them in any way they deemed appropriate.[8] In Europe, by contrast, the news triggered an escalating series of responses, as an array of first company and then state resources were mobilized, noisily if not always effectively, on both sides of the North Sea in support either of the executed men or the judges who had ordered their deaths.[9] It was this expansive infrastructure that burnished, promoted, and circulated the flawed and obviously self-serving testimony of two warring groups of witnesses.

The two versions of the trial that appeared on opposite sides of the North Sea differed on almost every substantive point. One portrayed Van Speult and De Bruyn as judicial murderers working to achieve a carefully calculated aim, the other as sensible jurists painstakingly following correct protocol in pursuit of the most justifiable of all verdicts. They combined, however, in one way: to launder the case by erasing any sign of judicial incompetence and with it the stain of fear that had so permeated the actual proceedings.

The "Amboyna Men"

News of the Amboina case reached Europe around the end of May 1624. By early June, Carleton, the English ambassador at The Hague, was in possession of the first "account of the pretended treason at Amboyna."[10] Within a few days, news of the trial had crossed the North Sea, where it sparked a mix of anger and outrage from EIC administrators and shareholders. The case plunged the organization into an immediate and sustained crisis. Its servants had been arrested, tortured, and then executed with apparent impunity by its chief rival, and there seemed no guarantee that such actions would not be repeated in other parts of Asia.[11] The organization's governor, Maurice (Morris) Abbott, led the way, his rhetoric soaring skywards as he declared that there was no parallel in history for the terrible deeds committed by the Dutch in Amboina.[12] While such statements found a receptive audience within the organization, it was clear that the company needed to act quickly to persuade the king, James I, to throw his "Royull help and favour" behind its claims for justice.[13]

While EIC officials were determined to fight back, they were handicapped by their reliance on Dutch accounts of what had happened. The initial reports that had filtered back into Europe had come from sources within the VOC and defended the proceedings on Kota Ambon.[14] Because of this, the first step was to commission a new account of the trial, which could be pressed into service to argue the case before the king. Such an effort required witnesses who could provide firsthand accounts of what had happened on this remote island thousands of miles away from Europe. Fortunately for the English company, these became suddenly available. Just weeks after the news had reached London, six survivors from the original trial—Edward Collins, John Beaumont, John Powle, William Webber, George Sherrock, and Ephraim Ramsey—disembarked in Plymouth. These "Amboyna men," as they were quickly dubbed, had set sail from Batavia in December 1623, reaching St. Helena in March and finally the English coast in June, where they swiftly made contact with the company's agents.[15]

While the Amboyna men had all been caught up in the conspiracy trial in some way, their involvement was very different. Of the six, four had been on the outer edges of the case. John Powle, Ephraim Ramsey, William Webber, and George Sherrock were all able to show that they had been nowhere near Kota Ambon when the crucial New Year's Day meeting had taken place and were later cleared as having no active involvement in the conspiracy. By contrast, Beaumont and Collins had been, at least in their retelling of events, brutally tortured until they were prepared to confess. Found guilty and sentenced to death, they had been given a reprieve at the last minute, just as they were about to march out to public execution. This experience placed the pair at the center of an aggressive effort to reframe what had happened.

By early July, the Amboyna men had arrived in London, where they reported to the Court of Committees, a group of leading EIC officials.[16] They were quickly dispatched to appear before the High Court of Admiralty, where they could be formally questioned by a judge, Sir Henry Marten.[17] The resultant depositions, which stretched across six days, from July 17 to 23, 1624, were designed to provide a firm basis for EIC complaints; the Amboyna men were required to answer fifteen identical questions detailing what had happened on the island.[18] First up on July 17 were Beaumont and Collins.

Both were tarnished figures. Collins had aggressively denounced his countrymen during the trial itself, while Beaumont had secured his freedom via a combination of convenient claims to infirmity and the lucky intervention of one of the Amboina judges, who seemed suspiciously friendly for a Dutch official plotting judicial murder. For both men, there were serious questions as to how they had survived when so many had been put to death. And there were their own undistinguished records to contend with. Collins in particular was a proven liar who, in the weeks before the trial, had been slated for dismissal for embezzling funds and cheating his countrymen. Appearing before the Admiralty Court, the pair confronted a crucial test. The right testimony could secure the warm embrace of an organization that had once seemed ready to discard them, but anything that contradicted an emerging EIC argument would leave the Amboyna men marooned on their own without support or patronage.

If this was an audition, Beaumont and Collins were clearly prepared. It had been more than a year since the original trial, and in the long voyage from Batavia to Plymouth they had smoothed out their testimonies, hammering out any inconsistencies and polishing them to a lustrous sheen.[19] What they said was explosive. In one voice, the pair declared with absolute certainty that the trial had been deliberately crafted by Dutch East India Company officials as a mechanism to rid themselves of their English competitors. They matched each other word for word: Beaumont testified that he "beleeveth in his conscience, that the bloody and murderous massacre predeposed, was premeditated by the Dutch," while Collins explained that "the mutherous and bloody Massacre aforesaid was premeditated by the Dutch before they questioned the English."[20]

Going further, Collins indicted Van Speult as the mastermind of the conspiracy. According to his testimony, Collins had heard the governor explain "longe before that Massacre that hee much desired to have Amboina, and the Factoryes thereaboute cleered of the English" as they had consistently "hindred the proffitt of the dutch."[21] The execution of Towerson and his countrymen was thus an act of murder, the bloody climax of a strategy designed to secure VOC advantage. All of this meant that the chief plotter was not Towerson but the governor himself, who had formulated secret plans against the English from his chambers in Castle Victoria. As evidence of this, the Amboyna men presented inflated descriptions of Dutch power on Amboina. Castle Victoria was, they insisted, "very stronge," supported by twenty-four cannons, more than two hundred soldiers, and a flotilla of VOC ships in the harbor.[22] Given this fact, it was impossible to believe that Van Speult, secure in such a well-defended position, could ever have believed that the English posed a real threat. If that was the case, it was clear that he had fabricated the charges in order to remove a key competitor.

It was powerful testimony that was buttressed by graphic accounts of brutal torture sessions. Beaumont, who had in fact been tortured, provided an accurate description of waterboarding and the sense of drowning that it induced. He explained that the interrogators had "powred water into him as aforesaid untill he was almost drowned, and could not indure that intollerable torture any long." Collins, however, described something quite different. In his version, Dutch interrogators had poured water into their victim's mouths until it "run downe into their mouthes in such aboundance that it drowned them, when their bellyes were full riseinge upp into their heades, and runinge out of their eares and noses untill they were bereaved of their sences."[23]

It was a gruesome picture, but it was also the wrong torture technique—not waterboarding, the act of simulated drowning, but rather the water cure, which forces the victim to consume huge quantities of water causing excruciating pain as the internal organs swell and distend.[24] Such techniques have their own long history. Collins's account closely resembles descriptions provided by American troops in the Philippines in the early twentieth century, who used the technique to interrogate suspected guerillas: "Now, this is the way we give them the water cure. Lay them on their backs, a man standing on each hand and each foot, then put a round stick in the mouth and pour a pail of water in the mouth and nose, and if they don't give up pour in another pail. They swell up like toads. I'll tell you it is a terrible torture."[25] Collins's account might not have been accurate, but his description of the water cure with its gory picture of distended bodies and water streaming out of ears and noses had a visceral power. Not surprisingly, then, it was repeated again and again by EIC representatives, who added it to their list of charges against the Dutch.

In addition to describing their own torture sessions, Beaumont and Collins claimed as well to have overheard the torture of their countrymen and seen its brutal aftereffects. This enabled the pair to craft an account that extended beyond their own experience to encompass everything that had happened in Castle Victoria. In this effort, they were joined by the remaining four Amboyna men, who swore that they had listened in on interrogation sessions in progress and seen the terrible impact of Dutch torture on English bodies. Following Collins's lead, they described the wholesale use of the water cure on the accused. As the water rose up, George

Sherrock explained, it "ran out at the eares, and nose, and made their eyes to stare as if they would have fallen out of their heades."[26] When this did not extract a confession, the Dutch used the flickering flame of a candle to brutally burn the accused until they were so badly injured, Ephraim Ramsey declared, that they "could not stirre out of the place where they lay, but stuncke insufferably haveinge wormes creepinge out of their wounds."[27]

Such descriptions extended beyond the core group of English merchants to the Japanese soldiers who had been interrogated first. Ramsey, for example, went on to explain that he had been imprisoned with Shichizō and the remainder of the Japanese contingent, who had been "miserably tormented with fire as aforesaid, insoemuch that their flesh rotted and did cleave from their bones, and stuncke and grewe full of maggots." While such accounts were suitably horrifying, they were almost certainly fabricated as well. The walls of the fortress were three feet thick, preventing any sound from escaping from one room to the next.[28] At the same time, it is difficult to believe that, even as the garrison watched nervously for any sign of a possible attack, they would have allowed a handful of English merchants to roam freely through the castle, visiting with suspected conspirators and observing their injuries. This point was confirmed by the Amboina judges, who explained that the handful of English merchants who had been acquitted were kept apart from the accused, so that there was no possibility of communication between the two groups.[29]

Although the bulk of the Admiralty depositions focused on the terrible nature of VOC torture, the Amboyna men also provided vivid accounts detailing their executed countrymen's last moments, including pious expressions of faith and declarations of absolute loyalty to their employer. John Beaumont testified that he had been granted access to Emmanuel Thomson, who had been brutally tortured with water and fire. Even as he lay in great pain, Thomson instructed Beaumont "to remember his duety to the honourable Company."[30] Such poignant details stuck deep in later imaginings of the trial. Writing in 1903, over three centuries later, one author honed in on this point, exclaiming, "Is there not pathos in the fact that the last words of most of these martyrs were for the Company!"[31] Not to be outdone, George Sherrock invented a moving dialogue between John Fardo and Samuel Coulson that ended with Coulson proclaiming that if he should be "found guilty of this cryme either more or lesse at thy Judgment seate soe lett me never be ptaker of thy heavenly Joyes."[32]

With its vivid accounts of devout English martyrs tortured by brutal and scheming Dutch interrogators, the Admiralty depositions offered up a deep vein of material that could be mined to craft a new version of the trial. Predictably, Collins, Beaumont, and the rest of the Amboyna men were welcomed with open arms, as their past offenses were discretely expunged from the record. For some of them, the turnaround was striking. In 1622, George Sherrock had been condemned as utterly unsuitable for employment. Writing to Towerson, his superiors instructed the chief merchant "not to trust [Sherrock] with any thing of charge, which belonge unto our maisters, and soe soone as we have others wee will send them, to remove him and some others, which are very unfitte to be ymployed in any busniss of ymportance."[33] After the Admiralty depositions, however, he was described as an "honest, diligent young man" and given employment as a purser's mate. For Edward Collins, the reversal was even more complete. Previously accused of stealing funds, he was now to be employed in the counting house, the very center of EIC financial activity, at a wage of ten shillings a week.[34] The remaining survivors were rewarded in different ways. John Beaumont asked for forty pounds that were owed to him out of one Edward Grant's wages, and a warrant for this was swiftly issued; John Powle received a promise of an investigation into the large sum that he claimed had been confiscated by the Dutch; and Ephraim Ramsey, the last of the six, was told that he would be presented to the king by Lord Holderness.[35]

Not surprisingly, the Amboyna men did everything possible to preserve their newfound status. Very quickly, a pattern was established in which they fed the Court of Committees with new snippets of Dutch brutality in return for additional support. In July 1624, for example, George Sherrock petitioned the EIC for help with goods and assets that had been seized in Amboina. To expedite the request, he offered up a fresh detail, claiming that in addition to waterboarding and burning, the Dutch "would gash the breasts of men, and having filled those gashes with powder, would put fire thereto."[36] It was a gruesome addition that was quickly incorporated into English accounts of the trial, and it earned Sherrock a generous award of ten pounds.

Over time, it became increasingly clear that rather than relying on this kind of piecemeal sponsorship, it would be cheaper to place the Amboyna men on a permanent stipend as professional witnesses. In December 1624, the EIC recorded that John Powle, William Webber, Ephraim Ramsey, and George Sherrock were to be offered ten shillings a week in return for a promise to remain in a constant state of readiness.[37] They lingered here, as the company's wards, year after year while the controversy dragged on. In May 1631, for example, more than eight years after the original trial, EIC officials decided that the weekly allowance of ten shillings should be extended yet again for Ramsey, Powle, and Beaumont, who remained frozen in the same status first conferred on them in 1624.[38]

Predictably it was Edward Collins, the great survivor, who managed to ride the Amboina gravy train longer and further than anyone else. Not content with a weekly stipend, he leveraged his position as an Amboina survivor in 1626 to become first a clerk and later the master of the company's first gunpowder mill at Chilworth.[39] There some old habits quickly reemerged, but despite ongoing questions about his misuse of money, he was able to petition successfully for an increased salary.[40] As the years passed, Amboina proved to be the most reliable of shields. Whenever he was called to account for his growing debts, Collins and his allies simply reminded their questioners that he was "one of those that suffered that cruel torture of Amboyna by the Dutch."[41] Faced by a figure that it had itself built up as a righteous martyr of VOC treachery, the EIC had little choice but to give in. Even with the organization's continued generosity, Collins managed to rack up huge debts far beyond his capacity to pay.[42] Despite bitter clashes in which EIC officials repeatedly explained that they had extended unprecedented favor in return for Collins's Amboina service, these debts remained unpaid until his death in 1636.[43]

While the Amboyna men had provided the raw materials, someone had to pull these accounts together into a single narrative that could be widely disseminated. That task was handed to John Skinner, an experienced EIC merchant who was charged with setting down the truth of what had happened at Amboina.[44] The result of his efforts was a lengthy account later republished as a pamphlet, *A True Relation of the Unjust, Cruell, and Barbarous Proceedings Against the English at Amboyna in the East-Indies, by the Neatherlandish Governour and Councel There.*[45] Packed with gruesome details, it delivered a powerful propaganda weapon that was pressed immediately into service.[46]

"Unjust, Cruell, and Barbarous"

By July 19, even as the last four survivors were still appearing before the Admiralty Court, Skinner's text was ready. It was, he claimed, a "bare and naked narration of the progresse and passages of this action" taken directly from the "sworn testimony of six credible witnesses"—that is, the Amboyna men with Beaumont and Collins at their head.[47] Over ten thousand words in length, *True Relation* welded the six Admiralty depositions into a single authoritative account of the arrest, torture, and execution of the accused plotters. At its center was a familiar message that the execution of the ten English merchants was the final act of a deliberate and carefully orches-trated plot designed to eject a commercial rival from Amboina. Given the vast scale of Dutch military strength of Amboina, there could be no pos-sibility that VOC officials had genuinely feared an attack. Instead, the "unsatiable covetousnesse of the Hollanders" had driven Van Speult to engineer a "cruell treacherie to gain the sole trade of the Molluccos, Banda, and Amboyna."

Much of Skinner's text was devoted to detailed accounts of torture and the torments supposedly visited upon English bodies by Dutch interroga-tors. Following Collins's lead, he explained that the individual victims had been forced to consume vast quantities of water until their bodies were "swollne twice or thrice as bigge as before," their "cheeks like great blad-ders," and their "eyes staring and strutting out."[48] In addition to condemn-ing Dutch interrogators as savage torturers, *True Relation* painted Towerson and his fellow merchants as righteous martyrs who had protested their innocence at every opportunity. As soon as the application of torture ceased, they proclaimed that "whatsoever they had formerly confessed, was most false."[49] And drawing deep on the reservoir of materials provided by the Amboyna men, it concluded with moving scenes in which the Towerson and the rest of the accused met their fate with doleful piety. Rejecting offers of wine to drown their sorrows, they spent their last night "in prayer, singing of Psalms, and comforting one another."[50] The result was a text filled with what Anthony Milton describes as "providential, martyrological tropes."[51]

While he took Collins and Beaumont as his most important sources, Skinner turned in secret to another informant carefully concealed from view in the text, which presented itself as the work of eye witnesses actu-ally present on Amboina at the time. This was Richard Welden, a disgraced EIC factor recently returned to London. Welden's crime was to have believed the charges against Towerson. Posted to the nearby Banda Islands, he had offered his "consent and Countenance" to the Amboina verdict when he was first informed of it.[52] According to reports that later filtered back to England, Welden had drunk the health of Van Speult while

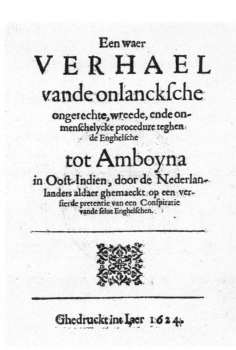

Een waer
VERHAEL
vande onlanckfche
ongerechte, wreede, ende on-
menfchelycke procedure teghen
de Enghelfche
tot Amboyna
in Ooft-Indien, door de Nederlan-
landers aldaer ghemaeckt op een ver-
fierde pretentie van een Confpiratie
vande felue Enghelfchen.

Ghedruckt int Iaer 1624.

Figure 6.1 Dutch translation of *A True Relation of the Unjust, Cruell, and Barbarous Proceedings*, pamphlet published from John Skinner's narrative. Nationaal Archief, Staten-Generaal, 1.01.02, inv. no. 12551.62.3.

treating Collins, Beaumont, and the other Amboina survivors "with imprisonment, blows, and hard speeches, to their utter discouragement."[53] Returning to London, Welden learned how badly he had miscalculated after he was condemned by his superiors for "carriage . . . so foul" that it had stained his reputation forever.[54] He had much to answer for. Instead of protesting the proceedings, he had in fact signed off on De Bruyn's judicial record when it was first shown to him, thereby providing his explicit consent for what had happened. Even more appalling, Welden had personally accepted a gift from Towerson's primary tormenter, Van Speult, even as his countrymen lay dead. All of this "bred a great detestation towards him" within the EIC hierarchy that threatened to ruin his career and make him a pariah.[55]

For Welden, the only way to repair relations and prove he was not a VOC sympathizer was by condemning the Dutch in Kota Ambon in the strongest possible terms. Even though he had not actually been present in Kota Ambon during the trial, Welden provided startling new testimony to Skinner, who confided to his superiors that this new account was the "most material and pregnant of all others."[56] It was a remarkable statement considering the exaggerated renditions of Dutch brutality already provided by Collins and Beaumont, but Welden seems to have given Skinner something new, a dramatic description of divine anger unleashed by VOC actions. In his retelling, the execution of the English merchants in Kota Ambon was accompanied by "a great darknesse, with a sudden and violent gust of winde and tempest" that almost wrecked the Dutch ships clustered in the harbor.[57] This was followed by a terrible illness that "swept away about a thousand people, Dutch and Amboyners." The meaning of such signs was unmistakable. They were "a token of the wrath of God for this barbarous tyranny of the Hollanders."[58]

Rushed to completion, *True Relation* proved an extraordinarily successful document. It layered a new and durable reading over the Amboina trial that presented it as a brutal act of judicial murder emanating from a confident VOC regime in full control of the territory. Once set down in print, it was an interpretation not easily shifted. Even now, close to four centuries later, Skinner's work continues to cast a long shadow, shaping English-language accounts all the way from the seventeenth century to modern representations that treat his account as an essentially factual description of events.[59]

In London, the Court of Committees, which met to discuss their wider strategy, was eager to use the formidable weapon Skinner had presented them with.[60] On July 20, just one day after the *True Relation* had been submitted, a petition was drawn up detailing the grave injustices done to the king's subjects at Amboina.[61] The next day EIC officials attending the king's bedroom at Wanstead handed over the petition and a copy of the *True Relation*, which was described as a "book, wherein was summarily set down the manner of the torments inflicted upon the English by the Dutch." They moved quickly to press their advantage. The king must act, EIC representatives insisted, to restore his honor, which had been violated by the torture and executions described in such graphic detail in Skinner's text. First, the king must secure justice against the murderers—that is, by making sure Van Speult, De Bruyn, and the remainder of the Amboina judges were properly punished. And second, the crown should force the Dutch East India Company or its home government to provide restitution for goods lost and trading opportunities denied by VOC action.[62]

Achieving such outcomes in the face of resistance would not be easy. If the EIC could look to the king for aid, so could the Dutch Company call on its own supporters within the States General and across the United Provinces. The overlap between the Dutch ruling elite and the VOC's directors (*bewindhebbers*) was a frequent topic of discussion for the Court of Committees, which sought ways to break these ties.[63] According to one report received from Amsterdam, "the Bewinthebbers are so mixed in the Government, and have knit to them all sorts of men of principal place" that there was no space to be found between state and company.[64] The only way to create one, EIC officials concluded, was by acquiring suitable bargaining chips. The king must, they insisted, seize some of the richly laden Dutch vessels passing through English ports and hold these until the States General was willing to give into their demands.[65] Without such leverage, the English company could expect no justice for Amboina.[66]

The king seemed to agree. Outraged by Skinner's shocking presentation, he pledged that he would have satisfaction for the unjust execution of his subjects and restitution for the losses that had been suffered. More importantly, if the States General did not respond appropriately, the king would act to seize Dutch vessels.[67] An initial deadline was set for August that year, by which time the States General should have taken action against Van Speult and the Amboina judges, who had done such damage to relations between the two states. When this date passed without any sign of movement from Dutch authorities, the Court of Committees resolved to step up the pressure.[68] In October, its members decided that three thousand copies of the *True Relation* should be circulated.[69] One-third of these were to be printed in a Dutch translation, carrying the fight directly into the United Provinces, where the pamphlet was intended to split the VOC from its supporters in the States General.[70] To give further weight to the charges, a woodcut image was commissioned, showing an unnamed English merchant being tortured with water and candles while another knelt in prayer, ready for execution. As Anthony Milton has shown, such depictions, which drew directly from a 1570 edition of John Foxe's *Book of Martyrs*, confirmed Towerson and his subordinates in their new role as righteous martyrs.[71]

In the United Provinces, VOC officials watched these developments with trepidation. Since the news of the original trial had broken, the Company had been able to count on the support of the States General, but there was growing resentment within that body and from other influential

Figure 6.2 Image depicting torture of the English, from *A True Relation of the Unjust, Cruell, and Barbarous Proceedings.* https://archive.org/details/trverelationofvnooeast /page/n7.

parties in Dutch politics, including the *Stadhouder,* Prince Maurits (1567–1625). The Amboina trial had disrupted a vital military alliance between the United Provinces and England, jeopardizing its long-running war against Spain. While EIC dreams of a "divorce betwixt the States and Bewinthebbers" had not materialized, the king's willingness to authorize seizures of Dutch ships threatened to change the political equation even as the circulation of Skinner's explosive allegations in translation forced the VOC back on the defensive. The danger was clear enough that, according to rumors circulating in the United Provinces, agents acting for the *bewindhebbers* had attempted to buy up all the translated copies of the *True Relation.*[72] What the Heeren 17 needed was a counter to Skinner's text, and their own witness who could dispute what the Amboyna men had said. And in September 1624, just as the king started to apply pressure, one of the former judges arrived back in the United Provinces ready to do precisely this.

The "Bloody Judge Maerschalke"

Fourteen VOC officials had signed their names at the bottom of each confession in De Bruyn's trial record.[73] First was Van Speult, who remained in his post at Amboina after the final verdict, but just below him was Laurens de Maerschalk, an upper merchant and the governor's putative second-in-command, who had returned to Europe in the aftermath of the case.[74] Like the EIC's star witnesses, De Maerschalk had not distinguished himself during his tenure as a company employee. Instead, after an initial rise through the ranks, his career had been cut short by criticism and disappointment.

Arriving in Asia in 1620, De Maerschalk first appeared as an assistant on the rolls of Castle Victoria in 1620, with a salary of twenty guilders per month. By 1621 he had been promoted to the position of merchant on a salary of fifty guilders a month, and at some point after this he was raised to the position of *opperkoopman*.[75] Despite this steady progress, he did not impress Van Speult, who reprimanded his subordinate publicly for his failings as an administrator.[76] VOC officials conventionally signed three-year contracts, which were renewed on multiple occasions, usually with increased wages each time. Competent administrators like Van Speult—or even far more mediocre figures whose main achievement was surviving the high mortality rate in Asia—tended to stay on, rising through the ranks of an organization desperately in need of qualified officials. No such path was available for De Maerschalk, however, either because he saw no future in the company or because the organization made it clear that he had none. The result was that in June 1623, as soon as his contract expired, the *opperkoopman* began the long journey back to Europe.

De Maerschalk reached Delft in September 1624 just as the EIC was moving to make more use of Skinner's inflammatory text. His arrival in the United Provinces sparked immediate protest in London. The Court of Committees wanted justice done against the officials who had presided over Amboina, and the "bloody judge Maerschalke" must be imprisoned immediately to face trial for his actions in Asia.[77] In Delft, however, local authorities had no intention of taking action against someone whose only crime had been to fight off a dangerous conspiracy. A furious back-and-forth ensued, with EIC officials demanding the jailing of De Maerschalk and the States General pointing to the limits of its influence when it came to provincial authorities. The dispute dragged on for months, with

English officials calling again and again for the arrest of a figure they presented as a murderer who should not be permitted to walk free.[78] After months of protesting, the English company was informed that De Maerschalk had at last been placed under house arrest in Delft.[79] It seemed like a victory, but in fact local authorities had simply requested that De Maerschalk stay inside his house "for a while."[80] Willing to cooperate, he had promised not to show himself on the streets, at least temporarily.

While the dispute over De Maerschalk dragged on, the VOC moved swiftly to put the former judge on the record, and in early November he was deposed in front of sympathetic magistrates in Delft.[81] As was the case with the Amboyna men, his testimony presented an opportunity to secure ongoing financial support in return for useful information, but for De Maerschalk the stakes were even higher. While Collins and Beaumont's trial was over, his lay ahead. The English company, with the support of the crown, was pushing aggressively for the arrest and prosecution of the Amboina judges, and within a few years De Maerschalk would find himself on trial for his actions in Asia.

One way forward was to place all the blame on De Bruyn by defending the legitimacy of the prosecution and its pursuit of a dangerous conspiracy, but offering up the incompetent advocate-fiscal as a scapegoat for every missed procedure and every broken protocol. De Maerschalk's own actions in the immediate wake of the trial's conclusion suggests that he realized very quickly that De Bruyn had bungled the case. On March 24, 1623, that is, just two weeks after the execution of the alleged conspirators, De Maerschalk had moved, apparently on his own initiative, to record in front of a witness a formal statement that he had heard John Beaumont personally confess his guilt. It was an extraordinary step to take so soon after a properly constituted trial had come to an end, and it revealed a clear awareness that the advocate-fiscal's record would not stand up to scrutiny without further evidence.[82]

But even if De Bruyn's incompetence was obvious, shifting all the blame to him carried its own risks. After all, De Maerschalk had been a senior administrator in Kota Ambon in 1623 and he should have acted to rein in the advocate-fiscal's excesses or made sure that the proper procedures had been followed. It was, therefore, far safer to go on the offensive by presenting a new version of the trial that exonerated everyone, including the advocate-fiscal, Van Speult, and of course De Maerschalk himself.

Making such a case, however, required the former judge to repair a number of lapses, gaps, and errors in the original legal process.

One of the primary complaints leveled against De Bruyn was that he had not followed standard Dutch legal practice by requiring the accused to confirm their confessions outside of the torture chamber when they were no longer under duress.[83] When he came to explain the case in 1624, however, De Maerschalk testified that in fact this had been done, not once but multiple times for each of the accused. In this new version, each of the accused had confirmed the charges "without torture or fetters, at many sittings, and full assemblies of the council at Amboyna, without revoking any thing, or desiring to diminish or augment any thing from or to their said confessions."[84]

While this filled in a missing step, De Maerschalk went further by declaring that Van Speult had taken extraordinary steps to make sure that each of the accused had been absolutely clear about their own guilt. The governor had, De Maerschalk claimed, required each of the confessions to be confirmed "four or five times."[85] Even after this, he went back again to ask each of the accused if they had confessed only out "fear of menaces, or terror of pain," with the intention of excusing anyone who was not prepared to validate their confession.[86] Rather than taking this opportunity to exonerate themselves, the alleged plotters, both English and Japanese, had simply shrugged and confirmed the charges. Because of this, there could be no question as to the accused's guilt. It was a significant reworking of the trial, but one that appears to have had as little basis in fact as the picture presented by the Amboyna men. There is no indication that Van Speult or De Bruyn had taken any of these steps, and the rushed nature of the legal proceedings makes it difficult to give any weight to this story of a meticulous process filled with multiple checks and confirmations.

While such claims served to strengthen the Dutch case, the former judge also struck back at Skinner's shocking descriptions of stoic English martyrs facing off against brutal Dutch torturers. Not surprisingly, De Maerschalk took aim at the EIC's star witness, Edward Collins, who had, he explained, confessed freely without the application of torture. Brought before Towerson, Collins had eagerly denounced the chief merchant as the ringleader of the plot.[87] And it was not just Collins who had admitted his guilt. Even Towerson himself had publicly reproached his subordinates for their "ill and disordinate lives, their whoredome and drunkenness," which had caused them to reveal the "intended enterprize."[88] And there was more. In the moments before he was executed, Towerson had taken personal responsibility for everything that had happened, admitting his role and asking his countrymen for their pardon.

Not only did this picture demolish Skinner's portrait of stoic martyrs, but De Maerschalk claimed as well that VOC authorities in Kota Ambon had in fact found documentary proof of English treachery. It came in the form of a secret letter supposedly written by Gabriel Towerson to Samuel Coulson, whose smuggled-out declaration of innocence had become a central plank of the EIC case. According to De Maerschalk, Towerson had castigated Coulson as the principal architect of the plot, and this letter was even now in the possession of Van Speult in Kota Ambon. If real, such a document would have shown clear evidence of a plot, albeit one with very different contours and an alternate ringleader; but, when pressed, no one seemed able to locate it. When he heard of the letter's existence, the governor-general demanded that it be sent immediately to Batavia for assessment, but there is no further mention of the document. Given how eager the VOC was to seize on any scrap of evidence, its disappearance means that either, as Coolhaas suggests, De Maerschalk made up the letter entirely or that he misrepresented the contents of a document that did little to support the notion of an organized conspiracy.[89]

While few of his claims could be backed up, De Maerschalk proved a compelling witness whose testimony served to push back against Skinner's narrative. In this much-revised version of the trial, De Bruyn and Van Speult had moved laboriously through the ranks of the accused, checking and rechecking their guilt until there could be no further doubt. Outside of the interrogation chamber, the English themselves had admitted their own involvement in the plot, not huddling together as innocent martyrs but denouncing each other for giving up their terrible secret. All of this strengthened the VOC case, but it also diverged significantly from the version presented in *The Confessions and Sentences*. It required no small leap to accept that the most meticulous of trials had been represented in the shoddiest of documents that had simply omitted to mention all the steps that had been taken to ensure the guilt of the accused. But for the VOC hierarchy and their allies in the States General, such claims offered a way to buttress a precarious legal edifice under attack by Skinner's charges. The result was that they embraced De Maerschalk and his version of events with open arms.

Like the Amboyna men, the former judge was converted into a professional witness placed permanently in readiness to provide additional details. Whereas they had attached themselves to their former employee, De Maerschalk became a ward of the States General. It proved an enduring status that far exceeded his original tenure in the Company. Having served the VOC for just three years, De Maerschalk remained in its defense on the States General payroll for close to a decade. Over this period, he became a regular presence in its deliberations as he demanded and regularly received five hundred guilders, a sum not far off the annual salary earned by a VOC merchant, to pay for his annual upkeep as well as individual funds for food and clothing.[90] Such requests provided a reliable stream of income. As late as April 1632, more than nine years after the original trial, he was still there, demanding and receiving a payment of 450 guilders from the States General.[91]

If De Maerschalk's 1624 deposition secured for him a new and more successful career as a witness, it also changed the way the Dutch company talked about the case by providing the centerpiece for a far more robust defense of the proceedings. Seizing on this enhanced version of a model trial, VOC authorities acted swiftly to make sure that no rival accounts could emerge from their side. De Maerschalk's testimony was immediately dispatched back to Batavia to be endorsed by the rest of the former judges there. Since the conclusion of the 1623 trial, the original Amboina judges had scattered. Some had remained in Kota Ambon, others had been posted to different parts of the VOC empire, and a few had died. In 1625, however, they were summoned back to Batavia to complete two urgent tasks.

First, they were required to answer a long list of 139 questions designed to counter the most sensational allegations contained within the *True Relation*. It was a mark of how seriously VOC officials took Skinner's text that they had insisted on having every surviving judge refute its claims point by point. The result was a mountain of depositions designed to undercut and dismiss Skinner's most lurid accusations.[92] The judges' second task was to sign off on De Maerschalk's account of the trial. One by one, they added their signatures to the bottom of a ten-point document that reproduced his Delft deposition almost word for word.[93] By the time it was sent back to Europe, there were seven names there, including Van Speult, five of the former judges, and the secretary who had recorded the original trial, although crucially not De Bruyn himself. The result was to elevate De Maerschalk's version of events while shutting out the possibility of competing accounts. How exactly the former judges responded to this retelling of events that pictured De Bruyn as a model prosecutor is not clear, but they surely recognized the value of a version of the case that effectively exonerated them from any charge of misconduct. In the war of the witnesses, they crowded predictably around De Maerschalk as the surest way to ward off the attacks contained in Skinner's document and the possibility of English retribution.

In London, Skinner had turned to the former Banda factor, Richard Welden, who, despite not actually being present in Kota Ambon in 1623, was eager to add inflammatory new details to the emerging account. In their efforts to defend against English accusations, the Heeren 17 adopted the same strategy as they looked toward additional witnesses to push back against Skinner's charges. They found their most useful informant in Frederik de Houtman, the former governor of the neighboring Moluccas, who had arrived in Kota Ambon in the weeks after the trial had concluded and had added his signature to *The Confessions and Sentences* on March 29, 1623.[94] Although he had not been involved in the actual trial, De Houtman, who arrived back in the United Provinces around the same time as De Maerschalk, was drafted into service to strengthen the Company's case.

Torture "Most Civil"

Frederik de Houtman (1571?–1627) was a VOC veteran whose long career had run parallel with the development and expansion of the Dutch company. He had participated in the first voyage to Asia at the end of the sixteenth century, before serving as governor over multiple territories, including Amboina itself from 1605 to 1611 and the Moluccas from 1621 to 1623. Perhaps more than any other VOC official aside from Van Speult, he was qualified to speak to the turbulent political environment that the governor found himself in at the outbreak of the Amboina trial. De Houtman's deposition, however, focused on something quite different: the torture technique used to extract the overwhelming majority of confessions.

The VOC veteran took aim first at Collins's fabrications. Dutch interrogators had never, De Houtman insisted, poured vast quantities of water into the victim's mouth in order to force a confession by swelling their internal organs. Instead, water had been trickled through a cloth pulled over the face, restricting breathing and stimulating the sense of drowning.[95] At the same time, De Houtman offered a powerful defense of the "torture by water" itself, which was, he insisted, a uniquely moderate technique of interrogation that stood apart from other techniques in use across Europe. He started by explaining that waterboarding was a standard part of VOC legal procedure that had "always been used by the Netherlanders in the Indies." Its widespread use hinged not on its brutal efficacy but rather on its nature as the "most certain and most civil" of all interrogation techniques. Because of this, a clear distinction could be drawn between this method and far harsher techniques. It was, he declared, a form of torment not "so hard or dangerous as is used here in these lands [the United Provinces] or the whole of Europe." In contrast to standard interrogation techniques that involved the dislocation or breaking of limbs, waterboarding caused no lasting physical harm. Since the "health of the person" was not damaged, nor any limb "lamed or bruised," the "torture of water" was nothing more than a psychological oppression that left no lasting imprint on the victim's body.[96] Real torture, in other words, left shattered bones, bloody wounds, and permanent scars on the body in its wake. The "torture of water" was something else entirely, a technique all of its own.

It was an intriguing defense that closely resembles the arguments made by the Bush administration centuries later when its officials came to justify the legality of waterboarding.[97] In some ways, it is surprising that De Houtman even felt the need to make this point. A wide range of torture techniques were entirely legal in the United Provinces, and by extension in Dutch possessions in Asia. If the Company followed De Maerschalk's version of events, which argued that all possible protocols had been correctly followed, there was nothing to defend. No one suggested that torture should be anything less than brutal if it had to extract a confession from a guilty party in the shortest possible time. But De Houtman's defense was of course designed to do something different by neutralizing Skinner's image of savage VOC torturers inflicting appalling pain. Armed with this defense of the "torture of water," Dutch officials could argue that not only had the trial been entirely legal but that the kind of torture technique that was used in Kota Ambon was far more moderate than anything used in courts across Europe. In this way, the 1623 conspiracy case could morph from Skinner's stage for torment into a judicial model in which the most "civil" of tortures was called into action only to confirm the absolute guilt of the accused.

VOC officials recognized immediately how helpful De Houtman's testimony was to its case. As with De Maerschalk's deposition, it was hurriedly dispatched to Asia to be endorsed by officials there. The document came first to the bailiff of Batavia, the senior legal official in Asia, who drew up his own statement:

> We bailiff of the city of Batavia to solemnly declare, under the oath taken on the assumption of our office and duties, that the form of torture using water has always been practiced by the Dutch in the Indies as being the most civil one, and that the same causes no such severe pain [*geen soo harde pijn*] as the form of torture normally applied throughout Europe which has always been judged to be much more severe, cruel and dangerous than that involving the use of water, whereby neither the person's health nor any of his limbs are harmed or damaged. Confirming the above with this our ordinary municipal seal, affixed in the space below, drawn up and testified in the town of Batavia on the 7th day of October 1625.[98]

Although he made no mention of this, the official in question was in fact one of the former Amboina judges, who had since moved on to take a position in the Company's headquarters.[99] Not surprisingly then, he showed no hesitation in endorsing De Houtman's positive description of waterboarding as very different from the "more severe, cruel and dangerous" techniques used across Europe. Instead it occupied, he declared confidently, a separate category. The "torture of water" was little more than a trick of the mind that left no lasting physical damage. The moment it concluded, the subject was restored to full health, with no broken limbs or other marks of physical torment.

The combined testimonies provided by De Maerschalk and De Houtman served to remake the VOC case, offering a powerful justification of the underlying legal procedure and the interrogation technique on which it depended. These two accounts were incorporated, essentially word for word, into a new and detailed defense of the case that was presented first to the States General on November 5, to shore up support before being handed over to EIC representatives in a French translation.[100] It later appeared in an English-language pamphlet titled *A Remonstrance of the Directors of the Netherlands East India Company Presented to the Lords States Generall of the United Provinces, in Defence of the Said Companie.* The *Remonstrance* became the official Dutch East India Company response to Skinner's claims, and its contents were reiterated again and again by VOC representatives as they sought to deflect any allegation of misconduct. Predictably, this new version of events generated an immediate reaction from the English company, which lashed out at De Maerschalk as an unreliable observer simply trying to defend his own actions, and at De Houtman's favorable interpretation of the "torture of water."[101] Instead of a uniquely moderate torture, waterboarding was, they insisted, far worse than a purely physical torment because it sapped the psychological capacity of the victim to resist.

The completion of the *Remonstrance* brought the first stage of the war of the witnesses to a close. By November 1624, just over eighteen months after the execution of the alleged plotters in front of Castle Victoria, clear battle lines had been drawn between two very different versions of the case. Although they diverged on the most basic of points, the EIC's *True Relation* and the Dutch company's *Remonstrance* combined in one way: to wipe away the signs of the original trial. For both organizations, it was better to overlay the disordered nature of De Bruyn's work with a clear story about Dutch brutality or English villainy. For officials attached to the English East India Company, it was far more valuable to present the trial as a deliberate, orderly, and systematic act of judicial murder that violated the king's honor and hence required action by the crown. A conspiracy orchestrated by the Dutch to expel their rivals offered a simpler and more compelling message than a blundering legal process propelled forward without a clear design.

On the other side, the presentation of the trial as methodical, deliberate, and marked by carefully observed safeguards offered the best way for the VOC to defend what had happened in Kota Ambon in 1623 in the face of systematic attacks from London. Swallowing their earlier criticism of De Bruyn, Dutch officials argued that the trial was a model case underpinned by the most moderate of tortures. In this way, both versions sought to unhook the trial from the turbulent environment that had shaped it, with lasting consequences for how the Amboina case has been understood.[102]

CHAPTER VII

Compensation and Calamity

All complaint, action, and demand of the English whomsoever, whether public or private, on the score of any injury or damage which they pretend to have suffered at Amboina . . . may be made void, terminated and committed to oblivion.

—REGULATION MADE BY THE COMMISSIONERS, 1654

We have stripped all the lands . . . of their cloves and nuts and emptied them of people.

—MEMORIAL OF ARNOLD DE VLAMING VAN OUDSHOORN, 1656

In 1654, John and Elizabeth Collins received unexpected news about their father, Edward, who had died years earlier while they were still children. The Dutch East India Company had agreed to pay them £465 in compensation for the injuries that he had suffered more than three decades earlier on Amboina.[1] It was part of a much larger settlement set in motion by the Treaty of Westminster, which had been signed in 1654, after the conclusion of the first Anglo-Dutch War. Rather than attempting to settle the Amboina impasse, the treaty had created a panel of arbitration, formed of four members from both sides, to resolve all outstanding differences between the two companies.[2] By the time the dust had settled on their deliberations, the panel had ruled in the EIC's favor, concluding that the Dutch company should pay the organization £85,000 in settlement of its losses and £3,615 to the heirs of the English merchants caught up in the Amboina trial, including £465 to John and Elizabeth Collins.

The Treaty of Westminster seems to mark the natural end point of the Amboina story. While the controversy was kept alive by a steady stream of outraged pamphlets that were published and republished during the second (1665–1667) and third (1672–1674) Anglo-Dutch Wars, the settlement concluded the formal dispute between the companies, which agreed as part of the arbitration process to drop any further complaints about what had happened in 1623. Because the treaty marked an important milestone in Anglo-Dutch relations, this is also one part of the Amboina story that is especially well known.[3] It forms a neat package: a war, a negotiation, and a final payout in favor of the long-standing complainant, with the negotiations meticulously documented in Dutch and English sources. But while the action that took place over a European negotiating table was significant, this was not the only place where the aftermath of the trial played out. Instead there is a second story, well documented by historians of Amboina and the Dutch colonial presence there but ignored in accounts of the 1623 trial that focus entirely on negotiations in Europe.

The conspiracy case that erupted in February 1623 was rooted in a wider sense of unease and anxiety that pervaded the settlement at Kota Ambon. By the time Shichizō first appeared on the walls of the castle, Van Speult and his subordinates had felt themselves perched on the edge of a precipice facing imminent disaster. The trial itself both drew from and magnified these dangers as De Bruyn conjured up a sprawling plot that pulled together a seething mass of colonial fears. This sense of crisis emerged out of the particular combination of factors detailed in the first half of this book, but it also reflected a shift in the nature of the Dutch colonial presence in Amboina. By 1623, the VOC stood at the beginning of a bloody thirty-year struggle to enforce the treaties it had signed, subdue or eradicate rival centers of power, and finally secure its monopoly over the clove trade. Over the subsequent decades the Company would fight a sequence of increasingly bitter conflicts, first labeled by Georg Everard Rumphius (1627–1702) as the Amboinese wars (*Ambonschen oorlog*), in 1625, 1636–1637, 1641–1646, and 1650–1656, against a combination of former allies, rivals, and its own colonial subjects.[4]

The final pacification of the unruly Hoamoal Peninsula, which had loomed so large in the buildup to the trial, came to a climax just as the Treaty of Westminster was being signed in Europe. As the commissioners sat down in London, the Dutch East India Company, responding to a bloody revolt that had broken out in 1651, moved to remake the political terrain in a conflict now known as the Hoamoalese War (1651–1656/8).[5] A series of climactic battles in 1654 and 1655, followed by a campaign of mass relocation, left behind what Dutch observers described as a depopulated wasteland.[6] By the time the conflict finally ground to a halt in 1656, the Company was master over a territory in which rival power centers had been either bound tightly to Castle Victoria or simply erased from the map.[7]

Both of these stories are important. This chapter shifts between the twin theaters of Asia and Europe in an attempt to trace the long aftermath of the case. It argues that the traditional focus on European negotiations should not obscure the far greater changes happening in Amboina as the remnants of the landscape that Van Speult had confronted in 1623 were swept away by the Hoamoalese War.

Breaking the Stalemate in Europe

By the closing months of 1624, both the Dutch and the English companies had armed themselves with their own sets of witnesses and their own accounts of what had happened. Any chance of breaking through the political deadlock depended on whether the king would make good on his promises to seize Dutch shipping, thereby delivering a powerful bargaining chip that might force concessions. A single vessel could carry hundreds of thousands of guilders worth of goods, and sustained naval action would paralyze the large volume of Dutch traffic passing through the North Sea. In late November 1624, the States General decided it was not worth taking the risk. Whereas its members had previously stalled by insisting that the events in Amboina were "so much enveloped in doubt and contradiction that it is impossible for them to proceed without further information," they now resolved to summon Van Speult and the remaining Amboina judges back to the United Provinces to answer for their actions.[8]

Although it was a concession, it was also the easiest way to defuse the escalating crisis without promising too much. The "king of Great Britain was," Dutch officials explained, "so discontented over the execution at Amboina, that he is ready to make reprisals against the Company's goods." It was not simply the VOC that was vulnerable to such action. Instead, the king "threatens to go further and to extend [his reprisals] against all the inhabitants of this state." Given these dangers, "there is no other way to settle with the king than to summon the governor of Amboina Van Speult and all others that were involved in the trial and execution of the English."[9] But because it would take years for the message to reach Batavia and then for the surviving Amboina judges to return to Europe, the decision also gave the States General considerable breathing room, opening up a space for English pressure to subside.

The Heeren 17, who believed they had presented a compelling defense to the States General in the *Remonstrance*, which had been handed over just weeks earlier, reacted furiously, declaiming the damage that had been done to the Company and insisting that the States General was failing in its most basic duty of protection.[10] However outraged, they were in no position to resist the recall demand, which was dispatched onto Batavia for immediate action. The first person the States General wanted back in Europe to defend his conduct was of course Van Speult, who, as the senior official involved in the trial, had emerged as the most visible target for English anger. By November 1624, when the States General decided to bring him home, the governor was still ensconced behind the walls of Castle Victoria, confronting a largely unchanged political environment that even eighteen months later appeared crowded with unresolved perils.

The Campaign Against Luhu

In their final verdict, the Amboina judges had indicted Luhu on the Hoamoal Peninsula as a key conspirator that had promised to dispatch hundreds of its warriors to Kota Ambon to join Towerson's plot and help drive the Dutch into the sea. In the subsequent months, Van Speult was insistent that action must be taken against the *kimelaha* and his supporters in Luhu, who were too dangerous to be left in a state of open defiance. The problem was that he lacked the soldiers necessary for a campaign against a militarized center that the governor himself estimated could muster 2,500 fighting men.[11] Without a significant infusion of troops, it was impossible to even contemplate an attack. In Batavia, itself struggling with manpower concerns, there were no reinforcements to be had.[12] Writing back, the governor's superiors explained they were unable to supply the forces needed to "redress the troubles." Instead, Van Speult was ordered to stay within the walls of the castle, thereby preserving his existing forces and not risking them on "dangerous enterprises."[13] In this way, he should restrict himself to "defensive rather than offensive war," taking no action that might leave the castle exposed to attack or deplete the ranks of what few troops he did possess.

Convinced that something had to be done, Van Speult pleaded with his superiors that a force of four or five hundred soldiers and five or six well-equipped yachts was all that was needed to properly stabilize Amboina.[14] He sketched out a comprehensive plan of action for this imagined army. First the Company's vessels should halt all maritime traffic coming into three key polities on the Hoamoal Peninsula: Lessidi, Kambelo, and Luhu.

With their trading links severed, Van Speult could attack Luhu and drive its inhabitants away. Once the military campaign was over, VOC troops should "ruin all their clove and fruit trees." With their settlement destroyed and no income from cloves to rebuild, Luhu would simply disappear from the map as its inhabitants would be forced to depart their former home.[15]

In Batavia, Van Speult's superiors were willing to endorse such action, but with no suitable force available it was clear to everyone that such plans would have to be put indefinitely on hold.[16] By March 1625, more than two years had passed since the original conspiracy trial and its verdict that Luhu had joined the plot against the Dutch. For all of Van Speult's bold statements about the need to strike back, Castle Victoria remined perilously weak, hemmed in by "feigned friends" and enemies on all sides. The situation was transformed overnight when a potent naval force appeared as if by chance in the region.[17] In early 1625, a fleet of "warlike Netherlands ships from the west of Peru" dropped anchor unexpectedly in Ternate.[18] This was the so-called *Nassause Vloot*, an armada of warships that had been jointly assembled by the VOC and the States General and sent westward from Europe with instructions to launch an all-out assault on Spanish possessions and shipping in the Pacific. After some successes in the Americas, the ships headed for Asia, crossing through the Straits of Magellan with most of the fleet intact. Arriving in the region, the *Nassause Vloot* was immediately seized upon by VOC officials desperate for reinforcements. By April 1625, part of the fleet had been detached and sent to Kota Ambon to reinforce the beleaguered governor there.[19]

The *Nassause Vloot* provided what Tristan Mostert describes as a military deus ex machina that suddenly altered the balance of power in Amboina.[20] For years, the governor had been forced to shelter behind the walls of Castle Victoria, unable to strike back against the plotters, who had, he believed, conspired with Towerson to murder or capture him and expel the Dutch from Amboina. Now, at last, Van Speult had sufficient strength to venture beyond Kota Ambon to punish Luhu, Kambelo, and other settlements on the Hoamoal Peninsula for their "insolence, murderousness and other pride."[21] The expedition was led jointly by Van Speult and his recently arrived successor, Jan van Gorcum, who would go on to serve as governor of Amboina from 1625 to 1628. It consisted of three ships and a number of sloops manned by 700 European sailors from the Nassau fleet, 150 soldiers from Castle Victoria, and 20 *kora-kora* rowed by loyal subjects drawn from the villages around Kota Ambon.[22] Opening the attack, VOC ships bombarded Luhu, raining over a hundred cannon shots on the fortified settlement before disgorging large numbers of troops to carry the assault onto land.[23] After the last sign of resistance had been stamped out, Luhu's strongholds and its surrounding villages were razed to the ground. The campaign did not end there. As long as the wealth of the clove orchards could be tapped, houses could be rebuilt, markets restarted, and old patterns of trade restored. In keeping with the plans he had laid out in his letters to Batavia, Van Speult moved to sever Luhu's economic lifeline by destroying "all the enemies' fruit tree."[24] It was backbreaking work, hacking down dense groves of clove trees, some of which stood as high as forty feet and had been in place for up to a hundred years.[25] It took weeks to complete the job, but by the end of the campaign tens of thousands of trees had been cut down, leaving the landscape denuded.[26]

After weeks of additional campaigning that took the fleet across the Hoamoal Peninsula, Van Speult handed over charge of the colony to his successor and departed Amboina for Batavia.[27] Once there, his tactics were enthusiastically endorsed by his superiors, who presented them to the Heeren 17 in 1626 as a blueprint for permanent VOC control over the Hoamoal Peninsula. The only way to "put an end to the continual unrest and to secure the cloves of Amboina for the Company" was to make use of what they described as "extreme remedies" (d'uutterste remedie). It was not simply Luhu that should be targeted in this manner. Instead, Batavia was clear that "Luhu, Kambelo, Lucelle, Lesidi, Eram and all their faithless Moorish supporters should be exterminated [verdelgd] and chased away [verdreven], all their clove and fruit trees extirpated, the land devastated."[28] Expressed in the language of extermination and expulsion, Batavia sketched out the outlines of a devastating campaign to pacify Hoamoal.[29] This belief in the need for "extreme remedies" would resurface periodically in VOC documents through later decades but was only transformed into official strategy during the Hoamoalese War in 1651, when a rebellion across Amboina pushed the organization to finally embrace these tactics.

Alongside their endorsement of Van Speult's tactics against Luhu, VOC authorities in Batavia, who were still unaware of the States General's decision to recall the former judges, feted the governor for his role in suppressing Towerson's dangerous conspiracy. Although there had been a spate of initial criticism aimed especially at De Bruyn, the Company had by this point largely fallen in line behind its administrators. It helped that the case had been significantly bolstered by De Maerschalk's intervention. While in Batavia, Van Speult added his signature to his subordinate's enhanced version of events, which presented the governor in the most positive light possible, as a methodical and careful administrator who had taken extraordinary steps to assure himself of the accused's guilt.

Even as they praised Van Speult for halting English treachery, VOC officials in Batavia moved quietly to make sure that such a high-profile case with its controversial aftermath would not be repeated. In the aftermath of Amboina, two regulations restricted the capacity of VOC administrators in outlying outposts to pursue conspiracy trials through the unlimited application of torture. First in 1625 and then again in 1632, the governor-general limited the instances in which torture could be used to extract confessions, while also requiring outlying officials to seek approval from Batavia before proceeding with cases of conspiracy or treason. The first order seemed specifically targeted at avoiding another controversy by insisting on the need for clear and "infallible presumptions" before proceeding to torture.[30] The result was not to put a stop to VOC conspiracy trials, which continued to recur across the seventeenth century, but rather to bring them more tightly under the control of the center.

Judging the Amboina Judges

In the years since the 1623 trial, Van Speult seems to have become convinced that any likelihood of English reprisal had faded. In his own letters, he had become increasingly confident not only that his swift actions had averted a bloody plot, but that any "objective and sensible [observer] will and shall celebrate our proceedings on this conspiracy and thank the Almighty that they opened our eyes and guarded [us] from their bloody hand." [31] Still, he did not object when the governor-general decided that it was safer to send him far away from the glare of English eyes on a long voyage to the port of Surat on the Indian coast. This meant that by the time the recall notice from the States General finally arrived in Batavia, Van Speult was already hundreds of miles away, en route to India. As a result, the governor-general was forced to dispatch a letter informing his subordinate that he had to return to the United Provinces immediately to answer questions about the case.

Although it made a determined effort to reassure Van Speult that he would be vindicated, the letter was ominous. It explained that the decision to bring him back had been made in response to English pressure, but also that the former governor would be required to answer for some "required formalities" that had been neglected in the original legal proceedings.[32] The implication was clear. Even with De Maerschalk's intervention, Van Speult was still on the hook for De Bruyn's flawed legal proceedings and would be required to explain in Europe exactly what had happened. It was bad enough to travel thousands of miles to answer such questions in the United Provinces, but the letter raised the terrible fear shared by all the Amboina judges. Would they have to answer for their actions before sympathetic judges in The Hague or would they be summoned to face their accusers in London, where an angry mob, whipped up by Skinner's pamphlet and a steady drip of news about Dutch atrocities on Amboina, would attack them in the streets?[33] Although he had argued that Towerson and the rest of the English merchants at Amboina should be sent to Batavia to face judgement there, Van Speult had signed off on their final execution, making him the first target of any push to punish the Amboina judges. The news was disturbing enough that the governor-general felt it necessary to remind Van Speult of his duty, writing that "we trust you will be willing to conform as an obedient subject of the sovereignty of the United Netherlands" to such instructions. As a further caution, Batavia warned him to guard against any possibility of coming under the "command of the English" on the long journey home. Exposing his person to English jurisdiction, even for a moment, could, the letter seemed to suggest, see Van Speult seized, bundled into a ship, and transported back to London before his employer could protest.

In an instant, the letter converted Van Speult from a respected VOC administrator assured of a future within the organization into a hunted man always watching for English agents lying in wait. The missive from the governor-general was carried aboard the *Zirickzee*, which departed for Surat in search of the former governor.[34] As with so much related to the Amboina case, there are contradictory accounts of what happened next. One suggests that the letter reached Van Speult in transit. According to George Forbes, the Scottish steward who was aboard the same vessel, the missive from the governor-general had a catastrophic effect. Arriving without warning, it brought Van Speult's confident expectations crashing down, plunging the former governor into a state of shock and turning his hair prematurely gray.[35] Within a few months he was bedridden and he died a broken man in July 1626.[36] Others within the Company suggested that Van Speult had fallen sick and died still ignorant of the letter and its summons.[37] Either way, it was a sudden end for a VOC administrator who had once seemed destined for greater things, and it meant that Van Speult never got to defend his actions in Europe.

Back in London, the Court of Committees remained convinced that the States General was simply stalling for time and only reprisals against Dutch shipping would spur genuine action from The Hague. To keep the pressure on, the organization commissioned a massive painting depicting in graphic detail the savage tortures of water and fire that had supposedly been wrought upon Towerson and his men. Although EIC officials insisted that their goal was only to create "a perpetual memory of that most bloody and treacherous villainy," it was clear that the painting was designed to hammer home Skinner's charges against the Dutch.[38] These attempts to ramp up the pressure were interrupted by King James I's unexpected death in March 1625 and the succession of his second son, Charles. Eager to secure immediate action from the new monarch, the English Company offered up detailed directions laying out exactly where the king's ships should lie in wait in order to seize Dutch shipping.[39] To make sure that nothing was missed, the EIC also dispatched two of the Amboyna men, Ephraim Ramsey and John Powle, to look out for any sign of the former judges who might be returning to the United Provinces. If they were discovered hiding in the holds of one of the ships, they should be arrested on sight and brought to London to stand trial.[40]

It quickly became clear that the new king had very different priorities.[41] In May, a VOC ship was spotted lying off Dover but it departed without interference. The next month, Charles received yet another Amboina petition with apparent indifference, looking briefly at the document before casually folding it and placing it in his pocket.[42] It was a sign of things to come. In September, the EIC was rocked by news of the Treaty of Southampton, which cemented a new alliance between England and the United Provinces against Spain.[43] It was a bitterly disappointing development for the English company, which had believed that it was at last on the cusp of securing action. To placate the Court of Committees, Charles attached a coda to the treaty, laying out a new deadline. If the States General had not taken action in eighteen months, he would act to "seek our revenge for the lives and property of our subjects, whether it be by a letter of reprisal or by means of our forces."[44]

The date for action was set for March 1627, more than four years after the conclusion of the Amboina trial. When this passed without any apparent movement, the king's ambassador, Lord Carleton, was dispatched to The Hague with instructions to threaten immediate reprisals. As before, the States General offered a strategic concession in response to mounting pressure. In late July 1627, it authorized a special tribunal formed of seven judges to investigate the original trial and the conduct of the VOC officials who had adjudicated it.[45] It marked a significant shift in the official Dutch response to the case. For the first time, the former judges found themselves in the dock forced to defend their actions. Van Speult was dead, but nine of his subordinates and a secretary had either arrived or were on their way back to the United Provinces.[46] Notably absent among their number was Isaaq de Bruyn, the inept advocate-fiscal who had done so much to shape the original proceedings. He had been summoned back to Europe but had died in circumstances that remain unclear. According to some reports, he had drowned when his ship went down on its way back from Asia.[47] De Bruyn's death meant that the trial's two leading actors, the governor and the advocate-fiscal, had departed the stage, leaving a cast of secondary characters headed by De Maerschalk to face the tribunal.

Both sides reacted predictably to the news that the former judges would be subject to legal action. The Dutch company protested the great injustice that had been done to its employees, while EIC observers argued that a tribunal consisting only of Dutch judges with no specific timeline for action was nothing more than a delaying mechanism that had been initiated by a States General too infiltrated by VOC sympathizers to take real action.[48] Because of this, the Court of Committees continued to press the king to seize ships. An opportunity soon presented itself as three richly laden Dutch vessels sailed into Stokes Bay.[49] This time, there was no sudden reversal, and the vessels were seized without a shot being fired.[50] Exactly as the EIC hoped, the act of reprisal spurred immediate action, and just over a week later, the States General appointed a fiscal, Laurens de Silla (Sylla), to take charge of the case.[51] Finally in October 1627, legal proceedings against the former judges formally commenced.[52]

For once, the EIC seemed to have the upper hand. The tribunal had started its investigation, and the presence of three rich merchant vessels held under guard in English ports seemed to guarantee progress. Things quickly settled, however, into an impasse. As one of his first steps, De Silla had interrogated the former judges who had made the long journey from Asia back to Europe. Although they had already responded to 139 questions in Batavia, they were now required to provide detailed answers to an even lengthier list of 189 separate inquiries.[53] The resultant depositions, which run to hundreds of pages, were largely unsurprising, confirming all the points made by De Maerschalk, De Houtman, and others, but they were closely scrutinized by both sides for advantage.[54] More important was De Silla's insistence that the key witnesses on the other side, the Amboyna men, must also travel to the United Provinces so they could tell their story before the tribunal.[55]

It was an obvious request. If the English survivors claimed to have witnessed such a clear miscarriage of justice, they should be prepared to relate this before the tribunal in the presence of the very individuals they now accussed.[56] De Silla's request, however, created a fresh dilemma that paralyzed the English side. The king was reluctant to allow his subjects to travel to the United Provinces, because it would mean an implicit surrender of jurisdiction.[57] Because of this, the king's representatives argued that the Admiralty depositions were suitable for inclusion in the tribunal and it was not necessary for the survivors to testify before Dutch judges. For their part, the Amboyna men proved far more willing to cross the North Sea, recognizing that a long stay in the United Provinces would afford new opportunities to milk their former employer for support. Even before the tribunal had been formally announced, Ephraim Ramsey had petitioned EIC officials that if the States General intended to do justice, he should be sent across the North Sea to ensure the right outcome.[58] Such eagerness to travel was predicated on the fact that it would dislodge further funds, and Ramsey was immediately provided with money to defray his costs. The king's officials remained obstinate, however, and the negotiations dragged on.

In 1628, EIC hopes were dashed yet again. For close to a year, the three Dutch vessels seized in Stokes Bay had remained impounded with their cargo held under guard and their sails removed. Suddenly, in July, the king informed the Court of Committees that these ships were to be released. To soften the blow, Charles dispatched seven high-ranking officials, including the Duke of Buckingham, to reassure the organization of "his Majesty's care for the Company."[59] Not surprisingly, such words provided little comfort for EIC officials, whose entire strategy depended on using these vessels to force concessions. The sudden shift in policy was made even harder to bear as rumors began to circulate that a bribe had been paid by the Dutch to secure the release of their ships. According to reports swirling through London, thirty thousand pounds had been handed over to the king, possibly in connection with some jewels that Charles had previously pawned in the United Provinces.[60] So outraged were EIC officials that they decided to take the risky step of notifying the king directly of these rumors. Responding angrily that he wished such a sum had been paid, as he was in dire need of funds, Charles reprimanded the Company for passing on gossip with so little grounding.[61] Placed on the defensive, EIC officials explained that they were simply conveying a widespread rumor that was generally "divulged in Amsterdam, and in the mouths of almost every man upon the Exchange."[62]

With the release of these vessels, the EIC's best chance of securing compensation disappeared. In The Hague, the tribunal continued to inch forward, although the removal of the threat of reprisal took away any sense of urgency. There was, however, some possibility of progress, if the Amboyna men and the VOC officials who had sat in judgment of them could be brought before the tribunal. Since 1624, both sides had clung to their own versions of what had happened, but bringing the warring groups of Amboina witnesses together might serve to at least establish some shared set of facts. The likelihood of this increased when the king permitted a number of the Amboyna men, including the supposedly enfeebled John Beaumont, to travel to the United Provinces, but their testimony remained conditional on the States General agreeing to a set of English demands designed to safeguard royal jurisdiction.[63] As negotiations continued, so did the demands for support. In October 1630, Powle, Ramsey, and Beaumont submitted a petition to the EIC requesting a continuance of their weekly allowance. It was met by a sharp reprimand for the lavish expenses incurred during their stay in Holland, but the Court of Committees had little choice but to continue payment. On the other side, the former judges with De Maerschalk at their head were equally insistent about the need for their own funds from the States General.

In the end, the States General refused to give in to the king's conditions, and Ramsey, Powell, and Beaumont never testified. With no opportunity to hear the English survivors' alternate version of events, the tribunal endorsed De Maerschalk's account of the trial, which stressed that extraordinary measures had been taken to confirm the accused's guilt. With this account in place, there was only one possible outcome, and in January 1632 the tribunal exonerated the Amboina judges.[64] It was a predictable but still bitterly disappointing result for the English Company, which believed it had been betrayed by a crown that had relieved pressure at key moments.

While the trial faded gradually from the spotlight, the EIC continued to hold fast to its grievances by compiling long lists of damages incurred by Dutch activities in Asia. The opportunity to revive the case came during the lead-up to the first Anglo-Dutch War, as anti-Dutch sentiments crested again. Charles was gone, executed in 1649, but, seeing a chance to secure Cromwell's support, the EIC published a new version of Skinner's narrative titled *Bloudy Newes from the East-Indies: Being a True Relation, and Perfect Abstract of the Cruel, Barbarous, and Inhumane Proceedings of the Dutch-Men Against the English at Amboyna.*[65] Put on the defensive, the VOC was forced to respond with its own reengineered pamphlet, which was printed a year later.[66] By the time war broke out in 1652, a renewed campaign of EIC propaganda had ensured that the Amboina conspiracy case had reemerged as a central point of dispute.

In the aftermath of the inconclusive conflict, which was fought entirely at sea, the two sides signed the Treaty of Westminster in April 1654. Buried in the long document were two clauses related to Amboina. The first assigned blame to Van Speult and the Amboina judges, with the States General committing to "take care that justice be done upon those who were partakers or accomplices in the massacre of the English at Amboyna."[67] While it seemed like a breakthrough, the fact that by 1654 all the original judges had long since died made this a hollow promise, easily given and lacking any substance. Far more important was the treaty's creation of a concrete mechanism for compensation, a panel of arbitration formed of four commissioners from each side that would meet in London to discuss the losses supposedly sustained by both companies across their long rivalry.

Negotiations commenced in May 1654. English representatives, who had more than three decades of complaints, petitions, and lists of damages to draw on, went on the offensive from the beginning, demanding the vast sum of £2,695,999 as compensation from the Dutch. By the time the negotiations concluded, they had emerged ahead, although the final figure was whittled down to £85,000 in general damages and £3,615 for the heirs of the English merchants caught up in the original trial. Of these, the largest single sum, £700, went to William Towerson, the nephew of Gabriel Towerson, the senior EIC official executed at Amboina. Remarkably, Edward Collins's children were next on the list, receiving £465 even though their father had not only survived the trial but had handsomely profited off it for decades afterward. Their award exceeded that offered to William Coulson, the surviving brother of Samuel Coulson, who had been tortured and executed at Amboina. It was another example of Collins's unique capacity to profit even after death off a case that proved so ruinous to almost everyone else caught up within it.

In attaching a final figure, the panel's members made it clear that no further petitions would be entertained on the matter.[68] The result was to draw a clear line below a dispute that had rolled on noisily for decades. Thousands of miles away in Amboina, however, a second process, far bloodier but much less well publicized, was unfolding. There, the Company was engaged in a series of conflicts stretching across three decades that combined to remake the political structure of the territory.[69] These culminated in a campaign of brutal pacification aimed squarely at the Hoamoal Peninsula, which had played such a prominent role in the weeks leading up to the 1623 trial.

Cured with Fire

Unlike Banda, where the absence of a central authority enabled a swift conquest by VOC armies under Coen in 1621, seventeenth-century Amboina was characterized by a proliferation of armed political centers capable of drawing on the wealth of the spice trade. Van Speult's 1625 campaign against Luhu had established one template for dealing with these centers, but instead of repeating such operations, the Company, always short of military resources and not certain of the efficacy of such tactics, settled into an uneasy peace by concluding an agreement with the new *kimelaha*, Leliato.[70] It seemed at first to stabilize the situation, but the underlying tension between VOC claims to monopoly rights over clove production and the refusal of spice-producing centers to accept this remained firmly in place.

In 1627, a commissioner, Gillis Seys, was dispatched from Batavia to Kota Ambon to inspect the state of the colony.[71] His subsequent report was underpinned by a familiar conviction that only harsh measures would serve to resolve the situation in Amboina. Like Van Speult before him, Seys concluded there was no possibility that the agreements guaranteeing monopoly rights to Castle Victoria would ever be properly enforced. Even bound by signed documents, the spice-producing centers scattered across the territory would never agree to sell cloves for the artificially depressed prices set by the Company. When it came to the "maintenance of the contracts," it was, he lamented, like "knocking on a dead man's door."[72] All of this meant that the only way to enforce the treaties was with force, and Seys laid out a series of steps that the organization must take to ensure its rights. Traders from Makassar and other rivals who pushed relentlessly into the Company's area of operations should be halted with violence, their ships burned, and the beaches barred to them. At the same time, the population of those areas that refused to accede to the VOC monopoly should be expelled and replaced with Christian subjects drawn from others parts of Ambon. The exchange would not be easy. At first these new inhabitants would have to endure resistance from the exiles who, like the Bandanese, "would not easily forget their old homes," but in the end, the cost would be repaid by expanded profits from the clove trade.[73]

While no attempt was made to set Seys's expansive recommendations into motion, it was clear to everyone that more conflict was inevitable.[74] In 1630, a new governor, Philip Lucasz, ordered a muster roll of all employees under his command. The completed list provides the clearest accounting of VOC personnel in Amboina since the depositions given by the former judges.[75] Strikingly, the total number had dropped—the muster roll included just 299 men scattered across all the Company's outposts in Amboina. While the garrison had not expanded in size, it had become more diverse, with a number of Portuguese and Spanish soldiers and at least one Scottish recruit. Intriguingly, the muster roll listed five Japanese soldiers, who were named as Gortsack from Japan, Jouste from Japan, Louis from Nagasaki, Siosabra from Hirado, and Mangurock from Sakai.[76] Although the Company had been banned from hiring directly in Japan, it could still find recruits within those Japanese communities already in Southeast Asia. The aggressive policies pursued by the Tokugawa regime had made it increasingly difficult for Japanese Christians to return to the archipelago, creating a ready if limited reserve of potential soldiers. The appearance of these soldiers in Kota Ambon in 1630 raises an obvious question about the fate of the unnamed Japan captain who had evaded the torture chamber by denouncing his countrymen. Was he listed here among these five? Certainly, there would have been ample reason for him to leave Castle Victoria. His initial three-year term of service would have expired, and the 1623 trial had shown just how cruelly the Company could treat its Asian recruits. But it is also possible that the captain might have hung on, trusting his capacity to prosper in an organization that had once seemed set to condemn him.

If the number of soldiers showed little change in the years since the trial, the slave population in Kota Ambon had continued to increase steadily in size. While the 1630 muster roll includes no reference to slaves, the report prepared by Seys three years earlier indicated the presence of "308 slaves that earn no salary."[77] It meant that in four years the slave population had roughly doubled in size, from around 150 at the time of the conspiracy trial. The 1630 muster roll did list Augustine Peres's successor as *marinho* over the slaves. Whereas Van Speult had entrusted the role to an Asian recruit from Bengal, his successor had decided it should be held by a European, Gillis Gillisen, whose name suggests he had been recruited in the United Provinces. It was another mark of how important the position was and how determined the Company was to prevent a repeat of the conspiracy at Amboina with its disloyal slave master joining his charges to threaten the security of the colony.

By 1632, the VOC was at war again with the *kimelaha* and settlements scattered across the Hoamoal Peninsula. Whereas the 1625 conflict had depended on the unexpected infusion of European sailors and soldiers carried aboard the *Nassause vloot*, no such force appeared ready to supplement the limited forces described in the muster roll. Instead, the Company came to rely ever more heavily on Asian military manpower in the form of the *hongi* expeditions, which were drawn primarily from the Christian communities located in the southern part of Ambon Island. Rather than being dispatched annually, these were now sent out two or three times in a single year on extended campaigns.[78] While the Company's capacity to muster these fleets represented a key measure of its power, such a sustained reliance on local military resources carried its own risks.[79] By February 1636, year after year of such operations had pushed the organization's Christian subjects into a state of revolt against VOC rule and the heavy burdens it had imposed.[80] It was, Knaap argues, the most dangerous crisis yet encountered for it threatened the foundations of the system that the VOC had constructed to maintain its rule.[81] The situation was only rescued by the arrival of the governor-general, Antonio van Diemen, with a large military force. Alongside this demonstration of VOC power, Van Diemen moved to convene a *landdag*—a meeting of Amboinese leaders—that responded to the crisis by limiting the requirements of the *hongi* expeditions to five weeks annually.[82]

With this danger averted, the Company worked over time to eliminate some of the armed political centers that dotted the territory. The next conflict broke out in Hitu, on the northern side of the islands of Ambon.[83] Heavily populated but lacking a single clear ruler, Hitu was described in VOC sources as a "free republic."[84] The area was officially governed by the representatives of four families, although in practice its politics were dominated by the so-called *kapitan Hitu*.[85] For the first three decades of VOC control, the role was occupied by Hitu Tepil, who held it from 1602 to 1633.[86] He was therefore one of the Company's oldest allies on Amboina, signing a treaty of alliance in 1601 that subsequently morphed into a monopoly contract in 1605.[87] The document pledged that Hitu would hand over all available cloves to the Dutch in return for the Company's help in delivering its lands "from the hands of their enemies, the Portuguese."[88] Despite this long history of connection, some within the organization condemned *kapitan Hitu* as a false ally, a "pernicious instrument" (*parnitieus instrument*) who traded secretly with outside merchants and should not be fully trusted.[89]

This simmering distrust ramped up after the death of Hitu Tepil and the succession of his son, Kakiali, who engaged in an increasingly active campaign of resistance to Dutch rule.[90] By 1641, the Company was again at war. Over the subsequent five years, VOC forces waged a bitter campaign across Hitu, sieging and razing a string of heavily fortified strongholds while fending off the increasing involvement of Makassar, which dispatched its own fleets to aid the Hituese.[91] By the time the conflict had come to an end in 1646, Hitu had been reduced from a semiautonomous ally into a conquered territory under Dutch control, with key settlements forcibly moved from the mountains to the coast, where they could be more easily controlled by VOC naval cannons.[92]

The erasure of Hitu as an alternate political center gave the VOC essentially undisputed control over the island of Ambon. This, combined with the defeat of a fleet sent from Makassar, also meant that the Company had finally achieved its long-claimed monopoly over the clove trade.[93] But even as VOC authority expanded, the *kimelaha* and his supporters on the Hoamoal Peninsula continued to frustrate Castle Victoria. The Hoamoalese War, which broke out in 1651, marked a significant escalation in the long rivalry as the Company came to embrace the "extreme remedies" that had first been outlined decades earlier.[94]

The Hoamoalese War was not part of a plan carefully crafted in Batavia to achieve final control over the territory. Rather, it stemmed from a panicked response to a rebellion that had broken out in 1651 across Amboina and which resulted in the destruction of a string of outposts and the brutal murder of more than 150 Company employees.[95] The revolt stemmed from a complex and escalating crisis that pitted the VOC and the Sultan of Ternate, Mandarsyah (r. 1648–1675), a recent and unpopular incumbent, against the *kimelaha*, Majira, and the sultan's nominal subjects across the Hoamoal Peninsula.[96] Acting on instructions from the Dutch, the sultan had authorized a reduction in the production of cloves. While this propped up VOC interests, it threatened the *kimelaha*'s position on Hoamoal, where the clove trade provided a vital source of revenue.[97] Over time, tensions flared into an open rebellion against Mandarsyah. Although the rebellion was suppressed, a number of the rebels fled to Hoamoal, where they joined up with Majira and were involved in the massacre of a large number of VOC merchants and soldiers.[98] Their numbers were later swelled by forces sent from Makassar, which saw an opportunity to expand its own influence by taking advantage of Dutch weakness.[99]

The rebellion sent a shock wave through the VOC system. With so many dead and key outposts burned to the ground, control over Amboina seemed once again in doubt. The task of restoring order was handed to the superintendent over Banda, Ambon, and Ternate, Arnold de Vlaming van Oudtshoorn, who was given instructions to pacify the territory once and for all. From a harsh beginning, the campaign rapidly escalated in scale and violence. According to one of De Vlaming's subordinates, who wrote a long account defending what had happened, "the innocent spilling of Dutch blood" required the harshest of all possible responses, including taking up "arms in Amboina against the murderers, demolishing their strongholds, cutting down their clove and fruit trees, spoiling their gardens."[100] It was a mandate for massive destruction aimed at "the wreck of the cities of the enemies," "the making of their lands unusable," and the demolition of alternate centers of political authority.[101]

De Vlaming's operations commenced with an assault on the island of Manipa, an island that had featured prominently in the buildup to the 1623 conspiracy trial. Here a number of VOC employees had been murdered in 1651, making it a natural starting point for a punitive campaign.[102] Arriving with five ships and 350 soldiers, VOC forces laid waste to the island, destroying not only the clove orchards that made it a node in the spice trade but also the sago trees upon which it depended for food. Within a few weeks there was mass starvation further compounded by drought and disease that swept through the island.[103] By the end of campaign, Manipa was devastated, left "so devoid of life-means that [it] did not resemble the same island."[104]

The Company's primary efforts were directed toward the Hoamoal Peninsula, which had been at the center of the revolt. One of its first targets was the institutional basis of the *kimelaha*'s power. For decades, the VOC had struggled with the difficult triangular relationship between Castle Victoria, the sultan in Ternate, and his increasingly independent proxy on the Hoamoal Peninsula—the *kimelaha*. In a treaty signed in 1652, the sultan of Ternate agreed that he would no longer appoint such an official. Instead, the VOC governor in Kota Ambon would assume a position as *stadhouder,* tasked to rule over the sultan's territories.[105] The agreement pulled away the foundation of the *kimelaha*'s authority and made the Company the effective overlord over Hoamoal. With the last remnant of influence removed, De Vlaming initiated a prolonged campaign of pacification aimed at Hoamoal. It culminated in two separate assaults on the fortified centers of Laala and Asahudi.[106]

The first took place in September 1654, just as the panel of arbitration convened in Europe to resolve the question of compensation over the conspiracy trial was coming to its final conclusion.[107] By the time the resistance had ended in Laala, an estimated seven hundred people were dead.[108] Asahudi would fall a year later to a combined force of around eight hundred European sailors fighting alongside the same number of Ambonese auxiliaries.[109] In both cases, the military campaign was accompanied by the destruction of settlements, the eradication of tens of thousands of clove trees, and the relocation of the surviving population from mountainous areas that could be easily defended to low-lying areas that the VOC could maintain control over.[110] As had happened in the aftermath of the conquest of Banda, such tactics served as well to inject hundreds of slaves into the VOC system. Some, like the two hundred fighters from Makassar captured at Asahudi, were sent on to Batavia, but others were distributed to local allies whose support had been critical in De Vlaming's long campaigns. This was the case after the assault on Laala, when four hundred women, men, and children were handed over to the Company's key supporters.[111]

The devastating impact of such campaigns was obvious. Writing to his superiors in May 1656 at the conclusion of the Hoamoalese War, De Vlaming explained that the conflict "has caused such a change in the state that it is not comparable to how it was."[112] It was an accurate assessment of how completely the conflict had transformed parts of Amboina.[113] The final outcome of De Vlaming's operations was a massive depopulation of the Hoamoal Peninsula, which had a pre-conflict population estimated at over ten thousand people.[114] By the time the campaign was over, Hoamoal had been turned, one observer suggested, into an "eternal waste land" [woestijne], desolate and uninhabited.[115] The imprint of VOC operations would remain visible for decades. From close to 80,000 in the 1630s, the population of Amboina declined to around 50,000 by 1670.[116] By 1708, more than five decades after the end of the Hoamoalese War, it had still not recovered to its pre-conflict levels.[117] Such operations served as well to eradicate rival centers of power within Amboina, flattening out the political landscape and elevating the Company to a role as absolute master over the territory. By the end of the conflict, the Hoamoal Peninsula, which had been such an important producer of cloves, generating 176,000 Amsterdam pounds of spices around 1620, had disappeared entirely as a node from the trade.[118] Stripped of its inhabitants, its strongholds razed to the ground and denuded of clove trees, the territory essentially disappeared as a factor in VOC calculations.[119]

Twin Aftermaths

In Europe, the memory of the Amboina trial never really faded. Although the arbitration panel's award in September 1654 marked the official end of the dispute, the case was far too useful to English propagandists for it to remain buried for long. Close to fifty years after Towerson's execution, a 1672 reprint of Skinner's pamphlet promised to reveal "the naked truth of this cause, hirtherto masked, muffled and obfuscated," while a year later John Dryden revived Skinner's charges for the stage.[120] Damning Van Speult and the Dutch as bloody murderers, the play titled simply Amboyna: A Tragedy presented the audience with, as one stage direction put it succinctly, "the English tortured, and the Dutch tormenting them."[121]

In Amboina, the Hoamoalese War spawned no equivalent contingent of writers determined to turn what had happened into an enduring controversy. In fact, its consequences were far greater. The revolt and the campaign of reprisal that it generated had a dramatic effect on the colony. For Rumphius, the longtime chronicler of Amboina, the conflict represented a moment of violent transformation that had at last restored order to a disordered landscape. For him, the Company's past tactics in Amboina had been too moderate. Instead of taking decisive action, VOC officials had relied on a strange mix of "persuasion, administered with punishment" that had served only to create a festering wound, a putrefying gangrene that would not heal. Under De Vlaming, however, the "old and stinking wound" had been cured with fire and the "Ambonese body brought to health."[122] In reality, these campaigns had ripped apart the fabric of the Hoamoal Peninsula, driving "deep," in the words of one modern writer, "into the Ambonese social structure."[123]

De Vlaming's work secured the Company's hold over Amboina for decades to come, and by 1656 VOC officials looked out across a very different environment.[124] This means that the Hoamoalese War marks an alternate end point for the longer story of the Amboina conspiracy trial, centered not on Europe but on Asia. While so much attention was focused on Europe, the VOC had transformed a swath of territory under its control. By the time De Vlaming departed Kota Ambon, the landmarks that Van Speult had confronted in 1623 as he looked out over an array of enemies, rivals, and "feigned friends" were gone, replaced with a new map. The jostling power centers scattered across Hoamoal that had loomed so large, with their thousands of warriors, in the weeks and months before Shichizō appeared on the walls of Castle Victoria had been eradicated, the peninsula depopulated and denuded of clove trees. Coming on the heels of the Ambonese Wars, which began this long process of transformation, De Vlaming's operations had replaced a world crowded with perils with a kind of "Pax Neerlandica" and a stage set for the display of VOC power.[125] It made the conspiracy trial three decades earlier, in which the Company's hold over Amboina appeared genuinely at risk, seem little more than a historical curiosity marooned in a very different time and place.

Epilogue

The Fearful Empire

For centuries now, there has been a strikingly durable image of the Amboina conspiracy trial that refuses to recede. This pictures Van Speult and De Bruyn as scheming plotters who engineered the successful ejection of the English from Kota Ambon via a carefully staged show trial. This version was driven home by a highly effective messaging campaign orchestrated by the English East India Company that embedded Skinner's *True Relation* into the record in a way that continues to shape modern accounts of Amboina.[1] But it endures as well because it matches a vision of the Dutch East India Company and its state sponsor, the United Provinces, as moving inexorably along a trajectory toward total control over the spice trade and what Jonathan Israel famously described as "Dutch primacy" in this period.[2] In this picture in which the Dutch East India Company rapidly achieved superiority over its challengers, Amboina appears as just another milestone on the inevitable path toward Dutch dominance in parts of Asia.

We do not have to look far to find images of Dutch confidence and success from this period, for they are scattered across museums in the Netherlands and beyond. A painting completed by Aelbert Cuyp at the height of VOC power around the middle of the seventeenth century, now hanging in the Rijksmuseum, provides one example. It depicts the commander of the fleet attired in Calvinist black and clutching the hand of his wife. He stands on the side of the painting with a parasol, a traditional symbol of Southeast Asian royalty, held above him by a deliberately diminutive Javanese slave dressed in European clothing complete with bowed shoes. In the background, the VOC headquarters of Batavia shimmers against a tropical landscape. The viewer's eye follows the commander's outstretched cane as he points toward the busy harbor, where a powerful fleet heaving with rich merchandise prepares to depart for Europe. We can make out the names of at least one of these vessels, the *Banda*, which lies deep in the water, its hold full of cargo, its decks crowded with sailors and passengers.[3] Anchored in a harbor that the VOC had wrested from the local ruler by force, the ship was a reminder of the Company's most famous early conquest, which had been subjugated by Jan Pieterszoon Coen in 1621 and then repopulated with thousands of imported slaves.

Such depictions show a familiar image of the confident, conquering European standing in a transformed landscape surrounded by the technologies of power and looming over colonial subjects. In fact, and despite such representations, VOC officials and merchants lived in a world filled with terrors. As they moved into the region, Dutch agents were plunged into an alien landscape that was crowded with sophisticated societies,

Figure 8.1 VOC senior merchant. Aelbert Cuyp, c. 1640–1660. Courtesy of the Rijksmuseum, Amsterdam. SK-A-2350.

long-established political and economic networks, and powerful states capable of mustering vast military resources. Clinging to the coast, they felt acutely and constantly vulnerable, besieged, as Coolhaas so accurately observed, by the "psychosis of fear."[4]

Looking beyond glossy images of Dutch confidence like the one painted by Cuyp reveals plentiful evidence of this. We see it first and most plainly in the writings of VOC officials like Jan Pieterszoon Coen who have long been held up as the iron men of empire. Looking around, Coen saw terrors lurking everywhere: murderous attacks or assassination attempts that could happen in the night, subjects that might rebel without warning, and allies that could morph suddenly into enemies. The result is that fear crackles through the pages of Coen's letters, shaping his interactions with Asia and those of the officials under his command. It can be seen as well in the conspiracies that seemed to proliferate across scattered colonies and outposts, as Dutch officials claimed to have uncovered an array of dangerous plots. Writing after the exposure of another supposed conspiracy in 1618, one administrator complained in exhaustion that "this is already the fourth assault that has been uncovered" in the past few months.[5] While some of these plots were surely genuine—the product of rival powers, disgruntled subjects, or local resistance to Dutch incursions—others were conjured up by VOC officials confronting a fearful landscape.

None of this makes the Dutch Empire in Asia unique. As many scholars have noted, colonial regimes were a strange melding of power and a sense of powerlessness.[6] While superior force enabled brutal conquest, it frequently came paired with a sense of acute vulnerability and a terror that however secure they appeared, the supports holding up such regimes might collapse at any moment. Because of this, fear formed a fundamental part of the colonial experience, even in situations where colonizing powers seemed to possess an overwhelming military advantage.

But if this was the case more generally, it is also true that each empire generated its own cast of monsters. For the Dutch East India Company, the Asian base of its empire provided a source of strength but also a deep well of colonial anxiety. In the first decades of the seventeenth century, as the VOC acquired its first territorial possessions, officials like Coen had dreamed of planting a string of European colonies in Asia populated with industrious Dutch migrants who could harvest the wealth of the spice trade while defending the boundaries of the Company's influence. When these dreams faltered, the Company moved instead to draw in Asian settlers, slaves, and soldiers to populate its settlements, perform its labor, and fight its wars. The result was a composite, a European empire with Asian roots, as a thin overlay of Dutch rule was stretched tightly over a much wider Asian base.[7]

There is another image of Dutch rule, painted by Andries Beeckman, that looks very different from Cuyp's vision.[8] Both show Batavia around the same period, in the middle of the seventeenth century, but in contrast to Cuyp's focus on European confidence, Beeckman depicts an empire heavily dependent on Asian inhabitants and structures. In the background, we see the squat castle that dominated the port city with its gates open as a thin column of Company officials and soldiers ride out. The focus, however, is on a busy market scene crowded with dozens of figures. On one side, there is a prosperous Japanese resident with swords stuffed in his sash. He is matched on the other edge of the painting by a pair of Chinese merchants locked in fierce negotiation. In the center, a Dutch official strolls leisurely with an Asian woman under a parasol, while a free Asian resident, presumably a *Mardijker*, stands with bright red shoes and holding a

Figure 8.2 The castle of Batavia. Andries Beeckman, c. 1661. Courtesy of the Rijksmuseum, Amsterdam. SK-A-19.

cane. Although the Dutch are present, it is Batavia's Asian residents who dominate the daily life and workings of the city.[9]

The Company's reliance on Asian structures allowed it to prosper; it also created a perennial anxiety, as a fear of dangers lurking within the walls of VOC settlements combined with a range of external threats to create a simmering sense of menace. This was the case in Kota Ambon in 1623, when a young Japanese soldier called Shichizō first appeared on the walls of the castle. There the VOC was in the process of turning itself from a trading organization with limited presence on land into an Asian power with direct control over a territory and tens of thousands of Asian subjects. In the months leading up to February 1623, Castle Victoria confronted an increasing threat from polities across the Hoamoal Peninsula determined to resist VOC attempts to enforce its monopoly rights over cloves, even as its population was swelled by slaves drawn from across Asia and by soldiers from Japan. Into this mix was thrust a group of English merchants propelled by an unwelcome treaty into the heart of a VOC settlement.

In this volatile environment, the questions of a single Japanese soldier pushed officials to bind together an array of colonial nightmares into one overarching plot. In the days after the first interrogation, fear combined with the clumsy work of an inept advocate-fiscal to unleash a paroxysm of judicial violence. One by one, a range of suspects were brutally tortured and then executed, even as a handful of the accused, most notably the Japan captain, Edward Collins, and John Beaumont, managed to thread their way through the confusion to emerge safe on the other side. In the end, we cannot know for sure if these investigations uncovered the traces of an inchoate conspiracy shared among some number of English merchants who nursed fantasies of ejecting the Dutch from Amboina, but, as I have argued here, the existence or absence of an actual plot did little to alter the fundamental trajectory of events. From the moment Shichizō first appeared to answer the governor's questions, Van Speult and the officials around him assumed that he must be part of a vast conspiracy drawing together multiple parties.

Recognizing the pervasive role of fear helps explain the chaotic nature of the Amboina trial. It also shows why the subsequent presentation in Europe and the case's long legacy in print are so misleading. Given the disordered nature of the original trial and the legal record that it generated, it is striking how successful the two companies were in creating new versions of the case and embedding them in popular understandings. Buoyed by the resources of the state, they combined to present an alternate accounting of Amboina that emphasized a deliberate and methodical process designed to achieve a singular end. While such versions proved compelling to many, they have little basis in reality. VOC officials like Van Speult or De Bruyn were not judicial murderers, plotting in cold blood to kill the English in Amboina and eject their employer from the rich spice trade, nor were they methodical professionals carefully following correct legal procedures and protocols undistracted by events around them. Instead, the trial was underpinned and animated by an overwhelming sense of crisis, which drove everything that happened.

In his groundbreaking 1942 article, Coolhaas first called attention to the "psychosis of fear" as a determining factor in understanding how VOC officials operated in isolated outposts like Kota Ambon. In the intervening decades, and even as scholarship has advanced in leaps and bounds, the popular vision of the Dutch East India Company has remained strikingly consistent. In 2006, then prime minister Jan Peter Balkenende called in an impromptu address to the Dutch House of Representatives for a revival of what he described as the "VOC mentality" (*VOC-mentaliteit*).[10] What he meant, as far as we can make out, was a revived dynamism, optimism, and above all confidence that permitted the Dutch to dominate global commerce in the seventeenth century and which would enable the modern-day Netherlands to recover, in his view, some of its luster by harnessing this spirit. Not surprisingly, such comments provoked a fierce response, as critics pointed to the terrible violence unleashed by officials like Coen in places like the Banda archipelago. Looking closely at the Amboina trial is a reminder that the "VOC mentality," if we can use such a term, was dominated as much by fear as by confidence, and that this fear dictated how Company officials interacted with the world around them including, as was the case here, unleashing a paroxysm of judicial violence designed to banish these terrors. It is, in other words, something to be studied and understood, certainly, but not to be emulated.

Notes

Introduction: The Company and the Colony

1. The VOC was based in the town of Kota Ambon (also called Ambon) on the island of Ambon in the wider VOC administrative area of Amboina (often spelled Amboyna in this period). The borders of VOC influence over Amboina expanded dramatically across the seventeenth century. It started with the southern parts of the island of Ambon, as well as Haruku, Saparua, and Nusalaut. Gerrit Knaap, *Kruidnagelen en Christenen: De VOC en de bevolking van Ambon 1656–1696* (Leiden: KITLV, 2004), 1. In its eventual form, the governorship of Amboina encompassed Ambon and a number of other islands, including Buru, Ambelau, Manipa, Kelang, Boano, Seram (also Ceram), Seram Laut, Nusalaut, and Honimoa. Multiple spellings for these islands appear in Dutch sources from this period.

2. Shichizō's name appears as Hytjeio, Hitieso, or a range of alternate spellings in VOC sources. I follow Iwao Seiichi that this is most likely 七蔵 (Shichizō). Iwao Seiichi, *Zoku Nanyō Nihon machi no kenkyū: Nanyō tōsho chiiki bunsan Nihonjin imin no seikatsu to katsudō* (Tokyo: Iwanami Shoten, 1987), 256.

3. Copie autentycq van de Confessien ende Sententien van Mr. Touwerson ende Complicen over de Moordadige Conspiratie op t' Casteel Amboyna voorgenomen, dat door Godes merckelijcke ende genadige beschicking opden xxiii Februario 1623 is aenden dach gecomen als mede de resolutien by den Hr. Gouvernr van Speult & den raet daer over genomen, NL-HaNA, VOC 1080, 136v. Hereafter, Copie autentycq van de confessien ende sententien.

4. Answer to question 91, deposition of Peter van Santen of Delft, 9 March 1628, British Library (hereafter BL), India Office Records (hereafter IOR), G/21/2, pt. 3.

5. This is how De Bruyn's role is described in the legal documents generated by the trial. In later periods, these officials in colonies outside Batavia were more commonly referred to as fiscals (*fiscaal*). John Ball, *Indonesian Legal History, 1602–1848* (Sydney: Oughtershaw Press, 1982), 27. Copie autentycq van de confessien ende sententien, NL-HaNA, VOC 1080, 137v.

6. Copie autentycq van de confessien ende sententien, NL-HaNA, VOC 1080, 138v.

7. Copie autentycq van de confessien ende sententien, NL-HaNA, VOC 1080, 146v.

8. Copie autentycq van de confessien ende sententien, NL-HaNA, VOC 1080, 161v. I have used the term "polity" to describe the range of political units scattered across the Hoamoal Peninsula. Given the diversity of political formations, this is an imperfect categorization at best. For an important discussion concerning the application of the label "state," see Gerrit Knaap, "De Ambonse eilanden tussen twee mogendheden; De VOC en Ternate, 1605–1656," in *Hof en Handel; Aziatische vorsten en de VOC 1620–1720*, ed. Elsbeth Locher-Scholten and Peter Rietbergen (Leiden: KITLV, 2004), 39–40.

9. In total, eight English merchants were spared. Some of these were deemed to have no knowledge of the plot, but others were pardoned by the governor just before they were due to be executed. It also appears that an older Japanese soldier was spared as well, although the trial document makes no direct reference to his fate.

10. *Waerachtich Verhael vande Tidinghen ghecomen wt de Oost-Indien* (1624). An English translation was published in the same year. *A True Declaration of the News That Came Out of the East Indies with the Pinnace Called the Hare* (London, 1624). Rupali Mishra, *A Business of State: Commerce, Politics, and the Birth of the East India Company* (Cambridge, MA: Harvard University Press, 2018), 223.

11. *Waerachtich Verhael vande Tidinghen ghecomen wt de Oost-Indien*, 7.

12. *A True Relation of the Unjust, Cruell, and Barbarous Proceedings Against the English at Amboyna in the East-Indies, by the Neatherlandish Governour and Councel There* (London: printed by H. Lownes for Nathanael Newberry, 1624), 1. This was published with an epistle to the reader, John Skinner's text, a translation of a Dutch pamphlet (*A True Declaration of the News That Came Out of the East Indies with the Pinnace Called the Hare*), and a response (*An Answer to the Dutch Relation, Touching the Pretended Conspiracie of the English at Amboyna in the Indies*).

13. The most famous image of Dutch torture appears in *True Relation* and will be discussed in chapter 6. The image on the cover is from a separate publication, *The Most Savage and Horrible Cruelties Lately Practised by the Hollanders upon the English in the East Indies* (Presborow, 1624). It can be found in Nationaal Archief, The Hague (hereafter NL-HaNA), Staten-Generaal, access no. 1.01.02, inv. no. 12551.62.3. The origins of this particular publication are murky. It was described by the EIC as a "pamphlet printed beyond the seas, expressing in effigy the several tortures inflicted upon the English at Amboyna and Lantar." W. N. Sainsbury, ed., *Calendar of State Papers Colonial, East Indies and Persia, 1625–1629* (London: H.M.S.O., 1884), 32. It appears to have been independently printed in Europe. My thanks to Alison Games for this reference.

14. For a superb analysis of this process and the first use of this term, see Alison Games, "Violence on the Fringes: The Virginia (1622) and Amboyna (1623) Massacres," *History* 99, no. 336 (2014): 505–29. This is the subject of Games's planned monograph currently titled *The Invention of the Amboyna Massacre.*

15. Charles Jenkinson, *A Collection of All the Treaties of Peace, Alliance, and Commerce, Between Great-Britain and Other Powers* (London: J. Debrett, 1785), 47.

16. John Dryden, *Amboyna, or the Cruelties of the Dutch to the English Merchants: A Tragedy,* in *The Works of John Dryden,* ed. Vinton Dearing, vol. 12 (Berkeley: University of California Press, 1994). See also Robert Markley, "Violence and Profits on the Restoration Stage: Trade, Nationalism, and Insecurity in Dryden's Amboyna," *Eighteenth-Century Life* 22, no. 1 (1998): 2–17.

17. W. P. Coolhaas, "Aanteekeningen en Opmerkingen over den zoogenaamdem Ambonschen Moord," *Bijdragen tot de Taal-, Land- en Volkenkunde van Nederlandsch-Indie* 101 (1942): 56–57. This was in fact the second Anglo-Boer War.

18. Giles Milton, *Nathaniel's Nutmeg* (London: Hodder & Stoughton, 1999). Milton relies heavily on the pamphlets produced on the English side, most notably *A True Relation of the Unjust, Cruell, and Barbarous Proceedings,* which he treats as essentially factual accounts of what happened in Amboina.

19. See for example Lawrence James, *The Rise and Fall of the British Empire* (New York: St. Martin's Griffin, 1995), 26. William Wilson Hunter, *A History of British India* (London: Longmans, Green, 1899), 1:408.

20. D. K. Bassett, "The 'Amboyna Massacre' of 1623," *Journal of Southeast Asian History* 1, no. 2 (1960): 3. P. J. Marshall, "The English in Asia to 1700," in *The Oxford History of the British Empire,* vol. 1, *The Origins of Empire,* ed. Nicholas Canny (Oxford: Oxford University Press, 1998), 271.

21. F. W. Stapel, "De Ambonsche 'Moord' (9 Maart 1623)," *Tijdschrift voor Indische Taal- Land- en Volkenkunde* 62 (1923): 209–26. Coolhaas, "Aanteekeningen en Opmerkingen." These were later translated and republished in M. A. P. Meilink-Roelofsz, M. E. van Opstall, and G. J. Schutte, eds., *Dutch Authors on Asian History: A Selection of Dutch Historiography on the Verenigde Oostindische Compagnie* (Dordrecht: Foris, 1988).

22. Anton Poot, *Crucial Years in Anglo-Dutch Relations (1625–1642): The Political and Diplomatic Contacts* (Hilversum: Verloren, 2013). See also Karen Chancey, "The Amboyna Massacre in English Politics, 1624–1632," *Albion* 30, no. 4 (1998): 583–98.

23. Anthony Milton, "Marketing a Massacre: Amboyna, the East India Company and the Public Sphere in Early Stuart England," in *The Politics of the Public Sphere in Early Modern England,* ed. Steven Pincus and Peter Lake (Manchester: Manchester University Press, 2007), 168–90. Mishra, *A Business of State.*

24. Games, "Violence on the Fringes."

25. Depositions taken in the High Court of Admiralty relating to the Massacre at Amboyna in 1623, BL IOR, G/21/2, pt. 3.

26. Transcriptions of both the 1625–1626 and 1628 depositions in the original Dutch are available in the Nationaal Archief. NL-HaNA, Staten-Generaal, 1.01.02, inv.

no. 12551.62. There are also contemporary English translations of these depositions available in the British Library. BL IOR, G/21/2.

27. The most important of these was George Forbes, a Scottish steward formerly
employed by the Dutch on Amboina. His deposition can be found in Sainsbury,
Calendar of State Papers, 1625–1629, 686–91.

28. See *A Remonstrance of the Directors of the Netherlands East India Company, Presented to
the Lords States Generall of the United Provinces, in Defence of the Said Companie, Touching the Bloudy Proceedings Against the English Merchants, Executed at Amboyna.
Together, with the Acts of the Processe, Against the Sayd English. And the Reply of the
English East India Company, to the Said Remonstrance and Defense* (London: printed
by John Dawson for the East India Company, 1632). It consisted of a VOC defense
of the case, an English translation of the original trial record, and an EIC response.

29. My very great thanks to Xing Hang at Brandeis University and Tristan Mostert
at Leiden University and their students for making this possible.

30. At the time of writing, there have been over five thousand recorded completions
of the trial engine.

31. As will be discussed, English merchants had attempted to trade with Luhu in
earlier years, but there is no correspondence from the EIC factory that suggests
any attempt to form a political alliance in this period.

32. Answer to question 49, deposition of Jan van Leeuwen, 15 March 1628, BL IOR,
G/21/2, pt. 3.

33. Bassett, "The 'Amboyna Massacre' of 1623."

34. Gabriel Towerson to Richard Fursland, 19 September 1622, BL IOR, G/21/3A: 351.

35. *A True Relation of the Unjust, Cruell, and Barbarous Proceedings,* 34.

36. Hunter, *A History of British India,* 1:388.

37. Answer to question 11, deposition of John Beaumont, depositions taken in the
High Court of Admiralty, BL IOR, G/21/2, pt. 3. See also *A True Relation of the
Unjust, Cruell, and Barbarous Proceedings.*

38. Beckles Willson, *Ledger and Sword or The Honourable Company of Merchants of England Trading to the East Indies (1599–1874)* (London: Longmans, Green, 1903), 1:156.

39. There are, it should be noted, a number of English-language studies that adopt
a far more measured approach that makes no such claims. See Mishra, *A Business
of State,* or the work of Alison Games.

40. James, *The Rise and Fall of the British Empire,* 26. J. R. Jones. *The Anglo-Dutch Wars
of the Seventeenth Century* (London: Longman, 1996), 147. There are numerous
similar summaries of the Amboina case. Another scholar explains that the "Dutch
East India Company guarded its advantages jealously and was often ruthless in
its pursuit of profit . . . Things turned ugly in 1623 when the VOC executed ten
to fifteen of the EIC's employees." Timothy Parsons, *The Rule of Empires: Those
Who Built Them, Those Who Endured Them, and Why They Always Fall* (New York:
Oxford University Press, 2012), 181.

41. Scholars writing in Dutch, who have argued that there was a genuine plot, have
never accepted this view that VOC authorities deliberately fabricated a conspiracy in order to push out the English.

42. Generale missive van Gouverneur-Generaal en Raden, 3 January 1624, Nationaal Archief, The Hague, Vereenigde Oostindische Compagnie (VOC) (hereafter NL-HaNA, VOC), access no 1.04.02, 1079, 36v.

43. Generale missive van Gouverneur-Generaal en Raden, 3 January 1624, NL-HaNA, VOC, 1079, 36.

44. In his monumental history of Amboina, Rumphius, who had participated in the last of these wars, described a series of five discrete conflicts (*Ambonschen oorlog*) forming part of a longer war. Georgius Rumphius, "De Ambonse Historie," *Bijdragen tot de Taal-, Land- en Volkenkunde van Nederlandsch-Indië* 64, no. 1/2 (1910): 36. Rumphius dated these wars from 1618, but I follow Knaap in emphasizing 1624 as the effective starting point of these conflicts. Gerrit Knaap, "Headhunting, Carnage and Armed Peace in Amboina, 1500–1700," *Journal of the Economic and Social History of the Orient* 46, no. 2 (2003): 168.

45. "Beschrijuinge vant eylant, stadt ende casteel van Ambona, midsgaders die eylanden onder den archipelago van Ambona sorterende, welcke landen vandien archipelago den Admirael Steuen vander Hagen van Amersfoort den 23en Februario ao. 1605," in P. A. Tiele, ed., "Documenten voor de geschiedenis der Nederlanders in het Oosten," *Bijdragen en Mededelingen van het Historisch Genootschap* 6 (1883): 365.

46. M. A. P. Meilink-Roelofsz, "Steven van der Haghen (1563–1624)," in *Vier eeuwen varen: Kapiteins, kapers, kooplieden en geleerden*, ed. L. M. Akveld (Bussum: De Boer, 1973), 26–49. There are numerous spelling of Van der Haghen's name but I follow Meilink-Roelofsz.

47. I follow Gerrit Knaap in referring to Ambon Town as Kota Ambon. Gerrit Knaap, "A City of Migrants: Kota Ambon at the End of the Seventeenth Century," *Indonesia*, no. 51 (1991): 105–28.

48. Knaap, *Kruidnagelen en Christenen*, 21.

49. Knaap, *Kruidnagelen en Christenen*. In this landmark study, Knaap considers the indigenous response to the colonial period, focusing on ruptures but also continuities. The first version of this book was published in 1986, the second in 2004 by KITLV. Gerrit Knaap, "Crisis and Failure: War and Revolt in the Ambon Islands, 1636–1637," *Cakalele* 3 (1992): 1–26; "Kora-kora en kruitdamp; De Verenigde Oost-Indische Compagnie in oorlog en vrede in Ambon," in *De Verenigde Oost-Indische Compagnie tussen Oorlog and diplomatie*, ed. Gerrit Knaap and Ger Teitler, 257–80 (Leiden: KITLV, 2002); "Headhunting, Carnage and Armed Peace in Amboina, 1500–1700," *Journal of the Economic and Social History of the Orient* 46, no. 2 (2003): 165–92; "De Ambonse eilanden tussen twee mogendheden"; "The Governor-General and the Sultan: An Attempt to Restructure a Divided Amboina in 1638," *Itinerario* 29, no. 1 (2005): 79–100. For a vital source compilation, see Gerrit Knaap, ed., *Memories van Overgave van gouverneurs van Ambon in de zeventiende en achttiende eeuw*, Rijks Geschiedkundige Publicatiën, Kleine Serie 62 (The Hague: Martinus Nijhoff, 1987). This is not a complete accounting of Knaap's many publications related to Amboina, which cannot, for reasons of space, be listed here in full.

50. Van Goor has produced a long-awaited biography of Jan Pieterszoon Coen that includes considerable material on Amboina. Jur van Goor, *Jan Pieterszoon Coen, 1587–1629: Koopman-Koning in Azië* (Amsterdam: Boom Publishers, 2015). Martine van Ittersum has contributed an important chapter on Amboina in her foundational study of Grotius. Martine J. van Ittersum, *Profit and Principle: Hugo Grotius, Natural Rights Theories and the Rise of Dutch Power in the East Indies, 1595–1615* (Leiden: Brill, 2006). For an indispensable study of the wider Malukan world, see Leonard Andaya, *The World of Maluku: Eastern Indonesia in the Early Modern Period* (Honolulu: University of Hawaii Press, 1993). In an important and innovative analysis, Jennifer Gaynor has argued that the frame for the war over spices should be expanded beyond the standard European protagonists. Jennifer Gaynor, *Intertidal History in Island Southeast Asia: Submerged Genealogies and the Legacy of Coastal Capture* (Ithaca, NY: Cornell University Press, 2016). See also J. Keuning, "Ambonese, Portuguese and Dutchmen: The History of Ambon to the End of the Seventeenth Century," in Meilink-Roelofsz, Van Opstall, and Schutte, *Dutch Authors on Asian History*. Widjojo's 2009 monograph also includes a section on Amboina in this earlier period. Muridan Satrio Widjojo, *The Revolt of Prince Nuku: Crosscultural Alliance-Making in Maluku, c. 1780–1810* (Leiden: Brill, 2009). Although he does not focus specifically on Amboina, Peter Borschberg's pioneering work on the early VOC includes much important material. Peter Borschberg, *Hugo Grotius, the Portuguese, and Free Trade in the East Indies* (Singapore: NUS Press, 2011). Peter Borschberg, *Journal, Memorial, and Letters of Cornelis Matelieff de Jong: Security, Diplomacy, and Commerce in 17th-Century Southeast Asia* (Singapore: NUS Press, 2015). See also an important source publication, which includes a superb introduction, by Hans Straver, Chris van Fraassen, and Jan van der Putten, *Ridjali Historie van Hitu: Een Ambonse geschiedenis uit de zeventiende eeuw* (Utrecht: Landelijk Steunpunt Educatie Molukkers, 2004).

51. H. T. Colenbrander and W. P. Coolhaas, eds., *Jan Pietersz. Coen: Bescheiden Omtrent Zijn Bedrijf in Indië*, 9 vols. (The Hague: Martinus Nijhoff, 1919–1954). Hereafter, *Coen: Bescheiden.*

52. Luise White, *Speaking with Vampires: Rumor and History in Colonial Africa* (Berkeley: University of California Press, 2000), 5.

53. In an important introduction, Cátia Antunes describes this tendency to treat the Company "as mostly a business enterprise, rather than an empire-building agent." Cátia Antunes, "Introduction: Exploring the Dutch Empire," in *Exploring the Dutch Empire: Agents, Networks and Institutions, 1600–2000*, ed. Cátia Antunes and Jos Gommans (London: Bloomsbury Academic, 2015). One work along these lines is Henk den Heijer, *De geoctrooieerde compagnie: De VOC en de WIC als voorlopers van de naamloze vennootschap*. Ars notariatus CXXVIII (Amsterdam: Stichting tot Bevordering der Notariële Wetenschap; Deventer: Kluwer, 2005). Not surprisingly, views of the VOC are informed by where the focus is placed, that is, on the European theater of corporate management or the Asian theater of direct expansion. For one example of the former, see the pioneering work of Gelderblom, De Jong, and Jonker, which focuses primarily on developments in corporate governance in Europe and treats the organization as essentially a

commercial one. Oscar Gelderblom, Abe de Jong, and Joost Jonker, "The Formative Years of the Modern Corporation: The Dutch East India Company VOC, 1602–1623," *Journal of Economic History* 73, no. 4 (2013): 1050–76. Such works have been hugely important in shedding light on how the Company developed in Europe but can be productively combined with studies that focus on the organization's activities in Asia.

54. J. A. van der Chijs, *Geschiedenis der stichting van de Vereenigde O.I. Compagnie* (Leiden: P. Engels, 1857), 130.

55. In adopting this view, I have been greatly influenced by the pioneering work of Jur van Goor. See Jur van Goor, "A Hybrid State: The Dutch Economic and Political Network in Asia," in *From the Mediterranean to the China Sea: Miscellaneous Notes*, ed. C. Guillot, D. Lombard, and R. Ptak (Wiesbaden: Harrassowitz Verlag, 1998), 192–214. In earlier publications he appears as Jurrien van Goor. See also the work of Julia Adams, who describes the VOC's "fused politico-economic character." Julia Adams, "Trading States, Trading Places: The Role of Patrimonialism in Early Modern Dutch Development," *Comparative Studies in Society and History* 36, no. 2 (1994): 337.

56. Van Goor, *Jan Pieterszoon Coen*, 522. Barendse states it particularly well when he notes that "in Europe the Companies were merchants; in Asia they were states." Rene Barendse, *The Arabian Seas, 1640–1700* (Leiden: CNWS, 1998), 299.

57. Such strategies were concentrated in Southeast Asia. As I have discussed in an earlier study, the VOC found itself confined to the margins in places like Tokugawa Japan in East Asia. Adam Clulow, *The Company and the Shogun: The Dutch Encounter with Tokugawa Japan* (New York: Columbia University Press, 2014).

58. Some of the most detailed studies have focused on the crucial role of Chinese settlers in VOC possessions like Batavia or Taiwan. Leonard Blussé, *Strange Company: Chinese Settlers, Mestizo Women and the Dutch in VOC Batavia* (Dordrecht: Foris, 1986); Tonio Andrade, *How Taiwan Became Chinese: Dutch, Spanish, and Han Colonization in the Seventeenth Century* (New York: Columbia University Press, 2008).

59. Michiel van Groesen, "Global Trade," in *The Cambridge Companion to the Dutch Golden Age*, ed. Hemer J. Helmers and Geert H. Janssen (Cambridge: Cambridge University Press, 2018). Van Groesen's comments are focused more on Asian labor within the organization, but I take the term to apply more broadly. Van Goor argues that the Company was transformed over time into an "Asian power" that was treated as "a 'normal' political power" by other states in Southeast Asia. Van Goor, "A Hybrid State," 214.

60. Van Goor's magisterial new biography presents the most comprehensive picture yet of this key administrator. Van Goor, *Jan Pieterszoon Coen*.

61. The governor-general was frequently described as the "king of Batavia." For details of this process, see Clulow, *The Company and the Shogun*, chapter 2.

62. There is an increasing willingness among scholars to characterize VOC campaigns in places like Banda as episodes of genocide. Michael J. Kelly, *Prosecuting Corporations for Genocide* (New York: Oxford University Press, 2016), 18. See also Van Groesen, "Global Trade." Although it comes from a later period, the Chinese massacre of 1740 is probably the most notorious example of mass violence

directed at Asian settlers. For a recent study, see Leonard Blussé, "Nevenactiviteiten overzee: Valckenier en Van Imhoff en de Chinezenmoord van 1740," in *Reizen door het maritieme verleden van Nederland,* ed. Anita van Dissel, Maurits Ebben, and Karwan Fatah-Black (Zutphen: Walburg Pers, 2015), 272–92.

63. Coolhaas, "Aanteekeningen en Opmerkingen," 55.

64. Jean Delumeau, *La peur en Occident, XIVe–XVIIIe siècles: La cité assiégée* (Paris: Fayard, 1978), 2.

65. Maurus Reinkowski and Gregor Thum, eds., *Helpless Imperialists: Imperial Failure, Fear and Radicalization* (Göttingen: Vandenhoeck & Ruprecht, 2013), 8. See also the important work of Kim Wagner. Kim Wagner, *The Great Fear of 1857: Rumours, Conspiracies and the Making of the Indian Uprising* (Bern: Peter Lang, 2010); Kim Wagner, "'Treading Upon Fires': The 'Mutiny'-Motif and Colonial Anxieties in British India," *Past & Present* 218, no. 1 (2013): 159–97. See also Robert Peckham, ed., *Empires of Panic: Epidemics and Colonial Anxieties* (Hong Kong: Hong Kong University Press, 2015). Tobias Green, "Fear and Atlantic History," *Atlantic Studies* 3, no. 1 (2006): 25–42.

66. Louis Roper and Lauric Henneton, eds., *Fear and the Shaping of Early American Societies* (Leiden: Brill, 2016). The quote comes from Mark Meuwese, "Fear, Uncertainty, and Violence in the Dutch Colonization of Brazil (1624–1662)," in Roper and Henneton, *Fear and the Shaping of Early American Societies,* 113. Raben shows how the city was constructed in response to colonial anxiety. Remco Raben, "Batavia and Colombo: The Ethnic and Spatial Order of Two Colonial Cities, 1600–1800" (PhD diss., Leiden University, 1996). Markus Vink, "A Work of Compassion? Dutch Slavery and Slave Trade in the Indian Ocean in the Seventeenth Century," *The History Cooperative* (2003), www.historycooperative.org /proceedings/seascapes. Special mention should be made of important work on the Chinese massacre at Batavia in 1740, an episode in which the role of fear cannot be overstated. Leonard Blussé, "Batavia, 1619–1740: The Rise and Fall of a Chinese Colonial Town," *Journal of Southeast Asian Studies* 12, no. 1 (1981): 159–78.

67. I have also been influenced by the work of Ann Laura Stoler, who notes that "rumor was not so much a source of what happened; it registered what people believed could have happened in the past and could happen in the future." Ann Laura Stoler, "'In Cold Blood': Hierarchies of Credibility and the Politics of Colonial Narratives," *Representations* 37 (1992): 181.

68. Examining the different permutations, Coolhaas writes that "it seems to me that Towerson was himself still not sure how he would take the castle. He probably had different possibilities." Coolhaas, "Aanteekeningen en Opmerkingen," 90.

69. For this caution about seeing empire builders as the victims of empire, see Paul Gilroy, *After Empire: Melancholia or Convivial Culture?* (Abingdon: Routledge, 2004).

70. Mary Beth Norton, *In the Devil's Snare: The Salem Witchcraft Crisis of 1692* (New York: Alfred A. Knopf, 2002).

71. Femme Gaastra, *The Dutch East India Company: Expansion and Decline* (Zutphen: Walburg Pers, 2003), 36. George Winius and Marcus Vink divide the Company's

development into three periods, beginning with an aggressive phase of expansion from 1600 to 1680. George Winius and Marcus Vink, *The Merchant Warrior Pacified: The VOC and Its Changing Political Economy in India* (Delhi: Oxford University Press, 1991).

72. Niels Steensgard famously praised the *Compagnie* for its rational use of violence, which he contrasted negatively with the Portuguese. Niels Steensgaard, *Carracks, Caravans, and Companies: The Structural Crisis in the European-Asian Trade in the Early 17th Century* (Copenhagen: Studentlitteratur, 1973). Reissued as *The Asian Trade Revolution of the Seventeenth Century: The East India Companies and the Decline of the Caravan Trade* (Chicago: University of Chicago Press, 1975).

73. This process can be said to have started decades earlier with the work of J. C. van Leur but it has gathered speed in recent years. For a recent work in this vein, see Tonio Andrade's brilliant study of Dutch defeat on Taiwan. Tonio Andrade, *Lost Colony: The Untold Story of China's First Great Victory Over the West* (Princeton, NJ: Princeton University Press, 2011). For VOC struggles in Japan, see Clulow, *The Company and the Shogun.* For a trenchant critique of views of VOC rationality, see Sanjay Subrahmanyam, "Forcing the Doors of Heathendom: Ethnography, Violence, and the Dutch East India Company," in *Between the Middle Ages and Modernity*, ed. Charles Parker and Jerry Bentley (Lanham, MD: Rowman & Littlefield, 2007).

74. Hunter, *A History of British India*, 427.

75. EIC leaders made the same case. Court minutes, 9 July 1624, BL IOR, B/9.

76. Edmund Scott, *An Exact Discourse of the Subtilties, Fashishions, Pollicies, Religion, and Ceremonies of the East Indians* (1606). Towerson was chief factor at Banten from 1605 to 1608. D. K. Bassett, "The Factory of the English East India Company at Bantam, 1602–1682" (PhD diss., University of London, 1955), ii.

77. For an examination of this episode, see Michael Neill, "Putting History to the Question: An Episode of Torture at Bantam in Java, 1604," *English Literary Renaissance* 25 (1995): 45–75.

78. For a study of conspiracy thinking in early modern Europe, see Barry Coward and Julian Swann, eds., *Conspiracies and Conspiracy Theory in Early Modern Europe: From the Waldensians to the French Revolution* (Aldershot: Ashgate, 2004).

79. As one recent example, see Mark Condos, *The Insecurity State: Punjab and the Making of Colonial Power in British India* (Cambridge: Cambridge University Press, 2017). Condos identifies "a pervasive and constant sense of anxiety, vulnerability and uncertainty about the survival of the colonial regime."

1. With Treaty or with Violence

The epigraph is taken from: Answer to question 104, deposition of Laurens de Maerschalk, March 1628, NL-HaNA, Staten-Generaal, 1.01.02, inv. no. 12551.62.

1. Coen to Heeren 17, 6 May 1621, in H. T. Colenbrander and W. P. Coolhaas, eds., *Jan Pietersz. Coen: Bescheiden Omtrent Zijn Bedrijf in Indië* (The Hague: Martinus

Nijhoff, 1919–1954), 1:625–26. Hereafter, *Coen: Bescheiden.* Coen also listed "286 captive Javanese," who most likely served as rowers on the Company's smaller vessels. As stated in the Note to the Reader, my descriptions of sender and recipient for the letters included in the Colenbrander and Coolhaas's compilation are intended to be indicative rather than comprehensive. The May 1621 letter, for example, came from Coen and a second administrator, Martinus Sonck.

2. As will be discussed later, whether Coen anticipated the bloody outcome of the campaign, which saw the erasure of most of Banda's population, remains a topic of contention among scholars.

3. In his writings, Coen emphasized the two-part nature of the campaign. For a description, see J. Keuning, "Ambonese, Portuguese and Dutchmen: The History of Ambon to the End of the Seventeenth Century," in *Dutch Authors on Asian History: A Selection of Dutch Historiography on the Verenigde Oostindische Compagnie,* ed. M. A. P. Meilink-Roelofsz, M. E. van Opstall, and G. J. Schutte (Dordrecht: Foris, 1988), 379.

4. Coen to Van Speult, 28 October 1622, *Coen: Bescheiden,* 3:252.

5. J. K. de Jonge and M. L. van Deventer, eds., *De opkomst van het Nederlandsch gezag in Oost Indië* (The Hague: Martinus Nijhoff, 1862–1909), 3:95.

6. Van Ittersum argues persuasively that "treaty-making should not be seen as an alternative to conquest and war, but was, in fact, integral to the process of European possession and indigenous dispossession." Martine J. van Ittersum, "Empire by Treaty? The Role of Written Documents in European Overseas Expansion, 1500–1800," in *The Dutch and English East India Companies: Diplomacy, Trade and Violence in Early Modern Asia,* ed. Adam Clulow and Tristan Mostert (Amsterdam: Amsterdam University Press, 2018). Arthur Weststeijn, "'Love Alone Is Not Enough': Treaties in Seventeenth-Century Dutch Colonial Expansion," in *Empire by Treaty: Negotiating European Expansion, 1600–1900,* ed. Saliha Belmessous (Oxford: Oxford University Press, 2014), 19–44.

7. There is a vast literature on the role of treaties and law in imperial expansion. For one representative work, see Antony Anghie, *Imperialism, Sovereignty and the Making of International Law* (Cambridge: Cambridge University Press, 2005).

8. Not all VOC officials shared this view. The Company was a fractious organization characterized by sharp disagreement between officials as to the correct policy. For an examination of internal VOC debates, see Martine J. van Ittersum, "Debating Natural Law in the Banda Islands: A Case Study in Anglo–Dutch Imperial Competition in the East Indies, 1609–1621," *History of European Ideas* 42, no. 4 (2016): 459–501.

9. The creation of the Company was driven as well by a desire to take the war against Spain into Asia. One of its chief architects argued, for example, that the creation of the VOC would serve to damage the Iberian powers and thereby secure the United Provinces. Peter Borschberg, *Journal, Memorial, and Letters of Cornelis Matelieff de Jong: Security, Diplomacy, and Commerce in 17th-Century Southeast Asia* (Singapore: NUS Press, 2015), 29.

10. Leonard Andaya, *The World of Maluku: Eastern Indonesia in the Early Modern Period* (Honolulu: University of Hawaii Press, 1993), 1.

11. "Tweede Schipvaerd der Hollanders," in Isaac Commelin, *Begin ende Voortgangh van de Vereenighde Nederlantsche Geoctroyeerde Oost-Indische Compagnie* (1646), 1:30.

12. Arthur Coke Burnell and P. A. Tiele, eds., *The Voyage of John Huyghen van Linschoten to the East Indies* (London: Hakluyt Society, 1885), 2:84.

13. Burnell and Tiele, *The Voyage of John Huyghen van Linschoten to the East Indies*, 2:86.

14. The Malukus are now split into two provinces, North Maluku and Maluku. North Maluku includes Ternate and Tidore, while Maluku includes Ambon and Banda.

15. Ternate was also a significant producer of cloves.

16. Femme Gaastra, *The Dutch East India Company: Expansion and Decline* (Zutphen: Walburg Pers, 2003), 34.

17. M. C. Ricklefs, *A History of Modern Indonesia Since c. 1200* (Stanford, CA: Stanford University Press, 2001), 29.

18. Jan de Vries and Ad van der Woude, *The First Modern Economy: Success, Failure, and Perseverance of the Dutch Economy, 1500–1815* (New York: Cambridge University Press, 1997), 385.

19. For a discussion of the extended process that led to the development of a permanent capital, see Oscar Gelderblom, Abe de Jong, and Joost Jonker, "The Formative Years of the Modern Corporation: The Dutch East India Company VOC, 1602–1623," *Journal of Economic History* 73, no. 4 (2013): 1050–76.

20. The *Heeren* 17 appear frequently as the *Heeren* XVII or the *Heren* XVII. For the purposes of this study, I will refer to them as the Heeren 17.

21. As will be discussed later in this chapter, part of the Spice Islands fell within the traditional sphere of influence of Ternate, which concluded a series of treaties with the VOC.

22. This and the next section draw on Adam Clulow, "The Art of Claiming: Possession and Resistance in Early Modern Asia," *American Historical Review* 121, no. 1 (2016): 17–38. My thanks to the journal's editors.

23. J. E. Heeres and F. W. Stapel, eds., *Corpus Diplomaticum Neerlando-Indicum* (The Hague: Martinus Nijhoff, 1907–1955), 1:71, 1:92.

24. Quoted in Peter Borschberg, *Hugo Grotius, the Portuguese, and Free Trade in the East Indies* (Singapore: NUS Press, 2011), 265.

25. Hugo Grotius, *Commentary on the Law of Prize and Booty*, ed. Martine Julia van Ittersum (Indianapolis, IN: Liberty Fund, 2006), 457.

26. Quoted in Borschberg, *Hugo Grotius*, 265.

27. Van Ittersum explains that such contracts "granted [the Company] an exclusive right for preemption, which applied to both present and future harvests. By virtue of these contracts, they had certainly alienated their sovereign rights in the economic sphere." Martine J. van Ittersum, *Profit and Principle: Hugo Grotius, Natural Rights Theories and the Rise of Dutch Power in the East Indies, 1595–1615* (Leiden: Brill, 2006), 385.

28. These are collected in a vast diplomatic compilation. Heeres and Stapel, *Corpus Diplomaticum Neerlando-Indicum*. The VOC argued that the religion of the signatories was essentially irrelevant, meaning that treaties signed between Christians

and Muslims had the same basic force. See Weststeijn, "'Love Alone Is Not Enough,'" 30.

29. Edward Keene, *Beyond the Anarchical Society: Grotius, Colonialism, and Order in World Politics* (Cambridge: Cambridge University Press, 2002).

30. Van Ittersum, *Profit and Principle*, 385.

31. In 1608, for example, Matelieff wrote that "whenever one concludes a treaty in the Indies, one should straightaway build a fort to go with it and then be careful not to give them occasion for malevolence. Then one will be good friends with them, as long as they fear and love you, for in my opinion love alone is not enough." Quoted in Borschberg, *Hugo Grotius*, 253.

32. P. A. Tiele, "Documenten voor de geschiedenis der Nederlanders in het Oosten," *Bijdragen en Mededelingen van het Historisch Genootschap* 6 (1883): 267. See also Weststeijn, "'Love Alone Is Not Enough,'" 33.

33. For a detailed examination of VOC relations with Banda in this period, see Van Ittersum, "Debating Natural Law in the Banda Islands." See also Vincent C. Loth, "Armed Incidents and Unpaid Bills: Anglo-Dutch Rivalry in the Banda Islands in the Seventeenth Century," *Modern Asian Studies* 29, no. 4 (1995): 705–40.

34. These are Naira (Banda Neira), Lontor or Bandar Besar, Gunung Api (Banda Api), Pulau Hatta, Ai (Pulau Ai), Run (Pulau Run), Pulau Karaka, Manukang, Pulau Syahrir (Pulau Pisang), and Naialaka. The islands had multiple names and spellings, and there is no single clear standard. See Vincent Loth, "Pioneers and Perkeniers: The Banda Islands in the 17th century," *Cakalele*, no. 6 (1995): 13–35.

35. François Pyrard, *The Voyage of Francois Pyrard of Laval to the East Indies, the Maldives, the Moluccas, and Brazil*, ed. and trans. Albert Gray (London: Hakluyt Society), 2.1:167.

36. John Villiers, "Trade and Society in the Banda Islands in the Sixteenth Century," *Modern Asian Studies* 15, no. 4 (1981): 729.

37. For a description of this fractious environment, see M. E. van Opstall, ed., "Laurens Reael in de Staten-Generaal: Het verslag van Reael over de toestand in Oost-Indië anno 1620," in *Nederlandse historische bronnen*, ed. A. C. F. Koch et al., vol. 1 (The Hague, Martinus Nijhoff, 1979), 1196. There was a running conflict between two confederations of villages, the *ulilima* and *ulisiva*.

38. Borschberg, *Journal, Memorials and Letters of Cornelis Matelieff de Jonge*, 261.

39. Villiers, "Trade and Society in the Banda Islands," 723.

40. For an analysis of Makassar's role in the spice trade, see Tristan Mostert, "Scramble for the Spices: Makassar's Role in European and Asian Competition in the Eastern Archipelago Up to 1616," in Adam Clulow and Tristan Mostert, eds., *The Dutch and English East India Companies: Diplomacy, Trade and Violence in Early Modern Asia* (Amsterdam: Amsterdam University Press, 2018). The list of traders comes from a contract expressly prohibiting external dealings signed in 1616. Contract bij commandeur Jan Dircksz. Lam met de vijf eijlanden van Banda, Nera, Poelewaij, Poderon ende Rossengijn in dato 3 Meij 1616, NL-HaNA, VOC 1072.

41. Borschberg, *Journal, Memorials and Letters of Cornelis Matelieff de Jonge*, 262.

42. Heeres and Stapel, *Corpus Diplomaticum Neerlando-Indicum*, 1:26.

43. Heeres and Stapel, *Corpus Diplomaticum Neerlando-Indicum*, 1:37.
44. Willard Hanna, *Indonesian Banda: Colonialism and Its Aftermath* (Philadelphia: Institute for the Study of Human Issues, 1978), 24.
45. This approach is reflected in Andaya's well-known article on VOC treaties. Leonard Andaya, "Treaty Conceptions and Misconceptions: A Case Study from South Sulawesi," *Bijdragen tot de taal-, land- en volkenkunde* 134/2, no. 3 (1978): 275–95.
46. For this formulation, see O. W. Wolters, *History, Culture, and Region in Southeast Asian Perspective* (Singapore: Institute of Southeast Asian Studies, 1982).
47. Both the sultan of Ternate and the Portuguese appear to have claimed tribute in return for offering protection to the Bandanese at different points during the sixteenth century. Villiers, "Trade and Society in the Banda Islands." For wider notions of protection, see Lauren Benton, Adam Clulow, and Bain Attwood, eds., *Protection and Empire: A Global History* (Cambridge: Cambridge University Press, 2017).
48. Van Ittersum, "Empire by Treaty?," 160.
49. Heeres and Stapel, *Corpus Diplomaticum Neerlando-Indicum*, 1:67.
50. Letter from the Heeren 17, 6 May 1615, *Coen: Bescheiden*, 4:311.
51. Van Ittersum argues that the "Bandanese were the victims of Anglo-Dutch imperial competition in Asia." Van Ittersum, "Debating Natural Law in the Banda Islands," 463.
52. See Clulow, "The Art of Claiming."
53. This move toward a violent resolution has been covered by a number of scholars, beginning with J. A. van der Chijs, *De vestiging van het Nederlandsche Gezag over de Banda eilanden, 1599–1621* (Batavia, 1886). See also Loth, "Pioneers and Perkeniers." For a more positive appraisal of VOC policy that defends it according to the standards of contemporary international law, see Lucas Kiers, *Coen op Banda: De conqueste getoetst aan het recht van den tijd* (Utrecht: A. Oosthoek, 1943).
54. P. A. Tiele and J. E. Heeres, eds., *Bouwstoffen voor de geschiedenis der Nederlanders in den Maleischen Archipel* (The Hague: Martinus Nijhoff, 1886–1895), 1:5; Loth, "Armed Incidents," 710.
55. De Jonge and Van Deventer, *De opkomst*, 3:389–90.
56. Heeren 17 to Coen, 30 April 1615, *Coen: Bescheiden*, 4:307.
57. Coen to Heeren 17, 26 October 1620, *Coen: Bescheiden*, 1:591. In an important study, Meilink-Roelofsz makes clear that while Coen is frequently criticized as the architect of these violent plans, such policies were, as can be seen in the cited quote, the product of an agenda "laid down by his masters in Holland." M. A. P. Meilink-Roelofsz, *Asian Trade and European Influence in the Indonesian Archipelago Between 1500 and About 1630* (The Hague: Martinus Nijhoff, 1962), 207.
58. In his authoritative biography, Van Goor argues that Coen could not have predicted what happened during the campaign. He notes that Coen had no "worked out plans" for what would happen after a successful expedition and that it "seems unlikely that Coen had planned the gruesome ending of his expedition beforehand." Jur van Goor, *Jan Pieterszoon Coen, 1587–1629: Koopman-Koning in Azië* (Amsterdam: Boom Publishers, 2015), 440, 463. While I agree that such an outcome was by no means inevitable, it is also difficult to envision an alternative in

which the Company's armies simply departed after signing another treaty. In this way, I struggle to imagine a scenario in which the VOC attempt to exert final control over Banda would not have resulted in sustained bloodshed.

59. The Banda campaign was central to Coen's ambitions in Asia. As a mark of its importance, it was, as Van Goor has shown, only one of two times that the governor-general actually left Java during his time in Asia. Van Goor, *Jan Pieterszoon Coen*, 433.

60. Van Goor, *Jan Pieterszoon Coen*, 445.

61. Heeres and Stapel, *Corpus Diplomaticum Neerlando-Indicum*, 1:162.

62. Coen to Heeren 17, 6 May 1621, *Coen: Bescheiden*, 1:629.

63. Coen to Van Speult, 20 April 1621, *Coen: Bescheiden*, 3:29–30. A total of 287 men, 256 women, and 246 children were transported to Batavia. Coen to Heeren 17, 6 May 1621, *Coen: Bescheiden*, 1:631.

64. Coen to Heeren 17, 16 November 1621, *Coen: Bescheiden*, 1:641. This is a figure from Coen's letters, but there are some variations in term of the total number.

65. Kiers, *Coen op Banda*, 288–89. This chapter does not have the space to assess whether or not such a conspiracy actually existed, but the evidence is far from persuasive.

66. Coen argued that as long as the Bandanese remained in their land it would be impossible to prevent the outbreak of rebellion. Coen to Heeren 17, 6 May 1621, *Coen: Bescheiden*, 1:630.

67. Loth, "Pioneers and Perkeniers." Coen to Heeren 17, 16 November 1621, *Coen: Bescheiden*, 1:643.

68. Coen to Heeren 17, 16 November 1621, *Coen: Bescheiden*, 1:644.

69. Knaap estimates a total population of 76,000 to 80,000 in 1634. Gerrit Knaap, "The Demography of Ambon in the Seventeenth Century: Evidence from Colonial Proto-Censuses," *Journal of Southeast Asian Studies* 26, no. 2 (1995): 238.

70. The problem was clearly recognized by Coen in a 1614 letter to his superiors: Coen to Heeren 17, 1 January 1614, *Coen: Bescheiden*, 1:10. For an overview of clove production, see Gerrit Knaap, *Kruidnagelen en Christenen: De VOC en de bevolking van Ambon 1656–1696* (Leiden: KITLV, 2004), 297.

71. See for example Gillis Seys, "'Verhael van den tegenwoordigen staet inde quarteren van Amboyna,' Oost-Indische Voyagie onder den Admirael Peter W. Verhoeven," in *Begin ende Voortgangh van de Vereenighde Nederlantsche Geoctroyeerde Oost-Indische Compagnie*, ed. Isaac Commelin (1646), 140. Letters from Herman van Speult in Amboina to Governor-General Pieter de Carpentier, 5 and 17 June, 5 July, and 9 September 1623, with an appendix from 14 September 1623, NL-HaNA, VOC 1080.

72. As will be discussed in chapter 4.

73. Gerrit Knaap, "De Ambonse eilanden tussen twee mogendheden; De VOC en Ternate, 1605–1656," in *Hof en Handel; Aziatische vorsten en de VOC 1620–1720*, ed. Elsbeth Locher-Scholten and Peter Rietbergen (Leiden: KITLV, 2004), 40.

74. See Van Speult's description in F. W. Stapel, ed., *Pieter van Dam's Beschryvinge van de Oostindische Compagnie* (The Hague: Martinus Nijhoff, 1927–1954), 2.1:136–60. The more precise translation would be "able-bodied men."

75. Gerrit Knaap, "Headhunting, Carnage and Armed Peace in Amboina, 1500–1700," *Journal of the Economic and Social History of the Orient* 46, no. 2 (2003): 168.

76. This was Sultan Said al-din Berkat Syah (r. 1584–1606). Andaya, *The World of Maluku*, 140.

77. Heeres and Stapel, *Corpus Diplomaticum Neerlando-Indicum*, 1:51–53.

78. Andaya, *The World of Maluku*, 153.

79. One English observer wrote about the "Kinge of Turnattee, whome the Hollanders doe protecte, or rather keepe as a prisoner, for the Kinge doth nothinge butt what the Hollanders please." William Foster, ed., *The Journal of John Jourdain (1608–1617), Describing His Experiences in Arabia, India, and the Malay Archipelago* (Cambridge: Hakluyt Society, 1905), 273.

80. Hans Straver, Chris van Fraassen, and Jan van der Putten, *Ridjali Historie van Hitu: Een Ambonse geschiedenis uit de zeventiende eeuw* (Utrecht: Landelijk Steunpunt Educatie Molukkers, 2004), 51–52.

81. W. P. Coolhaas, J. van Goor, J. E. Schooneveld-Oosterling, and H. K. s'Jacob, eds., *Generale Missiven van Gouverneurs-Generaal en Raden aan Heren XVII der Verenigde Oost-Indische Compagnie* (The Hague: Martinus Nijhoff, 1960–2007), 1:140. Hereafter, *Generale Missiven van Gouverneurs-Generaal en Raden*.

82. George Masselman, *The Cradle of Colonialism* (New Haven, CT: Yale University Press), 301.

83. Tiele and Heeres, *Bouwstoffen voor de geschiedenis der Nederlanders in den Maleischen Archipel*, 1:264. Heeres and Stapel, *Corpus Diplomaticum Neerlando-Indicum*, 1:170. There was a second less significant *kimelaha* on Buru.

84. For a description of the role of the *kimelaha*, see Gerrit Knaap, "Crisis and Failure: War and Revolt in the Ambon Islands, 1636–1637," *Cakalele* 3 (1992): 2–3. Straver, Van Fraassen, and Van der Putten, *Ridjali Historie van Hitu*, 5. Andaya, *The World of Maluku*, 157. In one of the more memorable exchanges, Van Speult explained to the *kimelaha* that he "no longer knew if we were friends or enemies." Tiele and Heeres, *Bouwstoffen voor de geschiedenis der Nederlanders in den Maleischen Archipel*, 1:319.

85. Stapel, *Pieter van Dam's Beschryvinge*, 2.1:152.

86. Stapel, *Pieter van Dam's Beschryvinge*, 2.1:152. Knaap suggests the existence of a rising political hierarchy, from village to federation of villages to federations of village federations. Knaap, "De Ambonse eilanden tussen twee mogendheden," 39.

87. Although they represented Ternate, which in turn depended on the Company, the *kimelaha* were forced to walk a precarious line between the demands of their royal masters and the interests of the Hoamoalese. While Ternate had signed a series of treaties with the VOC, the clove producers in the Hoamoal Peninsula depended on getting higher prices for their goods. Knaap writes that the *kimelaha* had to "choose between their own loyalty to the Sultan and supporting the cause of their subjects on Hoamoal." Knaap, "Crisis and Failure," 3.

88. Stapel, *Pieter van Dam's Beschryvinge*, 2.1:152.

89. Seys, "Verhael van den tegenwoordigen staet inde quarteren van Amboyna," 138; *Coen: Bescheiden*, 1:255.

90. Coen to Heeren 17, 26 July 1618, *Coen: Bescheiden*, 1:365.

91. Van Speult to Heeren 17, 30 September 1622, NL-HaNA, VOC 1078. In this letter, Van Speult explained that he had served the Company for ten years. *Generale Missiven van Gouverneurs-Generaal en Raden*, 1:138.

92. *Generale Missiven van Gouverneurs-Generaal en Raden*, 1:138; W. P. Coolhaas, "Aanteekeningen en Opmerkingen over den zoogenaamdem Ambonschen Moord," *Bijdragen tot de Taal-, Land- en Volkenkunde van Nederlandsch-Indie* 101 (1942): 76.

93. For an example of Coen's praise of Van Speult, see Coen to Heeren 17, 29 June 1623, *Coen: Bescheiden*, 1:784.

94. Answer to question 47, deposition of Jan Joosten, 9 February 1628, NL-HaNA, Staten-Generaal, 1.01.02, inv. no. 12551.62; Knaap, *Kruidnagelen en Christenen*, 25–26.

95. Van Speult to Coen, 4 June 1618, *Coen: Bescheiden*, 7.1:323–24.

96. Coen to Heeren 17, 26 July 1618, *Coen: Bescheiden*, 1:365.

97. Tiele and Heeres, *Bouwstoffen voor de geschiedenis der Nederlanders in den Maleischen Archipel*, 1:216.

98. Georgius Rumphius, "De Ambonse Historie," *Bijdragen tot de Taal-, Land- en Volkenkunde van Nederlandsch-Indië* 64, no. 1/2 (1910): 36. Rumphius labels this the first Ambonese war. In 1624, Van Speult described Hottomouri's actions as a rebellion against VOC authority. Beclach poincten over d'absurde ende hostile proceduiren der Ternatanen ende Louhesen in dato 16 September 1624, NL-HaNA, VOC 1083, 361.

99. Stapel, *Pieter van Dam's Beschryvinge*, 2.1:141. Keuning, "Ambonese, Portuguese and Dutchmen," 377.

100. Van Speult was not the first VOC administrator to deploy such fleets but he did significantly expand their use. As Knaap notes, the first *hongi* expeditions under VOC control were dispatched in 1607. Knaap, "Headhunting, Carnage and Armed Peace in Amboina," 170.

101. Knaap, "Headhunting, Carnage and Armed Peace in Amboina," 169.

102. The burden that was placed on these Christian communities would later spark a crisis in Amboina. See Gerrit Knaap, "The Governor-General and the Sultan: An Attempt to Restructure a Divided Amboina in 1638," *Itinerario* 29, no. 1 (2005): 79–100.

103. Individuals fleets could consist of thirty to forty *kora-kora*, each thirty meters in length and carrying up to ninety warriors, under VOC command. Put together this could amount to a mobile fighting force of several thousand men, although early expeditions were generally smaller. Knaap, "Headhunting, Carnage and Armed Peace in Amboina," 170.

104. Coen to Heeren 17, 6 September 1622, *Coen: Bescheiden*, 1:741.

105. Hanna writes that they were designed to inspire "calculated terror." Willard Hanna and Des Alwi, *Turbulent Times in Past Ternate and Tidore* (Banda Naira: Yayasan Warisandan Budaya Banda Naira, 1990), 158. Widjojo describes the hongi expeditions as a "well-planned and well-organized visitation of terror." Muridan Satrio Widjojo, *The Revolt of Prince Nuku: Crosscultural Alliance-Making in Maluku, c. 1780–1810* (Leiden: Brill, 2009), 40.

106. Letter from Heeren 17, 24 March 1620, *Coen: Bescheiden*, 4:444. A more literal translation would be to "hold in devotion."
107. Coen to Heeren 17, 6 September 1622, *Coen: Bescheiden*, 1:741.
108. Coen to Heeren 17, 16 November 1621, *Coen: Bescheiden*, 1:646–47.
109. Coen to Heeren 17, 16 November 1621, *Coen: Bescheiden*, 1:647.
110. Tiele and Heeres, *Bouwstoffen voor de geschiedenis der Nederlanders in den Maleischen Archipel*, 1:297.
111. Van Speult to Coen, 9 September 1622, *Coen: Bescheiden*, 7.1:1009. The limited sources mean that tracking these Bandanese refugees is extremely difficult. We know that many seem to have ended up in East Seram rather than Amboina proper, and that other Bandanese refugees settled in Makassar.
112. Van Speult to Coen, 21 July 1621, *Coen: Bescheiden*, 7.1:734.
113. Coen to Heeren 17, 20 June 1623, *Coen: Bescheiden*, 1:784.
114. *Generale Missiven van Gouverneurs-Generaal en Raden*, 1:139.
115. Coen to Heeren 17, 20 June 1623, *Coen: Bescheiden*, 1:784.
116. De Carpentier to Van Speult, 26 September 1623, NL-HaNA, VOC 850, 213. See also Letter from Herman van Speult in Amboina to Governor-General Pieter de Carpentier, 5 and 17 June, 5 July, and 9 September 1623, with an appendix from 14 September 1623, NL-HaNA, VOC 1080.
117. Rumphius, "De Ambonse Historie," 45. Georg Everard Rumphius (1627–1702) was a notable chronicler of Amboina and its history.
118. For a discussion of the spread of Christianity in Amboina, see K. A. Steenbrink and J. S. Aritonang, "The Arrival of Protestantism and the Consolidation of Christianity in the Moluccas, 1605–1800," in *A History of Christianity in Indonesia*, ed. Jan Sihar Aritonang and Karel Steenbrink (Leiden: Brill, 2008), 99–134. Brett Baker has called attention to the role of local rather than colonial drivers in an important recent dissertation. Brett Baker, "Indigenous-Driven Mission: Reconstructing Religious Change in Sixteenth-Century Maluku" (PhD diss., Australian National University, 2014).
119. Van Speult to Coen, 15 June 1622, Tiele and Heeres, *Bouwstoffen voor de geschiedenis der Nederlanders in den Maleischen Archipel*, 1:311–28.
120. Coen to Van Speult, 28 October 1622, *Coen: Bescheiden*, 3:249–50.
121. Coen to Van Speult, 28 October 1622, *Coen: Bescheiden*, 3:251.
122. Heeres and Stapel, *Corpus Diplomaticum Neerlando-Indicum*, 1:175–77.
123. For a description, see Tiele and Heeres, *Bouwstoffen voor de geschiedenis der Nederlanders in den Maleischen Archipel*, 1:316–19.
124. Stapel, *Pieter van Dam's Beschryvinge*, 2.1:145.
125. Coen to Heeren 17, 6 September 1622, *Coen: Bescheiden*, 1:742–43.
126. These attacks are recorded in a number of different places. Van Speult described them in a range of documents, among them his 1623 letter detailing the Amboina trial, his description of Amboina that is included in Stapel, *Pieter van Dam's Beschryvinge*, 2.1:153, and a long account he penned of various provocations by Luhu and the *kimelaha*: Beclach poincten over d'absurde ende hostile proceduiren der Ternatanen ende Louhesen in dato 16 September 1624, VOC 1083. They

are also described in later depositions made by the Amboina judges, including accounts by Pieter van Santen and Jan van Leeuwen.

127. *Generale Missiven van Gouverneurs-Generaal en Raden*, 1:138.

128. Letter from Herman van Speult in Amboina to Governor-General Pieter de Carpentier, 5 June 1623, NL-HaNA, VOC 1080, 97v. Answer to question 104, deposition of Jan van Leeuwen, March 1628, NL-HaNA, Staten-Generaal, 1.01.02, inv. no. 12551.62. Although the evidence is far from clear, Van Leeuwen was convinced that Kambelo had orchestrated the attack. Answer to question 14, deposition of Jan van Leeuwen, 1626, NL-HaNA, Staten-Generaal, 1.01.02, inv. no. 12551.62.

129. The sources are not clear on the precise timing but it seems that the incident in Kambelo took place before the incident in Luhu.

130. *Generale Missiven van Gouverneurs-Generaal en Raden*, 1:139.

131. Edmund Scott, *An Exact Discourse of the Subtilties, Fashishions, Pollicies, Religion, and Ceremonies of the East Indians* (1606), C1.

132. Answer to question 14, deposition of Roelant Tieller, December 1626, NL-HaNA, Staten-Generaal, 1.01.02, inv. no. 12551.62 Answer to question 14, deposition of Jan van Leeuwen, 1626, NL-HaNA, Staten-Generaal, 1.01.02, inv. no. 12551.62.

133. Answer to question 104, deposition of Pieter van Santen, 9 March 1628, BL IOR, G/21/2, pt. 3.

134. *Generale Missiven van Gouverneurs-Generaal en Raden*, 1:139.

135. Letter from Herman van Speult in Amboina to Governor-General Pieter de Carpentier, 5 June 1623, NL-HaNA, VOC 1080, 99v. *Generale Missiven van Gouverneurs-Generaal en Raden*, 1:139.

2. We Cannot Exist Well Without Slaves

The epigraph is taken from: Advice from Coen, 31 January 1623, H. T. Colenbrander and W. P. Coolhaas, eds., *Jan Pietersz. Coen: Bescheiden Omtrent Zijn Bedrijf in Indië* (The Hague: Martinus Nijhoff, 1919–1954), 3:294. Hereafter, *Coen: Bescheiden*.

1. VOC officials referred to Peres by the Portuguese title of *marinho*, which can be broadly translated as "guardian" or "overseer." Letter from Herman van Speult in Amboina to Governor-General Pieter de Carpentier, 5 June 1623, NL-HaNA, VOC 1080, 101v.

2. Trevor Burnard, *Mastery, Tyranny, and Desire: Thomas Thistlewood and His Slaves in the Anglo-Jamaican World* (Chapel Hill: University of North Carolina Press, 2004), 138. It could be argued that the term "slave societies" does not apply to this VOC settlement with a few hundred slaves at most, but, as I will argue here, slavery was an increasingly important feature of the Company's presence in Amboina by 1623. In using this term, I follow the lead of scholars such as Robert Ross, who has written widely on the Company's South African colony. Robert

Ross, *Cape of Torments: Slavery and Resistance in South Africa* (London: Routledge and Kegan Paul, 1983).

3. Answer to question 7, deposition of Jan Jacobsen Wyncoop, 1626, NL-HaNA, Staten-Generaal, 1.01.02, inv. no. 12551.62. Peres was invariably described as a Portuguese *marinho* or guardian of the slaves by the former judges in their depositions. In the original trial record he appears as "Augustyn Peris Maringhe van de slaven."

4. As such he, was a likely a mestizo, which is the term commonly used across the literature. See Leonard Andaya, *The World of Maluku: Eastern Indonesia in the Early Modern Period* (Honolulu: University of Hawaii Press, 1993), 283.

5. Hans Hägerdal, *Lords of the Land, Lords of the Sea: Conflict and Adaptation in Early Colonial Timor, 1600–1800* (Leiden: KITLV, 2012), 133. Hägerdal notes the ubiquitous nature of the mestizo population across the Portuguese empire. Examining the community in Timor, he argues that Portuguese identity frequently trumped actual heritage for these communities.

6. I have seen no reference to the fact that Peres had been imprisoned in the weeks before the trial. This is in part because this key detail is not mentioned in the original judicial record. Rather, it is confirmed in separate depositions by a pair of former Amboina judges. Answer to question 7, deposition of Jan Jacobsen Wyncoop, 1626, NL-HaNA, Staten-Generaal, 1.01.02, inv. no. 12551.62. Answer to question 7, deposition of Marten Jansz. Vogel, 1626, NL-HaNA, Staten-Generaal, 1.01.02, inv. no. 12551.62.

7. Advice from Coen, 31 January 1623, *Coen: Bescheiden*, 3:294.

8. Raben argues that the arrival of the Dutch caused a significant surge in the slave trade. Remco Raben, "Cities and the Slave Trade in Early-Modern Southeast Asia," in *Linking Destinies: Trade, Towns and Kin in Asian Histories*, ed. Peter Boomgaard, Dick Kooiman, and Henk Schulte Nordholt (Leiden: KITLV, 2008), 126.

9. Writing about Kota Ambon in the second half of the seventeenth century, Knaap describes a city dominated by thousands of slaves, where unfree laborers constituted more than half of the total population. For 1694, for example, he notes a total population of 5,487, of which 2,870 (about 52 percent) were slaves. Gerrit Knaap, "A City of Migrants: Kota Ambon at the End of the Seventeenth Century," *Indonesia*, no. 51 (1991): 123.

10. For a criticism of this older view of a more benevolent form of slavery, see Markus Vink, "'The World's Oldest Trade': Dutch Slavery and Slave Trade in the Indian Ocean in the Seventeenth Century," *Journal of World History* 14, no. 2 (2003): 175.

11. For earlier references to wide-scale slavery, see Gerrit Knaap, "Slavery and the Dutch in Southeast Asia," in *Fifty Years Later: Antislavery, Capitalism and Modernity in the Dutch Orbit*, ed. G. Oostindie (Leiden: KITLV Caribbean Series, 1995), 193–206. Leonard Blussé, *Strange Company: Chinese Settlers, Mestizo Women and the Dutch in VOC Batavia* (Dordrecht: Foris, 1986).

12. See important works by Ross and Worden. Ross, *Cape of Torments*. Nigel Worden, *Slavery in Dutch South Africa* (Cambridge: Cambridge University Press, 1985).

13. Vink, "'The World's Oldest Trade'"; Rik van Welie, "Patterns of Slave Trading and Slavery in the Dutch Colonial World, 1596–1863," in *Dutch Colonialism, Migration and Cultural Heritage,* ed. Gert Oostindie (Leiden: KITLV Press, 2008); Kerry Ward, *Networks of Empire: Forced Migration in the Dutch East India Company* (Cambridge: Cambridge University Press, 2008); Raben, "Cities and the Slave Trade in Early-Modern Southeast Asia." See also Richard Allen's important overview work and Henk Niemeijer's valuable study of Batavia. Richard Allen, *European Slave Trading in the Indian Ocean, 1500–1850* (Athens: Ohio University Press, 2014); Henk Niemeijer, *Batavia: Een koloniale samenleving in de zeventiende eeuw* (Amsterdam: Balans, 2005).

14. Vink explains that while "the Atlantic slave trade has been mapped out in relatively great detail in numerous studies, its Indian Ocean counterpart has remained largely uncharted territory and overlooked in Asian colonial historiography. Indeed, the sufferings of the slaves in Asia occurred mainly in silence, largely ignored by both contemporaries and modern historians." Vink, "'The World's Oldest Trade,'" 132.

15. The Company's attempt to recruit European settlers has been well documented by a number of scholars. See, for example, Jean Gelman Taylor, *The Social World of Batavia: Europeans and Eurasians in Colonial Indonesia,* 2nd ed. (Madison: University of Wisconsin Press, 2009). Gijs Kruijtzer, "European Migration in the Dutch Sphere," in *Dutch Colonialism, Migration and Cultural Heritage,* ed. Gert Oostindie (Leiden: KITLV Press, 2008), 97–154.

16. Peter Borschberg, *Journal, Memorial, and Letters of Cornelis Matelieff de Jong: Security, Diplomacy, and Commerce in 17th-Century Southeast Asia* (Singapore: NUS Press, 2015), 264.

17. J. K. de Jonge and M. L. van Deventer, eds., *De opkomst van het Nederlandsch gezag in Oost Indië* (The Hague: Martinus Nijhoff, 1862–1909), 3:390.

18. De Jonge and Van Deventer, *De opkomst,* 3:390.

19. Coen to Heeren 17, 31 July 1620, *Coen: Bescheiden,* 1:561.

20. *Discoers aen de E. Heeren Bewinthebberen touscherende den Nederlandtsche Indischen staet, Coen: Bescheiden,* 6:466. George Masselman, *The Cradle of Colonialism* (New Haven, CT: Yale University Press), 307. In an important study, Masselman first described this document as a "blueprint for Empire." Coen's plans for European settlers are detailed in Jur van Goor, *Jan Pieterszoon Coen, 1587–1629: Koopman-Koning in Azië* (Amsterdam: Boom Publishers, 2015), 179–80.

21. Coen to Heeren 17, 26 October 1620, *Coen: Bescheiden,* 1:586–87.

22. Knaap notes that "in times of danger the colonists could assist the VOC militarily, just as the casados were doing in the Portuguese towns." Knaap, "A City of Migrants," 111. See also Van Goor, *Jan Pieterszoon Coen,* 162 and 180.

23. Coen to Heeren 17, 11 May 1620, *Coen: Bescheiden,* 1:555; Coen to Heeren 17, 6 September 1622, *Coen: Bescheiden,* 1:731.

24. Coen to Heeren 17, 22 January 1620, *Coen: Bescheiden,* 1:534.

25. Kruijtzer, "European Migration in the Dutch Sphere," 104; Knaap, "A City of Migrants," 111.

26. Coen to Heeren 17, 11 May 1620, *Coen: Bescheiden*, 1:555.
27. Coen to Heeren 17, 1 January 1614, *Coen: Bescheiden*, 1:9.
28. Coen to Heeren 17, 6 September 1622, *Coen: Bescheiden*, 1:732.
29. Coen to Heeren 17, 1 January 1614, *Coen: Bescheiden*, 1:9.
30. Coen to Heeren 17, 6 September 1622, *Coen: Bescheiden*, 1:731–32; Taylor, *The Social World of Batavia*, 14.
31. Leonard Blussé points to a 1633 letter from the Heeren 17, which states that "it was of no use for the man in the street and expensive and prejudicial to the interests of the Company to send Dutch women." Leonard Blussé, "Batavia, 1619–1740: The Rise and Fall of a Chinese Colonial Town," *Journal of Southeast Asian Studies* 12, no. 1 (1981): 166. Kruijtzer dates the end of the "Company daughter" scheme to around the same year but notes that the notion of self-sustaining European colonies in Asia was periodically revived. Kruijtzer, "European Migration in the Dutch Sphere," 104.
32. See Coen's early comments regarding a proposed VOC headquarters in Asia. Coen to Heeren 17, 10 October 1616, *Coen: Bescheiden*, 1:215–16.
33. A similar process was evident in Taiwan. Its location close to the Chinese coast meant that the Company was able to draw large numbers of Chinese settlers to populate the island. This is detailed in Tonio Andrade, *How Taiwan Became Chinese: Dutch, Spanish, and Han Colonization in the Seventeenth Century* (New York: Columbia University Press, 2008).
34. Remco Raben, "Batavia and Colombo: The Ethnic and Spatial Order of Two Colonial Cities, 1600–1800" (PhD diss., Leiden University, 1996), 85. Blussé, "Batavia, 1619–1740," 160. As Blussé notes, such a characterization depends in part on excluding the slave population, which constituted a large part of Batavia's total residents.
35. Ambon had its own Chinese captain, but the Chinese population was more limited. As Knaap notes, the VOC there shifted to an "anti-Chinese policy" in the second half of the seventeenth century. Knaap, "A City of Migrants," 111. In contrast, Batavia was a "'cornerstone' of the Chinese trade network in Southeast Asia." Blussé, "Batavia, 1619–1740," 160.
36. W. P. Coolhaas, J. van Goor, J. E. Schooneveld-Oosterling, and H. K. s'Jacob, eds., *Generale Missiven van Gouverneurs-Generaal en Raden aan Heren XVII der Verenigde Oost-Indische Compagnie* (The Hague: Martinus Nijhoff, 1960–2007), 1:44. Hereafter, *Generale Missiven van Gouverneurs-Generaal en Raden*.
37. *Generale Missiven van Gouverneurs-Generaal en Raden*, 1:46–47. For further discussion of these comments, see Markus Vink, "A Work of Compassion? Dutch Slavery and Slave Trade in the Indian Ocean in the Seventeenth Century," *The History Cooperative* (2003), www.historycooperative.org/proceedings/seascapes. Such notions of course recurred across multiple European empires.
38. *Generale Missiven van Gouverneurs-Generaal en Raden*, 1:44.
39. Coen to Heeren 17, 10 October 1616, *Coen: Bescheiden*, 1:218.
40. Advice from Coen, 31 January 1623, *Coen: Bescheiden*, 3:294.
41. Advice from Coen, 31 January 1623, *Coen: Bescheiden*, 3:288.

42. Coen to Van Uffelen, 22 July 1622, *Coen: Bescheiden*, 3:209.

43. *Generale Missiven van Gouverneurs-Generaal en Raden*, 1:121. These comments come from Coen's successor as governor-general, Pieter de Carpentier.

44. In his words, "the slaves of the Portuguese in Macao were so trusted and useful" that they contributed to the defeat of the Dutch. Advice from Coen, 31 January 1623, *Coen: Bescheiden*, 3:294. Assessing what exactly happened in Macao and the precise role of the slaves is a task for a different study. For one assessment that seems to support Coen's view, see G. V. Scammell, "The Pillars of Empire: Indigenous Assistance and the Survival of the 'Estado da India' c. 1600–1700," *Modern Asian Studies* 22, no. 3 (1988): 485.

45. Coen to Heeren 17, 1 January 1614, *Coen: Bescheiden*, 1:9.

46. Resolutions, 9 January 1617, NL-HaNA, VOC 1070, 471.

47. Van Speult to Coen, 4 June 1618, *Coen: Bescheiden*, 7.1:336.

48. Resolutions, 9 January 1617, NL-HaNA, VOC 1070, 471.

49. Coen to Heeren 17, 29 September 1619, *Coen: Bescheiden*, 1:394. These were Van Speult's comments as reported by his superior.

50. Letter from Herman van Speult in Amboina to Governor-General Pieter de Carpentier, 5 June 1623, NL-HaNA, VOC 1080, 108.

51. Reid's volume on Southeast Asian slavery remains a vital work. In it, Reid examined "slavery, bondage and dependency" together, thereby acknowledging the overlapping categories that existed. Anthony Reid, ed., *Slavery, Bondage and Dependency in Southeast Asia* (St Lucia: Queensland University Press, 1983). In an important study, Peter Boomgaard draws a tripartite distinction between "slaves, who can be bought and sold, serfs, who can neither be traded nor leave their masters, and debt bondmen and bondwomen who in principle can regain freedom by paying off their debts." Peter Boomgaard, "Human Capital, Slavery, and Low Rates of Economic and Population Growth," *Slavery & Abolition* 24, no. 2 (2003): 87.

52. Artus Gijsels, "Grondig Verhaal van Amboyna," *Kroniek van het Historisch Genootschap Gevestigd te Utrecht* 6.2 (1871): 412.

53. Raben, "Cities and the Slave Trade in Early-Modern Southeast Asia," 126. Raben queries just how many slaves there actually were in pre-colonial societies around Southeast Asia. He "urges us to question the accepted idea of urban Southeast Asia relying on the import of slaves." Instead, he argues that "although there has been a lively trade in slaves in precolonial times, the coming of the Dutch caused an upsurge in the trade in humans" (122, 135).

54. Advice from Coen, 31 January 1623, *Coen: Bescheiden*, 3:294.

55. Fox distinguishes between "chained slaves" and "work slaves" while also noting that these distinctions broke down over time. James Fox, " 'For Good and Sufficient Reasons': An Examination of Early Dutch East India Company Ordinances on Slaves and Slavery," in Reid, *Slavery, Bondage, and Dependency in Southeast Asia*, 249.

56. A representative list of one group of chained laborers names "Pasquael Denis, Francisco Fernando, Domingo Parang, Francisco Rodrigo, married; Rodrigo Rodrigo, Deremia Rodrigo, Tugna Rodrigo, Dackelia Rodrigo, Deremia

Grande, Gregorie de Sine, Ysmael, Salvador Fernando, unmarried," all captured from the "frigate Ceylon" in 1616. Resolutions, 19 October 1619, *Coen: Bescheiden,* 3:546. See also Taylor, *The Social World of Batavia,* 18.

57. Coen to Heeren 17, 10 October 1616, *Coen: Bescheiden,* 1:196; Adriaen van der Dussen to Coen, 25 July 1616, *Coen: Bescheiden,* 7.1:167.

58. For a resolution to treat junks from Makassar as enemies, see Van Speult to Coen, 7 August 1618, *Coen: Bescheiden,* 7.1:380.

59. Torture by cord refers to the *strappado* technique whereby the victim is hosted up his or her arms and then dropped, resulting in an agonizing dislocation of limbs. Sentences, 11 February 1622, *Coen: Bescheiden,* 4:272.

60. Coen to Heeren 17, 26 March 1622, *Coen: Bescheiden,* 1:705.

61. Coen to Heeren 17, 26 March 1622, *Coen: Bescheiden,* 1:705.

62. Van Speult to Coen, 25 April 1619, *Coen: Bescheiden,* 7.1:415.

63. Van Speult to Coen, 10 August 1619, *Coen: Bescheiden,* 7.1:451.

64. Vink, "'The World's Oldest Trade,'" 143.

65. *Generale Missiven van Gouverneurs-Generaal en Raden,* 1:50.

66. Advice from Coen, 31 January 1623, *Coen: Bescheiden,* 3:293–94; Coen to Heeren 17, 10 October 1616, *Coen: Bescheiden,* 1:218.

67. Van Speult to Coen, 4 June 1618, *Coen: Bescheiden,* 7.1:331; Van Speult to Coen, 7 August 1618, *Coen: Bescheiden,* 7.1:378.

68. Van Goor, *Jan Pieterszoon Coen,* 424–25.

69. Coen to De Hase, 19 September 1618, *Coen: Bescheiden,* 2:446.

70. Coen to Heeren 17, 26 March 1622, *Coen: Bescheiden,* 1:708.

71. Coen to Soury, 18 October 1621, *Coen: Bescheiden,* 3:96.

72. Coen to Heeren 17, 26 March 1622, *Coen: Bescheiden,* 1:707–8. They were promptly sent on the *Eenhoorn* to Sonck in Banda. Coen to Sonck, 19 March 1622, *Coen: Bescheiden,* 3:147.

73. *Generale Missiven van Gouverneurs-Generaal en Raden,* 1:121.

74. Quoted in Vink, "A Work of Compassion?" Vink characterizes these as "vicious 'famine-slave' cycles."

75. Raben, "Cities and the Slave Trade in Early-Modern Southeast Asia," 125.

76. *Generale Missiven van Gouverneurs-Generaal en Raden,* 1:121.

77. Vink, "'The World's Oldest Trade,'" 142.

78. Coen to Heeren 17, 20 June 1623, *Coen: Bescheiden,* 1:780–81.

79. The roughly 20 percent mortality rate was far from unique. Van Welie discusses the "catastrophic mortality rates" of some of the Company's early voyages. Van Welie, "Patterns of Slave Trading and Slavery in the Dutch Colonial World," 189. Similar figures were recorded in the Atlantic slave trade.

80. This is not to say that slaves were continually acquired in such large numbers. Rather, there were significant high points followed by troughs in which fewer slaves were purchased.

81. Coen to Heeren 17, 20 June 1623, *Coen: Bescheiden,* 1:781.

82. Raben, "Batavia and Colombo," 120.

83. While the Company's slaving voyages to Coromandel depended on cyclical famines, the Bengal coast proved more reliable. Vink suggests that "between 1626

and 1662, the Dutch exported with reasonable regularity 150–400 slaves annually from the Arakan-Bengal coast." Vink, "'The World's Oldest Trade,'" 140. The proportion of South Asian slaves remained significant across this period. Of 211 slaves who were manumitted in Batavia between 1646 and 1649, 126 came from South Asia, including 86 from Bengal. The original figures were collected by Raben. Raben, "Batavia and Colombo." Van Welie suggests that "approximately 100,000 slaves were taken from South Asia by the Dutch." Van Welie, "Patterns of Slave Trading and Slavery in the Dutch Colonial World," 195.

84. Coen to Van Speult, 28 December 1622, *Coen: Bescheiden*, 3:273–74. The letter is discussed in Van Goor, *Jan Pieterszoon Coen*, 425–26.

85. Figures appear in the depositions provided by Laurens de Maarschalk, Jan van Leeuwen, Herman Cravanger, Pieter van Santen, Jan Joosten, Roland Tailler, Jan van Nieuwpoort, and Vincent Cortals. Cortals was the secretary for the original trial.

86. Van Speult to Coen, 17 July 1621, *Coen: Bescheiden* 7.1:731. This figure rose quickly in subsequent months. Coen to Heeren 17, 6 September 1622, *Coen: Bescheiden* 1:743. Coen to Heeren 17, 20 June 1623, *Coen: Bescheiden*, 1:784. The figure of 115 deaths was recorded in a 1623 letter but likely refers to 1622.

87. Knaap, "A City of Migrants," 125.

88. In this way, they excluded the Christian villagers living in settlements across Ambon proper. Some of these were located close to Castle Victoria. As discussed in the previous chapter, these settlements were regularly tapped for military labor in the governor's *hongi* expeditions. These villages are listed in Seys, "Verhael van den tegenwoordigen staet inde quarteren van Amboyna," in Isaac Commelin, *Begin ende Voortgangh van de Vereenighde Nederlantsche Geoctroyeerde Oost-Indische Compagnie* (1646).

89. The typical ranges provided by the judges were 90–100, 80–90, or around 100. By contrast, English pamphleteers insisted there were 200 soldiers in the castle, but there is no evidence to support this inflated figure.

90. Seys, "Verhael van den tegenwoordigen state," 131.

91. Coen to Heeren 17, 5 August 1619, *Coen: Bescheiden*, 1:492. Coen to Heeren 17, 26 October 1620, *Coen: Bescheiden*, 1:594.

92. Coen to Heeren 17, 20 June 1623, *Coen: Bescheiden*, 1:800.

93. One Amboina judge explained that there were between 149 and 182 men scattered around these various outposts. Answer to question 47, deposition of Jan Joosten, 1628, BL IOR, G/21/2, pt. 3. In a letter written in September 1624, Van Speult explained that there were 148 men scattered around the various forts and factories excluding Castle Victoria. Letter from Herman van Speult in Cambello to Governor-General Pieter de Carpentier, 16 September 1624, NL-HaNA, VOC 1083.

94. I follow Knaap in his translation of *Vrijburger*. Knaap, "City of Migrants," 111. Van Goor notes that Coen authorized the settling of these free citizens in Kota Ambon. Van Goor, *Jan Pieterszoon Coen*, 378.

95. Knaap, *City of Migrants*, 111.

96. The most common figure was ninety, although some estimates were as low as sixty.
97. Answer to question 12, deposition of Jan Joosten, 1628, BL IOR, G/21/2, pt. 3. Knaap calls them "non-Ambonese, 'foreign,' Asians." Knaap, "City of Migrants," 112.
98. In 1627, Seys listed 110 "free Mardijkers" in Kota Ambon. Seys, "Verhael van den tegenwoordigen state," 132.
99. F. W. Stapel, ed., *Pieter van Dam's Beschryvinge van de Oostindische Compagnie* (The Hague: Martinus Nijhoff, 1927–1954), 2.1:137.
100. Van Speult to Coen, 4 May 1620, *Coen: Bescheiden*, 7.1:549.
101. Answer to question 35, deposition of Jan Joosten, 9 February 1628, BL IOR, G/21/2, pt. 3.
102. Fox, "'For Good and Sufficient Reasons,'" 249.
103. Roelant Tieller suggested there were 150 slaves in Kota Ambon. Answer to question 29, deposition of Roelant Tieller, 1628, NL-HaNA, Staten-Generaal, 1.01.02, inv. no. 12551.62.
104. This was the case with the *Pegu*, which passed through Kota Ambon with thirty-eight Bandanese women and fourteen children in 1622. For instructions to send such slaves onto Banda, see Coen to Van Speult, 3 March 1622, *Coen: Bescheiden*, 3:144.
105. Letter from Herman van Speult in Amboina to Governor-General Pieter de Carpentier, 5 June 1623, NL-HaNA, VOC 1080, 108.
106. Coen to Sonck, 28 December 1622, *Coen: Bescheiden*, 3:382.
107. It was commanded by Jan van Nieuwpoort, who would reappear as one of the Amboina judges. Answer to question 2, deposition of Jan van Nieuwpoort, April 1628, BL IOR, G/21/2, pt. 3. According to this testimony the yacht arrived either on January 31 or February 1.
108. See for example Coen to Van Speult, 31 January 1622, *Coen: Bescheiden*, 3:133. Here he was instructed "to reduce the overall costs as much as is possible."
109. Coen to Van Speult, 28 December 1622, *Coen: Bescheiden*, 3:273.
110. Letter from Herman van Speult in Amboina to Governor-General Pieter de Carpentier, 5 June 1623, NL-HaNa, VOC 1080, 108v and 108.
111. See for example P. A. Tiele and J. E. Heeres, eds., *Bouwstoffen voor de geschiedenis der Nederlanders in den Maleischen Archipel* (The Hague: Martinus Nijhoff, 1886–1895), 2:78. The reference is to slaves from Malabar, who had died in significant numbers after arriving in Kota Ambon.
112. Letter from Van Speult, 4 May 1620, *Coen: Bescheiden*, 7.1:558.
113. Pieter Mijer, *Verzameling van instructien, ordonnancien en reglementen voor de regering* (Batavia, 1848), 39.
114. Some captives did manage to survive long enough to win preferential treatment. See for example Bastian Dias, who served faithfully for eight years. Resolutions, 7 January 1623, *Coen: Bescheiden*, 3:937.
115. Letter from Van Speult, 4 May 1620, *Coen: Bescheiden*, 7.1:558.
116. For an example of harsh VOC regulations designed to maintain control over slaves, see J. A. van der Chijs, H. T. Colenbrander, and J. de Hullu, eds.,

Nederlandsch Indisch plakaatboek, 1602–1811 (Batavia: Landsdrukkerij; The Hague: Martinus Nijhoff, 1885–1900), 1:573.

117. Letter from Van Speult, 4 May 1620, *Coen: Bescheiden*, 7.1:558–59.

118. Ross, *Cape of Torments*, 3. See also Nigel Worden and Gerald Groenewald, *Trials of Slavery* (Cape Town: Van Riebeeck Society, 2005).

119. Van Speult to Coen, 10 August 1619, *Coen: Bescheiden*, 7.1:446.

120. Van der Chijs, Colenbrander, and de Hullu, *Nederlandsch Indisch plakaatboek, 1602–1811*, 1:92.

121. Van Speult to Coen, 14 August 1620, *Coen: Bescheiden*, 7.1:631.

122. A number of former judges testified that the slaves were locked up in this way. See answer to question 35, deposition of Jan Joosten, 1628, BL IOR, G/21/2, pt. 3.

123. Manuel from Goa, a Portuguese interpreter implicated in a supposed plot to murder the Dutch in Bantem, was one example of many. Diverse attestatien tegen den conspirateur Manuel Japansche tolck beleijt den 12 Julij 1618 in Jacatra, NL-HaNa, VOC 1068, 127–35.

124. Resolutions, 13 August 1621, *Coen: Bescheiden*, 3:753.

125. Resolutions, 19 June 1621, *Coen: Bescheiden*, 3:739.

126. Communities such as the Topasses of southern India were referred to as "Portuguese" by the Dutch. Kruijtzer, "European migration in the Dutch sphere," 131. Kruijtzer notes that the "term 'Portuguese' as used by the Dutch was somewhat open-ended."

127. Resolutions, 19 June 1621, *Coen: Bescheiden*, 3:739.

128. Copie autentycq van de Confessien ende Sententien van Mr. Touwerson ende Complicen over de Moordadige Conspiratie op t' Casteel Amboyna voorgenomen, dat door Godes merckelijcke ende genadige beschicking opden xxiii Februario 1623 is aenden dach gecomen als mede de resolutien by den Hr. Gouvernr van Speult & den raet daer over genomen, NL-HaNa, VOC 1080, 164v. Hereafter, Copie autentycq van de confessien ende sentatien.

129. In the end, Van Speult announced that she would be returned to her "former masters of the said company, until such time that she shall be otherwise disposed of by the Governor." Copie autentycq van de confessien ende sentatien, NL-HaNA, VOC 1080, 164v.

130. Answer to question 7, deposition of Jan Jacobsen Wyncoop, 1626, NL-HaNA, Staten-Generaal, 1.01.02, inv. no. 12551.62. Answer to question 7, deposition of Marten Jansz. Vogel, 1626, NL-HaNA, Staten-Generaal, 1.01.02, inv. no. 12551.62.

131. Answer to question 135, deposition of Jan Joosten, December 1626, NL-HaNA, Staten-Generaal, 1.01.02, inv. no. 12551.62.

3. Dangerous and Difficult to Govern

The epigraph is taken from: Coen to Heeren 17, 1 January 1614, H. T. Colenbrander and W. P. Coolhaas, eds., *Jan Pietersz. Coen: Bescheiden Omtrent Zijn*

Bedrijf in Indië (The Hague: Martinus Nijhoff, 1919–1954), 1:32. Hereafter, *Coen: Bescheiden.*

1. For a description of these ceremonies, see J. A. van der Chijs, H. T. Colenbrander, and J. de Hullu, eds., *Dagh-register gehouden int Casteel Batavia vant passerende daer ter plaetse als over geheel Nederlandts-India*, 31 vols. (Batavia: Landsdrukkerij; The Hague: Martinus Nijhoff, 1887–1931), vol. 1 (1624–1629), 257.

2. Answer to question 19, deposition of Jan Joosten, February 1628, BL IOR, G/21/2, pt. 3.

3. The VOC commonly referred to these troops as "soldiers from Japan" (*soldaten van Japon*). Steven van der Haghen to the Amsterdam Chamber, 18 July 1616, NL-HaNA, VOC 1063, 53v. In this chapter, I use two terms, Japanese soldiers and Japanese mercenaries, to refer to them. The distinction between soldier and mercenary is frequently murky and this was especially the case when it came to VOC forces. The Dutch East India Company was a private, commercial company that waged war with a polyglot collection of soldiers drawn from Europe, including many from outside the United Provinces, and Asia. As a result, it is essentially impossible to draw a clear line between mercenaries and soldiers. Although I refer to these soldiers as Japanese throughout this chapter, I do not, as will be clear later, suggest that notions of Japanese identity were fixed or applied equally to all residents of the archipelago. Rather, I use the term because this is what the VOC called these troops, even as they recruited some soldiers who clearly had closer ties with other parts of Asia.

4. For the VOC's employment of Japanese soldiers, see W. Z. Mulder, *Hollanders in Hirado, 1597–1641* (Haarlem: Fibula-Van Dishoeck, 1984), 128–33. Adam Clulow, "Unjust, Cruel and Barbarous Proceedings: Japanese Mercenaries and the Amboyna Incident of 1623," *Itinerario* 31, no. 1 (2007): 15–34. Iwao Seiichi, *Zoku Nanyō Nihon machi no kenkyū: Nanyō tōsho chiiki bunsan Nihonjin imin no seikatsu to katsudō.* (Tokyo: Iwanami Shoten, 1987), 61–66. For a more general study of Asian military manpower in European armies, see Kaushik Roy, *Military Manpower, Armies and Warfare in South Asia* (London: Pickering & Chatto, 2013). For an important new study of Dutch warfare outside of Europe, see Gerrit Knaap, Henk den Heijer, and Michiel de Jong, eds., *Oorlogen overzee. Militair optreden door compagnie en staat buiten Europa, 1595–1814* (Amsterdam: Boom, 2015).

5. Gijs Kruijtzer, "European Migration in the Dutch Sphere," in *Dutch Colonialism, Migration and Cultural Heritage,* ed. Gert Oostindie (Leiden: KITLV, 2008), 111. In 1622, for example more than one-third of the garrison in Batavia consisted of Germans, Swiss, English, Scots, Irish, Danes, and other nationalities. J. de Hullu, "De Matrozen en Soldaten op de Schepen der Oost-Indische Compagnie," *Bijdragen tot de Taal-, Land- en Volkenkunde van Nederlandsch-Indië,* 69, nos. 2/3 (1914): 336. Soldiers brought from ports in the Dutch Republic required eight months on average to reach Batavia. Scholars estimate that about 7 percent of those embarking at the Netherlands did not survive the first leg of the voyage to the Cape of Good Hope, and another 3 to 4 percent perished on the way from the Cape to Batavia.

6. Coen to Heeren 17, 1 January 1614, *Coen: Bescheiden*, 1:16.
7. D. de Iongh, *Het Krijgswezen onder de Oostindische Compagnie* (The Hague: W. P. van Stockum, 1950), 61. Although dated, De Iongh's work remains a key resource.
8. Remco Raben, "Het Aziatisch Legion: Huurlingen, bondgenoten en reservisten in het geweer voor de Verenigde Oost-Indische Compagnie," in *De Verenigde Oost-Indische Compagnie tussen Oorlog and diplomatie*, ed. Gerrit Knaap and Ger Teitler (Leiden: KITLV, 2002), 188. Raben dates this vision to the middle of the seventeenth century. As this chapter suggests, it can be tied as well to the earlier recruitment of Japanese soldiers.
9. See for example Coen to Specx, 26 June 1620, *Coen: Bescheiden*, 2:748.
10. Laurens Reael to the Amsterdam Chamber, 18 July 1616, NL-HaNA, VOC 1063, 19.
11. Raben, "Het Aziatisch Legion," 182.
12. Raben notes that "hardly a war was fought without the assistance of a multitude of Asian soldiers." Remco Raben, "Batavia and Colombo: The Ethnic and Spatial Order of Two Colonial Cities, 1600–1800" (PhD diss., Leiden University, 1996), 142. As he argues, this process accelerated in the second half of the seventeenth century.
13. See for example studies of the contested relationship between EIC officials and Indian troops. Joseph Sramek, *Gender, Morality, and Race in Company India, 1765–1858* (Basingstoke: Palgrave Macmillan, 2011).
14. Hendrik Brouwer to Pieter Both, 29 January 1613, NL-HaNA, VOC 1056, 34v.
15. The fluid nature of the Company's operations in this period make it difficult to obtain a precise number. The available sources suggest that the Company could call on fewer than a thousand soldiers. Coen to Heeren 17, 1 January 1614, *Coen: Bescheiden*, 1:16. Pieter van Dam, *Beschrijvinge van de Oostindishe Compagnie*, ed. F. W. Stapel (The Hague: Rijksgeschiedkundige Publicatiën, 1927–1954), 1.2:525–26.
16. Emma Blair and James Robertson, eds., *The Philippine Islands, 1493–1898* (Cleveland, OH: A. H. Clark, 1903–1909), 10:212.
17. In the second half of the sixteenth century, Chinese maritime entrepreneurs such as Wang Zhi had pioneered new routes between Southeast Asia and Japan, but the volume of traffic remained relatively limited. The situation was transformed in the first decade of the seventeenth century with the creation of a stable framework for international commerce within Japan. This took the form of the *shuinjō* or maritime pass system, which required all outgoing merchant vessels to obtain special trading licenses authorizing the holder to undertake a single voyage from Japan to a stated destination. After 1604, the first year for which records exist, a total of 356 licenses were issued to Japan-based merchants. The overwhelming majority of these, just under 300, were intended for ships traveling to Southeast Asia, with 85 licenses issued for Cochinchina, 44 for Cambodia, 52 for the Philippines, and 56 for Siam. The classic study of these maritime links remains Iwao Seiichi, *Shuinsen bōekishi no kenkyū* (Tokyo: Yoshikawa Kōbunkan, 1985).
18. For an excellent analysis of Japanese mercenaries across the region see Stephen Turnbull, "The Japanese 'Wild Geese': The Recruitment, Roles and

Reputation of Japanese Mercenaries in Southeast Asia, 1593–1688" (unpublished paper).

19. Francois Caron and Joost Schouten, *A True Description of the Mighty Kingdoms of Japan and Siam* (London, 1663), 133–34.
20. Katō Eiichi has argued persuasively that the VOC used Hirado primarily as a strategic rather than a commercial outpost in its first decade. Katō Eiichi, "Rengō Oranda Higashi-Indo Kaisha no senryaku kyoten toshite no Hirado shōkan," in *Nihon zenkindai no kokka to taigai kankei*, ed. Tanaka Takeo (Tokyo: Yoshikawa Kōbunkan, 1987).
21. The term *Bakufu* (or "tent government") refers to the military government under the control of a shogun. The Bakufu ruled Japan in tandem with over two hundred semi-autonomous domainal lords. The Dutch frequently referred to the shogun as the emperor, even though they knew of the existence of the actual emperor in Kyoto.
22. Hendrik Brouwer to Pieter Both, 29 January 1613, NL-HaNA, VOC 1056, 34v. See also Copia da Carto do Bispo de Japao para el Rey, feita em Nangasaqui a 15 de Novembro de 1612. Ms Biblioteca de la Real Academica de la Historia, Jesuitas 9–2655 (Cortes, 566), 174–77.
23. For an examination of Bakufu responses to the activities of its subjects overseas, see Adam Clulow, "Like Lambs in Japan and Devils Outside Their Land: Violence, Law and Japanese Merchants in Southeast Asia," *Journal of World History* 24, no. 2 (2013): 335–58.
24. Nagazumi Yōko, "Ayutthaya and Japan: Embassies and Trade in the Seventeenth Century," in *From Japan to Arabia: Ayutthaya's Maritime Relations with Asia*, ed. Kennon Breazeale (Bangkok: Printing House of Thammasat University, 1999), 96.
25. We know that the craft was deployed in Southeast Asia but that it later sunk, with some loss of life. Specx to Coen, 12 October 1617, *Coen: Bescheiden*, 7.1:293.
26. Resolutions, Hirado factory, 12 August 1614, NL-HaNA, VOC 1058, 112. Mulder mistakenly identifies this craft as the *Hasewint*. In fact, it was shipped in the hold of that vessel. Mulder, *Hollanders in Hirado*, 130.
27. "Discourse to the Honorable Directors Concerning the State of the Netherlands Indies," *Coen: Bescheiden*, 6:468.
28. Coen returned periodically to this idea of using Japanese soldiers in some sort of attack against Manila. In 1621, he insisted that just two hundred Japanese or European solders could be deployed in operations against Manila. Coen to Willem Jansz., 11 June 1621, *Coen: Bescheiden*, 3:59.
29. Quoted in W. Theodore de Bary, Carol Gluck, and Arthur Tiedemann, eds., *Sources of Japanese Tradition: Volume 2, 1600 to 2000* (New York: Columbia University Press, 2005), 1:156.
30. See, for example, Laurens Reael to the Amsterdam Chamber, 18 July 1616, NL-HaNA, VOC 1063, 19.
31. We know of at least four shipments of Japanese soldiers, although there may have been more. The *Roode Leeuw met Pijlen* sailed in 1613 with the initial shipment of sixty-eight men recruited by Brouwer; the *Enckhuijsen* and *Fortuijne* transported

sixty-seven men (fifty-nine recruits plus some additional workers) in 1615; the *Nieuw Bantam* and *Galiasse* carried ninety troops in 1619; and in 1620 another shipment of roughly one hundred men was sent out aboard the *China*. Aenteck-eningen van de timmeragie ongelden montcosten provision ende maentgelden gedaen en betaelt inty equipperen van de joncke als nu genaempt de fortuijne, NL-HaNA, VOC 1062, 106–21. Coen to Heeren 17, 22 January 1620, *Coen: Bescheiden*, 1:519. Pieter de Carpentier and Jacob Dedel to the directors, 8 March 1621, NL-HaNA, VOC 1072, 376v. Iwao, *Zoku nanyō Nihon machi no kenkyū*, 6–7.

32. The Dutch East India Company's shipping between the Netherlands and Asia 1595–1795, http://resources.huygens.knaw.nl/das/detailVoyage/91220, accessed December 2014.
33. Robert Parthesius, *Dutch Ships in Tropical Waters: The Development of the Dutch East India Company (VOC) Shipping Network in Asia, 1595–1660* (Amsterdam: Amsterdam University Press, 2010), 107. The *last* was a variable Dutch unit to measure cargo capacity. As Parthesius notes in his invaluable study of VOC shipping, for a "general comparison with the modern measure of cargo capacity, the 'tonnage', the last value can be multiplied by two."
34. Parthesius, *Dutch Ships in Tropical Waters*, 107.
35. This document is the sole surviving example of an agreement signed between Japanese mercenaries and the VOC. Aenteckeningen van de timmeragie ongelden montcosten provision ende maentgelden gedaen en betaelt inty equipperen van de joncke als nu genaempt de fortuijne, NL-HaNA, VOC 1062, 106–21.
36. Originele missive door Jacques Specx, geschreven ten ancker liggende voor het veroverde Portugese fort op 't eijlant Tijdoor aen d'Ed. heeren bewinthebberen tot Amsterdam in dato 2 Augustus 1613, NL-HaNA, VOC 1056.
37. Ernest Satow, ed., *The Voyage of Captain John Saris to Japan* (London: Hakluyt Society, 1900), 172.
38. Satow, *The Voyage of Captain John Saris to Japan*, 179.
39. See, for example, Albert Markham, ed., *The Voyages and Works of John Davis* (London, 1880), 178–82; Isaac Commelin, ed., *Begin ende Voortgangh van de Vereenighde Nederlantsche Geoctroyeerde Oost-Indische Compagnie* (1646), 3:77.
40. Anthony Farrington, *The English Factory in Japan, 1613–1623* (London: British Library, 1991), 379.
41. In an important article, Ghulam Nadri has analyzed similar practices in Surat. Ghulam Nadri, "Sailors, Zielverkopers, and the Dutch East India Company: The Maritime Labour Market in Eighteenth-Century Surat," *Modern Asian Studies* 49, no. 2 (2015): 336–64.
42. Christoph Frick and Christoph Schweitzer, *A Relation of Two Several Voyages Made into the East-Indies* (London, 1700), 227.
43. Blair and Robertson, *The Philippine Islands, 1493–1803*, 5:271.
44. For a landmark study of Chinese settlers in Taiwan, see Tonio Andrade, *How Taiwan Became Chinese: Dutch, Spanish, and Han Colonization in the Seventeenth Century* (New York: Columbia University Press, 2008).

45. Iwao, *Zoku nanyō Nihon machi no kenkyū*, 257. For a recent study of the porcelain industry in Hirado, see Hwang Chŏng-dŏk, Chin-sun To, and Yun-sang Yi, *Imjin Waeran Kwa Hirado Mik'awach'i Sagijang: Segyejŏk Pomul ŭl Pijŭn P'irap Chosŏn Sagijang ŭl Ch'ajasŏ* [The Imjin Wars and captive Korean potters at Mikawachi, Hirado] (Sŏul-si: Tongbuga Yŏksa Chaedan, 2010).
46. One further example was Joan Maccau, whose name suggests a connection with Macao. Resolutions, Fort Jacatra, 18 July 1619, *Coen: Bescheiden*, 3:528.
47. Aenteckeningen van de timmeragie ongelden montcosten provision ende maentgelden gedaen en betaelt inty equipperen van de joncke als nu genaempt de fortuijne, NL-HaNA, VOC 1062, 120.
48. Japanese military leaders had adopted the use of volley fire independently of their European counterparts. Matthew Stavros, "Military Revolution in Early Modern Japan," *Japanese Studies* 33, no. 3 (2013): 243–61.
49. Mulder, *Hollanders in Hirado*, 130. Coen to Jacques Specx, 14 May 1616, *Coen: Bescheiden*, 2:105. See also *Coen: Bescheiden*, 7.1:501.
50. Farrington, *The English Factory in Japan*, 813.
51. Richard Cocks, *Diary Kept by the Head of the English Factory in Japan: Diary of Richard Cocks, 1615–1622* (Tokyo: University of Tokyo, 1980), 2:113.
52. Lenaert Camps to Coen, 15 October 1621, *Coen: Bescheiden*, 7.1:798; Cocks, *Diary of Richard Cocks*, 2:131.
53. Mulder, *Hollanders in Hirado*, 158.
54. Coen to Specx, 14 May 1616, *Coen: Bescheiden*, 2:111.
55. Quoted in C. R. Boxer, *The Dutch Seaborne Empire, 1600–1800* (London: Penguin, 1965), 78–79. Nicolaas de Graaf, *Reisen en Oost-Indise Spiegel* (1701), 30.
56. For a still valuable description of life aboard a VOC vessel, see Boxer, *The Dutch Seaborne Empire*.
57. Resolutions, Hirado factory, 20 August 1615, NL-HaNA, VOC 1061, 247–57.
58. Frick and Schweitzer, *A Relation of Two Several Voyages*, 9–10.
59. Specx to Coen, 1 October 1616, *Coen: Bescheiden*, 7.1:199.
60. Bruijn explains that the "combination of poor diet and substandard sleeping and living quarters plus the climate put a severe strain on the physical resilience of the crew." Iris Bruijn, *Ship's Surgeons of the Dutch East India Company: Commerce and the Progress of Medicine in the Eighteenth Century* (Leiden: Leiden University Press, 2009), 73.
61. We know from the sources that the 1613 contingent, which was shipped three years earlier, developed a number of tropical illnesses as they moved into warmer conditions. Originele missive door Jacques Specx, geschreven ten ancker liggende voor het veroverde Portugese fort op 't eijlant Tijdoor aen d'Ed. Heeren bewinthebberen tot Amsterdam in dato 2 Augustus 1613, NL-HaNA, VOC 1056.
62. Frick and Schweitzer, *A Relation of Two Several Voyages*, 30.
63. De Carpentier and Dedel to the Heeren 17, 8 March 1621, NL-HaNA, VOC 1072. Blair and Robertson, *The Philippine Islands, 1493–1898*, 19:70.
64. In his analysis of Indian sailors employed by the VOC, Nadri examines the imporant role played by *serangs* (chiefs of sailors), who both recruited crews and

maintained discipline. Nadri, "Sailors, Zielverkopers, and the Dutch East India Company."

65. Coen to Specx, 23 April 1617, *Coen: Bescheiden*, 2:234–35.
66. Coen to Specx, 14 May 1616, *Coen: Bescheiden*, 2:111.
67. Coen to Specx, 14 May 1616, *Coen: Bescheiden*, 2:111.
68. Specx to Coen, 1 October 1616, *Coen: Bescheiden*, 7.1:199–200.
69. Jaccatra Resolutions, 3 June 1616, *Coen: Bescheiden*, 4:125–26.
70. Jaccatra Resolutions, 10 June 1616, *Coen: Bescheiden*, 3:366.
71. Descriptions of both incidents can be found in J. W. IJzerman, ed., *Cornelis Buijsero te Bantam, 1616–1618* (The Hague: Martinus Nijhoff, 1923).
72. Iwao, *Zoku nanyō Nihon machi no kenkyū*, 402–3.
73. Specx to Coen, 1 October 1616, *Coen: Bescheiden*, 7.1:200.
74. Resolutions, Fort Jacatra, 18 July 1619, *Coen: Bescheiden*, 3:528.
75. Specx to Coen, 24 February 1620, *Coen: Bescheiden*, 7.1:501.
76. It should be noted that Coen continually asked his superiors to send more soldiers from Europe. In 1620, he called for the Heeren 17 to send seven hundred soldiers immediately. Coen to Heeren 17, 26 October 1620, *Coen: Bescheiden*, 1:601.
77. Coen to Specx, 30 March 1618, *Coen: Bescheiden*, 2:373.
78. Coen to Heeren 17, 22 January 1620, *Coen: Bescheiden*, 1:519.
79. Coen to Specx, 26 June 1620, *Coen: Bescheiden*, 2:748.
80. Pieter de Carpentier and Jacob Dedel to the directors, 8 March 1621, NL-HaNA, VOC 1072, 376v. Iwao, *Zoku nanyō Nihon machi no kenkyū*, 6–7. Mulder suggests that the vessel in question may have been the *Engel* rather than the *China*. Mulder, *Hollanders in Hirado*, 131. Mulder suggest as well that there was another contingent dispatched aboard the *Eendracht*. Although he dates it to a different year, one ship of this name did arrive in Ternate in 1617 carrying some Japanese recruits, and this may be the vessel in question.
81. The complete edict can be found in Nagazumi Yōko, "Hirado ni dentatsu sareta Nihonjin baibai buki yushutsu kinshirei," *Nihon rekishi* 611 (1999): 67–81.
82. Report by Jacques Specx in Hirado, 20 September 1621, NL-HaNA, VOC 1075, 91.
83. Coen to Camps, 2 June 1622, *Coen: Bescheiden*, 3:195.
84. Coen to Camps, 9 April 1622, *Coen: Bescheiden*, 3:165.
85. For one example of such praise, see Coen to Heeren 17, 18 December 1617, *Coen: Bescheiden*, 1:302.
86. As reported in Coen to Heeren 17, 1 January 1614, *Coen: Bescheiden*, 1:32.
87. Jan Van Hasell to Coen, 4 October 1620, *Coen: Bescheiden*, 7.1:648.
88. Specx to Coen, 1 October 1616, *Coen: Bescheiden*, 7.1:191.
89. Iwao suggests his name was Saquemond.[ne] Iwao, *Zoku nanyō Nihon machi no kenkyū*, 249.
90. Resolutions, 17 January 1620, *Coen: Bescheiden*, 3:581.
91. Van Speult to Coen, 4 May 1620, *Coen: Bescheiden*, 7.1:554.
92. Van Speult to Coen, 14 August 1620, *Coen: Bescheiden*, 7.1:629.
93. Van Speult to Coen, 4 May 1620, *Coen: Bescheiden*, 7.1:554.
94. Resolutions, 28 February 1621, *Coen: Bescheiden*, 3:686.

95. Resolutions, 14 March 1621, *Coen: Bescheiden*, 3:698–99.

96. P. A. Leupe, "De Verovering der Banda-Eilanden," *Bijdragen tot de Taal-, Land- en Volkenkunde van Nederlandsch-Indië* 2, no. 4 (1854): 427. There is a well-known modern painting of this scene that hangs in Banda today. See Tsuchiya Kenji and James Siegel, "Invincible Kitsch or as Tourists in the Age of Des Alwi," *Indonesia* 50 (1990): 61–76.

97. Resolutions, 5 June 1621, *Coen: Bescheiden*, 3:732.

98. Steven van der Haghen to the Amsterdam Chamber, 18 July 1616, NL-HaNA, VOC 1063, 53.

99. Originele missive van Jacques Specx uijt Firando aen gouverneur generaal Pieter Both in dato 2 Januarij 1615, NL-HaNA, VOC 1058.

100. Answer to question 22, deposition of Van Santen, 9 March 1628, BL IOR, G/21/2, pt. 3.

101. *A True Relation of the Unjust, Cruell, and Barbarous Proceedings Against the English at Amboyna in the East-Indies, by the Neatherlandish Governour and Councel There* (London: printed by H. Lownes for Nathanael Newberry, 1624), 5. While these pamphlets are unreliable when it comes to a set of familiar controversies, they do contain useful information on other topics.

102. Depositions provided by the Amboina judges confirm that Japanese troops were not allowed firearms and powder, except when on special duty.

103. Letter from Herman van Speult in Amboina to Governor-General Pieter de Carpentier, 5 June 1623, NL-HaNA, VOC 1080, 101v. It is equally possible that this was an attempt to justify his suspicions after the fact. When asked, most of the Amboina judges stated that they had seen no evidence that the Japanese favored the English over their masters. It may be, therefore, that the governor simply fabricated such interactions.

104. Sidney Miguel was named as a former servant of the EIC in the trial document. Copie autentycq van de Confessien ende Sententien van Mr. Touwerson ende Complicen over de Moordadige Conspiratie op t' Casteel Amboyna voorgenomen, dat door Godes merckelijcke ende genadige beschicking opden xxiii Februario 1623 is aenden dach gecomen als mede de resolutien by den Hr. Gouvernr van Speult & den raet daer over genomen, NL-HaNA, VOC 1080. At least one of the judges declared that his countryman, Pedro Conje, had also served the EIC, although he was characterized as a former slave.

4. The English Serpent

The epigraph is taken from: "Discourse to the Honorable Directors Concerning the State of the Netherlands Indies," in H. T. Colenbrander and W. P. Coolhaas, eds., *Jan Pietersz. Coen: Bescheiden Omtrent Zijn Bedrijf in Indië* (The Hague: Martinus Nijhoff, 1919–1954), 6:460. Hereafter, *Coen: Bescheiden*.

1. Letter from Gabriel Towerson at Amboina to Richard Fursland, 19 September 1622, BL IOR, G/21/3A, 356.

2. Letter from Gabriel Towerson at Amboina to Fursland, 19 September 1622, BL IOR, G/21/3A, 352.

3. As is standard practice, I use the term "English" to refer to the merchants employed by the English East India Company. Although this was the term used by the Dutch and by contemporary sources, it ignores the reality of the EIC's expansive labor pool, which drew employees from across the British Isles and indeed from Europe more generally.

4. For the classic study of EIC-VOC rivalry in Asia, see Holden Furber, *Rival Empires of Trade in the Orient, 1600–1800* (Minneapolis: University of Minnesota Press, 1976). See also Vincent Loth, "Armed Incidents and Unpaid Bills: Anglo-Dutch Rivalry in the Banda Islands in the Seventeenth Century," *Modern Asian Studies* 29, no. 4 (1995): 705–40.

5. Van Speult to Coen, 15 June 1622, *Coen: Bescheiden,* 7.2:965.

6. M. A. P. Meilink-Roelofsz, *Asian Trade and European Influence in the Indonesian Archipelago Between 1500 and About 1630* (The Hague: Martinus Nijhoff, 1962), 66. Van Goor is dubious of such an assessment, arguing instead that Coen's comments reflected the Heeren 17's policies and hence a basic structural contest between the companies. Jur van Goor, *Jan Pieterszoon Coen, 1587–1629: Koopman-Koning in Azië* (Amsterdam: Boom Publishers, 2015), 257.

7. Coen to Heeren 17, 22 October 1615, *Coen: Bescheiden* 1:133.

8. One can find similar comments on the other side. EIC officials regularly claimed the same of the Dutch: that they were false friends who worked in the shadows "persecutinge us, giveinge us a Judas kisse with faire words when behinde our backes they sell us." John Jourdain, *The Journal of John Jourdain, 1608–17: His Experiences in Arabia, India and the Malay Archipelago,* ed. William Foster (Cambridge: Hakluyt Society, 1905), 260. English traders in Ayutthaya described the Dutch as their "mortall enemis." Anthony Farrington, *The English Factory in Japan, 1613–1623* (London: British Library, 1991), 1:605.

9. Coen to Heeren 17, 22 October 1615, *Coen: Bescheiden,* 1:133.

10. Gaynor's important new study illuminates the role of "networks of maritime people" in "opposing European efforts to control the seventeenth-century spice trade." Jennifer Gaynor, *Intertidal History in Island Southeast Asia: Submerged Genealogies and the Legacy of Coastal Capture* (Ithaca, NY: Cornell University Press, 2016), 17. See also Tristan Mostert's in-progress PhD dissertation (Leiden University) focused on the rise of Makassar.

11. In recent years, a number of important works have focused on the complex nature of Anglo-Dutch relations in this period. They have pointed to the "vacillation between friendship and enmity" that was so characteristic of this relationship. What Marjorie Rubright calls the "paradoxes of proximity" created a dual vision of similarity and difference. Marjorie Rubright, *Doppelgänger Dilemmas: Anglo-Dutch Relations in Early Modern English Literature and Culture* (Philadelphia: University of Pennsylvania Press, 2015). See also Alison Games's important work: Alison Games, "Anglo-Dutch Connections and Overseas Enterprises: A Global Perspective on Lion Gardiner's World," *Early American Studies* 9, no. 2 (2011): 435–61.

12. Coen to Heeren 17, 18 December 1617, *Coen: Bescheiden*, 1:300.

13. Coen to Heeren 17, 26 March 1622, *Coen: Bescheiden*, 1:704–5.

14. *A True Relation of the Unjust, Cruell, and Barbarous Proceedings Against the English at Amboyna in the East-Indies, by the Neatherlandish Gouernour and Councel There* (London: printed by H. Lownes for Nathanael Newberry, 1624).

15. Games, "Anglo-Dutch Connections and Overseas Enterprises," 438.

16. Farrington, *The English Factory in Japan, 1613–1623*, 1:383–84.

17. Henry Stevens, *The Dawn of British Trade to the East Indies as Recorded in the Court Minutes of the East India Company, 1599–1603* (London: Henry Stevens, 1886), 8.

18. Furber, *Rival Empires of Trade*, 38.

19. K. N. Chaudhuri, *The English East India Company: The Study of an Early Joint-Stock Company* (London: Frank Cass, 1965), 45.

20. D. K. Bassett, "The Factory of the English East India Company at Bantam, 1602–1682" (PhD diss., University of London, 1955), 12.

21. The classic study of the EIC factory in Japan remains Derek Massarella, *A World Elsewhere: Europe's Encounter with Japan in the Sixteenth and Seventeenth Centuries* (New Haven, CT: Yale University Press, 1990). See also Timon Screech's groundbreaking new work (forthcoming) on the English in Japan, which focuses on paintings presented to the shogun.

22. Coen to Heeren 17, 22 October 1615, *Coen: Bescheiden*, 1:132.

23. Coen to Heeren 17, 22 October 1615, *Coen: Bescheiden*, 1:132. Furnivall calls the English the omnipresent "gadflies" for Dutch merchants in Asia. J. S. Furnivall, *Netherlands India: A Study of Plural Economy* (Cambridge: Cambridge University Press, 1939), 27.

24. Loth puts this especially well when he writes that "in every theatre, the English came later and were weaker." Loth, "Armed Incidents and Unpaid Bills," 709.

25. When the English arrived in Japan, for example, they were welcomed by the Dutch, who invited them to dinner while giving them an ad-hoc tutorial in local practices.

26. Thomas Dale, for example, fought in the United Provinces before turning up in Asia in command of a fleet designed to strike back against the Dutch. Games, "Anglo-Dutch Connections and Overseas Enterprises," 439.

27. For the Scottish steward, see W. N. Sainsbury, ed., *Calendar of State Papers Colonial, East Indies and Persia, 1625–1629* (London: H.M.S.O., 1884), 686. Van Leeuwen identified a soldier in VOC service who had been born in England. Answer to question 61, deposition of Jan van Leeuwen, 15 March 1628, BL IOR, G/21/2, pt. 3.

28. Van Goor, *Jan Pieterszoon Coen*, 261.

29. Coen to Heeren 17, 18 December 1617, *Coen: Bescheiden*, 1:304. W. N. Sainsbury, ed., *Calendar of State Papers Colonial, East Indies, China and Japan, 1617–1621* (London: H.M.S.O., 1870), 192.

30. Martine J. van Ittersum, *Profit and Principle: Hugo Grotius, Natural Rights Theories and the Rise of Dutch Power in the East Indies, 1595–1615* (Leiden: Brill, 2006), 372–73, 451–80.

31. Bassett, "The Factory of the English East India Company at Bantam," 44; Jourdain, *The Journal of John Jourdain*, lii.

32. Jourdain, *The Journal of John Jourdain*, 250–51.

33. George Masselman, *The Cradle of Colonialism* (New Haven, CT: Yale University Press, 1963), 302.

34. Jourdain, *The Journal of John Jourdain*, 252. Van Ittersum, *Profit and Principle*, 455–56.

35. Jourdain, *The Journal of John Jourdain*, 251.

36. Jourdain, *The Journal of John Jourdain*, 261.

37. "Discourse to the Honorable Directors Concerning the State of the Netherlands Indies," *Coen: Bescheiden*, 6:460.

38. Coen to Heeren 17, 18 December 1617, *Coen: Bescheiden*, 1:300–301.

39. Coen to Heeren 17, 18 December 1617, *Coen: Bescheiden*, 1:304.

40. Coen to Heeren 17, 22 January 1620, *Coen: Bescheiden*, 1:519.

41. Coen to Heeren 17, 18 December 1617, *Coen: Bescheiden*, 1:304.

42. Coen to Heeren 17, 22 October 1615, *Coen: Bescheiden*, 1:131. In 1615, Coen had recorded an English flag flying on the Hoamoal Peninsula.

43. The English were accused of providing cannons to the Bandanese, which were then used against the Dutch. *Coen: Bescheiden*, 1:131.

44. Coen to Heeren 17, 22 October 1615, *Coen: Bescheiden*, 1:133.

45. Resolution, 10 July 1618, *Coen: Bescheiden*, 3:440.

46. Sentences, 10 July 1618, *Coen: Bescheiden*, 4:151–54.

47. Sentences, 10 July 1618, *Coen: Bescheiden*, 4:151–52.

48. Sentences, 10 July 1618, *Coen: Bescheiden*, 4:151–54. A second Japanese interpreter called Martingo who worked for the EIC factory also played a key role as an intermediary.

49. For the judicial record, see: Diverse attestatien tegen den conspirateur Manuel Japansche tolck beleijt den 12 Julij 1618 in Jacatra, NL-HaNA, VOC 1068, 127–35.

50. Diverse attestatien tegen den conspirateur Manuel Japansche tolck beleijt den 12 Julij 1618 in Jacatra, NL-HaNA, VOC 1068, 128v.

51. W. N. Sainsbury, ed., *Calendar of State Papers Colonial, East Indies, China and Japan, 1622–1624* (London: H.M.S.O., 1878), 20. The quote comes from a different case, but one in which there were similar frustrations on the VOC side.

52. Sentences, 10 July 1618, *Coen: Bescheiden*, 4:154.

53. According to English sources, EIC merchants had been invited by the leaders of Kambelo and Luhu to set up a trading outpost in these settlements. F. C. Danvers and W. Foster, *Letters Received by the East India Company from Its Servants in the East* (London: S. Low, Marston, 1896–1902), 3:144. In Banda, for example, local leaders dispatched an embassy asking for English intervention and then worked to draw the EIC into a standoff with the Dutch. See Adam Clulow, "The Art of Claiming: Possession and Resistance in Early Modern Asia," *American Historical Review* 121, no. 1 (2016): 17–38.

54. Everard Deyn to Coen, 29 June 1614, *Coen: Bescheiden*, 7.1:3.

55. Coen to Heeren 17, 22 August 1617, *Coen: Bescheiden*, 1:269.

56. Coen to Heeren 17, 18 December 1617, *Coen: Bescheiden*, 1:305.

57. J. W. IJzerman, ed., *Cornelis Buijsero te Bantam, 1616–1618* (The Hague: Martinus Nijhoff, 1923), 56–57.

58. Resolution, 10 July 1618, *Coen: Bescheiden*, 3:440.

59. Coen to Heeren 17, 18 December 1617, *Coen: Bescheiden*, 1:301–2.

60. Coen to Heeren 17, 18 December 1617, *Coen: Bescheiden*, 1:305.

61. Bassett, "The Factory of the English East India Company at Bantam," 52. Masselman, *The Cradle of Colonialism*, 367.

62. Quoted in Bassett, "The Factory of the English East India Company at Bantam," 52. Van Goor notes that, for all his antagonism toward the English, Coen was shocked by this surprise attack. Van Goor, *Jan Pieterszoon Coen*, 317.

63. Richard Cocks, *Diary Kept by the Head of the English Factory in Japan: Diary of Richard Cocks, 1615–1622* (Tokyo: University of Tokyo, 1980), 3:276.

64. Coen left a small VOC garrison under siege in Jayakarta.

65. Masselman, *The Cradle of Colonialism*, 391.

66. Coen to Heeren 17, 5 August 1619, *Coen: Bescheiden*, 1:472.

67. This was a continuation of a long process. Two Anglo-Dutch colonial conferences had been convened in 1613 and 1615 but with limited results. For a detailed discussion, see Van Ittersum, *Profit and Principle*.

68. Masselman, *Cradle of Colonialism*, 406. Loth, "Armed Incidents and Unpaid Bills," 721.

69. The treaty can be found in Charles Jenkinson, *A Collection of Treaties of Peace, Commerce, and Alliance Between Great-Britain and Other Powers: From Year 1619 to 1734* (London: J. Almon and J. Debrett, 1781), 1–16.

70. Jenkinson, *A Collection of Treaties of Peace*, 3.

71. Jenkinson, *A Collection of Treaties of Peace*, 5. Furber, *Rival Empires of Trade*, 44.

72. Some VOC officials did celebrate the news. In Aceh, for example, Nicolaes Casembroot indicated his "great happiness with which I have understood the good peace between us and the English." Nicolaes Casembroot to Coen, 1 July 1620, *Coen: Bescheiden*, 7.1:614.

73. Van Goor has a different, more mixed appraisal, believing that Coen did welcome the news on one level as a way to prevent further bloodshed. Van Goor, *Jan Pieterzoon Coen*, 405.

74. Coen to Heeren 17, 11 May 1620, *Coen: Bescheiden*, 1:544.

75. Coen to Heeren 17, 11 May 1620, *Coen: Bescheiden*, 1:544.

76. Coen to Heeren 17, 21 January 1620, *Coen: Bescheiden*, 1:693–94.

77. Heeren 17 to Coen, 8 September 1622, *Coen: Bescheiden*, 4:554.

78. In Batavia, the treaty created a set of joint institutions designed to adjudicate disputes, including a Council of Defense consisting of four representatives from each side. It should be noted that some of the mechanisms put in place by the treaty, including the Fleet of Defense, did function, albeit imperfectly, and that the treaty might have survived if not for the shock of the Amboina trial. My thanks to Aaron Maher (Monash University) for extended discussions in 2015 on this point.

79. Jan van Hasell to Coen, 4 October 1620, *Coen: Bescheiden*, 7.1:640.

80. Coen to Heeren 17, 6 September 1622, *Coen: Bescheiden*, 1:734; Heeren 17 to Coen, 26 March 1622, *Coen: Bescheiden*, 1:704–5.

81. Van Speult to Coen, 2 March 1621, *Coen: Bescheiden*, 7.1:688.

82. Van Speult to Coen, 2 March 1621, *Coen: Bescheiden*, 7.1:689.

83. "The Particular Advice and Orders of General Coen to the Governors of the Moluccas, Amboina, and Banda," 23 February 1621, *Coen: Bescheiden*, 3:16–19. This is the first part of a much longer title for this document.

84. "The Particular Advice and Orders of General Coen," *Coen: Bescheiden*, 3:17–18.

85. The rent was set at 40 reals a month for Hitu, 20 for Luhu, 20 for Kambelo, and 15 for Larica, making a total of 1,140 annually. Van Speult to Coen, 17 July 1621, *Coen: Bescheiden*, 7.1:730.

86. Letter from Samuel Coulson at Amboina, 31 August 1622, British Library, Factory Records: Java, G/21/3A, 349. For Muschamp's account of his injury, see Jourdain, *The Journal of John Jourdain*, 370. For a brief sketch, see *Coen: Bescheiden*, 7.1:916.

87. Danvers and Foster, *Letters Received by the East India Company*, 6:121, footnote 2.

88. Edmund Scott, *An Exact Discourse of the Subtilties, Fashishions, Pollicies, Religion, and Ceremonies of the East Indians* (1606), F.

89. Scott, *An Exact Discourse of the Subtilties*, F3. Michael Neill, "Putting History to the Question: An Episode of Torture at Bantam in Java, 1604," *English Literary Renaissance* 25 (1995): 54.

90. Danvers and Foster, *Letters Received by the East India Company*, 6:228.

91. Van Speult to Coen, 9 September 1622, *Coen: Bescheiden*, 7.2:1015.

92. Answer to question 26, deposition of Jan Joosten, 9 February 1628, BL IOR, G/21/2, pt. 3.

93. Not all the merchants working for the EIC in Amboina shared such a positive view. John Weatherall wrote from Kambelo that the Dutch used "vs more like their slaves and servants than their fellows and friends." John Weatherall at Amboina, 18 August 1622, G/21/3A, 253r–v.

94. Gabriel Towerson to Fursland, 19 September 1622, BL IOR, G/21/3A, 352.

95. Towerson to Fursland, 19 September 1622, BL IOR, G/21/3A, 351.

96. Fursland to Towerson, 17 December 1622, BL IOR, G/21/3A, 455.

97. Coen to Van Speult, 15 March 1621, *Coen: Bescheiden*, 3:22–23.

98. Coen to Van Speult, 23 November 1621, *Coen: Bescheiden*, 3:117.

99. Coen to Van Speult, 28 October 1622, *Coen: Bescheiden*, 3:251.

100. Copie sententie tegens de gevangen Bandanesen in dato 9 September 1622 [in 't Casteel Nassouw op 't eijlant Neira in Banda], NL-HaNA, VOC 1078, 385–86.

101. P. A. Tiele and J. E. Heeres, *Bouwstoffen voor de geschiedenis der Nederlanders in den Maleischen Archipel* (The Hague: Martinus Nijhoff, 1886–1895), 1:340. Coen to Heeren 17, 20 June 1623, *Coen: Bescheiden*, 1:782.

102. Coen to Heeren 17, 20 June 1623, *Coen: Bescheiden*, 1:783.

103. Van Speult to Coen, 19 March 1621, *Coen: Bescheiden*, 7.1:691.

104. Van Speult to Coen, 19 March 1621, *Coen: Bescheiden*, 7.1:692.

105. Tiele and Heeres, *Bouwstoffen voor de geschiedenis der Nederlanders in den Maleischen Archipel*, 1:325.

5. The Trial

The epigraph is taken from: Letter from Herman van Speult in Amboina to Governor-General Pieter de Carpentier, 5 June 1623, NL-HaNA, VOC 1080, 102.

1. For the power of rumor, see Ann Laura Stoler, "'In Cold Blood': Hierarchies of Credibility and the Politics of Colonial Narratives," *Representations* 37 (1992): 179.
2. Answer to question 1, deposition of Maerten Jansen Vogel, 1626, NL-HaNA, Staten-Generaal, 1.01.02, inv. no. 12551.62. Huel's name appears with multiple spellings.
3. Answer to question 2, deposition of Roelant Tieller, December 1626, NL-HaNA, Staten-Generaal, 1.01.02, inv. no. 12551.62.
4. The council consisted of five members, including the governor and Laurens de Maerschalk, an upper merchant who will be discussed in more detail in the next chapter. Answer to question 9, deposition of Laurens de Maerschalk, March 1628, NL-HaNA, Staten-Generaal, 1.01.02, inv. no. 12551.62.
5. Copie autentycq van de Confessien ende Sentencien van Mr. Touwerson ende Complicen over de Moordadige Conspiratie op t' Casteel Amboyna voorgenomen, dat door Godes merckelijcke ende genadige beschicking opden xxiii Februario 1623 is aenden dach gecomen als mede de resolutien by den Hr. Gouvernr van Speult & den raet daer over genomen, NL-HaNA, VOC 1080, 135v. Hereafter, Copie autentycq van de confessien ende sentencien.
6. Copie autentycq van de confessien ende sentencien, NL-HaNA, VOC 1080, 136v.
7. Answer to question 27, deposition of Roelant Tieller, December 1626, NL-HaNA, Staten-Generaal, 1.01.02, inv. no. 12551.62.
8. Christopher Hitchens, "Believe Me, It's Torture," *Vanity Fair*, August 2008, http://www.vanityfair.com/news/2008/08/hitchens200808.
9. Quoted in the Senate Select Committee on Intelligence, *Committee Study of the Central Intelligence Agency's Detention and Interrogation Program* (2014), 3, https://www.intelligence.senate.gov/sites/default/files/press/foreword.pdf.
10. Rachel Kerr and James Gow, "Law and War in the Global War on Terror," in *International Law, Security and Ethics: Policy Challenges in the Post-9/11 World*, ed. Aidan Hehir, Natasha Kuhrt, and Andrew Mumford (London: Routledge, 2011), 72; *Committee Study of the Central Intelligence Agency's Detention and Interrogation Program*, 415.
11. Letter from Herman van Speult in Amboina to Governor-General Pieter de Carpentier, 5 June 1623, NL-HaNA, VOC 1080, 101v. The last detail as to the exact size of the pots comes from a later deposition. Attestation of Cornelius Thomas, smith at Amboyna, 1629, BL IOR, G/21/2, pt. 3.
12. Quoted in *Committee Study of the Central Intelligence Agency's Detention and Interrogation Program*, 494.
13. Answer to question 3, deposition of Jan Joosten, December 1626, NL-HaNA, Staten-Generaal, 1.01.02, inv. no. 12551.62. The use of Malay as a language of interrogation was first noted by Iwao, whose work forms an indispensable reference for studies of the Japanese in Southeast Asia. Iwao Seiichi, *Zoku Nanyō Nihon*

machi no kenkyū: Nanyō tōsho chiiki bunsan Nihonjin imin no seikatsu to katsudō (Tokyo: Iwanami Shoten, 1987), 259.

14. Diverse attestatien tegen den conspirateur Manuel Japansche tolck beleijt den 12 Julij 1618 in Jacatra, NL-HaNA, VOC 1068, 127–35.

15. Letter from Herman van Speult in Amboina to Governor-General Pieter de Carpentier, 5 June 1623, NL-HaNA, VOC 1080, 101v.

16. Letter from Herman van Speult in Amboina to Governor-General Pieter de Carpentier, 5 June 1623, NL-HaNA, VOC 1080, 101v.

17. There were reports on the English side that he had been seen gambling with the Japanese. W. N. Sainsbury, ed. *Calendar of State Papers Colonial, East Indies, China and Japan, 1622–1624* (London: H.M.S.O., 1878), 392.

18. Copie autentycq van de confessien ende sententien, NL-HaNA, VOC 1080, 136v.

19. Letter from Herman van Speult in Amboina to Governor-General Pieter de Carpentier, 5 June 1623, NL-HaNA, VOC 1080, 101v.

20. The Amboina judges, who provided long depositions detailing every aspect of the case, were similarly silent. As will be discussed in chapter 6, this is not especially surprising as they were determined to present a picture of the case as ordered and deliberate.

21. The fact that Forbes was present in this capacity in Kota Ambon is confirmed by the Amboina judges in their subsequent depositions.

22. W. N. Sainsbury, ed., *Calendar of State Papers Colonial, East Indies and Persia, 1625–1629* (London: H.M.S.O., 1884), 690.

23. One could argue that Forbes, who ended up in Britain, wanted to secure English East India Company support, but this account of the governor's apparent breakdown contributed nothing to the English version of the case, which presented Van Speult as a cold-blooded murderer who had fabricated the plot to eject the English from his dominion.

24. It was standard procedure for legal officials like the advocate-fiscal to take charge of cases in VOC settlements, but all the evidence suggests that De Bruyn exerted a much higher degree of control over proceedings than was normal. Certainly this was the conclusion reached by officials in Batavia in the aftermath of the trial. See Generale missive van Gouverneur-Generaal en Raden, 3 January 1624, NL-HaNA, VOC 1079, 36v.

25. I have found only one study of De Bruyn and his background. Although it includes a number of valuable details, Worp's article is focused on De Bruyn's son and has only a brief reference to Amboina. J. A. Worp, "Jan de Brune de Jonge," *Oud-Holland* 8 (1890): 81–103.

26. For an example of a successful recruit, see the brief career of Cornelis Dedel as described in Martine J. van Ittersum, "Debating Natural Law in the Banda Islands: A Case Study in Anglo-Dutch Imperial Competition in the East Indies, 1609–1621," *History of European Ideas* 42, no. 4 (2016): 472. Like so many other recruits, however, Dedel died just a few years after arriving in Asia.

27. As discussed in Adam Clulow, *The Company and the Shogun: The Dutch Encounter with Tokugawa Japan* (New York: Columbia University Press, 2014), chap. 2.

28. Quoted in Leonard Blussé, "Bull in a China Shop: Pieter Nuyts in China and Japan (1627–1636)," in *Around and About Formosa, Essays in Honor of Professor Ts'ao Yung-ho*, ed. Leonard Blussé (Taipei: SMC, 2003), 101. Blussé writes that the scheme to replace "hard drinking, but charismatic 'old hands' in high level positions by inexperienced but well-educated scions of the ruling class for the sake of institutionalising the operations of the Company turned out to be rather counter-productive."

29. W. P. Coolhaas, J. van Goor, J. E. Schooneveld-Oosterling and H. K. s'Jacob, eds., *Generale Missiven van Gouverneurs-Generaal en Raden aan Heren XVII der Verenigde Oost-Indische Compagnie* (The Hague: Martinus Nijhoff, 1960–2007), 1:577. Blussé, "Bull in a China Shop," 102.

30. Worp, "Jan de Brune de Jonge." This paragraph draws heavily on Worp's article, which uses an alternate spelling, Isaac de Brune.

31. He was not the only new employee who hoped for this transformation. Antonio Van Diemen, for example, escaped a failed business career to rise governor-general.

32. Coen to Governor Houtman, 31 January 1622, H. T. Colenbrander and W. P. Coolhaas, eds., *Jan Pietersz. Coen: Bescheiden Omtrent Zijn Bedrijf in Indië* (The Hague: Martinus Nijhoff, 1919–1954), 3:131. Hereafter, *Coen: Bescheiden*. Resolutions, 26 January 1622, *Coen: Bescheiden*, 3:817.

33. Van Speult to Coen, 15 June 1622, *Coen: Bescheiden*, 7.2:975.

34. Van Speult to Coen, 15 June 1622, *Coen: Bescheiden*, 7.2:978.

35. Van Speult to Coen, 15 June 1622, *Coen: Bescheiden*, 7.2:978.

36. As discussed earlier, this is the title that appears in the trial records, but the more common designation in the VOC empire for this position was *fiscaal*. Robert Ross, *Cape of Torments: Slavery and Resistance in South Africa* (London: Routledge and Kegan Paul, 1983), x.

37. Generale missive van Gouverneur-Generaal en Raden, 3 January 1624, NL-HaNA, VOC 1079, 36v.

38. *A Remonstrance of the Directors of the Netherlands East India Company Presented to the Lords States Generall of the United Provinces, in Defence of the Said Companie, Touching the Bloudy Proceedings Against the English Merchants, Executed at Amboyna* (London, 1632), 36. As will be discussed in the next chapter, De Maerschalk realized a few weeks after the execution of the alleged plotters just how badly the advocate-fiscal had managed the case and moved to augment it with new documents.

39. Generale missive van Gouverneur-Generaal en Raden, 3 January 1624, NL-HaNA, VOC 1079, 36v.

40. Copie autentycq van de confessien ende sententien, NL-HaNA, VOC 1080. This is a copy (or rather a copy of a copy) of the original document, which was drawn up in the immediate aftermath of the case by a scribe attached to Castle Victoria.

41. Generale missive van Gouverneur-Generaal en Raden, 3 January 1624, NL-HaNA, VOC 1079, 36v.

42. Scholars writing in Dutch have long noted many of the problems with this document and the proceedings it reflected. F. W. Stapel, "De Ambonsche 'Moord'

(9 Maart 1623)," *Tijdschrift voor Indische Taal- Land- en Volkenkunde* 62 (1923): 209–26.

43. Coolhaas notes the relative absence of trained legal professionals. W. P. Coolhaas, "Aanteekeningen en Opmerkingen over den zoogenaamdem Ambonschen Moord," *Bijdragen tot de Taal-, Land- en Volkenkunde van Nederlandsch-Indie* 101 (1942): 49–93. For a description of the legal system in VOC possessions, see Kerry Ward, *Networks of Empire: Forced Migration in the Dutch East India Company* (New York: Cambridge University Press, 2008); John Ball, *Indonesian Legal History, 1602–1848* (Sydney, Oughtershaw Press, 1982).

44. Generale missive van Gouverneur-Generaal en Raden, 3 January 1624, NL-HaNA, VOC 1079, 36v.

45. Pieter de Carpentier to Van Speult, 14 January 1624, NL-HaNA, VOC 1080, 182v. Coolhaas has a different transcription of one word in this quote. He has "*regels*" or "order." My reading is "*vigeur*" or vigor. Coolhaas, "Aanteekeningen en Opmerkingen over den zoogenaamdem Ambonschen Moord," 61.

46. For a representative trial that includes this kind of cross-examination record, see Diverse attestatien tegen den conspirateur Manuel Japansche tolck beleijt den 12 Julij 1618 in Jacatra, NL-HaNA, VOC 1068, 127–35. This form of interrogations is discussed in Nigel Worden and Gerald Groenewald, *Trials of Slavery* (Cape Town: Van Riebeeck Society, 2005). They note that the accused was required to answer questions set down by the fiscal that were designed to lead to an admission of guilt.

47. De Carpentier to Van Speult, 14 January 1624, NL-HaNA, VOC 1080, 182v.

48. De Carpentier to Van Speult, 14 January 1624, NL-HaNA, VOC 1080, 182v. This point was addressed again and again in the later depositions provided by the Amboina judges. They explained that confrontations were standard so as to reduce the reliance on torture. Answer to question 18, deposition of Jan Joosten, December 1626, NL-HaNA, Staten-Generaal, 1.01.02, inv. no. 12551.62.

49. Of the eleven Japanese mercenaries that confessed at the beginning of the trial record, for example, only nine are left by the end, leaving the reader with no other choice but to conjecture as to the fate of the missing pair, Soysimo and Sacoube.

50. Coolhaas, "Aanteekeningen en Opmerkingen over den zoogenaamdem Ambonschen Moord," 65–66.

51. Answer to question 1, deposition of Jan Jacobsen Wyncoop, 1626, NL-HaNA, Staten-Generaal, 1.01.02, inv. no. 12551.62.

52. Generale missive van Gouverneur-Generaal en Raden, 3 January 1624, NL-HaNA, VOC 1079, 36v and 36.

53. C. Brants, "Legal Culture and Legal Transplants," *Electronic Journal of Comparative Law* 14, no. 3 (December 2010), http://www.ejcl.org/143/art143–5.pdf. For a discussion of the 1570 Ordinance in relation to Amboina, see J. K. de Jonge and M. L. van Deventer, eds., *De opkomst van het Nederlandsch gezag in Oost Indië* (The Hague: Martius Nijhoff, 1862–1909), 5: viii–ix. De Jonge writes that "influential legal experts still assigned legality to the ordonnance of 1570." For a broader account of the code and its influence, see Marijke van de Vrugt, *De*

criminele ordonnantie van 1570 (Zutphen: Walburg Pers, 1978). An English translation of this code can be found in Jabez Henry, *Report on the Criminal Law at Demerara and in the Ceded Dutch Colonies* (London: Henry Butterworth, 1821), 4–57. Ward notes that the organization's administrators constructed a hierarchical system in which specific laws passed by the VOC had first precedence. When no such laws existed, the Company relied on laws from the United Provinces. Ward, *Networks of Empire*.

54. John Langbein, *Torture and the Law of Proof: Europe and England in the Ancien Regime* (Chicago: University of Chicago Press, 1977), 5.

55. Henry, *Report on the Criminal Law at Demerara*, 36–37. For a discussion in practice, see Susie Newton-King, "For the Love of Adam: Two Sodomy Trials at the Cape of Good Hope," *Kronos: Journal of Cape History*, no 28 (2002): 21–42.

56. Stapel, "De Ambonsche 'Moord,'" 219. De Jonge and Van Deventer, *De Opkomst*, 5:viii–ix.

57. Brants, "Legal Culture and Legal Transplants." For a description of how this process functioned in a different colonial setting, see Natalie Zemon Davis, "Judges, Masters, Diviners: Slaves' Experience of Criminal Justice in Colonial Suriname," *Law and History Review* 29, no. 4 (2011): 925–84. See also C. G. Botha, "Criminal Procedure at the Cape During the 17th and 18th Centuries," *South African Law Journal* 32 (1915): 322–43; George Pavlich, "Occupied Cape Judges and Colonial Knowledge of Crime, Criminals, and Punishment," *Sage Open* (2014), https://doi.org/10.1177/2158244013520612; Worden and Groenewald, *Trials of Slavery*. Newton-King notes that "the inquisitorial process and the extraordinary mode of procedure were imported lock, stock and barrel to the Dutch East India Company's overseas possessions." Newton-King, "For the Love of Adam."

58. Quoted in De Jonge and Van Deventer, *De Opkomst*, 5:xxv. Voorda's key writing is Bavius Voorda, *De Crimineele Ordonnantien van Koning Philips van Spanje. Verzeld van eene Verhandling over het Verstand van de Ordonnantie* (Leiden: Honkoop and van Tiffelen, 1792).

59. Simon van Leeuwen, *Het Rooms-Hollands-Regt* (Leiden: Hackens, 1664), 630.

60. Generale missive van Gouverneur-Generaal en Raden, 3 January 1624, NL-HaNA, VOC 1079, 36.

61. De Carpentier to Van Speult, 14 January 1624, NL-HaNA, VOC 1080, 182v.

62. Henry, *Report on the Criminal Law at Demerara*, 34. There has been some misunderstanding as to whether confirmation should happen within twenty-four hours or after twenty-four hours. The latter is correct. See Coolhaas, "Aanteekeningen en Opmerkingen over den zoogenaamdem Ambonschen Moord," n. 45.

63. As will be discussed in chapter 6, VOC officials would later claim that these confirmations had in fact taken in place.

64. For a superb recent account of Nagasaki's development and the Christian connection, see Reinier Hesselink, *The Dream of Christian Nagasaki: World Trade and the Clash of Cultures, 1560–1640* (Jefferson, NC: McFarland, 2015).

65. Massarella suggests that Miguel may have been employed at the English factory in Japan, although he cities no evidence aside from a reference in one of the Amboina pamphlets. Derek Massarella, *A World Elsewhere: Europe's Encounter*

with Japan in the Sixteenth and Seventeenth Centuries (New Haven, CT: Yale University Press, 1990), 188.

66. Some of the Amboina judges testified that he had formerly been a slave of Captain Towerson, but it seems more likely that he had simply been employed by the EIC. Answer to question 18, deposition of Laurens de Maerschalk, March 1628, BL IOR, G/21/2, pt. 3.

67. A Japanese captain such as Kusnoky Itsiemon was only paid ten reals per month.

68. Copie autentycq van de confessien ende sententien, NL-HaNA, VOC 1080, 138v.

69. Copie autentycq van de confessien ende sententien, NL-HaNA, VOC 1080, 142v.

70. Sinsa, for example, confessed that twelve Japanese agreed to hand over the castle to the English. Copie autentycq van de confessien ende sententien, NL-HaNA, VOC 1080, 141v.

71. Answer to question 18, deposition of Jan van Leeuwen, NL-HaNA, Staten-Generaal, 1.01.02, inv. no. 12551.62.

72. Sainsbury, *Calendar of State Papers, 1625–1629*, 686.

73. These three were Quiendayo, Sinsa, and Tsavinda.

74. Answer to question 3, deposition of Jan van Leeuwen, 1626, NL-HaNA, Staten-Generaal, 1.01.02, inv. no. 12551.62. Another Amboina judge, De Maerschalk, testified in 1628 that some free Japanese living in Kota Ambon had acted as interpreters, but this seems unlikely. Viewed on balance, Van Leeuwen's explanation seems the most persuasive.

75. It should be noted that any possible involvement of the captain was confined to subsequent interrogations after Shichizō. All the sources agree that Shichizō was questioned by himself.

76. One last Japanese soldier, Sacoube, was interrogated on February 25.

77. Copie autentycq van de confessien ende sententien, NL-HaNA, VOC 1080, 143v.

78. *An Answer to the Dutch Relation, Touching the Pretended Conspiracie of the English at Amboyna in the Indies* (London: printed by H. Lownes for Nathanael Newberry, 1624), 11. This was published alongside John Skinner's text.

79. EIC officials often complained about what they saw as Dutch attempts to pull them into VOC jurisdiction. Sainsbury, *Calendar of State Papers, 1622–1624*, 20. In fact, the response to the 1623 trial shows that this was not standard.

80. Samuel Coulson, John Clarke, and George Sherrocke were arrested in Hitu; William Griggs and John Sadler at Larica; John Powle, John Wetherall, and Thomas Ladbrooke were apprehended at Kambelo and brought in irons to Kota Ambon.

81. Deposition of John Beaumont, July 1624, BL IOR, G/21/2, pt. 3.

82. Answer to question 9, deposition of William Webber, July 1624, BL IOR, G/21/2, pt. 3

83. *An Answer to the Dutch Relation, Touching the Pretended Conspiracie of the English at Amboyna in the Indies*, 21.

84. This was January 11, 1623, in the Gregorian calendar. I will refer to it as the New Year's Day meeting, as that is how it was consistently presented in the records. Given the two calendars in use, there is some confusion as to the actual date for this meeting. Coolhaas agrees with my reading, but Bassett suggests it took place

on December 22, 1622. D. K. Bassett, "The 'Amboyna Massacre' of 1623," *Journal of Southeast Asian History* 1, no. 2 (1960): 2.

85. Copie autentycq van de confessien ende sententien, NL-HaNA, VOC 1080, 152v.

86. Copie autentycq van de confessien ende sententien, NL-HaNA, VOC 1080, 146v.

87. Answer to question 7, deposition of John Beaumont, July 1624, BL IOR, G/21/2, pt. 3.

88. Jean Gelman Taylor, *The Social World of Batavia: Europeans and Eurasians in Colonial Indonesia*, 2nd ed. (Madison: University of Wisconsin Press, 2009), 21.

89. Thomas Brockedon and Council at Jakatra to the East India Company in London, 14 December 1623, BL IOR, E/3/10, 54v.

90. Thomas Brockedon and Council at Jakatra to the East India Company in London, 14 December 1623, BL IOR, E/3/10, 54v. Towerson was reprimanded for placing too much faith in Collins. His superiors wrote that their agent had made a bad mistake when he had "so much recommended unto vs at your being here."

91. Answer to question 9, deposition of Edward Collins, BL IOR, G/21/2, pt. 3.

92. Answer to question 67, deposition of Jan van Leeuwen, 15 March 1628, BL IOR, G/21/2, pt. 3.

93. Answer to question 6, deposition of Edward Collins, July 1624, BL IOR, G/21/2, pt. 3.

94. For one of those later descriptions, see Beckles Willson, *Ledger and Sword or The Honourable Company of Merchants of England Trading to the East Indies (1599–1874)* (London: Longmans, Green, 1903), 167.

95. This detail comes from Collins and appears in *A True Relation of the Unjust, Cruell, and Barbarous Proceedings Against the English at Amboyna in the East-Indies, by the Neatherlandish Governour and Councel There* (London: printed by H. Lownes for Nathanael Newberry, 1624).

96. Copie autentycq van de confessien ende sententien, NL-HaNA, VOC 1080, 150v.

97. Answer to question 43, deposition of Jan Joosten, December 1626, NL-HaNA, Staten-Generaal, 1.01.02, inv. no. 12551.62.

98. Answer to question 48, deposition of Jan Joosten, December 1626, NL-HaNA, Staten-Generaal, 1.01.02, inv. no. 12551.62.

99. Quoted in *Committee Study of the Central Intelligence Agency's Detention and Interrogation Program*, 43.

100. Answer to question 113, deposition of Jan Joosten, 9 February 1628, BL IOR, G/21/2, pt. 3.

101. The decision to cut Clark's hair was picked up by English pamphleteers, who charged that De Bruyn and his fellow interrogators had done this because they were convinced that Clark was surely a "witch, [or] at least had some charm about him, or was enchanted that he could bear so much." Only by cutting his hair could this witchcraft be removed. *A True Relation of the Unjust, Cruell, and Barbarous Proceedings.*

102. Answer to question 42, deposition of Rolant Teiller, December 1626, NL-HaNA, Staten-Generaal, 1.01.02, inv. no. 12551.62.

103. Answer to question 9, deposition of Edward Collins, July 1624, BL IOR, G/21/2, pt. 3. Such gruesome descriptions were promptly turned into published images such as the one displayed on the cover of this book.

104. Answer to question 50, deposition of Jan Joosten, December 1626, NL-HaNA, Staten-Generaal, 1.01.02, inv. nr. 12551.62.

105. Copie autentycq van de confessien ende sententien, NL-HaNA, VOC 1080, 152v.

106. The original book with Coulson's inscription was sent over to the United Provinces and survives in the National Archives there today.

107. *A Remonstrance of the Directors of the Netherlands East India Company.*

108. Coolhaas, "Aanteekeningen en Opmerkingen over den zoogenaamdem Ambonschen Moord," 84. Coolhaas is dismissive of any assumption that the psalm book was forged.

109. Copie autentycq van de confessien ende sententien, NL-HaNA, VOC 1080, 155v.

110. Quoted in De Jonge and Van Deventer, *De Opkomst,* 5:xxiii. *A True Relation of the Unjust, Cruell, and Barbarous Proceedings,* 20. Although the existence of such a note was admitted by both sides, I have been unable to locate the original document in either the Dutch or English archive. This is in contrast to Coulson's psalm book, which remains freely accessible.

111. Copie autentycq van de confessien ende sententien, NL-HaNA, VOC 1080, 155v. Hitu's relationship with Castle Victoria is discussed in chapter 7. We know from this denial that De Bruyn pressed Towerson repeatedly on this point of local allies.

112. His presence shows just how capacious the VOC label of "English" was in this period.

113. Answer to question 60, deposition of Jan van Leeuwen, 15 March 1628, BL IOR, G/21/2, pt. 3.

114. Answer to question 9, deposition of Edward Collins, BL IOR, G/21/2, pt. 3.

115. The explanation preferred by VOC authorities was that Towerson had once reprimanded Thomson that his frequent drunkenness would give away the plot. Because of this, Thomson was so determined not to reveal the plot that he suffered terrible torture. Answer to question 61, deposition of Laurens de Maerschalk, 1628, BL IOR, G/21/2, pt. 3. Given the fact that Towerson had already confessed his involvement in the plot, it seems difficult to credit this explanation.

116. Copie autentycq van de confessien ende sententien, NL-HaNA, VOC 1080, 156v.

117. It also directly contradicted what Shichizō had confessed.

118. Answer to question 135, deposition of Jan Joosten, December 1626, NL-HaNA, Staten-Generaal, 1.01.02, inv. no. 12551.62.

119. Some writers have speculated that it would have been too dangerous to ship the English over to Batavia. This has little basis. Sending around a dozen unarmed merchants aboard a VOC vessel would not have been an especially hazardous enterprise, and such ships regularly transported far larger groups of prisoners captured during privateering expeditions. De Jonge notes the delay as the governor debated what to do. De Jonge and Van Deventer, *De Opkomst,* 5, xix.

120. Sainsbury, *Calendar of State Papers, 1625–1629,* 690.

121. Copie autentycq van de confessien ende sententien, NL-HaNA, VOC 1080, 160v.

122. As is so often the case with the trial, there are two accounts of Van Speult's recommendation. In *The Confessions and Sentences* the advocate-fiscal wrote that the governor recommended that action should be taken in Amboina and the English sentenced there. But in his own letters to the governor-general, Van Speult was clear that he had recommended precisely the opposite and that the matter should be referred to Batavia. Given De Bruyn's record of misleading statements, it is this second version of events that seems more credible. Letter from Herman van Speult in Amboina to Governor-General Pieter de Carpentier, 5 June 1623, NL-HaNA, VOC 1080, 102v. Most scholars to discuss this point have only referenced De Bruyn's statement.

123. Letter from Herman van Speult in Amboina to Governor-General Pieter de Carpentier, 5 June 1623, NL-HaNA, VOC 1080, 102v.

124. Copie autentycq van de confessien ende sententien, NL-HaNA, VOC 1080, 161v.

125. Four others were exempted. These were Ephraim Ramsey, John Powle, Thomas Ladbrook, and John Sadler, all of whom were away from Amboyna when the crucial New Year's Day meeting had taken place.

126. Copie autentycq van de confessien ende sententien, NL-HaNA, VOC 1080, 143v.

127. It is not clear why these three soldiers were chosen. The confessions give them different roles, but we can assume they were selected as likely leaders.

128. Copie autentycq van de confessien ende sententien, NL-HaNA, VOC 1080, 163v.

129. Answer to question 107, deposition of Jan Joosten, December 1626, NL-HaNA, Staten-Generaal, 1.01.02, inv. no. 12551.62.

6. The War of the Witnesses

The epigraphs are taken from: *A Reply to the Remonstrance of the Bewinthebbers or Directors of the Netherlands East-India Companie* (London: printed by John Dawson for the East India Company, 1632), 2; and D. K. Bassett, "The Factory of the English East India Company at Bantam, 1602–1682," (PhD diss., University of London, 1955), 71.

1. See, for example, declaration before Govert van Aps, 24 March 1623, NL-HaNA, Staten-Generaal, 1.01.02, inv. no. 12551.62.

2. Bassett, "The Factory of the English East India Company at Bantam," 71.

3. This was the formulation most commonly used to describe these six men. W. N. Sainsbury, ed., *Calendar of State Papers Colonial, East Indies, China and Japan, 1622–1624* (London: H.M.S.O., 1878), 404.

4. *A True Relation of the Unjust, Cruell, and Barbarous Proceedings Against the English at Amboyna in the East-Indies, by the Neatherlandish Governour and Councel There* (London: printed by H. Lownes for Nathanael Newberry, 1624), 38.

5. Such retellings of the case provide a key point of focus for Alison Games's planned monograph on the Amboina trial. Anthony Milton, "Marketing a Massacre: Amboyna, the East India Company and the Public Sphere in Early Stuart England," in *The Politics of the Public Sphere in Early Modern England*, ed. Steve Pincus

and Peter Lake, 168–90 (Manchester: Manchester University Press, 2007). Rupali Mishra, *A Business of State: Commerce, Politics, and the Birth of the East India Company* (Cambridge, MA: Harvard University Press, 2018). Miles Ogborn, *Indian Ink: Script and Print in the Making of the English East India Company* (Chicago: University of Chicago Press, 2007), 120–29. Edmond Smith, "Networks of the East India Company, c. 1600–1625" (PhD diss., Cambridge University, 2016).

6. The document was initially delivered in a French translation to the English East India Company. The French translation can be found in State Papers, Holland, SP 84/121/1, National Archives, Kew. It was enclosed in a letter sent from Carleton to Conway on November 1. An English translation was printed as *A Remonstrance of the Directors of the Netherlands East India Company Presented to the Lords States Generall of the United Provinces, in Defence of the Said Companie* (London: printed by John Dawson for the East India Company, 1632).

7. As such, it highlights the importance of state support to European expansion in the early modern period. Tonio Andrade, who has argued persuasively for this view, suggests that "Europeans' success in creating overseas empires was based less on technology than on geopolitics, and particularly on one factor: state support." Tonio Andrade, "Beyond Guns, Germs, and Steel: European Expansion and Maritime Asia, 1400–1750," *Journal of Early Modern History* 14 (2010): 165–86.

8. Adam Clulow, "Like Lambs in Japan and Devils Outside Their Land: Violence, Law and Japanese Merchants in Southeast Asia," *Journal of World History* 24, no. 2 (2013): 335–58.

9. Mishra argues that "Amboyna became the crucible in which the weaknesses in the mutually beneficial relationship between the Company and the regime . . . were tested." Mishra, *A Business of State*, 210.

10. Sainsbury, *Calendar of State Papers, 1622–1624*, 283. In general, I have converted the dates that appear in English documents into the Gregorian calendar, so as to standardize them with the dates coming out of the Dutch sources.

11. Rupali Mishra writes that the case prompted "an existential crisis for the Company." Mishra, *A Business of State*, 209.

12. Court minutes, 9 July 1624, BL IOR, B/9.

13. Court minutes, 9 July 1624, BL IOR, B/9.

14. *Waerachtich Verhael vande Tidinghen ghecomen wt de Oost-Indien* (1624). This was translated and later printed as a pamphlet entitled *A True Declaration of the News That Came Out of the East Indies with the Pinnace Called the Hare*. It stated that the Dutch had every right to try the case and that justice had been executed "according to the laws of the Netherlands." Sainsbury, *Calendar of State Papers, 1622–1624*, 283.

15. Sainsbury, *Calendar of State Papers, 1622–1624*, 292 and 404–5.

16. Court minutes, 30 June 1624, BL IOR, B/8.

17. Sainsbury, *Calendar of State Papers, 1622–1624*, xix.

18. Dated 7–13 July 1624 in the original document. Depositions taken in the High Court of Admiralty, BL IOR, G/21/2, pt. 3. They had been "appointed for formes sake, and to take away all objeccons from the Dutch." Court minutes, 30 June 1624, BL IOR, B/8; Sainsbury, *Calendar of State Papers, 1622–1624*, 299.

19. It is striking how closely the depositions borrowed emphasis and phrasing from each other while returning again and again to the same points. The depositions in the record are likely not word-for-word transcriptions, but the similarities between individual statements are nonetheless noteworthy. This can be seen, for example, in the description of the Japanese mercenaries employed in Amboina. For Beaumont, the Japanese were "poore souldiers most of them serving under the dutch, and there never was any familiarity betweene them and Captaine Towerson." For Collins, they were "poore fellowes of small accompt" with no familiarity with the English.

20. Answer to question 11, depositions of Edward Collins and John Beaumont, July 1624, BL IOR, G/21/2, pt. 3. Five of the six Amboyna men confirmed the same point. The sixth, Ephraim Ramsey, stated simply that he could not testify about such a question. Depositions taken in the High Court of Admiralty, BL IOR, G/21/2, pt. 3.

21. Answer to question 11, deposition of Edward Collins, July 1624, BL IOR, G/21/2, pt. 3.

22. Answer to question 2, deposition of Edward Collins, July 1624, BL IOR, G/21/2, pt. 3. Some other depositions suggested there were 250 soldiers.

23. Answer to question 6, deposition of Edward Collins, July 1624, BL IOR, G/21/2, pt. 3. Here, Collins was describing the torture used against the Japanese.

24. Henry Moore Teller, *The Problem in the Philippines* (Washington, DC: U.S. Government Printing Office, 1902), 54.

25. Teller, *The Problem in the Philippines*, 52.

26. Answer to question 6, deposition of Geroge Sherrock, July 1624, BL IOR, G/21/2, pt. 3.

27. Answer to question 6, deposition of Ephraim Ramsey, July 1624, BL IOR, G/21/2, pt. 3. For an imagined depiction of this widespread burning, see the cover image of this book.

28. Answer to question 29, deposition of Jan Joosten, December 1626, NL-HaNA, Staten-Generaal, 1.01.02, inv. no. 12551.62.

29. Answer to question 83, deposition of Jan Jacobsen Wyncoop, 1626, NL-HaNA, Staten-Generaal, 1.01.02, inv. no. 12551.62.

30. Answer to question 9, deposition of John Beaumont, July 1624, BL IOR, G/21/2, pt. 3.

31. Beckles Willson, *Ledger and Sword or The Honourable Company of Merchants of England Trading to the East Indies (1599—1874)* (London: Longmans, Green, 1903), 173.

32. Answer to question 9, deposition of George Sharrock, July 1624, BL IOR, G/21/2, pt. 3.

33. Fursland to Towerson, 17 December 1622, BL IOR, G/21/3A, 456. This letter includes multiple abbreviations which I have reproduced here in full.

34. Sainsbury, *Calendar of State Papers, 1622–1624*, 404–5.

35. Sainsbury, *Calendar of State Papers, 1622–1624*, 405.

36. Sainsbury, *Calendar of State Papers, 1622–1624*, 324. Collins testified in his deposition that gunpower had been put into the toes of the interrogated men and then set alight.

37. Sainsbury, *Calendar of State Papers, 1622–1624*, 461.
38. Sainsbury, *Calendar of State Papers, 1630–1634*, 157–58.
39. W. N. Sainsbury, ed., *Calendar of State Papers Colonial, East Indies and Persia, 1625–1629* (London: H.M.S.O., 1884), 203–4.
40. Sainsbury, *Calendar of State Papers, 1625–1629*, 416.
41. W. N. Sainsbury, ed., *Calendar of State Papers Colonial, East Indies and Persia, 1630–1634* (London: H.M.S.O., 1892), 366. His brother-in-law (usually identified as Billingsley) made particular use of this strategy.
42. Sainsbury, *Calendar of State Papers, 1630–1634*, 286.
43. Sainsbury, *Calendar of State Papers, 1630–1634*, 366.
44. Sainsbury, *Calendar of State Papers, 1622–1624*, 295. Skinner had sailed to Asia years earlier aboard the *Globe*. Smith, "Networks of the East India Company," 225.
45. Mishra, *A Business of State*, 227. When published, Skinner's text was atttached to an epistle to the reader, a translation of a Dutch pamphlet (*A True Declaration of the News That Came Out of the East Indies with the Pinnace Called the Hare*), and a response (*An Answer to the Dutch Relation, Touching the Pretended Conspiracie of the English at Amboyna in the Indies*).
46. Milton calls it "the first weapon in the Company's response." Milton, "Marketing a Massacre," 174.
47. *A True Relation of the Unjust, Cruell, and Barbarous Proceedings*, 33.
48. *A True Relation of the Unjust, Cruell, and Barbarous Proceedings*, 11.
49. *A True Relation of the Unjust, Cruell, and Barbarous Proceedings*, 17.
50. *A True Relation of the Unjust, Cruell, and Barbarous Proceedings*, 26.
51. Milton, "Marketing a Massacre," 176.
52. Court minutes, 11 August 1624, BL IOR, B/9.
53. Sainsbury, *Calendar of State Papers, 1622–1624*, 358.
54. Sainsbury, *Calendar of State Papers, 1622–1624*, 358.
55. Sainsbury, *Calendar of State Papers, 1622–1624*, 358. On August 16, the Company examined him for a diamond that he had supposedly received from Van Speult.
56. Sainsbury, *Calendar of State Papers, 1622–1624*, 295.
57. *A True Relation of the Unjust, Cruell, and Barbarous Proceedings*, 29. We cannot be certain exactly what Welden told Skinner as he did not provide a formal deposition, but it seems highly likely that these details came from him as they are not featured in any of the Admiralty depositions provided by the six Amboyna men. This would also be in line with Skinner's statement that Welden was especially useful to him.
58. Not surprisingly, the Dutch derided these supposed miracles. Rather than a sign of God's displeasure, the change in the weather was simply the advent of the monsoon. Van Leeuwen explained, for example, that there had been a change in the weather but that such changes were standard in the tropics. Answer to question 123, deposition of Van Leeuwen, 1626, NL-HaNA, Staten-Generaal, 1.01.02, inv. no. 12551.62. The former judges also ridiculed the notion of a mass illness, testifying that sickness was a standard part of life in the Indies.
59. Giles Milton, *Nathaniel's Nutmeg* (London: Hodder & Stoughton, 1999). See also Stephen Brown, *Merchant Kings: When Companies Ruled the World, 1600–1900*

(New York : Thomas Dunne Books, 2010). As a sign of the success of Skinner's narrative, Brown attributes it to a "conscience-stricken VOC employee."

60. This meeting is dated July 9 in the English sources. Sainsbury, *Calendar of State Papers, 1622–1624*, 303. Smith, "Networks of the East India Company," 226.

61. Sainsbury, *Calendar of State Papers, 1622–1624*, 302.

62. Court minutes, 9 July 1624, BL IOR, B/9; Sainsbury, *Calendar of State Papers, 1622–1624*, 302.

63. Gaastra notes that "close ties were formed between the ruling oligarchy of regents and the directors." Femme Gaastra, *The Dutch East India Company: Expansion and Decline* (Zutphen: Walburg Pers, 2003), 31.

64. Sainsbury, *Calendar of State Papers, 1625–1629*, 350.

65. Court minutes, 22 July 1624, BL IOR, B/9.

66. Sainsbury, *Calendar of State Papers, 1625–1629*, 42.

67. The king's answer and offer, 16 July 1624, State Papers, Domestic Correspondence, James I, SP 14, National Archives, Kew; Sainsbury, *Calendar of State Papers, 1622–1624*, 325.

68. Sainsbury, *Calendar of State Papers, 1622–1624*, 415. By October 1624, the king, via Buckingham, had issued the order to seize Dutch ships.

69. Court minutes, 8 October 1624, BL IOR, B/9; Mishra, *A Business of State*, 227.

70. Court minutes, 8 October 1624, BL IOR, B/9.

71. Milton, "Marketing a Massacre," 175.

72. Smith, "Networks of the East India Company," 234. Some of these translations can be found in NL-HaNA, Staten-Generaal, 1.01.02, inv. no. 12551.62.3.

73. As discussed in the previous chapter, not all fourteen were present throughout the trial.

74. *A Remonstrance of the Directors of the Netherlands East India*, 36.

75. These details come from NL-HaNA, Klapper Van Delden: Carthotheek Alfabetische Naamindex VOC-dienaren (17e eeuw), inv. no. 1.04.23.

76. Letter from Herman van Speult in Amboina to Governor-General Pieter de Carpentier, 5 June 1623, NL-HaNA, VOC 1080, 109.

77. Sainsbury, *Calendar of State Papers, 1625–1629*, 33.

78. Sainsbury, *Calendar of State Papers, 1625–1629*, 11.

79. Sainsbury, *Calendar of State Papers, 1625–1629*, 56.

80. Extract from resolutions from the States General, 27 April 1625, NL-HaNA, VOC 11138. This section draws heavily on these extracts, which appear in the VOC archives. They can be matched with printed copies of the States General's resolutions available at http://resources.huygens.knaw.nl/besluitenstatengeneraal1576-1630.

81. This deposition appears in a number of forms. It was presented first to the States General on November 5 and then handed over in a French translation to English representatives. The French translation is in State Papers, Holland, SP 84/121/1, National Archives, Kew. The deposition was then incorporated into a pamphlet translated into English as *A Remonstrance of the Directors of the Netherlands East India Company Presented to the Lords States Generall of the United Provinces, in Defence of the Said Companie*. The deposition is summarized in Sainsbury, *Calendar of State*

Papers. "Deposition of Laurens Mareschalk, aged about 30, having served as chief merchant or as the chief in Amboyna, and as one of the judges there, taken before the magistrates, &c. of Delft," Sainsbury, *Calendar of State Papers, 1622–1624,* 434–35.

82. Declaration before Govert van Aps, 24 March 1623, NL-HaNA, Staten-Generaal, 1.01.02, inv. no. 12551.62. This is certainly how Coolhaas interprets the move. W. P. Coolhaas, "Aanteekeningen en Opmerkingen over den zoogenaamdem Ambonschen Moord," *Bijdragen tot de Taal-, Land- en Volkenkunde van Nederlandsch-Indie* 101 (1942): 62–63.

83. Jabez Henry, *Report on the Criminal Law at Demerara and in the Ceded Dutch Colonies* (London: Henry Butterworth, 1821), 34.

84. *A Remonstrance of the Directors of the Netherlands East India,* 23. This comes from the English translation of his deposition.

85. *A Remonstrance of the Directors of the Netherlands East India,* 24.

86. *A Remonstrance of the Directors of the Netherlands East India,* 24.

87. *A Remonstrance of the Directors of the Netherlands East India,* 25.

88. *A Remonstrance of the Directors of the Netherlands East India,* 26.

89. Coolhaas, "Aanteekeningen en Opmerkingen over den zoogenaamdem Ambonschen Moord," n. 35. I have found what appears to be a Dutch translation of a letter that purports to be from Towerson to Coulson in the archive of the States General. NL-HaNA, Staten-Generaal, 1.01.02, inv. no. 12551.62. The absence of an original English-language document makes it difficult to give any credence to this document, as does the fact that it was largely ignored by VOC authorities desperate to prove English guilt. At the same time, the contents of the Dutch version are highly ambiguous and do not clearly show the existence of an English plot. If we accept that it is a translation of a genuine document, it was likely written in response to Towerson having been told that Coulson had denounced him in his confession.

90. Extract from resolutions from the States General, 6 May 1626, 23 November 1628, NL-HaNA, VOC 11138. A typical VOC merchant earned around fifty guilders a month or six hundred guilders a year.

91. Extract from resolutions from the States General, 23 April 1632, NL-HaNA, VOC 11138.

92. Depositions, 1625–1626, NL-HaNA, Staten-Generaal, 1.01.02, inv. no. 12551.62. There are multiple depositions contained in this folder, including from Van Leeuwen, Joosten. Teiller, Wyncoop, Crayvanger, and others.

93. The existence of this 1625 declaration has been noted by scholars, but the fact that it came almost completely from De Maerschalk has been missed. Deposition by the governor of Amboina and other officials, 10 September 1625, NL-HaNA, Staten Generaal, 1.01.02, inv. no. 12551.62.

94. Moluccas refers in this case to what is now called North Maluku, that is, Ternate and surrounding area.

95. Deposition and further explanation by Frederick Houtman, NL-HaNA, Staten-Generaal, 1.01.02, inv no. 12551.62.

96. The most common of these was probably the *strappado*, whereby the victim is hoisted up by his or her arms and then dropped, resulting in an agonizing dislocation.

97. Although there is no direct connection, this was in fact the first airing of a defense that would be deployed during the Bush administration to rationalize the authorization of techniques of "enhanced interrogation" used in the aftermath of the September 11 attacks. In August 2002, the White House Office of Legal Counsel released a document, later dubbed "the torture memo," that was designed to provide legal justification for a range of techniques, including waterboarding. For John Yoo and Jay S. Bybee, the memo's authors, the fact that waterboarding inflicted no actual physical harm was crucial. "As we understand it, when the waterboard is used, the subject's body responds as if the subject were drowning— even though the subject may be well aware that he is in fact not drowning. You have informed us that this procedure does not inflict actual physical harm. Thus, although the subject may experience the fear or panic associated with the feeling of drowning, the waterboard does not inflict physical pain." Since waterboarding was a torture of perception, which caused only the "fear or panic associated with the feeling of drowning," it was not comparable to more brutal forms of torture and hence it belonged in a special category all of its own. Jay S. Bybee to Alberto Gonzales, 1 August 2002, in Karen Greenberg and Joshua Dratel, *The Torture Papers: The Road to Abu Ghraib* (New York: Cambridge University Press, 2005), 172–217.

98. Declaration by the bailiff of Batavia, signed by Jan Pietersen Prins, secretary, 7 October 1625, NL-HaNA, Staten-Generaal, 1.01.02, inv. no 12551.62.1.

99. Coolhaas, "Aanteekeningen en Opmerkingen over den zoogenaamdem Ambonschen Moord," 68.

100. State Papers, Holland, SP 84/121/1, National Archives, Kew. Reference to the translation and submission of the document can be found in Extract from resolutions from the States General, 5 November 1624, NL-HaNA, VOC 11138.

101. Sainsbury, *Calendar of State Papers, 1622–1624*, 446–48.

102. The *Remonstrance* does mention the activities of the "Ternatens" on the Hoamoal Peninsula, but only to show that Towerson's plot could have succeeded because he had local allies.

7. Compensation and Calamity

The epigraphs are taken from: Charles Jenkinson, *A Collection of All the Treaties of Peace, Alliance, and Commerce Between Great Britain and Other Powers* (London: J. Debrett, 1785), 65; and "Memorie door Arnold De Vlaming Van Oudshoorn," in *Memories van Overgave van gouverneurs van Ambon in de zeventiende en achttiende eeuw*, ed. Gerrit Knaap, Rijks Geschiedkundige Publicatiën, Kleine Serie 62 (The Hague: Martinus Nijhoff, 1987), 192.

1. Jenkinson, *A Collection of All the Treaties of Peace*, 64.
2. Jenkinson, *A Collection of All the Treaties of Peace*, 47–48.
3. See, for example, Steven Pincus, *Protestantism and Patriotism: Ideologies and the Making of English Foreign Policy, 1650–1668* (Cambridge: Cambridge University Press, 1996).
4. Rumphius is now most famous for his contribution to botany but he also produced a history of Amboina and the Dutch presence there. In part this stemmed from his own participation in the Hoamoalese War. For Rumphius's life and career, including his involvement in this campaign, see Wim Buijze, *Leven en werk van Georg Everhard Rumphius* (The Hague: Boekhandel Couvée, 2006). Rumphius suggests there were six Amboinese wars, beginning in 1618 with the campaign against Houtomori. I follow Knaap in emphasizing the conflicts beginning in 1624. He writes that in order to "enforce the treaties it had concluded, the VOC resorted to violence, which from 1624 until 1658 resulted in a series of armed conflicts, which have been collectively labeled the Amboinese Wars." Gerrit Knaap, "Headhunting, Carnage, and Armed Peace in Amboina, 1500–1700," *Journal of the Economic and Social History of the Orient* 46, no. 2 (2003): 168.
5. Also known as the Great Ambon War. Gerrit Knaap, *Kruidnagelen en Christenen: De Verenigde Oost-Indische Compagnie en de bevolking van Ambon 1656–1696* (Leiden: KITLV, 2004), 29. Hans Hägerdal, *Lords of the Land, Lords of the Sea: Conflict and Adaption in Early Colonial Timor, 1600–1800* (Leiden: KITLV, 2012), 11.
6. Georgius Rumphius, "De Ambonse Historie," *Bijdragen tot de Taal-, Land- en Volkenkunde van Nederlandsch-Indië* 64, no. 1/2 (1910): 2:103.
7. The Hoamoalese War commenced in 1651 but concluded either in 1656 or 1658, depending on whether you include a subsequent campaign in Buru. By the end of this conflict, the VOC had not dispensed with all challengers. Rather, it still had to face Makassar, a significant maritime rival which was eventually defeated in the 1660s.
8. W. N. Sainsbury, ed., *Calendar of State Papers Colonial, East Indies, China and Japan, 1622–1624* (London: H.M.S.O., 1878), 367, 439.
9. J. K. de Jonge and M. L. van Deventer, eds., *De opkomst van het Nederlandsch gezag in Oost Indië* (The Hague: Martius Nijhoff, 1862–1909), 5:xxxvi. This quote comes from a document dated 23 November 1624.
10. Letter to the States General from the *bewindhebbers*, 15 March 1625, NL-HaNA, Staten-Generaal, 1.01.02, inv. no. 12563.14.
11. F. W. Stapel, ed., *Pieter van Dam's Beschryvinge van de Oostindische Compagnie* (The Hague: Martinus Nijhoff, 1927–1954), 2.1:151–52.
12. In his description of Amboina penned in August 1623, Van Speult explained that a significant force would be needed to properly subdue Luhu. Stapel, *Pieter van Dam's Beschryvinge*, 2.1:154.
13. Letter to Van Speult, 26 September 1623, NL-HaNA, VOC 850, 213.
14. P. A. Tiele and J. E. Heeres, eds. *Bouwstoffen voor de geschiedenis der Nederlanders in den Maleischen Archipel* (The Hague: Martinus Nijhoff, 1886–1895), 2:29.
15. Tiele and Heeres, *Bouwstoffen voor de geschiedenis der Nederlanders in den Maleischen Archipel*, 2:29.

16. Governor-general to Van Speult, 4 March, 1625, NL-HaNA, VOC 1085, 41.

17. This section draws from Tristan Mostert's in-progress PhD dissertation at Leiden University currently titled "The Great Spice War: Makassar, the Dutch East India Company and the Struggle for the Clove Trade" and a series of exchanges we had in 2018. I am grateful for his many insights.

18. W. N. Sainsbury, ed., *Calendar of State Papers Colonial, East Indies and Persia, 1625–1629* (London: H.M.S.O., 1884), 689. J. Keuning, "Ambonese, Portuguese and Dutchmen: The History of Ambon to the End of the Seventeenth Century," in *Dutch Authors on Asian History: A Selection of Dutch Historiography on the Verenigde Oostindische Compagnie*, ed. M. A. P. Meilink-Roelofsz, M. E. van Opstall, and G. J. Schutte (Dordrecht: Foris, 1988), 380.

19. Rumphius, "De Ambonse Historie," 1:51.

20. Mostert, "The Great Spice War."

21. Tiele and Heeres, *Bouwstoffen voor de geschiedenis der Nederlanders in den Maleischen Archipel*, 2:49.

22. Tiele and Heeres, *Bouwstoffen voor de geschiedenis der Nederlanders in den Maleischen Archipel*, 2:48.

23. Tiele and Heeres, *Bouwstoffen voor de geschiedenis der Nederlanders in den Maleischen Archipel*, 2:52. Knaap, "Headhunting, Carnage, and Armed Peace in Amboina," 178. Mostert, "The Great Spice War."

24. Tiele and Heeres, *Bouwstoffen voor de geschiedenis der Nederlanders in den Maleischen Archipel*, 2:53.

25. There were multiple ways to destroy clove trees. VOC sources make reference to "peeling" (*schillen*), a method of destroying the tree by cutting the bark around the trunk. This is a process also known as "girdling," which results in the death of the tree. In this case, however, the word used was *omgehouwen*, suggesting the trees were chopped down. I am grateful to Tristan Mostert for this insight.

26. Knaap, "Headhunting, Carnage, and Armed Peace in Amboina," 178.

27. Van Speult had planned to attack other settlements across the Hoamoal Peninsula but was forced to adjust his plans after suffering an unexpected setback on the island of Kelang.

28. De Jonge and Van Deventer, *De Opkomst*, 5.

29. Mostert notes that the plan to depopulate western Seram was clearly already on the table by 1626. Mostert, "The Great Spice War."

30. J. A. van der Chijs, H. T. Colenbrander, and J. de Hullu, eds., *Nederlandsch Indisch plakaatboek, 1602–1811* (Batavia: Landsdrukkerij; The Hague: Martinus Nijhoff, 1885–1900), 1:162. P. Mijer, *Verzameling van Instructiën, Ordonnanciën en Reglementen voor de Regering van Nederlandsch Indië* (Batavia, 1848), 50.

31. Letter from Herman van Speult in Cambello to Governor-General Pieter de Carpentier, 15 May 1624, NL-HaNA, VOC 1083, 338v.

32. Particular letter to the governor, Herman van Speult, 5 August 1625, NL-HaNA, VOC 853, 123–24v.

33. See comments to this effect from George Forbes. There is ample reason to believe that this fear was widely shared by the Amboina judges. Sainsbury, *Calendar of State Papers, 1625–1629*, 411–12.

34. Particular letter to the governor, Herman van Speult, 5 August 1625, NL-HaNA, VOC 853, 123–24v.

35. Sainsbury, *Calendar of State Papers, 1625–1629*, 418.

36. Stapel, *Pieter van Dam's Beschryvinge*, 2.1:136.

37. Further interrogation of Vincent Cortals, March 1628, NL-HaNA, Staten-Generaal, 1.01.02, inv. no. 12551.62. Cortals's description is vague at best but it does seem to suggest that Van Speult was unaware of the summons.

38. Sainsbury, *Calendar of State Papers, 1625–1629*, 32.

39. Sainsbury, *Calendar of State Papers, 1625–1629*, 53. The East India Company's directions for stay of the Holland ships outward bound, 8 April 1625, Colonial Office Series, CO 77/3/72, National Archives, Kew.

40. Sainsbury, *Calendar of State Papers, 1625–1629*, 54.

41. For a detailed description of this period, see Rupali Mishra, *A Business of State: Commerce, Politics, and the Birth of the East India Company* (Cambridge, MA: Harvard University Press, 2018), 244–55.

42. Sainsbury, *Calendar of State Papers, 1625–1629*, 78.

43. Anton Poot, *Crucial Years in Anglo-Dutch Relations (1625–1642): The Political and Diplomatic Contacts* (Hilversum: Verloren, 2013), 32.

44. Quoted in Poot, *Crucial Years in Anglo-Dutch Relations*, 34.

45. W. P. Coolhaas, "Aanteekeningen en Opmerkingen over den zoogenaamdem Ambonschen Moord," *Bijdragen tot de Taal-, Land- en Volkenkunde van Nederlandsch-Indie* 101 (1942): 70. For the names of the judges, see Sainsbury, *Calendar of State Papers, 1625–1629*, 393.

46. These were Herman Crayvanger, Laurens de Maerschalk, Jan van Leeuwen, Jan Jacobsen Wyncoop, Jan Joosten, Jacob Coper, Jan van Nieupoort, Pieter van Santen, Rolant Tailler, and Vincent Cortals. Multiple variations of their names appear in the records. By 1628, they had all reached the United Provinces.

47. J. A. Worp, "Jan de Brune de Jonge," *Oud-Holland* 8 (1890): 86.

48. Heeren 17 to governor-general, 10 August 1627, NL-HaNA, VOC 315.

49. Sainsbury, *Calendar of State Papers, 1625–1629*, 394.

50. Sainsbury, *Calendar of State Papers, 1625–1629*, 399–401.

51. Extract from resolutions from the States General, 2 October 1627, NL-HaNA, VOC 11138. Karen Chancey, "The Amboyna Massacre in English Politics, 1624–1632," *Albion* 30, no. 4 (1998): 595. He appears frequently as *fiscael* Sylla.

52. Extract from resolutions from the States General, 15 October 1627, NL-HaNA, VOC 11138.

53. They can be found in NL-HaNA, Staten-Generaal, 1.01.02, inv. no. 12551.62.

54. The Dutch versions are available in NL-HaNA, Staten-Generaal 1.01.02, inv. no. 12551.62. The English translations can be found in BL IOR, G/21/2, pt. 3.

55. Extract from resolutions from the States General, 10 February 1628, NL-HaNA, VOC 11138.

56. Sainsbury, *Calendar of State Papers, 1625–1629*, 495.

57. Extract from resolutions from the States General, 30 April 1630, NL-HaNA, VOC 11138. Sainsbury, *Calendar of State Papers, 1625–1629*, 474.

58. Sainsbury, *Calendar of State Papers, 1625–1629*, 349.

59. Court minutes, 16 July 1628, BL IOR, B/13.

60. Sainsbury, *Calendar of State Papers, 1625–1629,* 542.

61. Sainsbury, *Calendar of State Papers, 1625–1629,* 555.

62. Court minutes, 1 October 1628, BL IOR, B/13. It is difficult to know if a bribe was actually paid. Charles was short of funds and in 1626 he had pawned part of his crown jewels in return for a loan of 58,400 pounds. We also know that there were in fact negotiations connecting these jewels with VOC demands to release their ships. The key figure was Josias de Vosberghen, who was described as an agent for the king of Denmark and appears regularly in the resolutions of the States General. We cannot be certain, however, if it was these negotiations that eventually produced the release of the vessels. Steensgaard notes the correspondence "gives the impression that the release of the ships was not gratis for the Dutch Company, but that it was the King himself who pocketed the proceeds." Niels Steensgaard, *Carracks, Caravans, and Companies: The Structural Crisis in the European-Asian Trade in the Early 17th Century* (Copenhagen: Studentlitteratur, 1973), 120.

63. W. N. Sainsbury, ed., *Calendar of State Papers Colonial, East Indies and Persia, 1630–1634* (London: H.M.S.O., 1892), 43.

64. Coolhaas, "Aanteekeningen en Opmerkingen," 215.

65. *Bloudy Newes from the East-Indies: Being a True Relation, and Perfect Abstract of the Cruel, Barbarous, and Inhumane Proceedings of the Dutch-Men Against the English at Amboyna* (London: printed for George Horton, 1651).

66. *Engelsche-duymdrayery, ofte 't geen de Oost-Indische Compagnie in Nederland, van de Engelsche word nageseyd, aengaende de torture, die de conspirateurs in Amboyna* (Amsterdam, 1652).

67. Jenkinson, *A Collection of All the Treaties of Peace,* 47.

68. Jenkinson, *A Collection of All the Treaties of Peace,* 64.

69. Gerrit Knaap has written widely on this period, including his foundational work, *Kruidnagelen en Christenen.* See also Keuning, "Ambonese, Portuguese and Dutchmen." Hans Straver, Chris van Fraassen, and Jan van der Putten, *Ridjali Historie van Hitu: Een Ambonse geschiedenis uit de zeventiende eeuw* (Utrecht: Landelijk Steunpunt Educatie Molukkers, 2004). Carl Fredrik Feddersen, *Principled Pragmatism: VOC Interaction with Makassar 1637–68, and the Nature of Company Diplomacy* (Oslo: Nordic Open Access Scholarly Publishing, 2017). I am grateful for the comments of the anonymous readers for significantly improving this section.

70. Knaap, *Kruidnagelen en Christenen,* 27.

71. Seys, "Verhael van den tegenwoordigen state," in Isaac Commelin, *Begin ende Voortgangh van de Vereenighde Nederlantsche Geoctroyeerde Oost-Indische Compagnie.* (1646). This is the spelling that appears in the text, but other references are to Gillis van Zeys or Gillis Seijst.

72. Seys, "Verhael van den tegenwoordigen state," 140.

73. Seys, "Verhael van den tegenwoordigen state," 142. Seys's focus was on Hitu, where he believed a population of loyal VOC subjects could be most helpful to the Company.

74. Not everyone in the Company believed that such tactics would secure control over Amboina. As this section argues, it was only the particular circumstances of

the Hoamoalese War, coupled with Arnold de Vlaming van Oudtshoorn's belief in the need for aggressive tactics, that pushed the Company to finally embrace this strategy.

75. Rolle der soldaten ende offijcieren guarnisoen houdendende tot besetting van 't Casteel Amboijna ende omleggende quartieren, adij 15 September 1631, NL-HaNA, VOC 1100, 313–18.

76. See also Iwao Seiichi, *Zoku Nanyō Nihon machi no kenkyū: Nanyō tōsho chiiki bunsan Nihonjin imin no seikatsu to katsudō* (Tokyo: Iwanami Shoten, 1987), 260.

77. Seys, "Verhael van den tegenwoordigen state," 144.

78. Gerrit Knaap, "Crisis and Failure: War and Revolt in the Ambon Islands, 1636–1637." *Cakalele* 3 (1992): 7.

79. Mostert notes that the size of the *hongi* fleet can be seen as an important yardstick for VOC power. Mostert, "The Great Spice War."

80. Gerrit Knaap, "The Governor-General and the Sultan: An Attempt to Restructure a Divided Amboina in 1638," *Itinerario* 29, no. 1 (2005): 81; Knaap, "Crisis and Failure," 17–18; Keuning, "Ambonese, Portuguese and Dutchmen," 384–85.

81. Knaap, "Crisis and Failure," 1.

82. Knaap, "The Governor-General and the Sultan," 81. Knaap, "Crisis and Failure," 18. Similar ceremonies played out in Taiwan. Tonio Andrade, "Political Spectacle and Colonial Rule: The Landdag on Dutch Taiwan, 1629–1648," *Itinerario* 21, no. 3 (1997): 57–93.

83. For an invaluable resource on Hitu and this conflict, see Straver, Fraassen, and Putten, *Ridjali: Historie van Hitu.*

84. M. E. van Opstall, "Laurens Reael in de Staten-Generaal: Het verslag van Reael over de toestand in Oost-Indië anno 1620," in *Nederlandse historische bronnen*, ed. A. C. F. Koch et al., vol. 1 (The Hague, 1979–2002), 194.

85. Gerrit Knaap, "De Ambonse eilanden tussen twee mogendheden; De VOC en Ternate, 1605–1656," in *Hof en Handel; Aziatische vorsten en de VOC 1620–1720*, ed. Elsbeth Locher-Scholten and Peter Rietbergen (Leiden: KITLV, 2004), 46.

86. Gerrit Knaap, "Crisis and Failure," 4.

87. Knaap, "Headhunting, Carnage, and Armed Peace in Amboina," 174. Such treaties were signed by the leaders of Hitu including *kapitan Hitu.*

88. J. E. Heeres and F. W. Stapel, eds., *Corpus Diplomaticum Neerlando-Indicum* (The Hague: Martinus Nijhoff, 1907–1955), 1:31–32.

89. W. P. Coolhaas, J. van Goor, J E Schooneveld-Oosterling and H. K. s'Jacob, eds., *Generale Missiven van Gouverneurs-Generaal en Raden aan Heren XVII der Verenigde Oost-Indische Compagnie* (The Hague: Martinus Nijhoff, 1960–2007), 1:218.

90. Keuning, "Ambonese, Portuguese and Dutchmen," 386–87.

91. Jennifer Gaynor, *Intertidal History in Island Southeast Asia: Submerged Genealogies and the Legacy of Coastal Capture* (Ithaca, NY: Cornell University Press, 2016), 81. Knaap, "Headhunting, Carnage, and Armed Peace in Amboina," 178.

92. Knaap writes that "this was the end of Hitu as an independent political unit." Knaap, "The Governor-General and the Sultan," 94. Keuning, "Ambonese, Portuguese and Dutchmen," 390.

93. Bassett argues that the VOC had essentially achieved its monopoly over cloves by 1643. D. K. Bassett, "English Trade in Celebes, 1613–1667," *Journal of the Malayan Branch of the Royal Asiatic Society* 31, no. 1 (1958): 15. See also Knaap, *Kruidnagelen en Christenen*, 28; Knaap, "De Ambonse eilanden tussen twee mogendheden," 51; Feddersen, *Principled Pragmatism*, 31.

94. Knaap notes that the Company made use of a "tactic of destruction" (*vernietigingstactiek*). Knaap, *Kruidnagelen en Christenen*, 34.

95. Stapel, *Pieter van Dam's Beschryvinge*, 2.1:119.

96. Also written as Sultan Mandar Syah. Leonard Andaya, *The World of Maluku: Eastern Indonesia in the Early Modern Period* (Honolulu: University of Hawaii Press, 1993), 163.

97. For the *kimelaha's* independent power base on Hoamoal, see Andaya, *The World of Maluku*, 160.

98. Knaap, "De Ambonse eilanden tussen twee mogendheden," 54; Straver, Fraassen, and Putten, *Ridjali: Historie van Hitu*, 66.

99. It is worth noting, as Andaya does, that Makassar had itself been strengthened by the arrival of Bandanese refugees in the aftermath of Coen's conquest of Banda. Andaya, *The World of Maluku*, 164.

100. L. Bor, *Amboinse oorlogen, door Arnold de Vlaming van Oudshoorn als superintendent over d'Oosterse gewesten oorlogaftig ten eind gebracht* (Delft, 1663), 55–56.

101. Bor, *Amboinse oorlogen*, 55. For a different metric, see J. Collins, "Language Death in Maluku: The impact of the VOC," *Bijdragen tot de Taal-, Land- en Volkenkunde* 159, no. 2/3 (2003): 247–89.

102. Rumphius, "De Ambonse Historie," 2:11, 2:17.

103. Rumphius, "De Ambonse Historie," 2:22.

104. Rumphius, "De Ambonse Historie," 2:18; Knaap, *Kruidnagelen en Christenen*, 34.

105. Heeres and Stapel, *Corpus Diplomaticum*, 2:38; Knaap, "De Ambonse eilanden tussen twee mogendheden," 54.

106. Knaap, "Headhunting, Carnage and Armed Peace in Amboina," 180–81.

107. Jenkinson, *A Collection of All the Treaties of Peace*, 64.

108. Rumphius, "De Ambonse Historie," 2:79.

109. Bor, *Amboinse oorlogen*, 289.

110. "Memorie door Arnold De Vlaming Van Oudshoorn," 192. Knaap, *Kruidnagelen en Christenen*, 214. One account of one of De Vlaming's operations notes that "an uncountable number of sagu and clappus trees as well as 3000 clove trees were destroyed." Rumphius, "De Ambonse Historie," 2:42.

111. Gaynor, *Intertidal History*, 91. Gaynor has provided an excellent description of this campaign.

112. "Memorie door Arnold De Vlaming Van Oudshoorn," 189.

113. In his landmark study, Knaap cautions us not to overestimate the rupture of the VOC period. He points to continuities that persisted across this long period in Amboinese society. Knaap, *Kruidnagelen en Christenen*, 336.

114. Keuning suggests that 12,000 people were relocated. See Keuning, "Ambonese, Portuguese and Dutchmen," 393.

115. Rumphius, "De Ambonse Historie," 2:103.

116. Van Dam lists a population of 40,238 people in 1668. Stapel, *Pieter van Dam's Beschryvinge*, 2.1:133. Knaap estimates a total population of 76,000–80,000 in 1634 and 49,168 in 1671 (*Kruidnagelen en Christenen*, 129). Knaap suggests a total decline of around 30 percent of the population in the western part of Amboina ("Head-hunting, Carnage and Armed Peace in Amboina," 190).

117. Gerrit Knaap, "The Demography of Ambon in the Seventeenth Century: Evidence from Colonial Proto-Censuses," *Journal of Southeast Asian Studies* 26, no. 2 (1995): 238–39.

118. Knaap, *Kruidnagelen en Christenen*, 297.

119. "Memorie door Arnold De Vlaming Van Oudshoorn," 192.

120. *The Emblem of Ingratitude: A True Relation of the Unjust, Cruel, and Barbarous Proceedings Against the English at Amboyna in the East-Indies, by the Netherlandish Governour & Council There: Also a Farther Account of the Deceit, Cruelty, and Tyranny of the Dutch Against the English, and Several others, from Their First to Their Present Estate, with Remarks upon the Whole Matter: Faithfully Collected from Antient and Modern Records* (London: printed for William Hope, 1672).

121. Quoted in Robert Markley, "Violence and Profits on the Restoration Stage: Trade, Nationalism, and Insecurity in Dryden's Amboyna," *Eighteenth-Century Life* 22, no. 1 (1998): 2–17.

122. Rumphius, "De Ambonse Historie," 1:199. Rumphius was describing as well the effects of an earlier campaign led by Gerrit Demmer.

123. Keuning, "Ambonese, Portuguese and Dutchmen," 393.

124. Knaap argues that VOC control rested on four interlocking elements: military dominance, the establishment of the population in places that could be easily controlled, the exploitation of indigenous divisions, and the building of some degree of consensus with VOC subjects. Knaap, *Kruidnagelen en Christenen*, 37.

125. Knaap describes a "Pax Neerlandica" that was "based on fear rather than affection for the colonial overlords." Knaap, "Headhunting, Carnage and Armed Peace in Amboina," 181.

Epilogue: The Fearful Empire

1. For the most widely read account, see Giles Milton, *Nathaniel's Nutmeg* (London: Hodder & Stoughton, 1999). As dicussed earlier, this version is confined primarily to English-language scholarship.

2. Jonathan Israel, *Dutch Primacy in World Trade, 1585–1740* (Oxford: Clarendon Press, 2002).

3. Kees Zandvliet, ed., *The Dutch Encounter with Asia, 1600–1950* (Zwolle: Waanders, 2002), 181–82.

4. W. P. Coolhaas, "Aanteekeningen en Opmerkingen over den zoogenaamdem Ambonschen Moord," *Bijdragen tot de Taal-, Land- en Volkenkunde van Nederlandsch-Indie* 101 (1942): 55.

5. J. K. de Jonge and M. L. van Deventer, eds., *De opkomst van het Nederlandsch gezag in Oost Indië* (The Hague: Martius Nijhoff, 1862–1909), 1:87.

6. Reinkowski and Thum argue that the "feeling of 'helplessness' was a significant part of the imperial experience." Maurus Reinkowski and Gregor Thum, "Helpless Imperialists: Introduction," in *Helpless Imperialists: Imperial Failure, Fear and Radicalization*, ed. Reinkowski and Thum (Göttingen: Vandenhoeck & Ruprecht, 2012), 8.

7. At its extreme end, in places like Taiwan, this created a degree of interdependency that Tonio Andrade labels as co-colonization. Andrade, *How Taiwan Became Chinese: Dutch, Spanish, and Han Colonization in the Seventeenth Century* (New York: Columbia University Press, 2008). He argues that there should be no assumption that the "Dutch and Chinese were equal partners in the colony."

8. For an analysis, see Jean Gelman Taylor, "Painted Ladies of the VOC," *South African Historical Journal* 59, no 1 (2007): 47–78.

9. It was an accurate reflection of a city that visitors described as crammed with "inhabitants . . . of all Nations" living alongside a small section of European officials and settlers. Christopher Frick and Christoph Schweitzer, *A Relation of Two Several Voyages Made into the East-Indies* (London, 1700), 35.

10. Victor Enthoven, "Jan Pietersz. Coen: A Man They Love to Hate. The First Governor-General of Dutch East Indies as an Imperial Site of Memory," in *Sites of Imperial Memory: Commemorating Colonial Rule in the Nineteenth and Twentieth Centuries*, ed. Dominik Geppert and Frank Lorenz Müller (Manchester: Manchester University Press, 2015), 115.

Selected Bibliography

Archives

Note: Due to space constraints here, individual archival records, particularly VOC letters and resolutions, are cited in full in the notes.

Nationaal Archief, The Hague (NL-HaNA)

De archieven van de Verenigde Oostindische Compagnie (VOC), access number 1.04.02

Nationaal Archief, The Hague (NL-HaNA)

Archief van de Staten-Generaal, (1431) 1576–1796), access number 1.01.02
   12551.62 Stukken betreffende de bemoeiingen van de Staten-Generaal met de procedures tegen de Engelsen op Amboina in 1623
   12563.13 Proces Engelsen op Amboina, 1623–1629
   12563.14 Stukken betreffende de bemoeiingen van de Staten-Generaal met de geschillen tussen de V.O.C. en de Engelsen op Amboina, 1623–1629
   12563.18 Stukken betreffende de bemoeiingen van de Staten-Generaal met de geschillen tussen de V.O.C. en de Engelse Oost-Indische Compagnie, 1629–1640. Met retroacta, 1616–1637

National Archives (formerly Public Record Office), Kew

Colonial Office Series
   CO 77 East Indies
State Papers Domestic
   SP 14 Jacobean
State Papers Foreign
   SP 84 Holland

British Library, London (BL)

Asia, Pacific, and Africa Collections (formerly Oriental and India Office Collections)
India Office Records (IOR) Court Minutes, B series
   B/8 Court Book 6, July 1623 to June 1624
   B/9 Court Book 7, July 1624 to April 1625
   B/10 Court Book 8, April 1625 to June 1626
   B/11 Court Book 9, July 1626 to July 1627
   B/12 Court Book 10, July 1627 to July 1628
   B/13 Court Book 11, July 1628 to July 1629
IOR East India Company: General Correspondence 1602–1859, E Series.
   E/3/10, 1623–1625
Factory Records: Java (G/21)
   G/21/2, Parts 1–4: The controversies between the English and Dutch Companies,
     1618–1654
   G/21/3A Java Factory Records, 1613–1623

Printed Sources

Adams, Julia. "Trading States, Trading Places: The Role of Patrimonialism in Early Modern Dutch Development." *Comparative Studies in Society and History* 36, no. 2 (1994): 319–55.

Allen, Richard. *European Slave Trading in the Indian Ocean, 1500–1850.* Athens: Ohio University Press, 2014.

Andaya, Leonard. *The Heritage of Arung Palakka: A History of South Sulawesi (Celebes) in the Seventeenth Century.* The Hague: Martinus Nijhoff, 1981.

——. "Treaty Conceptions and Misconceptions: A Case Study from South Sulawesi." *Bijdragen tot de taal-, land- en volkenkunde* 134/2, no. 3 (1978): 275–95.

——. *The World of Maluku: Eastern Indonesia in the Early Modern Period.* Honolulu: University of Hawaii Press, 1993.

Andrade, Tonio. "Beyond Guns, Germs, and Steel: European Expansion and Maritime Asia, 1400–1750." *Journal of Early Modern History* 14 (2010): 165–86.

——. *How Taiwan Became Chinese: Dutch, Spanish, and Han Colonization in the Seventeenth Century*. New York: Columbia University Press, 2008.

——. *Lost Colony: The Untold Story of China's First Great Victory Over the West*. Princeton, NJ: Princeton University Press, 2011.

——. "Political Spectacle and Colonial Rule: The Landdag on Dutch Taiwan, 1629–1648." *Itinerario* 21, no. 3 (1997): 57–93.

Anghie, Anthony. "Francisco de Vitoria and the Colonial Origins of International Law." *Social and Legal Studies* 5, no. 3 (1996): 321–36.

——. *Imperialism, Sovereignty and the Making of International Law*. Cambridge: Cambridge University Press, 2005.

Antunes, Cátia, and Jos Gommans, eds. *Exploring the Dutch Empire: Agents, Networks and Institutions 1600–2000*. London: Bloomsbury Academic, 2015.

Aveling, H. "Seventeenth-Century Bandanese Society." *Bijdragen tot de Taal-, Land- en Volkenkunde* 123, no. 3 (1967): 347–65.

Baker, Brett. "Indigenous-Driven Mission: Reconstructing Religious Change in Sixteenth-Century Maluku." PhD diss., Australian National University, 2014.

Baker, Chris, Dhiravat na Pombejra, Alfons van der Kraan, and David Wyatt. *Van Vliet's Siam*. Chiang Mai: Silkworm Books, 2005.

Ball, John. *Indonesian Legal History, 1602–1848*. Sydney: Oughtershaw Press, 1982.

Barendse, Rene. *The Arabian Seas, 1640–1700*. Leiden: CNWS, 1998.

Bassett, D. K. "The 'Amboyna Massacre' of 1623." *Journal of Southeast Asian History* 1, no. 2 (1960): 1–19.

——. "English Trade in Celebes, 1613–1667." *Journal of the Malayan Branch of the Royal Asiatic Society* 31, no. 1 (1958): 1–39.

——. "The Factory of the English East India Company at Bantam, 1602–1682." PhD diss., University of London, 1955.

Benton, Lauren, Adam Clulow, and Bain Attwood, eds. *Protection and Empire: A Global History*. Cambridge: Cambridge University Press, 2017.

Blair, Emma, and James Robertson, eds. *The Philippine Islands, 1493–1898*. 55 vols. Cleveland, OH: A. H. Clark, 1902–1909.

Bloudy Newes from the East-Indies: Being a True Relation, and Perfect Abstract of the Cruel, Barbarous, and Inhumane Proceedings of the Dutch-Men Against the English at Amboyna. London: printed for George Horton, 1651.

Blussé, Leonard. "Batavia, 1619–1740: The Rise and Fall of a Chinese Colonial Town." *Journal of Southeast Asian Studies* 12, no. 1 (1981): 159–78.

——. "Bull in a China Shop: Pieter Nuyts in China and Japan (1627–1636)." In *Around and About Formosa, Essays in Honor of Professor Ts'ao Yung-ho*, ed. Leonard Blussé, 95–110. Taipei: SMC, 2003.

——. "Nevenactiviteiten overzee: Valckenier en Van Imhoff en de Chinezenmoord van 1740." In *Reizen door het maritieme verleden van Nederland*, ed. Anita van Dissel, Maurits Ebben, and Karwan Fatah-Black, 272–92. Zutphen: Walburg Pers, 2015.

——. *Strange Company: Chinese Settlers, Mestizo Women and the Dutch in VOC Batavia*. Dordrecht: Foris, 1986.

Bollingii, Friderici. "Friderici Bollingii Oost-Indisch reisboek." Trans. J. Visscher. *Bijdragen tot de Taal-, Land- en Volkenkunde van Nederlandsch Indië* 68 (1913): 331.

Boomgaard, Peter. "Human Capital, Slavery, and Low Rates of Economic and Population Growth." *Slavery & Abolition* 24, no. 2 (2003): 83–96.

Bor, L. *Amboinse oorlogen, door Arnold de Vlaming van Oudshoorn als superintendent over d'Oosterse gewesten oorlogaftig ten eind gebracht.* Delft, 1663.

Borschberg, Peter. *Hugo Grotius, the Portuguese, and Free Trade in the East Indies.* Singapore: NUS Press, 2011.

———. *Journal, Memorial, and Letters of Cornelis Matelieff de Jong: Security, Diplomacy, and Commerce in 17th-Century Southeast Asia.* Singapore: NUS Press, 2015.

Botha, C. G. "Criminal Procedure at the Cape During the 17th and 18th Centuries," *South African Law Journal* 32 (1915): 322–43.

Boxer, C. R. *The Dutch Seaborne Empire 1600–1800.* London: Penguin, 1965.

Brants, C. "Legal Culture and Legal Transplants." *Electronic Journal of Comparative Law* 14, no. 3 (December 2010). http://www.ejcl.org/143/art143–5.pdf.

Brown, Stephen. *Merchant Kings: When Companies Ruled the World, 1600–1900.* New York: Thomas Dunne Books, 2010.

Bruijn, Iris. *Ship's Surgeons of the Dutch East India Company: Commerce and the Progress of Medicine in the Eighteenth Century.* Leiden: Leiden University Press, 2009.

Buijze, Wim. *Leven en werk van Georg Everhard Rumphius.* The Hague: Boekhandel Couvée, 2006.

Burnard, Trevor. *Mastery, Tyranny, and Desire: Thomas Thistlewood and His Slaves in the Anglo-Jamaican World.* Chapel Hill: University of North Carolina Press, 2004.

Burnell, Arthur Coke, and P. A. Tiele, eds. *The voyage of John Huyghen van Linschoten to the East Indies.* 2 vols. London: Hakluyt Society, 1885.

Caron, Francois, and Joost Schouten. *A True Description of the Mighty Kingdoms of Japan and Siam.* London, 1663.

Chancey, Karen. "The Amboyna Massacre in English Politics, 1624–1632." *Albion* 30, no. 4 (1998): 583–98.

Chaudhuri, K. N. *The English East India Company: The Study of an Early Joint-Stock Company.* London: Frank Cass, 1965.

Chijs, J. A van der. *De vestiging van het Nederlandsche Gezag over de Banda eilanden, 1599–1621.* Batavia, 1886.

———. *Geschiedenis der stichting van de Vereenigde O.I. Compagnie.* Leiden: P. Engels, 1857.

———. "Kapitein Jonker, 1630?–1689." *Tijdschrift voor Indische Taal-, Land- en Volkenkunde uitgegeven door het Bataviaasch Genootschap van Kunsten en Wetenschappen* 28 (1883): 378.

———, ed. *Nederlandsch Indisch plakaatboek, 1602–1811.* 17 vols. Batavia: Landsdrukkerij; The Hague: Martinus Nijhoff, 1885–1900.

Chijs, J. A. van der, H. T. Colenbrander, and J. de Hullu, eds. *Dagh-register gehouden int Casteel Batavia vant passerende daer ter plaetse als over geheel Nederlandts-India.* 31 vols. Batavia: Landsdrukkerij; The Hague: Martinus Nijhoff, 1887–1931.

Chŏng-dŏk, Hwang, Chin-sun To, and Yun-sang Yi. *Imjin Waeran Kwa Hirado Mik'awach'i Sagijang: Segyejŏk Pomul ŭl Pijŭn P'irap Chosŏn Sagijang ŭl Ch'ajasŏ* [The Imjin Wars and captive Korean potters at Mikawachi, Hirado]. Sŏul-si: Tongbuga Yŏksa Chaedan, 2010.

Clulow, Adam. "The Art of Claiming: Possession and Resistance in Early Modern Asia." *American Historical Review* 121, no. 1 (2016): 17–38.

——. *The Company and the Shogun: The Dutch Encounter with Tokugawa Japan.* New York: Columbia University Press, 2014.

——. "Like Lambs in Japan and Devils Outside Their Land: Violence, Law and Japanese Merchants in Southeast Asia." *Journal of World History* 24, no. 2 (2013): 335–58.

——. "Unjust, Cruel and Barbarous Proceedings: Japanese Mercenaries and the Amboyna Incident of 1623." *Itinerario* 31, no. 1 (2007): 15–34.

Clulow, Adam, and Tristan Mostert, eds. *The Dutch and English East India Companies: Diplomacy, Trade and Violence in Early Modern Asia.* Amsterdam: Amsterdam University Press, 2018.

Cocks, Richard. *Diary Kept by the Head of the English Factory in Japan: Diary of Richard Cocks, 1615–1622.* Tokyo: University of Tokyo, 1980.

Colenbrander, H. T., and W. P. Coolhaas, eds. *Jan Pieterszoon Coen: Bescheiden Omtrent Zijn Bedrijf in Indië.* 9 vols. The Hague: Martinus Nijhoff, 1919–1954.

Collins, James. "Language Death in Maluku: The Impact of the VOC." *Bijdragen tot de Taal-, Land- en Volkenkunde* 159, no. 2/3 (2003): 247–89.

Collins, James, and Timo Kaartinen. "Preliminary Notes on Bandanese Language Maintenance and Change in Kei." *Bijdragen tot de Taal-, Land- en Volkenkunde* 154, no. 4 (1998): 521–70.

Commelin, Isaac, ed. *Begin ende Voortgangh van de Vereenighde Nederlantsche Geoctroyeerde Oost-Indische Compagnie.* 4 vols. 1646.

Condos, Mark. *The Insecurity State: Punjab and the Making of Colonial Power in British India.* Cambridge: Cambridge University Press, 2017.

Coolhaas, W. P. "Aanteekeningen en Opmerkingen over den zoogenaamdem Ambonschen Moord." *Bijdragen tot de Taal-, Land- en Volkenkunde van Nederlandsch-Indie* 101 (1942): 49–93.

Coolhaas, W. P., J. van Goor, J. E. Schooneveld-Oosterling, and H. K. s' Jacob, eds. *Generale Missiven van Gouverneurs-Generaal en Raden aan Heren XVII der Verenigde Oost-Indische Compagnie.* 13 vols. The Hague: Martinus Nijhoff, 1960–2007.

Coward, Barry, and Julian Swann, eds. *Conspiracies and Conspiracy Theory in Early Modern Europe: From the Waldensians to the French Revolution.* Aldershot: Ashgate, 2004.

Cushman, Richard, trans. *The Royal Chronicles of Ayutthaya: A Synoptic Translation.* Bangkok: Siam Society, 2000.

Dam, Pieter van. *Beschrijvinge van de Oostindishe Compagnie.* Ed. F. W. Stapel. The Hague: Rijksgeschiedkundige Publicatiën, 7 vols. 1927–1954.

Danvers, F. C., and W. Foster. *Letters Received by the East India Company from Its Servants in the East.* 6 vols. London: S. Low, Marston, 1896–1902.

Davis, Natalie Zemon. "Judges, Masters, Diviners: Slaves' Experience of Criminal Justice in Colonial Suriname." *Law and History Review* 29, no. 4 (2011): 925–84.

De Bary, W. Theodore, Carol Gluck, and Arthur Tiedemann, eds. *Sources of Japanese Tradition: Volume 2, 1600 to 2000.* New York: Columbia University Press, 2005.

Delumeau, Jean. *La peur en Occident, XIVe–XVIIIe siècles: La cité assiégée.* Paris: Fayard, 1978.

Dryden, John. "Amboyna, or the Cruelties of the Dutch to the English Merchants: A Tragedy." In *The Works of John Dryden*, ed. Vinton Dearing, vol. 12. Berkeley: University of California Press, 1994.

The Emblem of Ingratitude: A True Relation of the Unjust, Cruel, and Barbarous Proceedings Against the English at Amboyna in the East-Indies, by the Netherlandish Governour & Council There: Also a Farther Account of the Deceit, Cruelty, and Tyranny of the Dutch Against the English, and Several others, from Their First to Their Present Estate, with Remarks upon the Whole Matter: Faithfully Collected from Antient and Modern Records. London: printed for William Hope, 1672.

Engelsche-duymdrayery, ofte 't geen de Oost-Indische Compagnie in Nederland, van de Engelsche word nageseyd, aengaende de torture, die de conspirateurs in Amboyna. Amsterdam, 1652.

Enthoven, Victor. "Jan Pietersz. Coen: A Man They Love to Hate. The First Governor-General of Dutch East Indies as an Imperial Site of Memory." In *Sites of Imperial Memory: Commemorating Colonial Rule in the Nineteenth and Twentieth Centuries*, ed. Dominik Geppert and Frank Lorenz Müller, 115–35. Manchester: Manchester University Press, 2015.

Farrington, Anthony. *The English Factory in Japan, 1613–1623.* London: British Library, 1991.

Feddersen, Carl Fredrik. *Principled Pragmatism: VOC Interaction with Makassar 1637–68, and the Nature of Company Diplomacy.* Oslo: Nordic Open Access Scholarly Publishing, 2017.

Floris, Peter. *His Voyage to the East Indies in the Globe, 1611–1615.* Ed. W. H. Moreland. London: Hakluyt Society, 1934.

Foster, William, ed. *The Journal of John Jourdain (1608–1617), Describing His Experiences in Arabia, India and the Malay Archipelago.* London: Hakluyt Society, 1905.

Frick, Christoph, and Christoph Schweitzer. *A Relation of Two Several Voyages Made Into the East-Indies.* London, 1700.

Furber, Holden. *Rival Empires of Trade in the Orient, 1600–1800.* Minneapolis: University of Minnesota Press, 1976.

Furnivall, J. S. *Netherlands India: A Study of Plural Economy.* Cambridge: Cambridge University Press, 1939.

Gaastra, Femme. *The Dutch East India Company: Expansion and Decline.* Zutphen: Walburg Pers, 2003.

Games, Alison. "Anglo-Dutch Connections and Overseas Enterprises: A Global Perspective on Lion Gardiner's World." *Early American Studies* 9, no. 2. (2011): 435–61.

——. "Violence on the Fringes: The Virginia (1622) and Amboyna (1623) Massacres." *History* 99, no. 336 (2014): 505–29.

Gaynor, Jennifer. *Intertidal History in Island Southeast Asia: Submerged Genealogies and the Legacy of Coastal Capture.* Ithaca, NY: Cornell University Press, 2016.

Gelderblom, Oscar, Abe de Jong, and Joost Jonker. "The Formative Years of the Modern Corporation: The Dutch East India Company VOC, 1602–1623." *Journal of Economic History* 73, no. 4 (2013): 1050–76.

Gijsels, Artus. "Grondig Verhaal van Amboyna." *Kroniek van het Historisch Genootschap Gevestigd te Utrecht* 6, no. 2 (1871): 348–496.

Gilroy, Paul. *After Empire: Melancholia or Convivial Culture?* Abingdon: Routledge, 2004.

Goor, Jur van. "A Hybrid State: The Dutch Economic and Political Network in Asia." In *From the Mediterranean to the China Sea: Miscellaneous Notes*, ed. C. Guillot, D. Lombard, and R. Ptak, 192–214. Wiesbaden, Harrassowitz Verlag, 1998.

———. *Jan Pieterszoon Coen, 1587–1629: Koopman-Koning in Azië*. Amsterdam: Boom Publishers, 2015.

Graaf, Nicolaas de. *Reisen en Oost-Indise Spiegel*. 1701.

Green, Tobias. "Fear and Atlantic History." *Atlantic Studies* 3, no. 1 (2006): 25–42.

Greenberg, Karen, and Joshua Dratel. *The Torture Papers: The Road to Abu Ghraib*. New York: Cambridge University Press, 2005.

Grotius, Hugo. *Commentary on the Law of Prize and Booty*. Ed. Martine Julia van Ittersum. Indianapolis, IN: Liberty Fund, 2006.

Guha, Ranajit. "Not at Home in Empire." *Critical Inquiry* 23, no. 3 (1997): 482–93.

Hägerdal, Hans. *Lords of the Land, Lords of the Sea: Conflict and Adaption in Early Colonial Timor, 1600–1800*. Leiden: KITLV Press, 2012.

Hanna, Williard. *Indonesian Banda: Colonialism and Its Aftermath in the Nutmeg Islands*. Philadelphia: Institute for the Study of Human Issues, 1978.

Hanna, Willard, and Des Alwi. *Turbulent Times in Past Ternate and Tidore*. Banda Naira: Yayasan Warisandan Budaya Banda Naira, 1990.

Heeres, J. E., and F. W. Stapel, eds. *Corpus Diplomaticum Neerlando-Indicum*. 6 vols. The Hague: Martinus Nijhoff, 1907–1955.

Heijer, Henk den. *De geoctrooieerde compagnie: De VOC en de WIC als voorlopers van de naamloze vennootschap*. Ars notariatus CXXVIII. Amsterdam: Stichting tot Bevordering der Notariële Wetenschap; Deventer: Kluwer, 2005.

Helmers, Hemer J., and Geert H. Janssen, eds. *The Cambridge Companion to the Dutch Golden Age*. Cambridge: Cambridge University Press, 2018.

Henry, Jabez. *Report on the Criminal Law at Demerara and in the Ceded Dutch Colonies*. London: Henry Butterworth, 1821.

Hesselink, Reinier. *The Dream of Christian Nagasaki: World Trade and the Clash of Cultures 1560–1640*. Jefferson, NC: McFarland, 2015.

Hitchens, Christopher. "Believe Me, It's Torture." *Vanity Fair*, August 2008. http://www.vanityfair.com/news/2008/08/hitchens200808.

Hoogenberk, H. *De Rechtsvoorschriften voor de Vaart op Oost-Indië 1595–1620*. Utrecht: Kemink, 1940.

Hullu, J. de. "De Matrozen en Soldaten op de Schepen der Oost-Indische Compagnie." *Bijdragen tot de Taal-, Land- en Volkenkunde van Nederlandsch-Indië* 69, no 2/3 (1914): 318–65.

Hunter, William Wilson. *A History of British India*. 2 vols. London: Longmans, Green, 1899–1912.

IJzerman, J. W., ed. *Cornelis Buijsero te Bantam, 1616–1618*. The Hague: Martinus Nijhoff, 1923.

Iongh, D. de. *Het Krijgswezen onder de Oostindische Compagnie*. The Hague: W. P. van Stockum, 1950.

Ishizawa, Yoshiaki. "Les quartiers japonais dans l'Asie du Sud-Est au XVIIème siècle." In *Guerre et Paix en Asie du Sud-Est*, ed. Nguyen The Anh and Alain Forest, 85–94. Paris: Harmettan, 1998.

Israel, Jonathan. *Dutch Primacy in World Trade, 1585-1740.* Oxford: Clarendon Press, 2002.

Ittersum, Martine J. van. "Debating Natural Law in the Banda Islands: A Case Study in Anglo-Dutch Imperial Competition in the East Indies, 1609–1621." *History of European Ideas* 42, no. 4 (2016): 459–501.

——. "Empire by Treaty? The Role of Written Documents in European Overseas Expansion, 1500–1800." In *The Dutch and English East India Companies: Diplomacy, Trade and Violence in Early Modern Asia,* ed. Adam Clulow and Tristan Mostert. Amsterdam: Amsterdam University Press, forthcoming.

——. *Profit and Principle: Hugo Grotius, Natural Rights Theories and the Rise of Dutch Power in the East Indies, 1595–1615.* Leiden: Brill, 2006.

Iwao, Seiichi. *Shuinsen bōekishi no kenkyū.* Tokyo: Yoshikawa Kōbunkan, 1985.

——. *Zoku Nanyō Nihon machi no kenkyū: Nanyō tōsho chiiki bunsan Nihonjin imin no seikatsu to katsudō.* Tokyo: Iwanami Shoten, 1987.

Jacobs, Els M. *Merchant in Asia: The Trade of the Dutch East India Company During the Eighteenth Century.* Leiden: CNWS, 2006.

James, Lawrence. *The Rise and Fall of the British Empire.* New York: St. Martin's Griffin, 1995.

Jenkinson, Charles. *A Collection of All the Treaties of Peace, Alliance, and Commerce Between Great Britain and Other Powers.* London: J. Debrett, 1785.

——. *A Collection of Treaties of Peace, Commerce, and Alliance Between Great-Britain and Other Powers: From Year 1619 to 1734.* London: J. Almon and J. Debrett, 1781.

Jones, J. R. *The Anglo-Dutch Wars of the Seventeenth Century.* London: Longman, 1996.

Jonge, J. K. de, and M. L. van Deventer, eds. *De opkomst van het Nederlandsch gezag in Oost Indië.* 13 vols. The Hague: Martinus Nijhoff, 1862–1909.

Jourdain, John. *Journal of John Jourdain, 1608–17: His Experiences in Arabia, India and the Malay Archipelago.* Ed. William Foster. Cambridge: Hakluyt Society, 1905.

Katō, Eiichi. "Rengō Oranda Higashi-Indo Kaisha no senryaku kyoten toshite no Hirado shōkan." In *Nihon zenkindai no kokka to taigai kankei,* ed. Tanaka Takeo. Tokyo: Yoshikawa Kōbunkan, 1987.

Keeley, Brian. "Of Conspiracy Theories." *Journal of Philosophy* 96, no. 3 (1999): 109–26.

Keene, Edward. *Beyond the Anarchical Society: Grotius, Colonialism, and Order in World Politics.* Cambridge: Cambridge University Press, 2002.

Kelly, Michael. *Prosecuting Corporations for Genocide.* New York: Oxford University Press, 2016.

Kemasang, A. R. T. "The 1740 Massacre of Chinese in Java: Curtain Raiser for the Dutch Plantation Economy." *Bulletin of Concerned Asian Scholars* 14, no. 1 (1982): 61–71.

Kerr, Rachel, and James Gow. "Law and War in the Global War on Terror." In *International Law, Security and Ethics: Policy Challenges in the Post-9/11 World,* ed. Aidan Hehir, Natasha Kuhrt, and Andrew Mumford, 61–78. London: Routledge, 2011.

Keuning, J. "Ambonese, Portuguese and Dutchmen: The History of Ambon to the End of the Seventeenth Century." In *Dutch Authors on Asian History: A Selection of Dutch Historiography on the Verenigde Oostindische Compagnie,* ed. M. A. P. Meilink-Roelofsz, M. E. van Opstall, and G. J. Schutte, 362–97. Dordrecht: Foris, 1988.

Kiers, Lucas. *Coen op Banda: De conqueste getoetst aan het recht van den tijd.* Utrecht: A. Oosthoek, 1943.

Knaap, Gerrit. "A City of Migrants: Kota Ambon at the End of the Seventeenth Century." *Indonesia,* no. 51 (1991): 105–28.

———. "Crisis and Failure: War and Revolt in the Ambon Islands, 1636–1637." *Cakalele* 3 (1992): 1–26.

———. "De Ambonse eilanden tussen twee mogendheden; De VOC en Ternate, 1605–1656." In *Hof en Handel; Aziatische vorsten en de VOC 1620–1720,* ed. Elsbeth Locher-Scholten and Peter Rietbergen, 35–58. Leiden: KITLV, 2004.

———. "The Demography of Ambon in the Seventeenth Century: Evidence from Colonial Proto-Censuses." *Journal of Southeast Asian Studies* 26, no. 2 (1995): 227–41.

———. "The Governor-General and the Sultan: An Attempt to Restructure a Divided Amboina in 1638." *Itinerario* 29, no. 1 (2005): 79–100.

———. "Headhunting, Carnage and Armed Peace in Amboina, 1500–1700." *Journal of the Economic and Social History of the Orient* 46, no. 2 (2003): 165–92.

———. "Kora-kora en kruitdamp; De Verenigde Oost-Indische Compagnie in oorlog en vrede in Ambon." In *De Verenigde Oost-Indische Compagnie tussen Oorlog and diplomatie,* ed. Gerrit Knaap and Ger Teitler, 257–80. Leiden: KITLV, 2002.

———. *Kruidnagelen en Christenen: De Verenigde Oost-Indische Compagnie en de bevolking van Ambon 1656–1696.* Leiden: KITLV, 2004.

———, ed. *Memories van Overgave van gouverneurs van Ambon in de zeventiende en achttiende eeuw.* Rijks Geschiedkundige Publicatiën, Kleine Serie 62. The Hague: Martinus Nijhoff, 1987.

———. "Slavery and the Dutch in Southeast Asia." In *Fifty Years Later; Antislavery, Capitalism and Modernity in the Dutch Orbit,* ed. G. Oostindie, 193–206. Leiden: KITLV Caribbean Series, 1995.

Knaap, Gerrit, Henk den Heijer, and Michiel de Jong, eds. *Oorlogen overzee. Militair optreden door compagnie en staat buiten Europa, 1595–1814.* Amsterdam: Boom, 2015.

Kondō Morishige, ed. *Gaiban tsūshō.* Kaitei shiseki shūran, vol. 21. Tokyo: Kokusho Kankō kai, 1901. Reprint, Kyoto: Rinsen Shoten, 1983.

Kruijtzer, Gijs. "European Migration in the Dutch Sphere." In *Dutch Colonialism, Migration and Cultural Heritage,* ed. Gert Oostindie, 97–154. Leiden: KITLV, 2008.

Langbein, John. *Torture and the Law of Proof: Europe and England in the Ancien Regime.* Chicago: University of Chicago Press, 1977.

Leeuwen, Simon van. *Het Rooms-Hollands-Regt.* Leiden: Hackens, 1664.

Lepore, Jill. *New York Burning: Liberty, Slavery, and Conspiracy in Eighteenth-Century Manhattan.* New York: Alfred A. Knopf, 2005.

Leupe, P. A. "De Verovering Der Banda-Eilanden." *Bijdragen tot de Taal-, Land- en Volkenkunde van Nederlandsch-Indië* 2, no. 4 (1854): 384–430.

Loth, Vincent. "Armed Incidents and Unpaid Bills: Anglo-Dutch Rivalry in the Banda Islands in the Seventeenth Century." *Modern Asian Studies* 29, no. 4 (1995): 705–40.

———. "Pioneers and Perkeniers: The Banda Islands in the 17th Century." *Cakalele,* no. 6 (1995): 13–35.

Markham, Albert, ed. *The Voyages and Works of John Davis.* London, 1880.

Markley, Robert. "Violence and Profits on the Restoration Stage: Trade, Nationalism, and Insecurity in Dryden's Amboyna." *Eighteenth-Century Life* 22, no. 1 (1998): 2–17.

Marshall, P. J. "The English in Asia to 1700." In *The Origins of Empire*, ed. Nicholas Canny, vol 1 of *The Oxford History of the British Empire*. Oxford: Oxford University Press, 1998.

Massarella, Derek. *A World Elsewhere: Europe's Encounter with Japan in the Sixteenth and Seventeenth Centuries*. New Haven, CT: Yale University Press, 1990.

Masselman, George. *The Cradle of Colonialism*. New Haven, CT: Yale University Press, 1963.

Meilink-Roelofsz, M. A. P. *Asian Trade and European Influence in the Indonesian Archipelago Between 1500 and About 1630*. The Hague: Martinus Nijhoff, 1962.

——. "Steven van der Haghen (1563–1624)." In *Vier eeuwen varen: kapiteins, kapers, kooplieden en geleerden*, ed. L. M. Akveld. Bussum: De Boer, 1973.

Meilink-Roelofsz, M. A. P., M. E. van Opstall, and G. J. Schutte, eds. *Dutch Authors on Asian History: A Selection of Dutch Historiography on the Verenigde Oostindische Compagnie*. Dordrecht: Foris, 1988.

Melley, Timothy. *Empire of Conspiracy: The Culture of Paranoia in Postwar America*. Ithaca, NY: Cornell University Press, 2000.

Meuwese, Mark. "Fear, Uncertainty, and Violence in the Dutch Colonization of Brazil (1624–1662)." In *Fear and the Shaping of Early American Societies*, ed. Louis Roper and Lauric Henneton, 93–114. Leiden: Brill, 2016.

Mijer, P. *Verzameling van Instructiën, Ordonnanciën en Reglementen voor de Regering van Nederlandsch Indië*. Batavia, 1848.

Milton, Anthony. "Marketing a Massacre: Amboyna, the East India Company and the Public Sphere in Early Stuart England." In *The Politics of the Public Sphere in Early Modern England*, ed. Steve Pincus and Peter Lake, 168–90. Manchester: Manchester University Press, 2007.

Milton, Giles. *Nathaniel's Nutmeg*. London: Hodder & Stoughton, 1999.

Mishra, Rupali. *A Business of State: Commerce, Politics, and the Birth of the East India Company*. Cambridge, MA: Harvard University Press, 2018.

——. "Merchants, Commerce and the State: The East India Company in early Stuart England." PhD diss., Princeton University, 2010.

Moore, Rebecca. "Reconstructing Reality: Conspiracy Theories about Jonestown." *Journal of Popular Culture* 36, no. 2 (2002): 200–229.

The Most Savage and Horrible Cruelties Lately Practised by the Hollanders upon the English in the East Indies. Presborow, 1624.

Mostert, Tristan. "The Great Spice War: Makassar, the Dutch East India Company and the Struggle for the Clove Trade." PhD diss., Leiden University, in progress.

Mulder, W. Z. *Hollanders in Hirado, 1597–1641*. Haarlem: Fibula-Van Dishoeck, 1984.

Nadri, Ghulam. "Sailors, Zielverkopers, and the Dutch East India Company: The Maritime Labour Market in Eighteenth-Century Surat." *Modern Asian Studies* 49, no. 2 (2015): 336–64.

Nagazumi, Yōko. "Ayutthaya and Japan: Embassies and Trade in the Seventeenth Century." In *From Japan to Arabia: Ayutthaya's Maritime Relations with Asia*, ed. Kennon Breazeale, 89–105. Bangkok: Printing House of Thammasat University, 1999.

———. "Hirado ni dentatsu sareta Nihonjin baibai buki yushutsu kinshirei." *Nihon rekishi* 611 (1999): 67–89.

———. *Shuinsen.* Tokyo: Yoshikawa Kōbunkan, 2001.

Neill, Michael. "Putting History to the Question: An Episode of Torture at Bantam in Java, 1604." *English Literary Renaissance* 25 (1995): 45–75.

Newton-King, Susie. "For the Love of Adam: Two Sodomy Trials at the Cape of Good Hope." *Kronos: Journal of Cape History*, no 28 (2002): 21–42.

Niemeijer, Henk. *Batavia: Een koloniale samenleving in de zeventiende eeuw.* Amsterdam: Balans, 2005.

Norton, Mary Beth. *In the Devil's Snare: The Salem Witchcraft Crisis of 1692.* New York: Alfred A. Knopf, 2002.

Ogborn, Miles. *Indian Ink: Script and Print in the Making of the English East India Company.* Chicago: University of Chicago Press, 2007.

Opstall, M. E. van, ed. "Laurens Reael in de Staten-Generaal: Het verslag van Reael over de toestand in Oost-Indië anno 1620." In *Nederlandse historische bronnen*, ed. A. C. F. Koch et al., vol. 1. The Hague: Martinus Nijhoff, 1979.

Parsons, Timothy. *The Rule of Empires: Those Who Built Them, Those Who Endured Them, and Why They Always Fall.* New York: Oxford University Press, 2012.

Parthesius, Robert. *Dutch Ships in Tropical Waters. The Development of the Dutch East India Company (VOC) Shipping Network in Asia, 1595–1660.* Amsterdam: Amsterdam University Press, 2010.

Pavlich, George. "Occupied Cape Judges and Colonial Knowledge of Crime, Criminals, and Punishment." *Sage Open*, 2014. https://doi.org/10.1177/2158244013520612.

Peckham, Robert, ed. *Empires of Panic: Epidemics and Colonial Anxieties.* Hong Kong: Hong Kong University Press, 2015.

Pincus, Steven. *Protestantism and Patriotism: Ideologies and the Making of English Foreign Policy, 1650–1668.* Cambridge: Cambridge University Press, 1996.

Poot, Anton. *Crucial Years in Anglo-Dutch Relations (1625–1642): The Political and Diplomatic Contacts.* Hilversum: Verloren, 2013.

Pyrard, François. *The Voyage of François Pyrard of Laval to the East Indies, the Maldives, the Moluccas, and Brazil.* Ed. and trans. Albert Gray, assisted by H. C. P. Bell. 2 vols. London: Hakluyt Society, 1887.

Raben, Remco. "Batavia and Colombo: The Ethnic and Spatial Order of Two Colonial Cities, 1600–1800." PhD diss., Leiden University, 1996.

———. "Cities and the Slave Trade in Early-Modern Southeast Asia." In *Linking Destinies: Trade, Towns and Kin in Asian Histories*, ed. Peter Boomgaard, Dick Kooiman, and Henk Schulte Nordholt, 119–40. Leiden: KITLV, 2008.

———. "Het Aziatisch Legion: Huurlingen, bondgenoten en reservisten in het geweer voor de Verenigde Oost-Indische Compagnie." In *De Verenigde Oost-Indische Compagnie tussen Oorlog and diplomatie*, ed. Gerrit Knaap and Ger Teitler, 181–207. Leiden: KITLV, 2002.

Reid, Anthony, ed. *Slavery, Bondage and Dependency in Southeast Asia.* St Lucia: Queensland University Press, 1983.

Reinkowski, Maurus, and Gregor Thum, eds. *Helpless Imperialists: Imperial Failure, Fear and Radicalization.* Göttingen: Vandenhoeck & Ruprecht, 2012.

A Remonstrance of the Directors of the Netherlands East India Company, Presented to the Lords States Generall of the United Provinces, in Defence of the Said Companie, Touching the Bloudy Proceedings Against the English Merchants, Executed at Amboyna. Together, with the Acts of the Processe, Against the Sayd English. And the Reply of the English East India Company, to the Said Remonstrance and Defense. London: printed by John Dawson for the East India Company, 1632.

Ribeiro, Madalena. "The Japanese Diaspora in the Seventeenth Century." *Bulletin of Portuguese-Japanese Studies* 3 (2001): 53–58.

Ricklefs, M. C. *A History of Modern Indonesia Since c. 1200.* Stanford, CA: Stanford University Press, 2001.

Roper, Louis, and Lauric Henneton, eds. *Fear and the Shaping of Early American Societies.* Leiden: Brill, 2016.

Ross, Robert. *Cape of Torments: Slavery and Resistance in South Africa.* London: Routledge and Kegan Paul, 1983.

Roy, Kaushik. *Military Manpower, Armies and Warfare in South Asia.* London: Pickering & Chatto, 2013.

Rubright, Marjorie. *Doppelgänger Dilemmas: Anglo-Dutch Relations in Early Modern English Literature and Culture.* Philadelphia: University of Pennsylvania Press, 2015.

Rumphius, Georgius. "De Ambonse Historie." *Bijdragen tot de Taal-, Land- en Volkenkunde van Nederlandsch-Indië* 64, no. 1/2 (1910): 3–327.

——. "De Ambonse Historie." *Bijdragen tot de Taal-, Land- en Volkenkunde van Nederlandsch-Indië* 64, no. 3/4 (1910): 3–162.

Sainsbury, W. N., ed. *Calendar of State Papers Colonial, East Indies, China and Japan, 1617–1621.* London: H.M.S.O., 1870.

——, ed. *Calendar of State Papers Colonial, East Indies, China and Japan, 1622–1624.* London: H.M.S.O., 1878.

——, ed. *Calendar of State Papers Colonial, East Indies and Persia, 1625–1629.* London: H.M.S.O., 1884.

——, ed. *Calendar of State Papers Colonial, East Indies and Persia, 1630–1634.* London: H.M.S.O., 1892.

Satow, Ernest. "Notes on the Intercourse Between Japan and Siam in the Seventeenth Century." *Transactions of the Asiatic Society of Japan* 13 (1884): 189–210.

——, ed. *The Voyage of Captain John Saris to Japan.* London: Hakluyt Society, 1900.

Scammell, G. V. "The Pillars of Empire: Indigenous Assistance and the Survival of the 'Estado da India' c. 1600–1700." *Modern Asian Studies* 22, no. 3 (1988): 473–89.

Scott, Edmund. *An Exact Discourse of the Subtilties, Fashishions, Pollicies, Religion, and Ceremonies of the East Indians.* 1606.

Senate Select Committee on Intelligence. *Committee Study of the Central Intelligence Agency's Detention and Interrogation Program* (2014). https://www.intelligence.senate .gov/sites/default/files/press/foreword.pdf.

Sharples, Jason. "Discovering Slave Conspiracies: New Fears of Rebellion and Old Paradigms of Plotting in Seventeenth-Century Barbados." *American Historical Review* 120, no. 3 (2015): 811–43.

Silverblatt, Irene. "Colonial Conspiracies." *Ethnohistory* 53, no. 2 (2006): 259–80.

Smith, Edmond. "Networks of the East India Company, c. 1600–1625." PhD diss., Cambridge University, 2016.

Sramek, Joseph. *Gender, Morality, and Race in Company India, 1765–1858.* Basingstoke: Palgrave Macmillan, 2011.

Stapel, F. W. "The Ambon 'Massacre' (9 March, 1623)." In *Dutch Authors on Asian History: A Selection of Dutch Historiography on the Verenigde Oostindische Compagnie*, ed. M. A. P. Meilink-Roelofsz, M. E. van Opstall, and G. J. Schutte. Dordrecht: Foris, 1988.

——. "De Ambonsche 'Moord' (9 Maart 1623)." *Tijdschrift voor Indische Taal- Land- en Volkenkunde* 62 (1923): 209–26.

——, ed. *Pieter van Dam's Beschryvinge van de Oostindische Compagnie.* 7 vols. The Hague: Martinus Nijhoff, 1927–1954.

Stavros, Matthew. "Military Revolution in Early Modern Japan." *Japanese Studies* 33, no. 3 (2013): 243–61.

Steenbrink, K. A., and J. S. Aritonang. "The Arrival Of Protestantism and the Consolidation of Christianity in the Moluccas, 1605–1800." In *A History of Christianity in Indonesia*, ed. Jan Sihar Aritonang and Karel Steenbrink, 99–134. Leiden: Brill, 2008.

Steensgaard, Niels. *Carracks, Caravans, and Companies: The Structural Crisis in the European-Asian Trade in the Early 17th Century.* Copenhagen: Studentlitteratur, 1973.

Stevens, Henry. *The Dawn of British Trade to the East Indies as Recorded in the Court Minutes of the East India Company, 1599–1603.* London: Henry Stevens, 1886.

Stoler, Ann Laura. "'In Cold Blood': Hierarchies of Credibility and the Politics of Colonial Narratives." *Representations* 37 (1992): 151–89.

Straver, Hans, Chris van Fraassen, and Jan van der Putten. *Ridjali Historie van Hitu: Een Ambonse geschiedenis uit de zeventiende eeuw.* Utrecht: Landelijk Steunpunt Educatie Molukkers, 2004.

Subrahmanyam, Sanjay. "Forcing the Doors of Heathendom: Ethnography, Violence, and the Dutch East India Company." In *Between the Middle Ages and Modernity*, ed. Charles Parker and Jerry Bentley, 131–53. Lanham, MD: Rowman & Littlefield, 2007.

Taylor, Jean Gelman. "Painted Ladies of the VOC." *South African Historical Journal* 59, no 1 (2007): 47–78.

——. *The Social World of Batavia: Europeans and Eurasians in Colonial Indonesia.* 2nd ed. Madison: University of Wisconsin Press, 2009.

Teller, Henry Moore. *The Problem in the Philippines.* Washington, DC: U.S. Government Printing Office, 1902.

Tiele, P. A., ed. "Documenten voor de geschiedenis der Nederlanders in het Oosten." *Bijdragen en Mededelingen van het Historisch Genootschap* 6 (1883): 222–376.

Tiele, P. A., and J. E. Heeres. *Bouwstoffen voor de geschiedenis der Nederlanders in den Maleischen Archipel.* 3 vols. The Hague: Martinus Nijhoff, 1886–1895.

A True Declaration of the News That Came Out of the East Indies with the Pinnace Called the Hare. London, 1624.

A True Relation of the Unjust, Cruell, and Barbarous Proceedings Against the English at Amboyna in the East-Indies, by the Neatherlandish Governour and Councel There. London: printed by H. Lownes for Nathanael Newberry, 1624.

Tsuchiya, Kenji, and James Siegel. "Invincible Kitsch or as Tourists in the Age of Des Alwi." *Indonesia* 50 (1990): 61–76.

Turnbull, Stephen. "The Japanese 'Wild Geese': The Recruitment, Roles and Reputation of Japanese Mercenaries in Southeast Asia, 1593–1688." Unpublished paper.

Valentijn, François. *Oud en Nieuw Oost-Indien*. Dordrecht: Joannes van Braam and Gerard onder de Linden, 1724–1726.

Villiers, John. "Trade and Society in the Banda Islands in the Sixteenth Century." *Modern Asian Studies* 15, no. 4 (1981): 723–50.

Vink, Markus. "A Work of Compassion? Dutch Slavery and Slave Trade in the Indian Ocean in the Seventeenth Century." *The History Cooperative* (2003). www.historycooperative.org/proceedings/seascapes.

——. "'The World's Oldest Trade': Dutch Slavery and Slave Trade in the Indian Ocean in the Seventeenth Century." *Journal of World History* 14, no. 2 (2003): 131–77.

Voorda, Bavius. *De Crimineele Ordonnantien van Koning Philips van Spanje. Verzeld van eene Verhandling over het Verstand van de Ordonnantie*. Leiden: Honkoop and van Tiffelen, 1792.

Vries, Jan de, and Ad van der Woude. *The First Modern Economy: Success, Failure, and Perseverance of the Dutch Economy, 1500–1815*. New York: Cambridge University Press, 1997.

Vrugt, Marijke van de. *De criminele ordonnantie van 1570*. Zutphen: Walburg Pers, 1978.

Wagner, Kim. *The Great Fear of 1857: Rumours, Conspiracies and the Making of the Indian Uprising*. Bern: Peter Lang, 2010.

——. "'Treading Upon Fires': The 'Mutiny'-Motif and Colonial Anxieties in British India." *Past & Present* 218, no. 1 (2013): 159–97.

Ward, Kerry. *Networks of Empire: Forced Migration in the Dutch East India Company*. Cambridge: Cambridge University Press, 2008.

Welie, Rik van. "Patterns of Slave Trading and Slavery in the Dutch Colonial World, 1596–1863." In *Dutch Colonialism, Migration and Cultural Heritage*, ed. Gert Oostindie, 155–259. Leiden: KITLV, 2008.

Weststeijn, Arthur. "'Love Alone Is Not Enough': Treaties in Seventeenth-Century Dutch Colonial Expansion." In *Empire by Treaty. Negotiating European Expansion, 1600–1900*, ed. Saliha Belmessous, 19–44. Oxford: Oxford University Press, 2014.

White, Luise. *Speaking with Vampires: Rumor and History in Colonial Africa*. Berkeley: University of California Press, 2000.

Widjojo, Muridan Satrio. *The Revolt of Prince Nuku: Crosscultural Alliance-Making in Maluku, c. 1780–1810*. Leiden: Brill, 2009.

Willson, Beckles. *Ledger and Sword or The Honourable Company of Merchants of England Trading to the East Indies (1599–1874)*. 2 vols. London: Longmans, Green, 1903.

Winius, George, and Marcus Vink. *The Merchant Warrior Pacified: The VOC and Its Changing Political Economy in India*. Delhi: Oxford University Press, 1991.

Wolters, O. W. *History, Culture, and Region in Southeast Asian Perspective*. Singapore: Institute of Southeast Asian Studies, 1982.

Worden, Nigel. *Slavery in Dutch South Africa*. Cambridge: Cambridge University Press, 1985.

Worden, Nigel, and Gerald Groenewald. *Trials of Slavery*. Cape Town: Van Riebeeck Society, 2005.

Worp, J. A. "Jan de Brune de Jonge." *Oud-Holland* 8 (1890): 81–103.

Zandvliet, Kees, ed. *The Dutch Encounter with Asia, 1600–1950*. Zwolle: Waanders, 2002.

Index

De Houtman, Frederik, 170–71, 172, 173, 184
Delumeau, Jean, 18
De Maerschalk, Laurens, 27, 124, 171, 239n4, 241n38, 244n74, 256n46; reward for, 166, 169; on torture, 152, 172, 173; trial of, 165–66, 183; and Van Speult, 165, 166, 179–80, 181; as witness, 165–70, 184, 185, 252n93
De Silla, Laurens, 183–84
De Vlaming von Oudtshoorn, Arnold, 20, 174, 191–93, 194, 257n74
Dias, Bastian, 225n114
"Discourse to the Honorable Directors Concerning the States of the Netherlands Indies" (Coen), 54, 80, 81
Dryden, John, 4, 193
Dutch East India Company (Vereenigde Oost-Indische Compagnie; VOC), 1–12; alleged anti-EIC conspiracy of, 9–10, 11, 152, 155–56, 160, 162, 173, 195; Asiafication of, 15–16, 44; attacks on employees of, 47–48, 191, 217n126; brutality of, 68–69, 87; capitalization of, 30, 99, 100; charter of, 15, 20, 30, 74, 100; colonization of Amboina by, 11–13, 27–49, 188, 201n1; "Company daughters" of, 55, 221n31; compensation from, 20, 162, 174, 186–87, 192; as corporation and state, 15, 30–31, 206n53; defense of, 3, 19–21, 151–54, 165–73, 176, 183; disagreements within, 210n8, 257n74; effects on Amboina of, 187–94; vs. EIC, 17, 19, 28, 96–114, 119, 120, 136; EIC cooperation with, 108, 237n78; employees of, 64, 111, 122–23, 146, 188, 241n28; and European settlers, 53–59; fears of, 11, 14–19, 37–38, 49, 105–6, 110–14, 115–22, 135, 143–44, 195–200; "feigned friends" of, 98, 104,

105, 106, 109, 119, 178, 194; history of, 13–14; legal system of, 124, 125–26, 133, 243n53; local rivals of, 27–49, 141–42, 194, 197, 253n102; mentality of, 200; monopolies of, 29, 53, 101, 175, 187–88, 190, 195, 199, 211n27, 259n93; mortality rates in, 63, 223n79; on orderly nature of trial, 19–21, 151, 153, 167, 173; organizational efficiency of, 20–21; political and military power of, 8, 15–17, 28–31, 74, 98, 100–101, 103, 107, 155–56, 160, 162, 178, 187, 260n124; propaganda of, 3, 5, 98, 140, 172–73, 174, 176, 186, 193, 199–200; recruiters for, 84; resistance to, 28, 40, 43, 46–49; seizure of ships of, 163, 164, 176, 182, 183–85, 257n62; and slave trade, 52, 57–58, 59–63, 67, 222n53; sources on, 13–14; state support for, 30, 163, 195; war captives of, 59–60, 65, 66, 106; witnesses of, 6, 165–73, 176
Dutch language, 118–19

Elizabeth I (England), 99
Enckhuijsen (ship), 81, 82, 86, 87, 89, 229n31
England: Admiralty Court in, 5, 136–37, 152, 154, 155, 157, 158, 159–60, 184; state support for EIC in, 5, 21
English East India Company (EIC): alleged VOC conspiracy against, 2, 9–10, 11, 152, 155–56, 160, 162, 173, 195, 200; in Amboina, 2, 17, 40, 98, 101, 103, 109–10; in Asia, 98–106; attack on Batavia by, 106–7; capitalization of, 99–100; charter of, 99; compensation paid to, 20, 174, 192; Court of Committees of, 154, 158, 162, 163, 165, 182–85; and English state, 5, 21; and Japanese soldiers, 90, 95, 129; and judges, 162, 163, 182, 183, 184–86; merchants'

torture of, 1–2, 116–18, 133, 157; and
Van Speult, 1, 94–95, 115–16
Siam (Ayutthaya), 77–78, 79
Skinner, John, 159–64, 165, 182, 186;
sources of, 152, 160–62, 170, 250n57.
See also *True Relation of the Unjust,
Cruell, and Barbarous Proceedings Again
the English*
slaves, 50–72; in Africa, 52, 61; in
Amboina, 56, 57, 59, 61, 62, 63, 218n2;
Asian, 15, 16, 198, 199; in Banda
Islands, 27, 38, 51, 53, 56, 57, 60–63,
65, 196; Bandanese, 60, 66, 225n104;
in Batavia, 57, 61, 62, 63, 224n83; in
Castle Victoria, 19, 51, 52, 64, 67;
categories of, 65–66; and Coen, 51,
57–59, 61, 62, 63, 65; and conspiracy,
141, 143; and EIC, 111, 139; vs.
European settlers, 56–59; fear of, 14,
15, 52, 53, 69–70, 139; fugitive, 69–70;
from India, 51, 60, 61, 62, 66–67, 69;
in Kota Ambon, 50–53, 59, 63, 64, 67,
69–70, 189, 219n9; mortality rates of,
66; and Peres, 70–72, 143, 226n122;
and Portuguese, 57, 59, 66, 70,
222n44; revolts by, 17, 50, 68–69;
sources of, 59–63, 66, 74, 223n83; in
Southeast Asia, 59, 222n51; and Van
Speult, 51, 52, 58–61, 63, 66–70, 94;
war captives as, 59–60, 65, 66, 192
slave trade: Asian, 58–59, 222n53;
Atlantic vs. Indian Ocean, 220n14;
in Indian Ocean, 51, 62, 69, 220n14;
and VOC, 51, 52, 57–63, 67, 222n53
Smith, Edmond, 152
soldiers: Asian, 15, 16, 73–74, 75, 95, 198;
in Castle Victoria, 14, 19, 64, 73, 75,
95; European, 74, 80, 82–83, 227n5,
232n76; mortality rates of, 74, 227n5
soldiers, Japanese, 1–2, 4, 7, 72, 73–95,
141, 202n9; and Banda Islands, 27, 38;

ban on recruitment of, 91–92;
captain of, 132, 135, 137, 188, 199; in
Castle Victoria, 14, 19, 73, 75, 95;
and Coen, 73, 74–75, 80, 81, 89–92,
94, 229n28; confessions of, 143, 167,
242n49; contracts of, 82–83, 89–90;
and EIC, 106, 139; ethnicities of, 85,
227n3; European attitudes towards,
84–85, 249n19; execution of, 144,
145, 146; fear of, 14, 15, 17, 75;
guarantors for, 83, 84; illnesses of,
231nn60–61; interpreters for, 118–19,
132, 244n74; loyalty of, 75; as
merchants, 79; and Philippines,
229n28; and Portuguese, 80–81, 90,
129; problems with, 75, 82–92;
recruitment of, 76–81, 78, 80, 83–84,
91–92, 229n31; reenlistment of, 90;
restrictions on, 115–16; return to
Japanese of, 90–91; signatures of,
129–30; and silver mine, 93; torture
of, 129–32, 157; and Towerson, 95,
133, 134, 249n19; weapons of, 85–86,
95, 233n102
Sonck, Martinus, 11, 66, 113
South Africa, 52, 69
Soysimo, 242n49
Spanish: and Anglo-Dutch relations, 97,
99, 100, 101, 108, 164, 182; and EIC,
103, 104, 105, 106, 139; and Japanese
soldiers, 76–77, 80–81, 90; in
Ternate, 41; vs. VOC, 28, 30, 31,
80–81, 178, 210n9; as VOC
employees, 188; as war captives, 59,
65, 66
Specx, Jacques, 81–87, 89–92, 94
spice trade, 9–10; in Amboina, 12, 29,
38–39; in Banda Islands, 12, 27–29,
34; and EIC, 98, 101–2, 152, 200; and
European settlers, 53–54, 197; in
Hoamoal Peninsula, 14, 40, 193, 199;

spice trade (*cont.*)

and Japanese soldiers, 80; and
Makassar, 40, 98; in Ternate, 215n87;
and Treaty of Defense, 108–10; VOC
monopoly of, 29, 53, 101, 175,
187–88, 190, 195, 199, 211n27,
259n93; and VOC treaties, 29–33,
44, 46

Steensgard, Niels, 209n72

Tailler, Rolant, 256n46

Taiwan, 20, 122–23, 221n33, 261n7

Ternate, xviii, 27, 33, 46, 178, 253n102;
and Luhu, 41–42, 43; sultans of, 40,
41, 191–92, 213n47; VOC treaties
with, 41, 211n21, 215n87. See also
kimelaha

Thomson, Emmanuel, 142, 146, 157,
246n115

Tidore, xviii, 33, 40, 70

Tokugawa Ieyasu, 78

torture: American use of, 116, 117, 118,
156, 253n97; in Bandanese
conspiracy, 113; and confessions, 116,
127–28, 130, 131, 136–46; and
confirmation, 10, 128, 131, 167; and
confrontations, 126, 242n48; Dutch
defense of, 170–73; by English, 22;
and fear, 17, 199, 200; and half-proof,
127, 128, 133; illustrations of, 117,
202n13, 246n103, 249n27; legal
conventions on, 127–28; propaganda
on, 22, 128, 138, 142, 159; of
Shichizō, 1–2, 118, 119; VOC
regulations on, 180; water, 1–2, 60,
116–18, 130, 131, 133, 136–39, 142,
152, 156–58, 160, 163, 170–73, 182,
253n97; witnesses on, 137, 156,
167–68

Towerson, Gabriel, 4, 11; accusations
against, 2, 8, 130, 133, 137–38, 139,

145; background of, 111;
compensation to heir of, 186; and
EIC employees, 120, 133, 136, 158,
245n90, 246n115; evidence against, 8,
252n89; execution of, 145–46, 155,
193; and Japanese soldiers, 2, 95, 133,
134, 249n19; local allies of, 142, 144,
253n102; and Luhu, 14, 177; as
martyr, 22, 160, 163; and New Year's
Day meeting, 134–35, 140; and slaves,
143; torture by, 22; torture of, 10,
140–42, 182; and Van Speult, 8,
96–97, 112, 178, 179, 181; witnesses
on, 160, 167–68

Towerson, William, 111, 186

Toyotomi Hideyoshi, 76, 84, 85

treaties, VOC protection/tribute, 15–16,
27–49, 211n27; with Banda Islands,
34–35, 37, 80; and EIC, 97, 101–2;
enforcement of, 27–29, 35, 44–47, 74,
80, 175, 188, 212n31; with Luhu, 42,
44; and religion, 211n28; resistance
to, 14, 19, 27, 28, 40, 43, 46–49, 199;
in Southeast Asia, 32, 35; and spice
trade, 29–33, 44, 46; with Ternate,
41, 211n21, 215n87; and violence,
28–29, 32–33, 254n4; and war
captives, 59–60, 65, 66, 106

Treaty of Defense (1619), 17, 97, 103–4,
107–10, 114, 144; Coen on, 108–9,
110, 112; and Fleet of Defense, 108,
237n78

Treaty of Southampton (1625), 182

Treaty of Westminster (1654), 174–75, 186

trial, Amboina, 1–3, 115–47; aftermath
of, 3–4, 20, 75, 98–99, 174–94, 195;
archive on, 5–6; defense of, 19–21,
151, 153, 167, 171, 173; and
executions, 2–3, 146–47; procedures
in, 10, 11, 19–21, 151, 153, 167, 173,
199; relocation of, 143–45, 246n119,